THE STRUCTURE
AND PROPERTIES OF
WATER

THE STRUCTURE
AND PROPERTIES OF
WATER

D. EISENBERG

AND

W. KAUZMANN

1969
OXFORD UNIVERSITY PRESS
New York and Oxford

Preface

WATER is the most abundant compound on the surface of the Earth and it is the principal constituent of all living organisms. The oceans alone contain $1 \cdot 4 \times 10^{24}$ grammes or roughly 320 000 000 cubic miles of water. Another $0 \cdot 8 \times 10^{24}$ grammes is held within the rocks of the Earth's crust in the form of water of hydration. The human body is about 65 per cent water by weight, some tissues such as brain and lung being composed of nearly 80 per cent water.

Men of science since Thales have recognized the importance of water in both our internal and external environments, and have studied this substance extensively. Our purpose in writing this book is to summarize from the voluminous literature on water some of the most important and reliable data on this substance and to present the theories that are most effective in correlating these data. We have made no attempt to produce a compendium of data such as that compiled by Dorsey (1940), but we have tried instead to relate the properties of water to its structure. Some important properties of water, such as thermal conductivity and surface tension of the liquid, are not discussed because they have not yet contributed to our understanding of the liquid structure; other properties such as infra-red and Raman spectra are covered in detail because they reveal so much about the structures of ice and liquid water. Though some data on both electrolyte and non-electrolyte solutions are undoubtedly helpful in understanding the structure of water, we have not ventured into the vast literature concerning aqueous solutions.

Realizing that scientists in many fields are interested in water, we have included in the text some background material in physical chemistry which is required in order to follow the discussions of a number of topics. We believe that nearly all material in this book should be accessible to those who have had a first course in physical chemistry.

We have inserted an Addendum at the end of the text; it lists a number of very recent articles on the structure and properties of water, and a few articles overlooked by us during preparation of the main body of the text. The articles are grouped according to the sections of the text to which they correspond.

During the preparation of this manuscript we have had the pleasure of discussing many interesting questions about water with a large number of friends and colleagues. These people are too numerous to mention individually, but we wish to thank in particular Professor S. I. Chan, Professor C. A. Coulson, Professor R. E. Dickerson, Professor B. Kamb, Dr. J. J. Kozak, Professor R. M. Pitzer, Dr. L. Salem, and Dr. G. E. Walrafen. We also wish to thank Lucy Eisenberg for a great deal of expert editorial advice.

DAVID EISENBERG

WALTER KAUZMANN

June 1968

Acknowledgements

THANKS are due to the following for permission to reproduce the material indicated, or to use it in preparing illustrative material.

Professor R. F. W. Bader (Figs. 1.6, 1.8a, and 1.9); Professor K. E. Bett (Fig. 4.21); Professor P. W. Bridgman (Fig. 4.16b); Professor R. Brill (Fig. 3.10); Dr. B. N. Brockhouse (Fig. 4.20); Professor C. A. Coulson (Fig. 1.4); Professor J. O. Hirschfelder (Fig. 1.36); Professor B. Kamb (Figs. 3.5b, 3.7, 3.8. 3.9, and 3.11); Dr. L. D. Kislovskii (Fig. 4.18); Dr. K. Kume (Fig. 3.21); Dr. I. M. Mills (Fig. 1.1); Dr. A. H. Narten (Fig. 4.3); Professor G. Nemethy (Fig. 4.5); Dr. P. G. Owston (Figs. 3.1 and 3.3); Professor G. C. Pimentel (Fig. 3.2); Professor J. A. Pople (Fig. 4.8); Professor J. C. Slater (Figs. 2.6, 2.9, and 2.10); Dr. T. T. Wall (Figs. 4.2, 3a, b and 4.24); Dr. G. E. Walrafen (Figs. 4.22a, b, 4.23c, d, and 4.25); Dr. B. E. Warren (Fig. 4.6); Dr. E. Whalley (Figs. 3.14, 3.15, and 3.20); Professor A. H. Wilson (Fig. 2.11); Professor M. W. Zemansky (Fig. 3.4); G. Bell and Sons (Fig. 4.16b); Cambridge University Press (Fig. 2.11); Elsevier Publishing Company (Fig. 1.1); W. H. Freeman and Company (Fig. 3.2); McGraw Hill Publishing Company (Figs. 2.6, 2.9, 2.10, 3.4); John Wiley and Sons Incorporated (Fig. 1.3b); *Acta Crystallographica* (Figs. 3.5b and 3.7); *Advances in Physics* (Figs 3.1 and 3.3); *Journal of the American Chemical Society* (Figs. 1.8a, 1.8b, 1.9); *Angewandte Chemie* (Fig. 3.10); *Canadian Journal of Chemistry* (Fig. 1.6); *Journal of Chemical Physics* (Figs. 3.14, 3.15, 3.20, 4.5, 4.6, 4.22a, b, 4.23a, b, 4.24, 4.25); *Discussions of the Faraday Society* (Fig. 4.3); *Nature* (Fig. 4.21); Oak Ridge National Laboratory Report (Fig. 4.4); *Optics and Spectroscopy* (Fig. 4.18); *Journal of Physical Society, Japan* (Figs. 3.21 and 4.20); *Proceedings of the National Academy of Science of the U.S.* (Fig. 3.9); *Proceedings of the Royal Society* (Fig. 4.8); *Science* (Fig. 3.8).

Contents

Glossary of Notation

A	Helmholtz free energy
Å	Ångstrom unit $= 10^{-8}$ cm
C_P	Heat capacity at constant pressure
C_V	Heat capacity at constant volume
c'	Velocity of light
D	Coefficient of self-diffusion
D	Debye unit $= 10^{-18}$ e.s.u. cm
E	Internal energy
e	Protonic charge
e	Base of natural logarithms $= 2 \cdot 71828$
e.s.u.	Electrostatic unit of charge
e.u.	Entropy unit $= $ cal mol^{-1} deg^{-1}
G	Gibbs free energy
g	Kirkwood correlation parameter
H	Enthalpy
h	Planck's constant
I	Moment of inertia
k	Boltzmann's constant. Various force constants
kbar	Kilobar $= 10^9$ dyn cm^{-2}
$\mathbf{m}$	Molecular dipole moment in a condensed phase
N	Avogadro's number
N^*	Number of molecules per unit volume
n	Refractive index
P	Pressure
Q	Quadrupole moment
R	Gas constant
S	Entropy
T	Temperature, in °K unless stated otherwise
t	Temperature in °C. Time
U	Potential energy
V	Molar volume
v	Vibrational quantum number
$\mathscr{V}$	Electrostatic potential
X_A	Mole fraction of component A
α	Molecular polarizability
β	Coefficient of cubical expansion
γ_S	Coefficient of adiabatic compressibility
γ_T	Coefficient of isothermal compressibility

δ	Chemical shift
ϵ	Dielectric constant
ϵ_0	Static dielectric constant
ϵ_∞	High-frequency dielectric constant
η	Coefficient of viscosity
κ	Direct current conductivity
μ	Dipole moment of isolated molecule
ν	Vibrational mode or frequency
ρ_0	Bulk density
$\rho(\bar{R})$	Local density
$\left.\begin{array}{l}\tau_D\\\tau_V\end{array}\right\}$	Relaxation times for motions of water molecules; see Section 4.1 (a)
τ_d	Dielectric relaxation time
χ	Magnetic susceptibility
ψ	Molecular orbital
Ψ	Molecular wave function

Notations pertaining to the water molecule and hydrogen bond

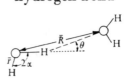

$\bar{r}$	O–H bond length
2χ	H–O–H bond angle
$\bar{R}$	Separation of oxygen nuclei of neighbouring water molecules
$180°-\theta$	Hydrogen bond angle

THE STRUCTURE
AND PROPERTIES OF
WATER

1. The Water Molecule

IN order to interpret the properties of steam, ice, and liquid water, we must understand the water molecule. In this chapter we describe an isolated water molecule in two complementary ways: first in terms of properties that have been deduced from experiments, and second in terms of properties deduced from the electronic theory of chemical valence. The first group of properties is based on measurements made on water vapour at sufficiently low pressures or high temperatures to ensure that interactions between molecules are largely absent. These properties include, for example, the relative positions of the nuclei, and the polarity of the molecule as a whole; but they do not include much information about the disposition of electronic charge within the molecule. Thus for a more detailed picture of the water molecule we must turn to the description given by theory. This provides such details as the shape of the electronic charge cloud of water, and an indication of which parts of the charge contribute most heavily to the total polarity of the molecule. Of course, the separation of these interdependent descriptions is artificial, but it serves to emphasize which portion of our understanding of water is based on observation, and which is based on reasonably accurate models of the molecule.

1.1. The water molecule: description based on experiment

(a) Composition

The experiments of Cavendish and Lavoisier in the 1780s established that water is composed of hydrogen and oxygen. Although the careful data of Cavendish were sufficient to prove that two volumes of hydrogen combine with one volume of oxygen, he did not point this out, and it was left to Gay-Lussac and Humboldt to make this discovery in 1805 (Partington 1928). Dumas, in 1842, found that the ratio of the combining weights of hydrogen and oxygen in water is very nearly 2 to 16.

With the discovery of the stable isotopes of oxygen in 1929 and of deuterium in 1932, it was apparent that naturally occurring water is actually a mixture of several species differing in molecular weight.

There are at present three known isotopes of hydrogen (^{1}H, ^{2}H (deuterium), and ^{3}H (tritium)), and six of oxygen (^{14}O, ^{15}O, ^{16}O, ^{17}O, ^{18}O, and ^{19}O). Tritium is radioactive with a half-life of 12·5 years. The isotopes ^{14}O, ^{15}O, and ^{19}O are also radioactive, but are short-lived and do not occur significantly in natural water.

The relative abundance of the stable isotopes in water was discussed at length by Shatenshtein *et al.* (1960). The precise isotopic content of natural water depends on the origin of the sample but within the limits of variation, the abundances of $H_2^{18}O$, $H_2^{17}O$, and HDO may be stated as 0·20 per cent, 0·04 per cent, and 0·03 per cent respectively. Since preparation of pure $H_2^{16}O$ is exceedingly difficult, virtually all experimental measurements on water have been made on the naturally occurring substance.

A few words should be said about the terminology used in this book. The term *water* refers either to H_2O in all its phases or simply to liquid H_2O, according to the context. *Ice* refers to any of the solid forms of H_2O, not necessarily to ordinary ice I. The terms *steam* and *water vapour* are used interchangeably for gaseous water. Occasionally the term *heavy water* is used for D_2O.

(b) Energetics of formation

Suppose we slowly bring together two hydrogen atoms and one oxygen atom, all in their electronic ground states, to form a water molecule in its electronic, vibrational, rotational, and translational ground state (that is, the process takes place at 0 °K). The energy change of this hypothetical reaction, called the *energy of formation at* 0 °K, is obtained by combining thermochemical and spectroscopic data (Wagman *et al.* 1965):

$$H_2 + \tfrac{1}{2}O_2 \rightarrow H_2O; \quad \Delta E = -57{\cdot}102 \text{ kcal mol}^{-1} \text{ (from heat of combustion)}$$

$$O \rightarrow \tfrac{1}{2}O_2; \quad \Delta E = -58{\cdot}983 \text{ kcal mol}^{-1} \text{ (from spectroscopic heat of dissociation)}$$

$$H + H \rightarrow H_2; \quad \Delta E = -103{\cdot}252 \text{ kcal mol}^{-1} \text{ (from spectroscopic heat of dissociation)}$$

$$\overline{O + H + H \rightarrow H_2O; \; \Delta E = -219{\cdot}337 \text{ kcal mol}^{-1}}$$

The negative sign indicates, of course, that formation of the molecule is accompanied by a net decrease of energy. In stating a value for the energy of formation, we have been careful to specify that the temperature is 0 °K, because at any higher temperature the energy of formation is somewhat more negative, owing to the difference of the combined translational energies of the atoms and the combined rotational and translational energies of the molecule. Moreover, heats of formation are usually measured at constant pressure and are, therefore, actually enthalpies of formation. The enthalpy of formation at a given tempera- ture is slightly more negative than the corresponding energy of formation, owing to the pressure–volume term. The enthalpy of formation of water at 25 °C is −221·54 kcal mol⁻¹ (see Table 1.1).

The *electronic binding energy* of a water molecule is the difference be- tween the energy of the molecule with its nuclei stationary and the sum of the energies of its constituent atoms. It is slightly larger than the energy of formation at 0 °K. This is because even at 0 °K the molecule possesses a residual vibrational energy called the zero-point energy, which is not included in the energy of formation as we have defined it. The zero-point energy is evaluated from spectroscopic data (see Section 1.1 (*d*)); when it is subtracted from the energy of formation at 0 °K, the electronic binding energy is obtained (Table 1.1).

TABLE 1.1

Energies associated with the formation of a water molecule

(1)	Energy of formation from atoms at 0 °K	−219·34† kcal mol⁻¹
(2)	Zero-point vibrational energy	13·25‡
(3)	Electronic binding energy $= (1) - (2)$	−232·59
(4)	Enthalpy of formation at 25 °C	−221·54†
(5)	Bond energy of O–H bond at 0 °K $= \frac{1}{2} \times (1)$	109·7
(6)	Dissociation energy of H–O	101·5§
(7)	Dissociation energy of H–OH $= (1) - (6)$	117·8

† Wagman *et al.* (1965).   ‡ Section 1.1 (*d*).   § Cottrell (1958).

The O–H *bond energy* of water is taken as half the energy of formation of the molecule, because water has two O–H bonds; its value is 109·7 kcal mol⁻¹ at 0 °K. A quantity closely related to the bond energy is the *dissociation energy*, which is defined as the energy to break a bond at 0 °K. Curiously enough, neither of the O–H bonds of water has a dissociation energy equal to the O–H bond energy. Cottrell (1958, p. 187) summarized the experimental evidence on this topic and con- cluded that the most accurate value of the energy for the dissociation of H–O into H and O is 101·5±0·5 kcal mol⁻¹. Since energy must be conserved, the sum of the dissociation energies of the two bonds of water is equal to the energy of formation, and so the energy for the dissociation of H–OH into H and OH is 117·8 kcal mol⁻¹.

Pauling (1960, p. 622) explained the inequality of the two dissociation energies as follows: the dissociation of the second O–H bond permits the oxygen atom to undergo an energetically favourable electronic rearrangement, thereby reducing the second dissociation energy. When the second O–H bond is broken, the resulting oxygen atom has a $1s^2 2s^2 2p^4$ electronic configuration. One of the Russell–Saunders states corresponding to this configuration is ^3P, and this state is stabilized by resonance of the two unpaired electrons. Pauling estimated that the stabilization energy is about $17 \cdot 1$ kcal mol^{-1}. Thus if the second dissociation produced an oxygen atom in its valence state rather than in the more stable ^3P state, the corresponding dissociation energy would be

$$101 \cdot 5 + 17 \cdot 1 = 118 \cdot 6 \text{ kcal mol}^{-1}.$$

This is essentially equal to the energy of the first dissociation.

(c) Molecular dimensions

The bond lengths and the bond angle of the water molecule are known with remarkable accuracy from the vibration–rotation spectra of normal and isotopic water vapour. The enormous labour of measuring and assigning the thousands of spectral lines was done by Darling and Dennison (1940), Benedict, Gailar, and Plyler (1956), and a number of others. Dennison (1940) and Herzberg (1950) discuss the procedure for deducing the moments of inertia, and hence the molecular dimensions, from the spectra; here we will be concerned only with the results.

TABLE 1.2

Molecular dimensions of D_2O, H_2O, *and* HDO†

Molecule		D_2O	H_2O	HDO
Moments of inertia	I_e^{x*}	5·6698	2·9376	4·2715
$\times 10^{40}$ g cm^2‡	I_e^{z*}	3·8340	1·9187	3·0654
	I_e^{y*}	1·8384	1·0220	1·2092
Bond length $\times 10^8$ cm	$\bar{r}_e$	0·9575	0·95718	0·9571
Bond angle	$2\alpha_e$	104·474°	104·523°	104·529°

† Determined by Benedict *et al.* (1956).

‡ The x^*-axis passes through the molecular centre of mass and is perpendicular to the plane of the molecule. In H_2O and D_2O, the z^*-axis is the bisector of the bond angle in the plane, and the y^*-axis is perpendicular to the other two. In HDO the z-* and y^*-axes are rotated about the x^*-axis by 21·09°. The subscript e denotes that the corresponding quantity refers to the equilibrium (vibrationless and rotationless) state.

The nuclei of a water molecule form an isosceles triangle, with a slightly obtuse angle at the oxygen nucleus. Table 1.2 shows the molecular dimensions of D_2O, H_2O, and HDO found by Benedict *et al.*

(1956). All entries in this table refer to the *equilibrium state* of the molecule, the hypothetical state in which the molecule is vibrationless as well as rotationless, lacking even zero-point vibrational energy. The fiction of the equilibrium state is adopted because the average molecular dimensions are slightly dependent on the vibrational and rotational states of the molecule. This dependence is small, but is significant when accurate measurements are considered. The superscripts x^*, z^*, and y^* to the moments of inertia in Table 1.2 refer to the axes of the moments: for H_2O and D_2O the x^*-axis is perpendicular to the plane of the molecule, the z^*-axis lies in this plane and is the bisector of the bond angle, and the y^*-axis is perpendicular to the other two. These axes are respectively parallel to the x-, z-, and y-axes of Fig. 1.2 (*a*) (p. 13), but have their origin at the molecular centre of gravity instead of at the nucleus of the oxygen atom. Note that the largest moment is about the x^*-axis and the smallest is about the y^*-axis.

The equilibrium bond lengths and bond angles of the three isotopic molecules are very nearly equal. This result is consistent with the Born–Oppenheimer approximation, which predicts that the electronic structure of a molecule is independent of the masses of its nuclei. Benedict *et al.* estimated the uncertainty in the values of $\bar{r}_e$ to be $\pm 0.0003 \times 10^{-8}$ cm, and the uncertainty in the values of $2\alpha_e$ to be $\pm 0.05°$. They believe that the best values of the equilibrium dimensions are: $\bar{r}_e = 0.9572 \times 10^{-8}$ cm, and $2\alpha_e = 104.52°$.

As mentioned above, the dimensions of the water molecule depend on the quantum state of the molecule. Their dependence on vibrational states is small. For each vibrational state, the molecular dimensions may be described by three 'effective moments of inertia' (Herzberg 1950, vol. ii, p. 461). Darling and Dennison (1940), using data slightly less accurate than those now available, gave the following expressions for the effective moments of inertia of the water molecule as functions of its vibrational states:

$$I^{x^*} \times 10^{40} \text{ g cm}^2 = 2.9436 + 0.0611(v_1 + \tfrac{1}{2}) + 0.0385(v_2 + \tfrac{1}{2}) + $$
$$+ 0.0441(v_3 + \tfrac{1}{2}); \quad (1.1\,a)$$
$$I^{z^*} \times 10^{40} \text{ g cm}^2 = 1.9207 + 0.0398(v_1 + \tfrac{1}{2}) - 0.0249(v_2 + \tfrac{1}{2}) + $$
$$+ 0.0077(v_3 + \tfrac{1}{2}); \quad (1.1\,b)$$
$$I^{y^*} \times 10^{40} \text{ g cm}^2 = 1.0229 + 0.0213(v_1 + \tfrac{1}{2}) - 0.1010(v_2 + \tfrac{1}{2}) + $$
$$+ 0.0486(v_3 + \tfrac{1}{2}). \quad (1.1\,c)$$

Here v_1, v_2, and v_3 are the quantum numbers for the three normal modes of vibration (see the following section).

In the higher rotational levels, the water molecule suffers considerable centrifugal distortion and its dimensions depart significantly from their values in the equilibrium state. For example, in the level corresponding to a rotational quantum number $J = 11$, the bond angle can be decreased by as much as $5 \cdot 58°$, and the bond length may be increased by $0 \cdot 006 \times 10^{-8}$ cm (Herzberg 1950, vol. ii, p. 50); these distortions are associated with a sub-level in which the molecule rotates essentially around its y^*-axis.

Though very little is known about the electronically excited states of the water molecule, it is certain that the molecular dimensions in such states differ from those in the ground state. Bell (1965) studied the electronically excited states that are associated with the band origins at 1240 and 1219 Å in the vacuum ultraviolet spectrum of water vapour. He concluded that in the excited state associated with the band origin at 1240 Å, the O–H bond length is increased by $0 \cdot 065 \pm 0 \cdot 010$ Å, and the H–O–H angle is increased by $5 \cdot 2 \pm 1 \cdot 8°$. In the other excited state, the O–H bond length is increased by $0 \cdot 067 \pm 0 \cdot 010$ Å, and the H–O–H angle is increased by $8 \cdot 5 \pm 1 \cdot 8°$.

Up to this point we have been concerned with the relative positions of the atomic nuclei in a water molecule. Some indication of the mean positions of the electrons relative to the nuclei is also available from experiments. From magnetic and spectroscopic data, one can determine $\left\langle \Psi^0 \left| \sum_i r_i^2 \right| \Psi^0 \right\rangle$, where Ψ^0 is the electronic wave function for the ground state of the molecule, and r_i^2 is the square of the distance of the ith electron from the molecular centre of mass. The quantity $\left\langle \Psi^0 \left| \sum_i r_i^2 \right| \Psi^0 \right\rangle$, which can be denoted $\langle r^2 \rangle$ for simplicity, is the mean value of the square of the electronic distance from the molecular centre of mass. For the water molecule $\langle r^2 \rangle$ has the value $5 \cdot 1 \pm 0 \cdot 7 \times 10^{-16}$ cm² (Eisenberg *et al.* 1965).

(d) Molecular vibrations

The nuclei of molecules, far from occupying fixed positions with respect to each other, are in a continual state of vibration, even at 0 °K. An important feature of these vibrations is that they can be described by a limited number of basic vibrations known as the normal modes. A normal mode is a vibration in which all the nuclei oscillate with the same frequency and the same phase. The water molecule has three normal modes and every possible vibration of the molecule can be described as a superposition of these three modes.

The normal modes of vibration of water are shown in Fig. 1.1. Because the motion of the nuclei in the ν_1 and ν_3 vibrations is nearly along the direction of the O–H bonds, these modes are often referred to as O–H stretching vibrations. Similarly, because the H nuclei in ν_2 move in directions almost perpendicular to the bonds, ν_2 is referred to as the

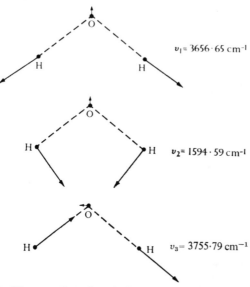

FIG. 1.1. The normal modes of vibration of H_2O. The bonds are represented by dashed lines. The arrows show the relative directions and displacements of the nuclei during a given vibration. If the arrows were drawn to the same scale as the bond lengths they would be only a fraction of the length shown for a molecule in its ground vibrational state. Redrawn from Mills (1963).

H–O–H bending vibration. In fact, ν_1 involves a small amount of H–O–H bending, and ν_2 involves a small amount of O–H stretching. The mode ν_3 is called the asymmetric stretching vibration to distinguish it from the symmetric stretching vibration ν_1.

The transition of a water molecule from its vibrational ground state to the excited state described by the ν_2 mode is associated with the infra-red absorption band centred at 1594·59 cm^{-1}. During this transition, the quantum number v_2 characterizing the ν_2 mode changes from 0 to 1, while the quantum numbers v_1 and v_3 characterizing the ν_1 and ν_3 modes remain equal to zero. Similarly, the transition from the ground state to the state in which only the first normal mode is excited—the state with quantum numbers $v_1 = 1, v_2 = 0, v_3 = 0$—is associated with the absorption band centred at 3656·65 cm^{-1}. Table 1.3 lists the frequencies

of a few of the observed vibrational absorption bands of isotopic water
molecules and gives the quantum numbers characterizing the upper
states. Table 1.3 does not contain all of the known absorption bands of
water; less intense bands extend all the way into the green part of the
visible spectrum, and account, at least in part, for the blue colour of
water.

TABLE 1.3

Observed vibrational bands of D_2O, H_2O, *and* HDO†

Quantum numbers of upper state‡			Absorption frequencies of band centres in cm^{-1}		
v_1	v_2	v_3	D_2O	H_2O	HDO
0	1	0	1178·33	1594·59	1402·20
1	0	0	2671·46	3656·65	2726·73
0	0	1	2788·05	3755·79	3707·47
0	2	0	..	3151·4	2782·16
0	1	1	3956·21	5332·0	5089·59
0	2	1	5105·44	6874	6452·05
1	0	1	5373·98	7251·6	6415·64
1	1	1	6533·37	8807·05	..
2	0	1	7899·80	10613·12	..
0	0	3	..	11032·36	..

† The data for D_2O and HDO, and the first three rows of data for H_2O, are those of
Benedict *et al.* (1956). The remaining data for H_2O are from Herzberg (1950).
‡ In every case the lower state is the ground state, having all three quantum num-
bers = 0.

A simple expression, involving nine empirical constants, describes
the frequencies of vibrational transitions quite accurately. Let us
denote by $G(v_1, v_2, v_3)$ the energy above the vibrationless equilibrium
state of the state with quantum numbers v_1, v_2, and v_3. Then

$$G(v_1, v_2, v_3) = \sum_{i=1}^{3} \omega_i(v_i + \tfrac{1}{2}) + \sum_{i=1}^{3} \sum_{k \geqslant i}^{3} x_{ik}(v_i + \tfrac{1}{2})(v_k + \tfrac{1}{2}) \qquad (1.2)$$

where the sums are over normal modes. The ωs in this equation are
often called the *harmonic frequencies*; they are the frequencies with which
the molecule would vibrate if its vibrations were perfectly harmonic
(see below). The xs are the *anharmonic constants* and describe the effect
on the vibrational frequencies of the departure from purely harmonic
form of the vibrations. Table 1.4 contains the vibrational constants
for H_2O, D_2O, and HDO; the constants were determined by Benedict
et al. (1956) from the frequencies of a large number of bands in the
vibrational spectra of the isotopes of water.

TABLE 1.4

Vibrational constants of D_2O, H_2O, *and* HDO *for eqn* (1.2)†

Molecule	D_2O	H_2O	HDO
ω_1	2763·80‡	3832·17	2824·32
ω_2	1206·39	1648·47	1440·21
ω_3	2888·78	3942·53	3889·84
x_{11}	−22·58	−42·576	−43·36
x_{22}	−9·18	−16·813	−11·77
x_{33}	−26·15	−47·566	−82·88
x_{12}	−7·58	−15·933	−8·60
x_{13}	−87·15	−165·824	−13·14
x_{23}	−10·61	−20·332	−20·08

† Determined by Benedict *et al.* (1956). All entries are in cm⁻¹.
‡ This value is a revision of the one given by Benedict *et al.* See Kuchitsu and Bartell (1962, footnote 23).

The frequency of the transition between any two vibrational states can be obtained from eqn (1.2) and the constants in Table 1.4. For example, the frequency ν_1 for the transition from the ground state to the state in which $v_1 = 1$, $v_2 = 0$, and $v_3 = 0$, is

$$\nu_1 = G(1,0,0) - G(0,0,0) = \omega_1 + 2x_{11} + \tfrac{1}{2}x_{12} + \tfrac{1}{2}x_{13}. \qquad (1.3\,\text{a})$$

Similarly,

$$\nu_2 = G(0,1,0) - G(0,0,0) = \omega_2 + 2x_{22} + \tfrac{1}{2}x_{12} + \tfrac{1}{2}x_{23} \qquad (1.3\,\text{b})$$

and

$$\nu_3 = G(0,0,1) - G(0,0,0) = \omega_3 + 2x_{33} + \tfrac{1}{2}x_{13} + \tfrac{1}{2}x_{23}. \qquad (1.3\,\text{c})$$

Note that the anharmonic constants are negative. This means that the higher vibrational energy levels are all somewhat closer together than they would be if molecular vibrations were purely harmonic.

Equation (1.2) also yields an expression for the zero-point energy of vibration:

Zero-point energy

$$= G(0,0,0) = \tfrac{1}{2}(\omega_1 + \omega_2 + \omega_3) + \tfrac{1}{4}(x_{11} + x_{22} + x_{33} + x_{12} + x_{13} + x_{23}). \qquad (1.4)$$

When the constants of Table 1.4 are inserted in this equation, the zero-point energy of H_2O is found to be 4634·32 cm⁻¹, or 13·25 kcal mol⁻¹. Similarly, the zero-point energies of D_2O and HDO are found to be 3388·67 cm⁻¹ and 4032·23 cm⁻¹ respectively.

The forms of the vibrations of a molecule, and hence the frequencies of the associated absorption bands, depend on the change in potential energy of the molecule during the vibration. This means that the spectrum of a molecule contains a great deal of information about the potential energy function that describes its vibrations. In practice, the procedure for obtaining this information is quite involved, so that simplifying assumptions are usually necessary.† An assumption commonly made, called the harmonic approximation, is that the force tending to restore a bond length or bond angle to its equilibrium value is proportional to its deviation from that value. Using the harmonic approximation, Dennison (1940) showed that the potential energy of the water molecule can be expressed as

$$2\Delta U = k_{\bar{r}}(\Delta \bar{r}_1^2 + \Delta \bar{r}_2^2) + k_\alpha(\bar{r}_e \Delta \alpha)^2 + 2k_{\bar{r}'} \Delta \bar{r}_1 \Delta \bar{r}_2 + 2k_{\bar{r}\alpha}(\bar{r}_e \Delta \alpha)(\Delta \bar{r}_1 + \Delta \bar{r}_2),$$

$$(1.5)$$

where ΔU is the change of potential energy in ergs, $\Delta \bar{r}_1$ is the change in cm of the bond length of one of the O–H bonds, $\Delta \bar{r}_2$ is the corresponding quantity for the other bond, $\Delta \alpha$ is the change in radians of the H–O–H angle, and $\bar{r}_e$ is the equilibrium O–H distance. The k terms are force constants given by (all in units of 10^5 dyn cm^{-1})‡

$$k_{\bar{r}} = 8\cdot454,$$
$$k_{\bar{r}'} = -0\cdot101,$$
$$k_\alpha = 0\cdot761,$$
$$k_{\bar{r}\alpha} = 0\cdot228.$$

This function allows us to calculate the approximate increase in energy for any distortion of the water molecule from its equilibrium configuration. Note that the third term on the right in eqn (1.5) tells us that changes in the two O–H bond lengths do not produce independent effects on the potential energy; if one of the two bonds is stretched, then (because of the negative sign of $k_{\bar{r}'}$) less energy is required to stretch the second bond by a given amount. Similarly, the positive value of $k_{\bar{r}\alpha}$ in the fourth term on the right in eqn (1.5) tells us that more energy is required to stretch a bond if the bond angle is increased, and if one or both O–H bonds are stretched, more energy is required to increase the bond angle.

An explanation for the signs of the $k_{\bar{r}'}$ and $k_{\bar{r}\alpha}$ force constants can be found in the hybrid nature of the O–H bonds (see Section 1.2 (b)). As the H–O–H angle is increased, the p-character of the bonds is decreased and hence the bond-lengths tend to decrease. This accounts for the positive sign of $k_{\bar{r}\alpha}$. Similarly, when an O–H bond is extended, its p-character increases, and so does the p-character of the other bond.

† This procedure is described briefly by Mills (1963) and extensively by Wilson, Decius, and Cross (1955).

‡ The values given here were calculated by Kuchitsu and Morino (1965) from more accurate data than those available to Dennison (1940).

Hence an increase in the length of one bond favours an increase in the length of the other, so that the sign of $k_{\bar{r}'}$ is negative.

Potential functions that describe the vibrations of the water molecule in fuller detail have been devised by several authors.[†] These functions include terms proportional to the third and fourth powers of the nuclear displacements in addition to the terms in eqn (1.5) and consequently they take into account the anharmonicity of the vibrations. The function of Kuchitsu and Morino (1965), like eqn (1.5), has $\Delta\alpha$, $\Delta\bar{r}_1$, and $\Delta\bar{r}_2$ as independent variables; it may be written as follows:

$$2\Delta U = 2\Delta U^0 + \frac{2}{\bar{r}_e}\{k_{\bar{r}\bar{r}\bar{r}}(\Delta\bar{r}_1^3+\Delta\bar{r}_2^3)+k_{\bar{r}\bar{r}\bar{r}'}(\Delta\bar{r}_1+\Delta\bar{r}_2)\Delta\bar{r}_1\Delta\bar{r}_2+$$

$$+k_{\bar{r}\bar{r}\alpha}(\Delta\bar{r}_1^2+\Delta\bar{r}_2^2)\bar{r}_e\Delta\alpha+k_{\bar{r}\bar{r}'\alpha}\Delta\bar{r}_1\Delta\bar{r}_2\,\bar{r}_e\Delta\alpha+$$

$$+k_{\bar{r}\alpha\alpha}(\Delta\bar{r}_1+\Delta\bar{r}_2)\bar{r}_e^2\Delta\alpha^2+k_{\alpha\alpha\alpha}\bar{r}_e^3\Delta\alpha^3\}+$$

$$+\frac{2}{\bar{r}_e^2}\{k_{\bar{r}\bar{r}\bar{r}\bar{r}}(\Delta\bar{r}_1^4+\Delta\bar{r}_2^4)+k_{\bar{r}\bar{r}\bar{r}\bar{r}'}(\Delta\bar{r}_1^2+\Delta\bar{r}_2^2)\Delta\bar{r}_1\Delta\bar{r}_2+k_{\bar{r}\bar{r}\bar{r}'\bar{r}'}\Delta\bar{r}_1^2\Delta\bar{r}_2^2+$$

$$+k_{\bar{r}\bar{r}\alpha\alpha}(\Delta\bar{r}_1^2+\Delta\bar{r}_2^2)\bar{r}_e^2\Delta\alpha^2+k_{\bar{r}\bar{r}'\alpha\alpha}\Delta\bar{r}_1\Delta\bar{r}_2\,\bar{r}_e^2\Delta\alpha^2+k_{\alpha\alpha\alpha\alpha}\bar{r}_e^4\Delta\alpha^4\}, \quad (1.6)$$

where $2\Delta U^0$ represents the right-hand side of eqn (1.5), and the ks are the higher order force constants (in units of 10^5 dyn cm^{-1}):

$$k_{\bar{r}\bar{r}\bar{r}} = -9{\cdot}55\pm0{\cdot}06 \qquad k_{r\bar{r}\bar{r}\bar{r}} = 15{\cdot}4\pm0{\cdot}3$$

$$k_{\bar{r}\bar{r}\bar{r}'} = -0{\cdot}32\pm0{\cdot}16 \qquad k_{\bar{r}\bar{r}\bar{r}\bar{r}'} = 0{\cdot}8\pm0{\cdot}6$$

$$k_{\bar{r}\bar{r}\alpha} = 0{\cdot}16\pm0{\cdot}03 \qquad k_{\bar{r}\bar{r}\bar{r}'\bar{r}'} = 1{\cdot}3\pm1{\cdot}1$$

$$k_{\bar{r}\bar{r}'\alpha} = -0{\cdot}66\pm0{\cdot}01 \qquad k_{\bar{r}\bar{r}\alpha\alpha} = -1{\cdot}7\pm0{\cdot}8$$

$$k_{\bar{r}\alpha\alpha} = 0{\cdot}15\pm0{\cdot}20 \qquad k_{\bar{r}\bar{r}'\alpha\alpha} = -0{\cdot}5\pm1{\cdot}7$$

$$k_{\alpha\alpha\alpha} = -0{\cdot}14\pm0{\cdot}01 \qquad k_{\alpha\alpha\alpha\alpha} = 0{\cdot}0\pm0{\cdot}2.$$

These constants were determined from the anharmonic constants in Table 1.4 and from the vibration–rotation interaction constants of water (Benedict et al. 1956).

In closing our discussion of molecular vibrations, it should be mentioned that electron diffraction measurements have given some additional information on the vibrations of the water molecule. Shibata and Bartell (1965) found, for example, that the root-mean-square amplitudes of vibrations of H_2O and D_2O in their ground vibrational states are $0{\cdot}067$ Å and $0{\cdot}056$ Å respectively.

[†] Plíva (1958), Kuchitsu and Bartell (1962), Papoušek and Plíva (1964), and Kuchitsu and Morino (1965).

(e) Electrical properties

The electrical properties of a molecule, such as its dipole and quadru-pole moments, are useful in characterizing its charge distribution, and also in describing the electric field around the molecule. In this section we give values for the electrical properties of the water molecule and discuss the information they provide about its charge distribution. Discussion of the electric field in the vicinity of a water molecule is given in Sections 1.2 (a) and 2.1 (a).

The mere existence of a permanent dipole moment in water provides structural information about the molecule: it demonstrates the absence of a molecular centre of symmetry. Thus the well-established permanent moment of water rules out the possibility of a linear H–O–H structure. This is, of course, consistent with the value of about 104·5° for the H–O–H angle, derived from the rotation–vibration spectrum.

Many investigators have measured the value of the permanent electric dipole moment of water, μ, and the more precise of these measure-ments give values in the range $\mu = 1\cdot84$ ($\pm0\cdot02$) $\times 10^{-18}$ e.s.u. cm (see McClellan 1963). Among the most accurate data are those of Sänger and Steiger (1928). These authors used the Debye method, in which the dielectric constant of the vapour is measured as a function of temperature. Moelwyn-Hughes (1964) re-examined their treatment of the data, and believes that the most probable value of μ is $1\cdot83_4 \times 10^{-18}$ e.s.u. cm. Stark-effect measurements of the dipole moment of water yield values in the same range. A dipole moment is conventionally defined as pointing from the negative towards the positive end of the molecule, and little doubt exists that the negative end of water is the oxygen atom, with its lone-pairs of electrons.

The values of quadrupole and octupole moment of molecules also provide useful information about their charge distributions (Buckingham 1959). The quadrupole moments of a molecule are the electrical ana-logues of the moments of inertia, and may be defined as

$$Q_{\alpha\beta} = \int r_\alpha r_\beta \rho(\mathbf{r}) \, d\tau, \qquad (1.7)$$

where $\rho(\mathbf{r})$ is the total charge density of the molecule, r_α is the α-Cartesian component (x, y, or z) of the vector $\mathbf{r}$, and $d\tau$ is an element of volume. Adopting the x, y, z coordinate system shown in Fig. 1.2 (a), the water molecule has three non-vanishing quadrupole moments, Q_{xx}, Q_{yy}, and Q_{zz}. The octupole moments $R_{\alpha\beta\gamma}$ may be similarly defined:

$$R_{\alpha\beta\gamma} = \int r_\alpha r_\beta r_\gamma \rho(\mathbf{r}) \, d\tau. \qquad (1.8)$$

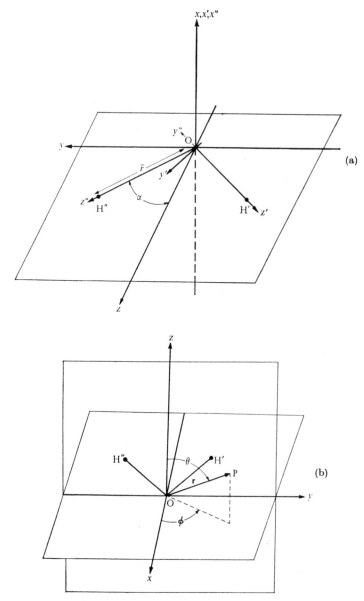

Fig. 1.2. Coordinate systems used to describe the water molecule in this book. (a) Cartesian coordinates. The molecule lies in the plane $x = 0$, with the z-axis bisecting the H–O–H angle. One of the hydrogen nuclei, H′, lies on the z'-axis, and the other on the z''-axis. The y'-axis lies in the molecular plane and is mutually perpendicular to the x'- and z'-axes, and similarly for the y''-axis. (b) Spherical polar coordinates. The molecule lies in the plane $x = 0$. Point P is distance $|\mathbf{r}|$ from the oxygen nucleus, θ is the angle between $\mathbf{r}$ and the z-axis, and ϕ is the angle between the projection of $\mathbf{r}$ in the x–y plane and the x-axis.

The only non-vanishing octupole moments of water are

$$R_{zzz}, \quad R_{xxz} = R_{xzx} = R_{zxx}, \quad \text{and} \quad R_{yyz} = R_{yzy} = R_{zyy}.$$

Experimental values for the quadrupole and octupole moments of the water molecule are not yet available. We may, however, readily derive the mean value of the quadrupole moments,

$$\bar{Q} = \tfrac{1}{3}(Q_{xx} + Q_{yy} + Q_{zz}),$$

from existing data. To do this we must multiply the quantity $\langle r^2 \rangle$ mentioned in Section 1.1 (c) by the value of the electronic charge, $-e$, and then add to this the nuclear contribution to the mean value of the moments:

$$\bar{Q} \equiv \tfrac{1}{3}(Q_{xx} + Q_{yy} + Q_{zz}) = \tfrac{1}{3}\Big(-e\langle r^2 \rangle + e \sum_n Z_n r_n^2\Big). \tag{1.9}$$

In this equation Z_n is the atomic number of the nth nucleus, and r_n^2 is the square of its distance from the molecular centre of mass. The second term on the right-hand side of the equation represents the contribution of the nuclei to $\bar{Q}$ and is easily evaluated from the molecular dimensions given in Table 1.2. Inserting the value of $\langle r^2 \rangle$ from Section 1.1 (c) into eqn (1.9), we find $\bar{Q} = -5 \cdot 6 \ (\pm 1 \cdot 0) \times 10^{-26}$ e.s.u. cm^2.

In the absence of experimental values for the individual quadrupole and octupole moments of water, we are forced to turn to quantum-mechanical calculations for even a rough idea of their magnitudes. Table 1.5 shows values of the quadrupole and octupole moments of water calculated by Glaeser and Coulson (1965) from a fairly accurate wave function for the molecule. The values of the higher moments depend on the choice of origin; Glaeser and Coulson chose the nucleus of the oxygen atom as origin. The values of the quadrupole moments in Table 1.5 have been transformed to refer to the molecular centre of mass as origin, so that their mean value may be compared to the experimental value of $\bar{Q}$. It can be seen that the calculated $\bar{Q}$ is equal within the stated un-certainty to the experimental value. It should be noted that the negative signs of the higher moments show that the contribution to them from the electrons is numerically greater than the contribution from the nuclei. The near equality of the quadrupole moments indicates that the charge distribution of the water molecule is not far from spherical; this is evident from eqn (1.7), which shows that Q_{xx}, Q_{yy}, and Q_{zz} for a sphere are all equal.

The change of the dipole moment of a molecule during the course of a vibration is related to the intensity of the corresponding absorption band. More precisely, the square of the change of dipole moment with

TABLE 1.5

Electric and magnetic properties of the water molecule† (*in C.G.S. units*)

Property		Value
μ_z	Dipole moment[a]	$1\cdot83_4 \times 10^{-8}$ e.s.u. cm
$\bar{Q} = \frac{1}{3}(Q_{xx}+Q_{yy}+Q_{zz})$	Mean quadrupole moment	
	Experimental	$-5\cdot6$ $(\pm1\cdot0)$ ⎫
	Calculated[b]	$-5\cdot8$ ⎬ $\times 10^{-26}$ e.s.u. cm²
$\left.\begin{array}{l} Q_{xx} \\ Q_{yy} \\ Q_{zz} \end{array}\right\}$	Quadrupole moments‡ (calculated)[b]	$\left\{\begin{array}{l} -6\cdot56 \\ -5\cdot18 \\ -5\cdot73 \end{array}\right\} \times 10^{-26}$ e.s.u. cm²
$\left.\begin{array}{l} R_{xxz},R_{zxx},R_{zxx} \\ R_{yyz},R_{yzy},R_{zyy} \\ R_{zzz} \end{array}\right\}$	Octupole moments§ (calculated)[b]	$\left\{\begin{array}{l} -1\cdot08 \\ -0\cdot50 \\ -2\cdot75 \end{array}\right\} \times 10^{-34}$ e.s.u. cm³
$\bar{\alpha} = \frac{1}{3}(\alpha_{xx}+\alpha_{yy}+\alpha_{zz})$	Mean polarizability[a]	$1\cdot444 \times 10^{-24}$ cm³
$\left.\begin{array}{l} \dfrac{\partial^2 V}{\partial z'^2} \\[4pt] \dfrac{\partial^2 V}{\partial y'^2} \\[4pt] \dfrac{\partial^2 V}{\partial x'^2} \end{array}\right\}$	Electric field gradients at the deuterons in D_2O^c	$\left(\begin{array}{l} 1\cdot59\ (\pm0\cdot04) \\ -0\cdot70\ (\pm0\cdot04) \\ -0\cdot89\ (\pm0\cdot06) \end{array}\right) \times 10^{15}$ e.s.u. cm⁻³
$\left.\begin{array}{l} \chi^p_{xx} \\ \chi^p_{yy} \\ \chi^p_{zz} \end{array}\right\}$	Paramagnetic susceptibilities‡[d]	$\left\{\begin{array}{l} 2\cdot46 \\ 0\cdot77 \\ 1\cdot42 \end{array}\right\} \times 10^{-6}$ e.m.u. mol⁻¹

† Subscripts refer to axes shown in Fig. 1.2 (*a*).
‡ Origin is the molecular centre of mass.
§ Origin is the nucleus of the oxygen atom.
[a] Moelwyn-Hughes (1964).
[b] Calculated by Glaeser and Coulson (1965) from the 'c.i. 7' wave function of Mc-Weeny and Ohno (1960).
[c] Posener (1960). It should be noted that the principal axes of the field gradient tensor differ very slightly from the z'- and y'-axes of Fig. 1.2 (*a*). The field gradient axes are rotated about the x'-axis by an angle $\theta = 1°\ 7'\pm1°\ 10'$.
[d] Eisenberg *et al.* (1965).

change in a normal coordinate is proportional to the integrated intensity of the band (Wilson *et al.* 1955). For a number of molecules these integrated intensities have provided interesting information about the change of moments with bond stretching and bond bending. Unfortunately the absolute values of intensities for vibrational absorption bands of H_2O have not as yet been determined. Moreover, they may be difficult to interpret in terms of the electronic structure of the molecule once they have been determined. Coulson (1959 *a*) has discussed these difficulties in detail. He pointed out that the assumption often made in the interpretation of intensities—that the total dipole moment of the molecule is equal to the vector sum of the moments of the bonds—is not a good one for water. One reason is that the lone-pairs of electrons on the oxygen atom are thought to contribute significantly to the total dipole moment (see Section 1.2 b), and that these contributions change during a vibration.

The polarizability, α, is another constant fundamental to the description of the electrical properties of a molecule. It is defined as the induced dipole moment per unit field strength, when the molecule is placed in a uniform electric field. The mean polarizability $\bar{\alpha}$ of a molecule can be determined, along with its dipole moment, from the Debye method, or alternatively, from the well-known Lorenz–Lorentz equation using index of refraction measurements. The former method involves a long extrapolation and thus tends to be less accurate. For example, Sänger and Steiger (1928) found $\bar{\alpha} = 1 \cdot 43 \times 10^{-24}$ cm^3 for water, whereas Moelwyn-Hughes (1964), using all but one point of their data, found $\bar{\alpha} = 1 \cdot 68 \times 10^{-24}$ cm^3. The value of $\bar{\alpha}$ for water, derived from refractive index data extrapolated to infinite wavelength, is $1 \cdot 444 \times 10^{-24}$ cm^3 (ibid.).

The polarizability, like the moment of inertia and the quadrupole moment, is a tensor, having a component along each of three principal axes. The methods we have just mentioned for determining α give the average value of the three components. It is possible, by combining the value of $\bar{\alpha}$ with both the Kerr constant and data on the depolarization of Rayleigh scattering, to deduce the three components of α (Böttcher 1952). These data are not yet available for water vapour, although Orttung and Meyers (1963) measured the Kerr constant of liquid water. Their work indicates that the anisotropy of polarizability is small, so that each component of the polarizability does not differ greatly from $\bar{\alpha}$.

An interesting quantity pertaining to the charge distribution within a molecule is the gradient of the electrostatic field at the nuclei of the atoms. This quantity, for a given nucleus possessing a quadrupole moment, is proportional to the quadrupole coupling energy of the nucleus, which may be deduced from the hyperfine structure of the pure rotational spectrum of the molecule (Orville-Thomas 1957; Kauzmann 1957). A deuterium nucleus has a quadrupole moment, and hence this quantity can be evaluated for the deuterium nuclei in D_2O. Posener (1960) has done this, and his results, expressed as the second derivatives of the electrostatic potential, $\mathscr{V}$, at the deuteron, are shown in Table 1.5. The field gradient is also a tensor and thus has three principal components.

For the sake of completeness we should mention the magnetic properties of water. Like most low molecular weight molecules, water has no unpaired electrons and is thus diamagnetic. The magnetic susceptibility χ is a tensor, and the component along each axis can be written as the sum of a negative diamagnetic contribution and a smaller, positive paramagnetic contribution. Thus $\chi_{xx} = \chi_{xx}^{d} + \chi_{xx}^{p}$, etc. The paramagnetic contributions for the principal axes of the water molecule are given in Table 1.5. The individual diamagnetic contributions are not known, although their mean value, $\bar{\chi}^{d}$, can be found by subtracting the mean of the paramagnetic contributions from the observed mean susceptibility. The mean susceptibility in liquid water,

$$\bar{\chi} = \tfrac{1}{3}(\chi_{xx} + \chi_{yy} + \chi_{zz}),$$

is about -13×10^{-6} e.m.u. mol^{-1} (Selwood 1956), and this property changes only slightly with phase. If we suppose that $\bar{\chi}$ of water vapour is within 15 per cent of $\bar{\chi}$ of liquid water, then we find $\bar{\chi}^{d}$ is

$$-14 \cdot 6 \ (\pm 1 \cdot 9) \times 10^{-6} \text{ e.m.u. mol}^{-1}.$$

As shown by eqn (2.9), $\bar{\chi}^{d}$ is proportional to $\langle r^2 \rangle$; this proportionality was used to derive the value of $\langle r^2 \rangle$ given in Section 1.1 (c).

(f) Comparison of molecular energies

It is helpful to keep in mind the relative magnitudes of the energy changes associated with, for instance, the vibrational excitation, dissociation, and ionization of the water molecule. In this section we compare the values of a number of these energy changes. Our purpose is not so much to describe the changes as to give a feeling for the amounts of energy they require, and the relation of these amounts to the total energy of the molecule.

To begin with, let us establish the total energy of the water molecule. The *total energy* of a molecule is defined as the difference between the energy of the motionless molecule and that of the electrons and nuclei at infinite separation and at rest. It consists of the kinetic energy of the electrons, and the Coulombic potential energies of the electrons with each other, of the electrons with the nuclei, and of the nuclei with each other. We find the total molecular energy in two steps. (1) We determine the sum of the energies of the separated atoms; this is the energy of formation of the three separated atoms from their appropriate nuclei and electrons. From atomic spectra (Moore 1949) it has been determined that the sum of the ground state energies of two hydrogen atoms and one oxygen atom is $-2070 \cdot 5$ eV.† (2) Adding this number to the electronic binding energy

† eV = electronvolt. 1 eV = 23·0609 kcal mol^{-1}. An energy difference of 1 eV corresponds to the absorption of radiation having a frequency of 8065·73 cm^{-1} (Wagman *et al.* 1965).

of the water molecule, we obtain the total molecular energy. The electronic binding energy is $-10\cdot1$ eV (Table 1.1); hence the total energy
of the water molecule is $-2080\cdot6$ eV. Note that the binding energy
is less than $0\cdot5$ per cent of the total energy. The numerical value of the
total energy is important because it corresponds to the quantity that
is the result of all quantum-mechanical energy calculations. In fact,
one of the principal criteria for choosing an approximate quantum-
mechanical wave function is that the energy calculated from it agrees
closely with this value.

The part of the total energy arising from the mutual Coulombic
repulsion of the nuclei can be easily calculated from a knowledge of the
equilibrium positions of the nuclei and their charges: its value for water
is $250\cdot2$ eV, and is positive in sign. The remaining part of the total energy
is called the *total electronic energy*; its value, by subtraction of the nuclear
repulsion from the total energy, is $-2330\cdot8$ eV.

We can use the virial theorem (e.g. Kauzmann 1957) to separate the
contributions to the total energy of the kinetic energy (KE) of the
electrons and the Coulombic potential energy (PE) of the electrons with
each other and with the nuclei. The virial theorem states that when
the molecule is in its equilibrium configuration,

$$\text{Total energy} = -\text{KE} = \tfrac{1}{2}(\text{PE}+\text{nuclear repulsion energy}).$$

Thus KE $= 2080\cdot6$ eV and PE $= -4411\cdot4$ eV.

The energies associated with electronic processes such as electronic
excitation and ionization are comparable in magnitude to the binding
energy. Excitation of electrons from a non-bonding orbital on the oxygen
atom to two of the Rydberg orbitals (high-energy orbitals about the
whole molecule) is thought to be the cause of two band systems observed
in the vacuum ultraviolet spectrum of water vapour (e.g. Bell 1965).
These bands have their origins at 1240 and 1219 Å, so that the energies
of excitation are both about 10 eV. The first ionization potential of the
water molecule, the energy required to remove the most loosely bound
electron from the molecule, is only slightly larger: it is $12\cdot62$ eV, and
probably corresponds to the removal of one of the non-bonding electrons
(Price and Sugden 1948; Watanabe and Jursa 1964). Three higher
ionization potentials of water have been observed at about 14, 16, and
18 eV (Table 1.6). The assignment of these potentials is less certain, but
the second and fourth ionizations are thought to involve dissociation of
the molecule as well (Price and Sugden 1948). Inner electrons are more
tightly bound and therefore have still higher ionization potentials.

For the purpose of comparison with the ionization potentials and energy of electronic excitation, the dissociation energies of the water molecule, expressed in electronvolts, are also given in Table 1.6. They are both somewhat less than half of the first ionization potential.

TABLE 1.6

Comparison of molecular energies of water (in electronvolts)

(1) Energy of formation at 0 °K	$-9{\cdot}511$†
(2) Zero-point vibrational energy	$+0{\cdot}575$‡
(3) Electronic binding energy = (1)−(2)	$-10{\cdot}086$
(4) Sum of ground state energies of separated atoms	$-2070{\cdot}46_8$§
(5) Total molecular energy at 0 °K = (3)+(4)	$-2080{\cdot}55_1$
(5a) Contribution of kinetic energy = −(5)	$+2080{\cdot}6$
(5b) Contribution of potential energy = $2\times(5)-(6)$	$-4411{\cdot}4$
(6) Energy of nuclear repulsion	$+250{\cdot}2$
(7) Total electronic energy = (5)−(6)	$-2330{\cdot}8$

Energy of electronic excitation at 1240 Å	$10{\cdot}0$
Ionization potentials : 1st	$12{\cdot}62$‖
2nd	$14{\cdot}5\pm0{\cdot}3$††
3rd	$16{\cdot}2\pm0{\cdot}3$††
4th	$18{\cdot}0\pm0{\cdot}5$††
Dissociation energies :	
Of H–OH at 0 °K	$5{\cdot}11$
Of H–O at 0 °K	$4{\cdot}40$

Energy of lowest vibrational transition	$0{\cdot}198$
Energy of a rotational transition	$\sim0{\cdot}005$

Internal energy change, per molecule, on vaporization at the boiling point	$0{\cdot}39$
Internal energy change, per molecule, on fusion of ice I at 0 °C	$0{\cdot}06$
Internal energy change, per molecule, on transition from ice I to ice II at −35 °C	$0{\cdot}0007$

† Wagman *et al.* (1965). The conversion factors used in preparing this table are from this reference.
‡ Section 1.1 (*d*).
§ Moore (1949).
‖ Watanabe and Jursa (1964).
†† Price and Sugden (1948).

Up to this point we have considered the water molecule to be in its vibrationless equilibrium state, but as noted in Section 1.1 (*d*) the molecule is always vibrating. At low temperatures the molecule possesses a zero-point vibrational energy of 0·575 eV. At high temperatures, or in the presence of electromagnetic radiation of the proper frequency, the molecule undergoes transitions to higher vibrational levels. The transition to the lowest vibrationally excited state requires an energy of 1595 cm^{-1}, or about 0·20 eV. The transitions from the ground state to the next three lowest vibrational levels require about 0·39, 0·45, and 0·47 eV respectively. Evidently the energy changes associated with vibrational transitions are much less than those associated with purely electronic processes, such as ionization. On the other hand, these energy changes are much greater than those required for transitions between the rotational levels, some rotational energies being as small as $\sim$ 0·005 eV.

In passing, we should note that the energy changes accompanying the phase transitions of water are also small compared to those connected with the electronic processes of the water molecule. The internal energy change on the vaporization of liquid water at 100 °C is 0·39 eV/molecule, comparable to the smaller vibrational transitions. The internal energy change on the fusion of ice I at the melting point is 0·06 eV/molecule, and the internal energy change for the transition of ice I to ice II at -35 °C and 2100 atm is 0·0007 eV/molecule.

We close this section by inquiring what states of ionization, dissociation, vibration, and rotation we should expect to find in a mole of dilute water vapour at room temperature. It is well known that if the energy change for a given transition is large compared to kT, where k is Boltzmann's constant and T is the absolute temperature, then thermal agitation is not sufficient to cause a significant population in the upper state. Since the value of kT at room temperature is approximately $\frac{1}{40}$ eV, which is small compared to the energy of the lowest vibrational transition, the vast majority of water molecules at this temperature are in the ground vibrational state. It can be shown without difficulty (Brand and Speakman 1960) that only 0·047 per cent of the water molecules are in excited vibrational states at 300 °K. By the same argument, the number of electronically excited, ionized, or dissociated molecules is vanishingly small. This is not the case for rotational transitions, where the transition energies are small compared to kT. Here molecules are distributed over a number of rotational states: about twenty-five states are populated by at least 1 per cent of the molecules at room temperature. As might be expected, the effect of centrifugal distortion on the molecular dimensions is small at 300 °K. The average bond length is increased by about 0·00082 Å over the equilibrium value, and the average bond angle is decreased by 0·099° (Toyama et al. 1964). The decrease in bond angle is presumably associated with rotation about the y^*-axis.

1.2. The water molecule: description based on theory

(a) Electrostatic models

One type of model for the water molecule, commonly used to represent the electric field around the molecule, consists of a small number of

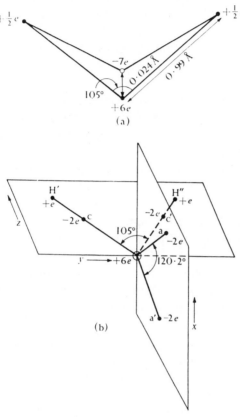

Fig. 1.3. Point-charge models of the water molecule. (a) Model proposed by Verwey (1941). (b) Model proposed by Pople (1951): the distances from the oxygen nucleus to H, c, and a are 0·97 Å, 0·374 Å, and 0·111 Å, respectively. Reproduced from Hirschfelder, Curtiss, and Bird (1954).

point-charges. The charges are located in agreement with the equilibrium bond lengths and bond angle, and they are adjusted in sign and magnitude to produce electrical neutrality and the experimental dipole moment. An example of this sort of model is that of Verwey (1941), shown in Fig. 1.3 (a). Like other models mentioned in this section, this model was designed to be used in calculations of intermolecular forces. In the model, a point-charge of $+6e$, where e is the protonic charge, is placed at the oxygen nucleus, and charges of $+\frac{1}{2}e$ are placed on each of the hydrogen nuclei. The bond length is taken to be 0·99 Å and the bond angle is 105°. A charge of $-7e$ is placed on the bisector of the bond angle, 0·024 Å from the oxygen nucleus, giving a dipole moment of 1·87 D. A slightly more complex model of this type was proposed by Pople (1951, see Fig. 1.3 (b)). In addition to charges on the nuclei, this model represents each pair of bonding and lone-pair electrons by a point-charge of $-2e$. Other point-charge models were used by Bernal and Fowler (1933), Rowlinson (1951), Bjerrum (1951), Campbell (1952), and Cohan et al. (1962).

These models have been used to estimate intermolecular forces in ice and liquid water, but the accuracy of the calculated forces is uncertain because the models drastically oversimplify the true charge distribution of the molecule. The oversimplification is apparent when we consider the moments of charge associated with them. All these models were adjusted to give the experimental dipole moment, but when their quadrupole and octupole moments are calculated, it is found that they differ greatly—sometimes even in sign—from the corresponding moments calculated from fairly accurate wave functions (see Glaeser and Coulson 1965).

A model which may be a slightly more accurate representation of the true charge distribution, and which is still convenient for calculations of intermolecular forces, is the multipole-expansion model used by Coulson and Eisenberg (1966 a). In this model, the charge distribution is represented by a point-dipole, a point-quadrupole, and a point-octupole, all situated at the nucleus of the oxygen atom. The electrostatic potential, $\mathscr{V}$, of this model at any point distance r from the oxygen nucleus is given by the expression

$$
\begin{aligned}
\mathscr{V} = {} & \frac{\mu_z \cos\theta}{r^2} + \frac{1}{2r^3}\{(Q_{zz}-Q_{xx})(1-3\sin^2\theta\cos^2\phi) + \\
& + (Q_{zz}-Q_{yy})(1-3\sin^2\theta\sin^2\phi)\} + \\
& + \frac{1}{2r^4}\{(R_{zzz}-3R_{zxx})(\cos\theta-5\sin^2\theta\cos^2\phi\cos\theta) + \\
& + (R_{zzz}-3R_{zyy})(\cos\theta-5\sin^2\theta\sin^2\phi\cos\theta)\}.
\end{aligned} \tag{1.10}
$$

Here the Qs and Rs are the molecular quadrupole and octupole moments, and θ and ϕ are the angles shown in Fig. 1.2 (b). The components of the electric field in spherical polar coordinates can be found by differentiating eqn (1.10) with respect to r, θ, and ϕ.

The simple models described here furnish a rough description of the electrostatic potential in the vicinity of the molecule, but apart from that, they tell us little more about the molecule than we already know from experiments. For more information and for a detailed picture of the electronic distribution within the molecule, we must turn to quantum-mechanical models of water.

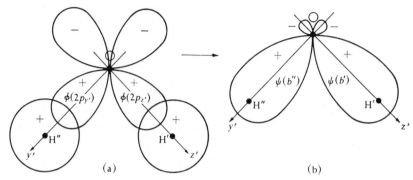

FIG. 1.4. Formation of bond m.o.s from oxygen $2p$ orbitals and hydrogen $1s$ orbitals. Reproduced, with changes of notation, from Coulson (1961).

(b) Molecular orbital theory†

To obtain wave functions that describe the electronic motions in atoms and molecules exactly, it is necessary to solve Schroedinger's equation for the relevant system. This is not yet possible for the water molecule, so we must rely on techniques that produce approximate wave functions. A commonly used technique is to suppose that the electrons move in molecular orbitals (m.o.s), two electrons with opposed spins in each orbital, and that these m.o.s are formed from a linear combination of the atomic orbitals (a.o.s) belonging to the constituent atoms. Even a simple description of water in terms of these m.o.s provides a useful qualitative picture of the electronic distribution of the molecule, and indicates the relation of this distribution to the value of the equilibrium bond angle, the value of the dipole moment, and the tetrahedral co-ordination of water molecules in condensed phases. We consider this qualitative approach in this section, and postpone until Section 1.2 (d) a discussion of the accurate calculation of physical properties from more complex m.o. wave functions.

To a first approximation, we may consider each of the O–H bonds of water as consisting of a m.o. formed from one of the $2p$ orbitals of the oxygen atom and the $1s$ orbital of a hydrogen atom. Of the eight electrons

† The first part of this section follows the presentation of Coulson (1961). For an introduction to molecular orbital theory readers are referred to this work.

belonging to the oxygen atom, two are in the spherical $1s$ orbital bound
tightly to the nucleus, another two are in the less tightly bound spherical
$2s$ orbital, and another two are in the $2p_x$ orbital which is perpendicular
to the plane of the paper in Fig. 1.4 (a). The remaining two electrons are
distributed, one each, in the $2p_{y'}$ and $2p_{z'}$ orbitals as shown in Fig. 1.4 (a);
since they are initially unpaired, these electrons are free to couple with
the $1s$ electrons of the two hydrogen atoms, forming the O–H bonds.
The two O–H bond m.o.s have the form

$$\psi(b') = \lambda\phi(\text{H}':1s)+\mu\phi(\text{O}:2p_{z'}), \qquad (1.11\,\text{a})$$

$$\psi(b'') = \lambda\phi(\text{H}'':1s)+\mu\phi(\text{O}:2p_{y'}), \qquad (1.11\,\text{b})$$

where the ϕs are the a.o.s, λ and μ are parameters, the ratio λ/μ is a
measure of the polarity of the orbitals, and $\phi(\text{O}:2p_{y'})$, for example,
means the $2p$ a.o. of the oxygen atom, pointing along the y'-axis.

If these bond m.o.s exactly described the O–H bonds of water, we
would expect water to have a bond angle of 90°. The fact that the
observed angle is roughly 105° tells us that this description misses an
essential feature. One possibility is that repulsive interactions of the
hydrogens are sufficient to increase the bond angle. Heath and Linnett
(1948), however, using a potential function for the vibrations of water
(eqn (1.5)), showed that this repulsion can account for an increase in bond
angle of no more than 5°. They suggested that a more important factor
is the mixing, or *hybridizing*, of the $2s$ orbital of the oxygen atom with
the $2p_{y'}$ and $2p_{z'}$ orbitals as the bonds are formed. This has the effect
of opening the bond angle and also of increasing the amount by which
the oxygen orbitals overlap the hydrogen orbitals, hence creating
stronger bonds.

The hybridization of the $2s$ and $2p$ orbitals of the oxygen atom has
still another important result: the two oxygen orbitals containing pairs
of valence electrons ($2s$ and $2p_x$ electrons prior to hybridization) form
two lobes on the side of the oxygen atom away from the hydrogen atoms.
These lobes, called the lone-pair hybrids, are symmetrically located
above and below the molecular plane, and form roughly tetrahedral
angles with the bond-hybrids (see Fig. 1.5). It is this tetrahedral character of water, with two positive vertices—the hydrogens—and two
negative vertices—the lone-pair hybrids—that gives rise to the tetrahedral coordination of water molecules in ice and liquid water. Recog-
nition of this important structural feature of the water molecule led
Pople (1951) and Lennard-Jones and Pople (1951) to postulate the
point-charge model of Fig. 1.3 (b).

Pople (1950) and Duncan and Pople (1953) formulated expressions for the hybridized m.o.s in water, using the linear combination of a.o.s method. Those of the lone-pair hydrids, l' and l'', are given by

$$\psi(l') = \cos\epsilon_l\,\phi(O:2s) + \sin\epsilon_l\,\phi(O:2p[l']), \qquad (1.12\,\text{a})$$

$$\psi(l'') = \cos\epsilon_l\,\phi(O:2s) + \sin\epsilon_l\,\phi(O:2p[l'']), \qquad (1.12\,\text{b})$$

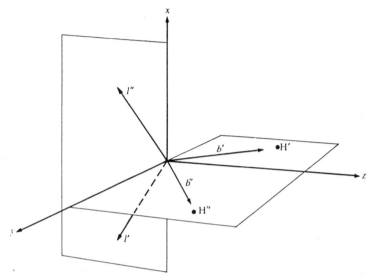

FIG. 1.5. Approximate directions of hybrid orbitals in water: b' and b'' are bond hybrids; l' and l'' are lone-pair hybrids.

where ϵ_l is a constant describing the hybridization and $\phi(O:2p[l'])$ is an oxygen $2p$ orbital in the direction l' (see Fig. 1.5). The m.o.s of the bonds, b' and b'', are linear combinations of the oxygen hybrid orbitals and the hydrogen $1s$ orbitals; they are given by

$$\psi(b') = \lambda[\cos\epsilon_b\,\phi(O:2s) + \sin\epsilon_b\,\phi\{O:2p(b')\}] + \mu\phi(H':1s), \quad (1.13\,\text{a})$$

$$\psi(b'') = \lambda[\cos\epsilon_b\,\phi(O:2s) + \sin\epsilon_b\,\phi\{O:2p(b'')\}] + \mu\phi(H'':1s). \quad (1.13\,\text{b})$$

Here ϵ_b describes the hybridization, and λ/μ is a measure of the polarity of the bond. Using Slater's expression for the atomic orbitals, the orthogonality conditions of the m.o.s, and the experimental values for the bond length, bond angle, and dipole moment, Duncan and Pople evaluated the constants of eqns (1.12) and (1.13). They found $\cos\epsilon_b = 0.093$, indicating that the bond orbitals are formed mainly from atomic p-functions. The value of $\cos\epsilon_l$ is 0.578, indicating that the lone-pairs have nearly an sp^3 character, and the angle between the lone-pair hybrids is $120.2°$. Duncan and Pople assumed that the bond orbitals point directly toward the hydrogen atoms; more complex wave functions indicate that this may not be exactly so.

Fig. 1.6 is a contour map of the valence electron density in the H–O–H plane for a wave function nearly identical to that of Duncan and Pople.

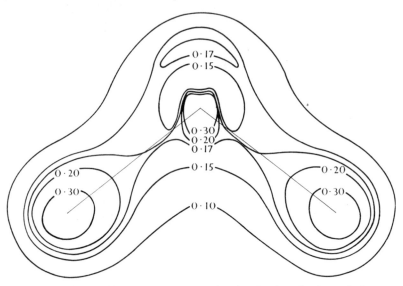

FIG. 1.6. Electron-density contour map, showing density of valence electrons in the molecular y–z plane for a wave function nearly identical to that of Duncan and Pople. Densities are given in atomic units. From Bader and Jones (1963).

The electron density is highest near the atoms, along the bonds, and in the region of the lone-pairs. In the following section we will summarize more recent calculations that suggest the Duncan–Pople wave function underestimates the electron density in the region adjacent to the oxygen nucleus in the direction of the hydrogen atoms, and overestimates it in the region on the opposite side of the oxygen nucleus.

Pople (1950) analysed the changes of electronic structure that accompany departures in the bond angle from its equilibrium value. As the bond angle is increased, $\cos \epsilon_b$, and hence the contribution to the bonds from the oxygen $2s$ orbital, is increased. At the same time, $\cos \epsilon_l$, and hence the contribution to the lone-pair hybrids of the $2s$ electrons, is decreased, resulting in greater repulsion between the lone-pairs. As the bond angle continues to increase, the angle between the lone-pairs and the bonds is decreased, giving rise to further repulsive interactions. In a similar manner, a decrease in the bond angle from its equilibrium value causes increased repulsive interactions between the hybrid bond orbitals. According to Pople, it is these repulsions between the hybrid orbitals which largely determine the equilibrium bond angle and the lone-pair angle in the molecule.

Equations (1.12) and (1.13) may also be used to determine which orbitals contribute to the polarity of the molecule, and in what measure they do so. In the first approximation to the bond orbitals of water, eqns (1.11 a, b), the dipole moment of the molecule arises completely from the moments of the bonds and the moment of the nuclei, because the orbitals of the other electrons (the $1s$, $2s$, and $2p_x$ electrons of the oxygen) are symmetrical about the oxygen atom and so make no contribution to the total moment. When hybridized orbitals are formed, however, the hybrids are not symmetrical about the oxygen atom and therefore can contribute to the moment (Coulson, 1951). Duncan and Pople (1953), taking the total moment to be 1·84 D, found that the contributions of the lone-pair orbitals, the bond orbitals, and the nuclei are 3·03 D, −6·82 D, and 5·63 D, respectively. More complex wave functions suggest that the lone-pair moment is not so large, but that it probably accounts for some of the total moment.

(c) Electron density distribution

A slightly different picture of the water molecule emerges when restrictions on its electron density distribution are determined by considering the forces that the distribution exerts on the nuclei. This method makes use of the fact that when the molecule is in its equilibrium configuration, the net force acting on every nucleus must vanish. Now the forces on a given nucleus arising from the other nuclei are repulsive, so that the electronic charge must be distributed in such a way that it balances these repulsive forces. Bader (1964 a), using a relationship known as the Hellmann–Feynman theorem,† showed that when electronic charge is located in what he calls the *binding region* of the water molecule, it opposes the repulsive forces of the nuclei and tends to bind the molecule together. Electronic charge outside this region is said to be in the *antibinding region*; this charge tends to increase at least one of the internuclear distances and thus to force the nuclei apart. Fig. 1.7 shows the binding and antibinding regions of the water molecule. In the molecular plane (Fig. 1.7 (a)) the binding region includes most of the area between the nuclei: it is enclosed by two rays which subtend an

---

† The Hellmann–Feynman theorem states that the force acting on a nucleus in an isolated molecule is the sum of the electrostatic forces arising from the other nuclei and the classical force arising from the (quantum-mechanical) electronic charge density.

angle of 76° at the oxygen nucleus. In the x–z plane of the molecule (Fig. 1.7 (b)) the boundary between the binding and antibinding regions is very nearly the x-axis, the binding region being the area in which z is positive.

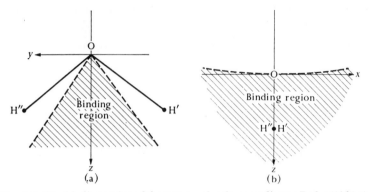

FIG. 1.7. The binding region of the water molecule, according to Bader (1964 a). The dashed line separates the binding region (shaded) from the antibinding region. (a) The plane containing the nuclei. (b) The x–z plane.

We have now delineated the region in which electronic charge must be concentrated in order that the molecule be stable. Bader (1964a) pointed out that this gives a criterion for judging proposed wave functions for water: any acceptable wave function must concentrate sufficient charge in the binding region to overcome the Coulombic repulsion of the nuclei. Bader developed the following procedure for testing wave functions. He noted that the charge density distribution of an oxygen atom and two hydrogen atoms (denoted $\rho_0(\mathbf{r})$), placed in the positions they would occupy in a water molecule but retaining their atomic distributions, does *not* place sufficient charge in the binding region to overcome the nuclear repulsion. He reasoned that the charge density associated with any accurate wave function for water must concentrate more charge in the binding region than does the atomic distribution $\rho_0(\mathbf{r})$. Let us denote the charge density associated with a proposed wave function by $\rho(\mathbf{r})$. Now it is clear that the quantity

$$\Delta\rho(\mathbf{r}) = \rho(\mathbf{r}) - \rho_0(\mathbf{r})$$

must be positive in the binding region if the charge density ρ is an accurate description of water. If the proposed charge density ρ leads to a negative $\Delta\rho$ in the binding region, the wave function from which ρ is derived cannot be an accurate description of water.

In order to determine the characteristics that an acceptable density distribution for the water molecule must possess, Bader (1964 a) calculated $\Delta\rho$ for several wave functions. He found that wave functions similar to that of Duncan and Pople (1953) yield negative values of $\Delta\rho$ in the binding region, and hence are not completely adequate descriptions of water. He was able, however, to produce positive values of $\Delta\rho$ in the binding region when several modifications were made in the Duncan and Pople wave function. These modifications include:

1. Greatly reducing the amount of s-character in the oxygen orbitals which overlap the hydrogen atoms. This allows the angle between the oxygen bonding orbitals to be less than the H–O–H angle (that is, the electron densities involved in the O–H bonds are bent inwards, away from the lines joining the oxygen and hydrogen nuclei).
2. Permitting some delocalization of the bond m.o.s (that is, not requiring that the bonds are entirely localized between two atoms).
3. Taking the lone-pair orbitals to be almost pure sp_x hybrids, so that the angle between the lone-pairs is almost 180° (that is, the lone-pairs are directed above and below the molecular plane with almost no component in the plane pointing away from the protons).

Fig. 1.8 shows plots of $\Delta\rho$ for a charge distribution having these modifications: $\Delta\rho$ is positive throughout the binding region. For this particular charge distribution the bonding hybrids from the oxygen are 97 per cent $2p$ in character and the angle between them is 64°. This means that each bond is bent inwards by about 20°. The oxygen lone-pairs are 50 per cent $2s$ and 50 per cent $2p$ in character. A plot of the *total* valence electron density in the x-z plane for the same distribution is shown in the left side of Fig. 1.9. The right side is a similar plot for another charge distribution in which both the lone-pair and bond hybrids of the oxygen are roughly sp^3 in character and in which the bond hybrids point toward the hydrogens. The latter charge distribution predicts a negative value of $\Delta\rho$ in the binding region and is thus unacceptable. Note that the angle between the lone-pairs in the acceptable charge distribution is considerably greater than in the unacceptable one.

Bader concluded that an acceptable wave function for water must have a charge distribution with the following characteristics: the lone-pair orbitals must be close to sp hybrids, the orbitals of the oxygen atom which overlap with the hydrogens must be nearly pure $2p$ orbitals, and the angle between these orbitals must be considerably less than the H–O–H angle. These conclusions are largely borne out by the more

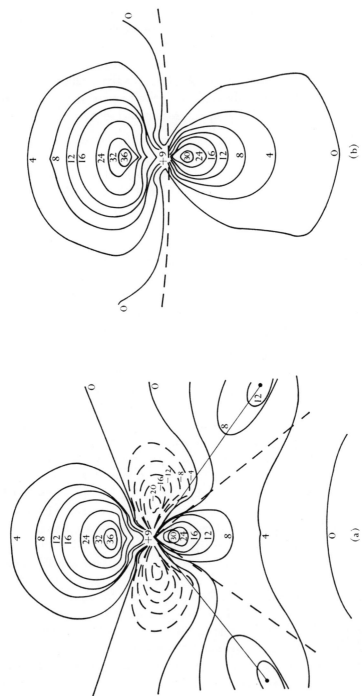

FIG. 1.8. Plots of $\Delta\rho$ for Bader's charge distribution with bent bonds (see text). The $\Delta\rho$ values are in atomic units $\times 100$. (a) In the plane containing the nuclei. The hydrogen nuclei are situated at the ends of the two solid straight lines, which meet at the oxygen nucleus. The dashed straight lines are the boundaries of the binding region, which lies between them (cf. Fig. 1.7 (a)). (b) In the x–z plane. The dashed line separates the binding and antibinding regions (cf. Fig. 1.7 (b)). Redrawn from Bader (1964 a).

complex wave function of Ellison and Shull (Ellison and Shull 1955, Burnelle and Coulson 1957). This wave function predicts lone-pairs of 53 per cent $2p$ character and oxygen bonding orbitals of almost 100 per cent $2p$ character, forming an angle of 69°.

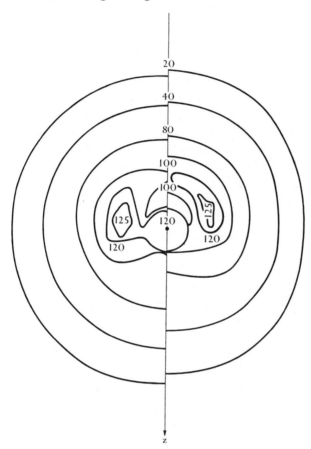

Fig. 1.9. The left side is a plot of the total valence electron density in the x–z plane for Bader's charge distribution with bent bonds. The right side is the corresponding plot for the charge distribution mentioned in the text in which the bonds and lone-pairs are sp^3 hybridized. From Bader (1964 a).

(d) *Accurate wave functions and the calculation of physical properties*

The calculation of molecular properties requires very accurate wave functions and elaborate computational techniques. Accurate wave functions are needed because most properties of interest to chemists are associated with energy changes that are small compared to the total molecular energy. For example, if we wish to calculate the electronic binding energy of the water molecule to an accuracy of ± 50 per cent, we must be able to calculate the total molecular energy to within $\sim 0\cdot25$ per cent. Calculations of this accuracy have become possible during the last few years, largely as a result of the development of techniques for evaluating the difficult integrals which occur in the quantum-mechanical expressions for energy and other properties. Let us now briefly consider some of the best wave functions so far devised for water, and the values of physical properties calculated from them. Table 1.7 contains a summary of these wave functions and their associated properties.

The work of Ellison and Shull (1955) was one of the earliest attempts to formulate an accurate description of the water molecule. In setting up their molecular orbital wave function, Ellison and Shull first grouped the a.o.s of the atoms into seven 'symmetry orbitals'. These are linear combinations of the Slater a.o.s taken so as to belong to irreducible representations of the symmetry group of the molecule. Then m.o.s were formed by taking linear combinations of symmetry orbitals possessing the same symmetry. The coefficients of the symmetry orbitals which produce the lowest electronic energy were found by Roothaan's (1951) method. This technique is often called the SCF (self-consistent field) m.o. method. All ten electrons were considered in this treatment and all integrals were retained in the calculation, although some of the multicentre integrals were approximated. The mathematical expression for the wave function, Ψ, is a determinant

$$\Psi = \frac{1}{\sqrt{10!}} \begin{vmatrix} \psi_1(1) & \psi_1(2) & \psi_1(3) & . & . & . & \psi_1(10) \\ \bar\psi_1(1) & \bar\psi_1(2) & & . & . & . & \bar\psi_1(10) \\ & . & & & & & \\ & . & & & & & . \\ . & & & & & & . \\ . & & & & & & . \\ & . & & & & & . \\ \bar\psi_5(1) & \bar\psi_5(2) & & . & . & . & \bar\psi_5(10) \end{vmatrix} \tag{1.14}$$

where $\psi_1(2)$, for example, represents the first molecular orbital occupied by the second electron. Electrons in orbitals with bars have a spin component of the opposite sign of those in orbitals without bars. Such a wave function is useful for calculating molecular properties such as the ionization energy, but is not easily visualized because the m.o.s are not localized in particular regions of the molecule. Both Ellison and Shull, and Burnelle and Coulson (1957), transformed the wave function to 'equivalent orbitals' which are more nearly localized. The calculations indicate that the lone-pairs contribute 1·69 D to the total moment, and, as discussed in the previous section, that the bonds are bent inwards.

Utilizing recent methods of computing molecular integrals, Pitzer and Merrifield (1966) were able to calculate physical properties from Ellison and Shull's wave function with improved accuracy (see Table 1.7). Pitzer (1966) went on to calculate several properties from this wave function after optimizing the orbital exponents of the a.o.s (Ellison and Shull had determined their orbital exponents by Slater's rules). The resulting values of the dipole moment, force constants, and field gradients are in good agreement with experiment.

McWeeny and Ohno (1960) constructed a number of wave functions for water, taking care to emphasize the localization of bonds and lone-pairs. They used the same a.o.s as Ellison and Shull and were thus able to use the integrals of the earlier work. We should note, however, that as some of these integrals were evaluated by approximate methods, their numerical results are subject to small uncertainties. McWeeny and Ohno first hybridized the seven a.o.s on the hydrogen and oxygen atoms to form seven new a.o.s which are orthogonal and spatially directed in such a way that

(1) four of them can be overlapped in pairs to describe the bonds,
(2) two of them describe equivalent lone-pairs,
(3) one describes an oxygen inner shell.

From the new a.o.s they formed seven different wave functions of increasing complexity. Three of these are SCF wave functions analogous to the Ellison and Shull wave function; two are configuration-interaction wave functions that take into account the effects of several pairings of electrons. Table 1.7 gives values for physical properties calculated from the function built up from seven configurations (the 'c.i. 7' wave function). This wave function is a sum of eight determinants, the first of which is similar to eqn (1.14).

Several authors have bypassed the difficulty of evaluating multicentre integrals by constructing m.o.s from a.o.s that are all centred at the same point in space. Inherent in this method, however, is a new difficulty: many more a.o.s must be used to achieve an adequate representation of the molecular charge distribution. Moccia (1964), for example, expressed the m.o.s of water as a linear combination of Slater-like functions, all centred at the nucleus of the oxygen atom. He used a total of

Table 1.7

Values of physical properties calculated from wave functions[a]

Authors	Type of wave function	Total energy (eV)[b]	Binding energy (eV)	Bond length (Å)
Ellison and Shull (1955)	SCF m.o.			
	(a) Experimental dimensions	−2062·5	−7·7	(0·95
	(b) Best energy	−2063·0	−8·2	(0·95
Pitzer and Merrifield (1966)	Same as Ellison and Shull, with integrals more accurately evaluated	−2058·59		(0·95
McWeeny and Ohno (1960)	Configuration-interaction with seven configurations	−2061·5	−6·3	(0·95
Moccia (1964)	One-centre, SCF m.o. centred at the oxygen nucleus	−2065·85		0·95
Hake and Banyard (1965)	United atom, centred at the oxygen nucleus	−2041·16		(0·95
Moskowitz and Harrison (1965)	SCF m.o. with			
	(a) 952/32 basis[e]	−2069·11		(0·95
	(b) 95/31 basis[e]	−2068·87		0·95
Bishop and Randić (1966)	One-centre m.o., consisting of 19 determinants	−2064·18		0·91
Whitten, Allen, and Fink (1966)	SCF m.o. with a Gaussian basis	−2068·05		(0·96
Pitzer (1966)	(a) Ellison and Shull's wave function with orbital exponents optimized at the experimental geometry	−2059·88		(0·95
	(b) Same, but with exponents reoptimized at each geometry	−2059·95	−4·49	0·99
Experimental		−2080·55	−10·1	0·95

[a] Molecular dimensions in parentheses have been assumed in the calculation.

[b] The energies which were reported in original papers in atomic units have been converted to eV using the factor 1 a.u. = 27·210 eV.

[c] Derived from the mean diamagnetic susceptibility reported by Hake and Banyard (1965).

[d] Eisenberg *et al.* (1965).

[e] See original paper for definition of these terms.

[f] The quantity reported in the original paper is $2(k_{\bar{r}} + k_{\bar{r}'})$; the present authors have combined this with the experimental value of $k_{\bar{r}'}$ to yield $k_{\bar{r}}$.

[g] Calculated by C. W. Kern.

[h] Calculated by S. Aung, R. M. Pitzer, and S. I. Chan.

Bond angle (degrees)	Dipole moment (D)	1st ionization potential (eV)	Force constants (10^5 dyn cm^{-1})	Other quantities and $\langle r^2 \rangle$
(105)	1·52	11·79		$\langle r^2 \rangle = 5\cdot4^c \times 10^{-16}$ cm^2
120	1·32	11·64		
(105)	1·434			
(105)	1·76			$\langle r^2 \rangle = 5\cdot4$
106·53	2·085	12·73		$\langle r^2 \rangle = 5\cdot5^c$
(105·05)				$\langle r^2 \rangle = 4\cdot4^c$
(105)	1·99	13·7		
108·4	2·44	14·5	$k_{\bar{r}} = 9\cdot8^f$	
(105)			$k_{\bar{r}} = 8\cdot9^f$	
112	2·50			
(104·52)	1·916^g		For (b): $k_{\bar{r}} = 8\cdot26$ $k_{\bar{r}'} = -0\cdot19$ $k_\alpha = 1\cdot22$ $k_{\bar{r}\alpha} = 0\cdot36$	For (a): Field gradients at the deuterons:^{h} $\partial^2 V/\partial z'^2 = 1\cdot69 \times 10^{15}$ e.s.u. $\partial^2 V/\partial y'^2 = -0\cdot74$ $\partial^2 V/\partial x'^2 = -0\cdot95$
100·32				
104·52	1·83$_4$	12·62	$k_{\bar{r}} = 8\cdot45$ $k_{\bar{r}'} = -0\cdot10$ $k_\alpha = 0\cdot76$ $k_{\bar{r}\alpha} = 0\cdot23$	$\langle r^2 \rangle = 5\cdot1 \pm 0\cdot7 \times 10^{-16}$ cm^2

twenty-eight Slater-like functions. The coefficients of those in a given m.o. were found by Roothaan's method. His wave function yields remarkably accurate values for the total energy and the equilibrium dimensions of water.

Hake and Banyard (1965) and Bishop and Randić (1966) also proposed one-centre wave functions for the water molecule. Hake and Banyard's wave function, like Moccia's, is a single determinantal function, but it is much simpler in that each m.o. is composed of only one a.o. The orbital exponents of the a.o.s were varied to produce the lowest possible total energy. Bishop and Randić's wave function is a sum of nineteen determinants, each being composed of Slater-like orbitals.

Moskowitz and Harrison (1965), and Whitten, Allen, and Fink (1966), attacked the problem of multicentre integrals in a different way. They expressed their m.o.s as linear combinations of Gaussian functions. Multicentre integrals involving Gaussians are evaluated much more easily than those involving Slater orbitals. Whitten *et al.* calculated a good value for the total energy of water by varying the coefficients of several predetermined groups of Gaussian functions in each m.o. Moskowitz and Harrison reported calculations with many different sets of basis functions; the results associated with two of their wave functions are given in Table 1.7.

(e) The charge distribution: a summary

As discussion of the charge distribution of the water molecule is scattered throughout this chapter, it may be helpful to summarize some of the important points here. The electronic charge of the molecule is not confined to the nuclear plane, as is shown by the electron-density contour maps in Figs. 1.6, 1.8, and 1.9, and also by the quadrupole and octupole moments. Thus any model of the water molecule that represents the charge distribution by a planar configuration of fixed charges is inadequate. The experimental evidence that the water molecule is almost isotropically polarizable is another indication that any planar charge distribution gives an unrealistic picture of the molecule.

A prominant structural feature of water is the two lobes of charge formed by the lone-pair electrons. These lobes project above and below the molecular plane, and probably project away from the hydrogens to some extent. This means that they contribute to the dipole moment of water. The importance of their contribution is, however, an unsettled matter; it cannot be measured because only the total moment is an observable quantity. If the lone-pairs do contribute to the dipole moment, then the total molecular moment cannot be considered to consist of only the vector sum of the two bond moments. Similarly, as the lone-pairs are undoubtedly quite polarizable, they also contribute to the total polarizability of the molecule in each direction. During the course of molecular vibrations the instantaneous values of the total dipole moment and polarizability change, and the contributions of the lone-pairs to these properties presumably also change, owing to changes in hybridization as the nuclei move.

The bonds of the molecule also have interesting properties. In the first place, careful calculations indicate that they do not lie precisely along lines drawn from the oxygen nucleus toward the hydrogen nuclei, but are bent inwards. In terms of the molecular orbital description of the molecule, this is expressed by the fact that the bonding orbitals of the oxygen atom form a smaller angle with one another than the H–O–H angle. In addition, the bonds are not independent of each other. This is evident from the difference in the dissociation energies of the two bonds, and also from the normal mode analysis of the vibrational spectrum, which shows that the equilibrium bond length of one bond is dependent on the length of the other bond. It is also evident from theoretical work, where it is found that acceptable results are not obtained if bonding electrons are treated as being entirely localized.

2. The Real Vapour

HAVING discussed the nature of a water molecule in the ideal vapour, where molecules do not interact, we next consider the real vapour. The properties of the real vapour, like those of ice and liquid water, are affected by the forces acting between the molecules. Indeed, studies of water in the vapour state have made an important contribution to what is known about the interactions of water molecules. In this chapter we shall first consider the origin of these forces, and their relation to the second and third virial coefficients of steam. Then we shall discuss the thermodynamic properties of the real vapour in detail. We shall not consider other properties of the vapour, such as its viscosity and thermal conductivity, because these properties have not yet proved to be very useful in understanding ice, liquid water, or the forces between water molecules.

2.1. Forces between water molecules

(a) Origin and description of the forces

It is convenient to represent the force of interaction between molecules A and B by a potential energy function, U_{AB}. This function depends on the intermolecular separation, $\bar{R}$, and for polar substances on the mutual orientation of the molecules. Orientations are often expressed in terms of the angles shown in Fig. 2.1. The net force between A and B along the line of centres, $\mathbf{F}_{AB}$, is given by

$$\mathbf{F}_{AB} = -\frac{\partial U_{AB}(\bar{R}, \text{angles})}{\partial \bar{R}}. \tag{2.1}$$

The function U_{AB} is negative in sign when the net force is attractive. Torques exerted on the molecules by each other are given by the partial derivatives of U_{AB} with respect to the angles.

In this section we describe the form of the potential energy function for the interaction of a pair of water molecules. Information about this function has come partly from interpretation of experimental virial coefficients with the aid of statistical mechanics, partly from calculations with models of the water molecule, and partly from analogy to potential functions of simpler systems. This information, as we shall see presently, is far from complete. There is no assurance, moreover, that the potential function for a group of water molecules is simply the sum of the potential

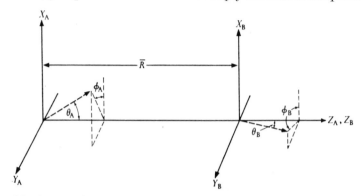

Fig. 2.1. A convenient coordinate system for representing the separation and mutual orientation of two dipolar molecules. The dashed arrows give the directions of the dipole moments.

functions for all pairs in the group. In other words, forces between water molecules may not be *pairwise additive*. As a result, even a perfectly accurate U_{AB} would predict with perfect accuracy only those physical properties, like the second virial coefficient, that depend solely on the interactions of pairs of molecules. Fortunately most components of intermolecular forces are pairwise additive to some extent (Table 2.1), so that even the physical properties depending on the interaction of a group of molecules may be interpreted semiquantitatively in terms of the potential functions we discuss here.

Before examining the detailed functional form of U_{AB} it may be helpful to say something about its general character. The value of U_{AB} is conventionally taken as zero for infinite separation of the molecules. As two water molecules approach to within several molecular diameters, U_{AB} can be either positive (molecules repelling) or negative (molecules attracting), depending on the molecular orientations. Clearly the mean value of U_{AB} must be negative for two molecules, for water vapour molecules attract each other sufficiently to condense into liquid water. Furthermore, U_{AB} must be positive at very small separations regardless of mutual orientation, since water and ice have finite volumes. The small compressibility of ice indicates that U_{AB} increases rapidly at small separations. These general features of U_{AB} are shown by the solid curves of Fig. 2.2.

TABLE 2.1

Characteristics of forces between water molecules

Force	R-dependence of potential energy		Attractive $(-)$ or repulsive $(+)$	Pairwise additive
	Molecules stationary	Molecules rotating		
Long-range forces:				
Electrostatic:			$-$ or $+$	Yes
Dipole–dipole	R^{-3}	R^{-6}		
Dipole–quadrupole	R^{-4}	R^{-8}		
Quadrupole–quadrupole	R^{-5}	R^{-10}		
Dipole–octupole	R^{-5}	R^{-10}		
Induction:				
Dipole–induced dipole	R^{-6}	R^{-6}	$-$	No
Dispersion†	R^{-6}	R^{-6}	$-$	Yes
Short-range forces:				
Overlap repulsion	$\sim e^{-\rho \bar{R}}$ or $\sim R^{-n}$		$+$	Nearly
Hydrogen bonding	complex		$-$	No

† The R^{-6} term in the dispersion energy is the leading term of a series; the next term is proportional to R^{-8}.

Long-range forces

The total force between two molecules is often considered to be the resultant of several component forces, and U_{AB} is then written as the sum of terms, each term representing one component. The component forces are regarded as being either *long-range* or *short-range*. Short-range forces are those that come into play only when the electronic charge clouds of the two molecules overlap; we shall discuss them below. Long-range forces may be rigorously described in terms of properties of isolated water molecules. In wave-mechanical terminology, this means that the molecules are far enough apart for electron exchange to be neglected, so that the wave function for the two-molecule system may be written as a simple product of the wave functions of the isolated molecules. Derivations of the contributions of these forces to U_{AB} are given by Hirschfelder *et al.* (1964).

Let us consider the results. The long-range forces between two water molecules in their ground states consist of *electrostatic, induction*, and *dispersion* forces. Electrostatic forces predominate at large separations. They arise from the interaction of the permanent electric moments of the molecules. The contribution to the potential function from electrostatic forces may be written as a series:

$$U_{\text{electrostatic}} = U_{\mu\mu} + U_{\mu Q} + U_{QQ} + \dots \qquad (2.2)$$

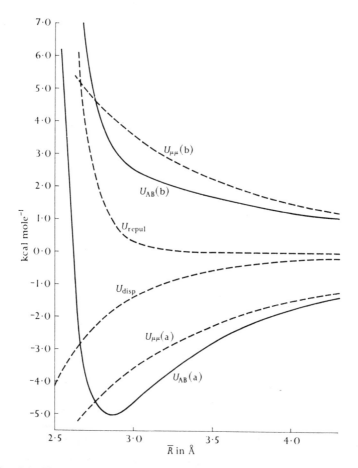

FIG. 2.2. The potential energy of interaction for two water molecules having fixed mutual orientations, as given by Stockmayer's potential (eqn (2.17)). The lower solid curve, $U_{\text{AB}}(a)$, shows the total potential energy for a pair of molecules with parallel dipole moments; the upper solid curve, $U_{\text{AB}}(b)$, shows the same function for a pair of molecules with anti-parallel dipole moments. The dashed curves show the dispersion, repulsive, and dipole–dipole contributions to the total potential energy. In Stockmayer's function, the dispersion and repulsive forces are independent of the mutual orientations of the molecules, and thus make the same contributions to $U_{\text{AB}}(a)$ as to $U_{\text{AB}}(b)$.

Each term on the right-hand side is a function of the separation and mutual orientation of the molecules, as well as certain electric moments.

The first and most consequential term of eqn (2.2) describes the interaction of the dipoles of the two molecules. It has the form

$$U_{\mu\mu} = \frac{\mu^2}{\bar{R}^3}\{\sin\theta_A \sin\theta_B \cos(\phi_A - \phi_B) - 2\cos\theta_A \cos\theta_B\} \qquad (2.3)\dagger$$

$$= \frac{\mu^2}{\bar{R}^3} \times f, \qquad (2.3\,\text{a})$$

where f is the function of angles in brackets. In this equation μ is the dipole moment of an isolated water molecule, the angles are those shown in Fig. 2.1, and $\bar{R}$ is the intermolecular distance. Throughout the present chapter we shall take $\bar{R}$ as the distance between the oxygen nuclei of the molecules. Table 2.2 presents values of $U_{\mu\mu}$ for several intermolecular distances and orientations. Note that the energy is highest (attraction weakest) in configuration (b) of Fig. 2.3 where the dipoles are head to head. The energy is lowest when the dipoles are head to tail (configuration (a)). In fact, $U_{\mu\mu}$ is twice as low in this position as in configuration (f), the most common relative orientation of two water molecules in ice.

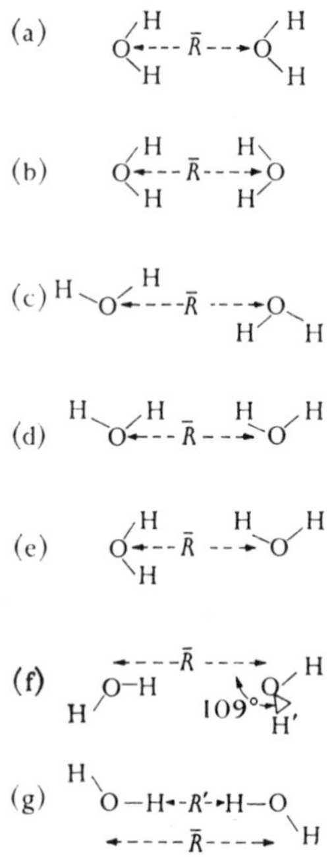

The next term in eqn (2.2), $U_{\mu Q}$, describes the interaction of a dipole with the quadrupole moment of another molecule, and U_{QQ} describes the interaction of the quadrupole moments of the quadrupole moments. We have evaluated these terms for the same set of mutual orientations (Table 2.2) using the calculated quadrupole moments of Table 1.5 and standard expressions for these terms (e.g. Margenau 1939). The values of $U_{\mu Q}$ and U_{QQ} are much smaller than $U_{\mu\mu}$ and they fall off more rapidly with intermolecular separation than does $U_{\mu\mu}$: they are proportional to $\bar{R}^{-4}$ and $\bar{R}^{-5}$ respectively, whereas $U_{\mu\mu}$ is proportional to $\bar{R}^{-3}$ (Table 2.1). Still other terms in the series of eqn (2.2) describe dipole–octupole forces, quadrupole–octupole forces, etc.

FIG. 2.3. The mutual orientations of two water molecules for which energies of interaction are given in Table 2.2 (all atoms are in the plane of the paper except H′ of configuration (f)).

† In this equation, and all others of this section except where noted, the potential energy is in units of ergs if the moments are in electrostatic units and the other quantities are in CGS units. The units of potential energy may be converted to kcal/mol-of-interaction by multiplying by $1\cdot44 \times 10^{13}$.

We have not yet treated the electrostatic forces between rotating molecules in a gas at a temperature T. It might be expected that electrostatic forces between rotating molecules vanish, since the forces are as strongly attracting in some orientations as they are repelling in others. In fact a net attraction arises because molecules are more likely to be found in orientations of low energy than in orientations of high energy. If we assume that $\bar{R}$ is nearly constant during molecular rotation, we can express the statistical average of $U_{\mu\mu}$ for rotating molecules, denoted $\langle U_{\mu\mu} \rangle$, by

$$\langle U_{\mu\mu} \rangle = \frac{\int U_{\mu\mu} \exp(-U_{\mu\mu}/kT) \, d\Omega}{\int \exp(-U_{\mu\mu}/kT) \, d\Omega}, \tag{2.4}$$

where $d\Omega = \sin\theta_A \sin\theta_B \, d\theta_A \, d\theta_B \, d\phi_A \, d\phi_B$. For temperatures at which kT is much greater than the difference of the maximum and minimum values of $U_{\mu\mu}$, $\langle U_{\mu\mu} \rangle$ becomes

$$\langle U_{\mu\mu} \rangle = -\frac{2}{3kT} \frac{\mu^4}{\bar{R}^6}. \tag{2.4 a}$$

Evidently the statistical average of $U_{\mu\mu}$ for rotating molecules decreases much more rapidly with distance than does $U_{\mu\mu}$ itself. The right-hand column of Table 2.2 shows values of $\langle U_{\mu\mu} \rangle$ at 300 °K. It is seen that for an intermolecular separation of 10 Å, $\langle U_{\mu\mu} \rangle$ is only 3 per cent of the maximum value of $U_{\mu\mu}$.

The second component of long-range forces consists of induction forces. They arise from the interaction of the permanent electric moments of each molecule with induced electric moments of the other. In contrast to the electrostatic forces, which may be either attractive or repulsive, depending on molecular orientations, induction forces are invariably attractive. The most important induction force is the interaction of the dipole moment of one molecule (say A) with the dipole it induces on the other (B). Assuming that water molecules are characterized by an isotropic polarizability $\bar{\alpha}$, we can write the potential function for this force as

$$U_{\mu\alpha} = -\frac{\mu^2 \bar{\alpha}(3 \cos^2\theta_A + 1)}{2\bar{R}^6}. \tag{2.5}$$

Of course, a similar term exists for the interaction of the induced moment on A with the permanent dipole moment of B. It should be noted that an exact expression for the induction energy would contain relevant components of the polarizability tensor, rather than its mean value. For rotating molecules the dipole–induced dipole energy is given by

$$\langle U_{\mu\alpha} \rangle = -\frac{2\mu^2 \bar{\alpha}}{\bar{R}^6}. \tag{2.6}$$

TABLE 2.2

Calculated contributions to the energy of interaction of two water molecules

(The molecules are separated by a distance $\bar{R}$ and are mutually oriented as shown in Fig. 2.3. All entries are in units of kcal/mol-of-interaction.)

(a) Long-range forces

Contribution	$\bar{R}$ (Å)	Mutual orientation						$\langle U \rangle$ at 300 °K
		(a)	(b)	(c)	(d)	(e)	(f)	
$U_{\mu\mu}$	5	−0·78	0·78	−0·39	0·39	0	−0·39	(−0·17)†
	10	−0·10	0·10	−0·05	0·05	0	−0·05	−0·003
	15	−0·03	0·03	−0·01	0·01	0	−0·01	−0·000
$U_{\mu Q}$	5	0	0·09	0	0	0·12	−0·07	
	10	0	0·01	0	0	0·01	−0·00	
	15	0	0·00	0	0	0·00	−0·00	
U_{QQ}	5	0·01	0·01	0·02	0·02	−0·01	−0·01	
	10	0·00	0·00	0·00	0·00	−0·00	−0·00	
$U_{\mu\alpha}$	5	−0·02	−0·02	−0·00	−0·00	−0·01	−0·01	−0·01
	10	−0·00	−0·00	−0·00	−0·00	−0·00	−0·00	−0·00
U_{disp}	5	−0·08	−0·08	−0·08	−0·08	−0·08	−0·08	−0·08
	10	−0·00	−0·00	−0·00	−0·00	−0·00	−0·00	−0·00
Total	5	−0·87	0·78	−0·45	0·33	0·02	−0·56	(−0·26)†

(b) Short-range forces

Contribution	$\bar{R}$ (Å)	Mutual orientation	Energy
U_{repul} (from eqn (2.10))‡	2·76	All	4
U_{repul} (from eqn (2.13))	2·76	g	219
		c	5
		f	6

† Equation (2.4 a) is not strictly applicable for $\bar{R} = 5$ Å and 300 °K because kT is not larger than the difference of the maximum and minimum values of $U_{\mu\mu}$.

‡ With $A^* = 4$ kcal mol^{-1} and $n = 9$.

Substituting values of μ and $\bar{\alpha}$ from Table 1.5 we get

$$U_{\mu\alpha} = -\frac{9 \cdot 7 \times 10^{-60}}{\bar{R}^6} \text{ergs,} \qquad (2.6\,a)$$

where $\bar{R}$, as before, is in centimetres. Note that the dipole–induced dipole energy, whether between rotating or stationary molecules, is proportional to $\bar{R}^{-6}$. From Table 2.2 it is clear that at distances of 5 Å or more, induction forces account for only a small part of the total long-range force. This is not the case in ice and liquid water, where the molecules are closer to each other and the induction forces between water molecules are relatively much more important. In these phases the proximity and correlated orientations of water molecules produce very large induced dipole moments which, in turn, contribute significantly to intermolecular forces (Section 3.4 (a)).

Dispersion forces, or London forces as they are sometimes called, are the third contribution to the long-range energy. They arise from the correlated movement of electrons in neighbouring molecules. A simplified explanation of dispersion forces is that, at a given instant, the configuration of electrons of molecule A results in an instantaneous dipole moment. This instantaneous moment induces a dipole moment in molecule B and interacts with it. London (1937) showed that the resulting potential energy function, U_{disp}, is negative and can be represented by a series having a leading term proportional to $\bar{R}^{-6}$,

$$U_{disp} = -\frac{c}{\bar{R}^6} + \dots. \qquad (2.7)$$

Evaluation of the exact expression for U_{disp} requires a knowledge of the molecular wave function for ground and excited electronic states, so that approximate formulas for U_{disp} are usually employed. One such formula is the Kirkwood–Müller expression:

$$U_{disp} = \frac{3mc'^2}{N\bar{R}^6}\bar{\alpha}\bar{\chi}^d, \qquad (2.8)$$

where m is the electronic mass, c' is the velocity of light, N is Avogadro's number, and $\bar{\chi}^d$ is the mean diamagnetic contribution to the magnetic susceptibility. The assumption that U_{disp} is independent of molecular orientation is probably not greatly in error for water molecules. Now $\bar{\chi}^d$ is proportional to the molecular property $\langle r^2 \rangle$ which was mentioned in Section 1.1 (c):

$$\bar{\chi}^d = -\frac{Ne^2}{6mc'^2}\langle r^2 \rangle. \qquad (2.9)$$

Combining eqns (2.8) and (2.9), and substituting the values for $\bar{\alpha}$ and $\langle r^2 \rangle$ given in Table 1.5 and Section 1.1 (c), we find that the Kirkwood–Müller expression gives $84 \cdot 9 \times 10^{-60}$ erg cm^6 for the coefficient c of eqn (2.7). We have used this value of c to compute the values of U_{disp} shown in Table 2.2.

Table 2.3 contains several estimates for the coefficient c describing the dispersion energy. The first value is the one we have just derived from the Kirkwood–Müller formula. The values predicted by other approximate expressions, the London and the Slater–Kirkwood formulas, are smaller. Salem (1960) showed that the Kirkwood–Müller formula yields a value of c which is the upper limit of the true value. Also listed are values of c^*—the proportionality constant for all intermolecular energies varying with $\bar{R}^{-6}$—derived from the second virial coefficient of steam (see following section). The constant c^* is the sum of c and the coefficient for the dipole–induced dipole energy. On the basis of eqn (2.6 a), the latter coefficient contributes roughly 10×10^{-60} erg cm^6 to c^*. Thus each value of c^* in Table 2.3 should yield a value of c smaller by about 10×10^{-60} erg cm^6. The values of c obtained from virial coefficients and the various theoretical expressions cover a wide range. There is, however, reason to believe that the actual value is near to the one predicted by the Kirkwood–Müller formula. In the case of atoms and molecules for which better experimental c values are known, the values of c predicted by the Kirkwood–Müller formula tend to be slightly too large but in better accord with experiment than coefficients obtained from the other simple expressions (Salem 1960). The coefficient predicted by London's formula is often too small by a factor of 2; the Slater–Kirkwood coefficient is better but also tends to be an underestimate.

TABLE 2.3

Proposed coefficients for dispersion and other $\bar{R}^{-6}$-dependent forces between water molecules

(All entries are in units of 10^{-60} erg cm^6.)

Method of evaluation	c (Dispersion energy coefficient of eqn (2.7))	c^* (Proportionality constant for all energies† varying with $\bar{R}^{-6}$)
Theoretical expressions:		
Kirkwood–Müller formula (eqn (2.8))	84·9	
Slater–Kirkwood formula (eqn (2.12))	63	
London formula (London 1937)	47	
Second virial coefficient:		
Stockmayer (1941)		70·4
Margenau and Myers (1944)		45
Rowlinson (1949)		72·8
Rowlinson (1951 a)		80·4

† The coefficient c^* is the sum of c and the coefficient of the dipole–induced dipole energy. The latter coefficient—on the basis of eqn (2.6 a)—is roughly 10×10^{-60} erg cm^6.

Short-range forces

When two water molecules approach within about 3 Å, short-range forces dominate. A rigorous expression for the interaction energy at short range would involve a wave function for all twenty electrons of the two molecules and would be very complicated. Roughly speaking, we can attribute the short-range forces between water molecules to a combination of electronic overlap repulsions and the contributions of electron delocalization to the hydrogen bond energy (see Section 3.6 (c)). Let us consider the overlap repulsions first. They arise from the tendency of the electrons in one molecule to avoid those in the other, as dictated by the Pauli principle. They come into play as the charge clouds of the two molecules begin to overlap and they increase rapidly as the molecules approach more closely: the repulsive potential energy is often described by a term proportional to either $e^{-\rho R}$ or $\bar{R}^{-n}$, where ρ and n are constants, n being between 9 and 24.

Kamb (1965 b) proposed a function of the form

$$U_{\text{repul}} = A^* \left(\frac{\sigma}{\bar{R}} \right)^n, \tag{2.10}$$

where $\sigma = 2 \cdot 76 \times 10^{-8}$ cm, to describe the overlap repulsions between water molecules. He derived two pairs of coefficients and exponents ($A^* = 2 \cdot 7$ kcal mol^{-1}, $n = 10$; and $A^* = 4 \cdot 0$ kcal mol^{-1}, $n = 9$) from the experimental difference in energy of ices I and VII (Section 3.2), and different assumptions about the attractive forces between molecules. Equation (2.10) may be a reliable description of the repulsive forces between non-hydrogen bonded molecules in ice VII, but in all probability it poorly describes repulsion between water molecules having other mutual orientations.

To obtain a rough idea of the dependence of overlap repulsion on the mutual orientation of two water molecules, we can adapt a method applied by Hendrickson (1961) and others to hydrocarbons. In this method forces between non-bonded atoms are assumed to be described by the Buckingham potential function

$$U_{\text{repul+disp}} = A^* e^{-\rho R'} - \frac{c}{R'^6}, \tag{2.11}$$

where A^*, ρ, and c are constants and R' is the separation in Ångstrom units between the interacting atoms. The overlap repulsion (plus dispersion force) between two water molecules is then given by the sum of the interactions of each atom in one molecule with each atom of the other molecule. To use this approach we must evaluate the constants in eqn (2.11) for H–H, O–H, and O–O interactions. The second term on the right-hand side describes, of course, the dispersion attractions between the atoms. The coefficient c may be roughly determined from the Slater–Kirkwood expression:

$$c = \tfrac{3}{2}e^2\sqrt{a_0}\left[\frac{\alpha_A\,\alpha_B}{(\alpha_A/N_A)^{\frac{1}{2}}+(\alpha_B/N_B)^{\frac{1}{2}}}\right], \qquad (2.12)$$

where e is the electronic charge, a_0 is the radius of the first Bohr orbit, α_A and α_B are the polarizabilities of the interacting atoms, and N_A and N_B are the numbers of electrons in the outer sub-shell of the atoms. Let us take Ketelaar's (1953) recommended values of α: $0\cdot59\times10^{-24}$ cm^3 for oxygen in a hydroxyl group and $0\cdot42\times10^{-24}$ cm^3 for hydrogen. These values lead to the coefficients of R'^{-6} in eqn (2.13). We follow Hendrickson (1961) in adopting the ρ coefficients from experiments on the scattering of rare gases. The value for hydrogen–hydrogen repulsion is from the scattering of helium, the value for oxygen–oxygen repulsion is from the scattering of neon, and the value for hydrogen–oxygen repulsion is the geometric mean of the two. Finally the values of A^* are determined from the condition that $\mathrm{d}U/\mathrm{d}R'$ must vanish at $R' = R_0$, where R_0 is the sum of the van der Waals radii of the interacting atoms. We take $1\cdot25$ Å for the van der Waals radius of hydrogen and $1\cdot4$ Å for that of oxygen. The final potential functions are:

$$U_{\text{repul+disp}}\ (\text{kcal mol}^{-1}) = \begin{cases} \text{H–H:}\ \ 10\times10^3 e^{-4\cdot6R'}-49/R'^6 \\ \text{O–H:}\ \ 8\cdot2\times10^3 e^{-4\cdot1R'}-94/R'^6 \\ \text{O–O:}\ \ 6\cdot8\times10^3 e^{-3\cdot6R'}-201/R'^6 \end{cases}, \quad (2.13)$$

where R' is the separation of the interacting atoms in Ångstroms. The first of these equations is identical to the one derived by Hendrickson (1961).

The first term of eqns (2.13) provides a very rough indication of the dependence of the overlap repulsion between two water molecules on their mutual orientation. Consider two molecules with their oxygen nuclei $2\cdot76$ Å apart, the separation of neighbouring molecules in ordinary ice I. When they are oriented, as in (g) of Fig. 2.3, with hydrogens in the head-on position, eqns (2.13) predict a repulsive energy of 219 kcal mol^{-1}. This arises almost entirely from the repulsive interaction of the hydrogen atoms. Now rotate the molecules, keeping $\bar{R} = 2\cdot76$ Å, until the pair is in configuration (c) of Fig. 2.3. According to eqns (2.13) the repulsion falls off to about 5 kcal mol^{-1}. Clearly the repulsive energy is very sensitive to mutual orientations. When the two molecules are placed in configuration (f) of Fig. 2.3, the most common mutual orientation of neighbouring molecules in ice I, eqns (2.13) predict a repulsion of 6 kcal mol^{-1}.

In closing our discussion of short-range forces between water molecules, a few words must be said about hydrogen bonding. Although ample proof exists for hydrogen bonds in ice and liquid water, the present authors are unaware of any direct evidence for a hydrogen bond between two water molecules in the vapour phase. Spectroscopic studies, in fact, indicate that hydrogen bonds are rare or non-existent in water vapour. This conclusion is based on the observation that the formation of a hydrogen bond between a molecule containing a hydroxyl group (X–O–H) and another atom is generally accompanied by a marked decrease in O–H stretching frequency and a slight increase in X–O–H bending frequency (Pimentel and McClellan 1960; Sections 3.5 (a) and 4.7 (a)). Similar but smaller frequency shifts have been observed during the formation of dimers and other small polymers of water molecules.

Van Thiel, Becker, and Pimentel (1957) observed these shifts in a study of the infra-red spectra of water molecules trapped in a matrix of nitrogen at 20 °K. These authors assigned the observed absorption bands centred at 3546 and 3691 cm^{-1} to the stretching modes of $(H_2O)_2$ dimers. The frequencies are considerably lower than the ν_1 and ν_3 stretching modes of isolated H_2O molecules (3657 and 3756 cm^{-1} respectively). They assigned the observed band at 1620 cm^{-1} to a bending mode of the dimer; this frequency is somewhat higher than the bending mode of the isolated molecule (1595 cm^{-1}). Van Thiel et al. believe the dimer has a cyclic, double hydrogen-bonded structure:

$$
\begin{array}{c}
H \\
\quad \diagdown \\
\quad\quad O\!-\!H \\
\quad\quad \vdots \quad \vdots \\
\quad\quad H\!-\!O \\
\quad\quad\quad\quad \diagdown \\
\quad\quad\quad\quad\quad H
\end{array}
$$

On the basis of these facts, one would expect that spectroscopic methods could detect the presence of any appreciable number of hydrogen-bonded molecules in water vapour. Thus is it interesting that a careful comparison of the infra-red spectra of dilute and concentrated water vapour in the region of the ν_2 mode revealed no differences in frequencies of absorption: Benedict et al. (1952) compared the solar spectrum of the atmosphere (dilute water vapour at an average temperature of 14 °C) and the spectrum of nearly saturated steam (1 atm pressure and 110 °C) in the region of the ν_2 mode. They measured the line frequencies and intensities from 770 to 2200 cm^{-1} for both cases, and the only differences they observed were slight intensity variations, attributable to the change in temperature. Benedict et al. concluded that if dimers having quantized rotational states are present in saturated steam at one atmosphere, their concentration relative to the monomer must be less than 1 per cent.

It should be noted that the term 'hydrogen bond' has been used in the preceding paragraphs to mean a specific association of a hydrogen atom of one molecule with one of the lone-pairs of electrons on the other, as occurs in ice. The second virial coefficient of steam (see following section) leaves no doubt that dimers are present in water vapour, but there is no evidence that these dimers contain hydrogen bonds of the sort found in ice. Indeed, the temperature dependence of the second virial coefficient can be reproduced by potential functions including only terms like those we have discussed above. Any potential function constructed from terms discussed above would favour the head-to-tail mutual orientation of two water molecules (position (a) of Fig. 2.3), rather than the mutual orientations existing in ice (e.g. position (f) of Fig. 2.3). Hydrogen bonds between water molecules may be stable only in clusters, where the average number of hydrogen bonds is larger than in a dimer. Owing to the paucity of information on hydrogen bonds between molecules in steam, we shall postpone consideration of potential functions for hydrogen-bonded water molecules until the chapter on ice.

(b) *Virial coefficients*

The virial coefficients of water vapour are a source of information about the potential function for the interactions of water molecules. These coefficients appear in the virial equation of state, an expression that describes pressure–volume–temperature data for water vapour at moderate pressures. It has the form

$$\frac{PV}{RT} = 1 + \frac{B(T)}{V} + \frac{C(T)}{V^2} + ..., \tag{2.14}$$

where V is the molar volume, R is the gas constant, and $B(T)$, $C(T)$,... are the second, third, . . . virial coefficients. These coefficients are functions of temperature and they depend on the intermolecular potential. The second virial coefficient, $B(T)$, can be determined by a simple procedure: for each temperature at which $B(T)$ is required, the function $\{(PV/RT) - 1\}V$ is plotted on the ordinate against $1/V$ on the abscissa; then the ordinate intercept is $B(T)$. According to Keyes (1958), the second virial coefficient of water vapour can be expressed as

$$B(T) = 2 \cdot 062 - (2 \cdot 9017 \times 10^3/T)\exp(1 \cdot 7095 \times 10^5/T^2) \text{ cm}^3 \text{ g}^{-1} \quad (2.15)$$

over the temperature range 323–733 °K. Fig. 2.4 shows that $B(T)$ is negative throughout this range but increases with rising temperature.

Interpretation of the second virial coefficient in terms of the intermolecular potential

The second virial coefficient is closely related to the potential function for the interaction of a pair of molecules. Using methods of classical

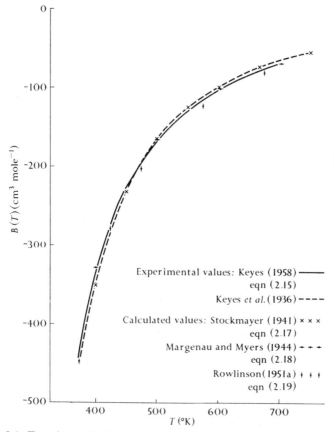

FIG. 2.4. Experimental and calculated values for the second virial coefficient of steam. The experimental values indicated by the dashed curve are those of Keyes *et al.* (1936) and are described by the empirical equation

$$B(T) = 1\cdot89 - (2\cdot641 \times 10^3/T) \times \exp(1\cdot858 \times 10^5/T^2) \text{ cm}^3 \text{ g}^{-1}.$$

The calculated values have been fitted to this equation. More recent experimental values are shown by the solid curve.

statistical mechanics it can be shown (e.g. Hirschfelder *et al.* 1964) that $B(T)$ is given by the expression

$$B(T) = \tfrac{1}{4}N \int\limits_0^\infty \int\limits_0^\pi \int\limits_0^\pi \int\limits_0^{2\pi} \{1 - \exp(-U_{AB}/kT)\}\bar{R}^2 \times$$
$$\times \sin\theta_A \sin\theta_B \, d(\phi_A - \phi_B) \, d\theta_A \, d\theta_B \, d\bar{R}. \quad (2.16)$$

In this equation U_{AB} is the potential energy function for a pair of stationary molecules, N is Avogadro's number, and the angles are those shown in Fig. 2.1. Stockmayer (1941) showed that the quantum-mechanical correction to this equation changes $B(T)$ values for H_2O only about 1 per cent for temperatures between 400 and 750 °K. His arguments are strictly applicable only for the potential function of eqn (2.17), but other workers have assumed that the quantum-mechanical correction is negligible for similar potential functions.

The physical meaning of eqn (2.16) is that a large negative value of $B(T)$ reflects strong attractive forces between molecules. This is clear if we recall that attractive forces correspond to negative values of U_{AB}. When U_{AB} is negative, $\exp(-U_{AB}/kT)$ is greater than unity and the factor $1-\exp(-U_{AB}/kT)$ in the integral is negative. Hence orientations with negative U_{AB} make negative contributions to $B(T)$. By the same token, the increasing values of $B(T)$ at higher temperatures reflect decreasingly negative values of U_{AB}/kT.

Equation (2.16) has been widely used to derive information about the potential functions for pairs of molecules. The usual procedure is to start with an assumed potential function, U_{AB}, containing several undetermined constants. The assumed function is inserted in eqn (2.16). The undetermined constants are chosen to produce the best possible fit of the calculated $B(T)$ values to the experimental values. Experience has shown that almost any reasonable form for U_{AB} will produce $B(T)$ values that can be fitted to experiment. This means, of course, that the temperature variation of the second virial coefficient is not a stringent test of the validity of U_{AB}. Nevertheless, if the functional form of the assumed U_{AB} is basically correct, this procedure should result in a fairly accurate potential function.

Let us review several applications of this procedure to potential functions for a pair of water molecules. Stockmayer (1941) chose a potential function of the form

$$U_{AB} = -\frac{\mu^2}{\bar{R}^3}f - \frac{c^*}{\bar{R}^6} + \frac{c^*\sigma^{18}}{\bar{R}^{24}}, \qquad (2.17)$$

where c^* and σ are undetermined constants and f represents the expression in brackets of eqn (2.3) that describes the dependence of the dipole–dipole interaction on the relative molecular orientations. The first term on the right-hand side of (2.17) is $U_{\mu\mu}$; other contributions to $U_{electrostatic}$ (eqn (2.2)) are neglected. The second term is the sum of the induction and dispersion energies, both of which are assumed to be independent of molecular orientations. The last term represents the repulsive interaction of the molecules, and is also taken as being independent of orientations. Stockmayer obtained a very close fit of calculated and experimental $B(T)$ values (Fig. 2.4) for $c^* = 70 \cdot 4 \times 10^{-60}$ erg cm^6 and $\sigma = 2 \cdot 76$ Å. He estimated that the contribution of dispersion forces to c^* is 47×10^{-60} erg cm^6, in close agreement with London's formula (see Table 2.3), but less than half of the coefficient of $\bar{R}^{-6}$ in the Kirkwood–Müller expression. The quantity σ is called the *collision diameter* of the molecule; it is the intermolecular separation at which U_{AB} would vanish if μ were zero. It is noteworthy that the value of σ found by Stockmayer is exactly equal to the separation of hydrogen-bonded molecules in ordinary ice (Section 3.1).

The quality of the fit of calculated $B(T)$ values to the experimental values does not seem to be particularly sensitive to the nature of the repulsive term. A good fit can be achieved for most plausible repulsive terms merely by adjusting the coefficient c^* of the $\bar{R}^{-6}$ term. Rowlinson (1949) obtained a good fit using a potential identical to eqn (2.17) except that he used a repulsive term of the form $c^* \sigma^6 / \bar{R}^{12}$, with $c^* = 72 \cdot 8 \times 10^{-60}$ erg cm^6 and $\sigma = 2 \cdot 65 \times 10^{-8}$ cm. Stockmayer (1941), in a second calculation, achieved an excellent fit simply by representing the repulsive forces as those between infinitely hard spheres of diameter $3 \cdot 16$ Å. In this case c^* was taken as $110 \cdot 3 \times 10^{-60}$ erg cm^6. Repulsive forces may be described with equal success by exponential functions, as is evident from what follows.

Margenau and Myers (1944) attempted to extract information about the repulsive forces between water molecules from second virial coefficient data. They developed a potential function for long-range forces from theoretical considerations; then they sought an expression for the repulsive interactions which produced a good fit between calculated and experimental $B(T)$ values (see Fig. 2.4 for the fit they obtained). Their final potential function can be written:

$$U_{AB} = \begin{cases} \text{for } \bar{R} > 2 \cdot 8 \times 10^{-8} \text{ cm:} \\[2mm] -\left(\dfrac{\mu^2}{\bar{R}^3} + \dfrac{e}{\bar{R}^5}\right)f - \dfrac{c^*}{\bar{R}^6} - \dfrac{d}{\bar{R}^8} + A^* \exp(-\rho \bar{R}); \\[4mm] \text{for } \bar{R} < 2 \cdot 8 \times 10^{-8} \text{ cm:} \\[2mm] -\dfrac{c^*}{\bar{R}^6} - \dfrac{d}{\bar{R}^8} + A^{*\prime} \exp(-\rho' \bar{R}), \end{cases} \qquad (2.18)$$

where
$$\mu = 1{\cdot}87 \times 10^{-18} \text{ e.s.u. cm}, \qquad e = 8{\cdot}5 \times 10^{-52} \text{ erg cm}^5,$$
$$c^* = 45 \times 10^{-60} \text{ e.s.u. cm}^6, \qquad d = 95 \times 10^{-76} \text{ erg cm}^8,$$
$$A^* = 3{\cdot}25 \times 10^{-9} \text{ erg}, \qquad \rho = 3{\cdot}6 \times 10^8 \text{ cm}^{-1},$$
$$A^{*\prime} = 2{\cdot}4 \times 10^{-6} \text{ erg}, \qquad \rho' = 6{\cdot}7 \times 10^8 \text{ cm}^{-1},$$

and f represents the function in brackets in eqn (2.3). In this function the exponential terms describe repulsive forces, $e/\bar{R}^5$ describes electrostatic forces other than dipole–dipole forces, $c^*/\bar{R}^6$ describes induction and dispersion forces, and $d/\bar{R}^8$ describes higher-order dispersion forces. From what we have said in the previous paragraph, the strategy of Margenau and Myers can succeed only if the long-range forces have been accurately described. Unfortunately, recent information about these forces between water molecules makes it doubtful that this is the case in the Margenau–Myers equation: the $e/\bar{R}^5$ term is based on an over-simplified model of the water molecule (that of Bernal and Fowler 1933) and does not have the correct dependence on molecular orientations. Moreover, in view of our discussion in the previous section, their coefficient c^* is probably too small. It might be fruitful to repeat Margenau and Myers's plan, incorporating more recent information on long-range forces.

Rowlinson (1951 a) used a potential function similar to Stockmayer's (eqn (2.17)), but with the repulsive energy proportional to $\bar{R}^{-12}$ and with an additional term describing dipole–quadrupole forces. Rowlinson's function can be written:

$$U_{\text{AB}} = -\frac{\mu^2}{\bar{R}^3} f - \frac{e'}{\bar{R}^4} g - \frac{c^*}{\bar{R}^6} + \frac{c^* \sigma^6}{\bar{R}^{12}}, \qquad (2.19)$$

where $c^* = 80{\cdot}4 \times 10^{-60} \text{ erg cm}^6$, $\sigma = 2{\cdot}725 \times 10^{-8} \text{ cm}$, $e' = 4{\cdot}97 \times 10^{-44}$ erg cm^4, and g is a function of angles describing the dependence of the dipole–quadrupole energy on molecular orientations. Rowlinson computed the coefficient of the dipole–quadrupole term from a point-charge model for water and he assumed that vapour molecules rotate about their z-axes (Fig. 1.2 (a)) so that they may be treated as being axially symmetric. Both of these approximations limit the accuracy of this term. The values of c^* and σ were determined by fitting calculated values of $B(T)$ to experimental values. The resulting value of σ is 1 per cent less than Stockmayer's value, but still close to the separation of hydrogen-bonded molecules in ice. The resulting value of c^* is 14 per cent larger than Stockmayer's value, so apparently the effect of the dipole–quadrupole term is to increase c^*. This value of c^*, like the values calculated by Stockmayer (1941) and Margenau and Myers (1944), is smaller than that predicted by the Kirkwood–Müller formula.

Interpretation of the second virial coefficient in terms of dimerization

An interesting, though less rigorous, interpretation of the second virial coefficient of steam was given by Rowlinson (1949). He first assumed that the electrostatic interaction energy of two water molecules is significant only in configurations for which the non-polar energy is negligible. Presumably these are configurations such as (*a*) of Fig. 2.3, in which the dipole–dipole energy is by far the most important attractive force. This assumption allowed him to treat the observed second virial coefficient as the sum of contributions from the electrostatic forces and from the non-polar forces. He then assumed that the contribution from the non-polar forces is given adequately by the Berthelot equation of state, because the Berthelot equation accurately describes the second virial coefficients of non-polar gases. Thus the difference between the observed second virial coefficient and that calculated by the Berthelot equation is the contribution arising from electrostatic forces and hydrogen bonding. Rowlinson assumed that these forces cause a small, reversible dimerization. Let us call the products of this dimerization 'strong dimers' to distinguish them from the paired molecules resulting from non-polar forces. Treating the strong dimers by the law of mass action, Rowlinson derived the relation

$$B(\text{Experimental}) - B(\text{Berthelot}) = -RT/K_\mathrm{P}, \qquad (2.20)$$

where R is the gas constant, T is the temperature in °K, and K_P is the dissociation constant for a strong $(H_2O)_2$ dimer. Rowlinson evaluated the empirical constants in the Berthelot equation from the critical temperature and pressure of steam, and found that the observed temperature dependence of the second virial coefficient of steam is reproduced satisfactorily by eqn (2.20) when K_P is of the form

$$\log_{10} K_\mathrm{P} = 5 \cdot 650 - 1250/T, \qquad (2.21)$$

where the units of K_P are atmospheres.

The energy and entropy of dissociation of a strong dimer are readily calculated from eqn (2.21). The entropy of dissociation at 373 °K is 25·8 e.u. and the energy of dissociation at the same temperature is 4·98 kcal mol^{-1}. The close correspondence of this energy to the maximum depth of Stockmayer's potential for two molecules in the head-to-tail mutual orientation (Fig. 2.2) is suggestive: strong dimers may exist in such a configuration.

We can also estimate the mole fraction of strong dimers, X_{dimer}, present in steam at any temperature T and pressure P by combining the following relations with eqn (2.21):

$$\frac{(X_{\text{monomer}})^2}{(X_{\text{dimer}})} = \frac{K_{\text{P}}}{P}; \quad \text{and} \quad X_{\text{monomer}} + X_{\text{dimer}} = 1. \quad (2.22)$$

The estimated mole fraction of strong dimers at several temperatures and pressures is shown in Table 2.4. At the critical point (647·3 °K and 218·3 atm), the mole fraction of strong dimers is about 0·04.

TABLE 2.4

Estimated mole fraction of 'strong dimers' present in water vapour

(Based on eqns (2.21) and (2.22))

Pressure (atm)	Temperature (°K)							
	400	450	500	550	600	650	700	750
1·0	0·003	0·0013	0·0007	0·0004	0·0003	0·0002	0·0002	0·0001
5·0		0·007	0·004	0·002	0·001	0·0009	0·0007	0·0005
25·0			0·017	0·010	0·007	0·005	0·003	0·003
50·0				0·020	0·013	0·009	0·007	0·005
75·0					0·020	0·014	0·010	0·008
100·0					0·026	0·018	0·013	0·010
150·0						0·027	0·020	0·015
200·0						0·035	0·026	0·020
250·0						0·043	0·032	0·025

It should be emphasized that the foregoing interpretation of the second virial coefficient is not rigorous, and that no direct evidence exists for strong dimers in water vapour. If such dimers do indeed exist, they may be difficult to detect, since the results in Table 2.4 indicate that the mole fraction of strong dimers at 400 °K and 1 atm would be only about 0·003.

The third virial coefficient

We shall consider the scant information on the third virial coefficient of steam before leaving the topic of intermolecular forces. The third virial coefficient, $C(T)$, depends on the potential functions for the interaction of both two molecules and three molecules (e.g. Hirschfelder *et al.* 1964). The approximate value of $C(T)$ at a temperature T can be found as follows: first the function $\{(PV/RT)-1\}V$ is plotted against $1/V$. As mentioned above, the extrapolated value of this function at $1/V = 0$ is $B(T)$. Moreover, as can be seen from eqn (2.14), the extrapolated slope of this function at $1/V = 0$ is $C(T)$. Mr. C. Starke, in collaboration with the present authors, found approximate values for $C(T)$ of steam by this procedure, using the P–V–T data reported by Bain (1964); the results are shown in Fig. 2.5. It can be seen that the uncertainty in $C(T)$ is

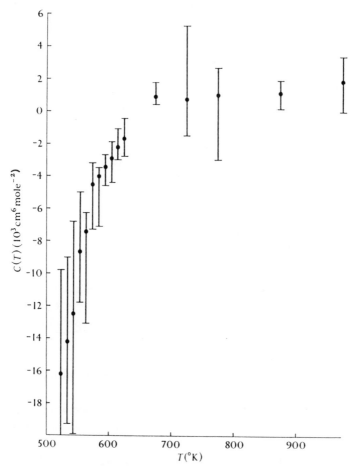

FIG. 2.5. Values of the third virial coefficient of steam determined by Mr. C. Starke and the present authors from the P–V–T data reported by Bain (1964). The points show the most probable value of $C(T)$ at temperature T, and the vertical lines indicate the limits of uncertainty in $C(T)$.

quite large, particularly at lower temperatures. Nevertheless, some qualitative statements about $C(T)$ can be made. $C(T)$ is negative at temperatures below about 650 °K and decreases rapidly as T decreases; at 600 °K $C(T)$ is roughly -3×10^3 cm^6 mol^{-2}. These values are in accord with values derived by Rowlinson (1951 b) from an equation of state for steam.

The only values of $C(T)$ for steam calculated from potential functions are those of Rowlinson (1951 b). He used a potential function similar to eqn (2.17), but with repulsive energy proportional to $\bar{R}^{-12}$, and he assumed that all forces are pairwise additive. His calculated values do not agree at all with experiment: $C(T)$ is calculated to be about $+3.4 \times 10^3$ cm^6 mol^{-2} at 650 °K and *increases* as T decreases. At much lower temperatures $C(T)$ falls off and changes sign near 380 °K. Thus these calculations predict that $C(T)$ is positive in the region between 650 and 380 °K, whereas it appears actually to be negative in this region, as is $B(T)$. According to Rowlinson (1954), the physical implication of a simultaneously positive $C(T)$ and negative $B(T)$ is that the association of a dimer AB with a third molecule is hindered by the mutual interaction of A and B. In other words, six molecules cannot be arranged in two triplets to produce as low a total energy as that given by three pairs. Thus, the fact that $C(T)$ is actually negative below 650° K suggests that the tendency of water molecules to cluster together is stronger than the calculations predict.

The source of this discrepancy may lie in either, or both, of the following.

(1) Short-range forces, perhaps hydrogen bonds similar to ones in ice, may influence the interactions of molecules in water vapour. The second virial coefficient can be correctly computed even though these forces are incompletely described by the potential function. The third virial coefficient, however, may be a more exacting test of the potential function and hence cannot be calculated without inclusion of these forces.

(2) The assumption of pairwise additive forces used by Rowlinson in calculating $C(T)$ is not valid. In other words, some attractive force may act among three water molecules which is not present in a pair of molecules. For example, a hydrogen bond between two molecules may be strongly enhanced by the presence of a third molecule polarizing both the others.

(c) *Forces between water molecules: a summary*

Our understanding of the forces between water molecules is still rudimentary. In nearly all studies to date, the intermolecular potential has been represented by a sum of terms, one term for each component of the force. The component forces are considered to be long-range or short-range, depending upon whether or not electron exchange between the molecules can be neglected. The functional forms of the long-range forces are known from theory, but our ignorance of constants that appear in the expressions prevents us from evaluating these forces accurately. For example, the functional form of the dipole–quadrupole force is known, but the precise values of the quadrupole moments of the water molecule are not known. Similarly, the dipole–induced dipole induction force depends on the still unknown anisotropy of the polarizability of the water molecule. Theoretical estimates of the coefficient of the $\bar{R}^{-6}$ dispersion energy also vary widely, as do estimates derived from the second virial coefficient, so that this interaction, too, can only be approximately evaluated. The dipole–dipole force can, of course, be accurately evaluated, because the dipole moment of the water molecule is known. This force is the dominant one at large distances. Present knowledge of short-range forces is even more limited. The expressions we have discussed for short-range forces should be regarded as extremely crude.

The second and third virial coefficients of water vapour seem to indicate that water molecules cluster together to a small extent below about 650 °K. The virial coefficient data disclose little about the structure of these polymers and, in particular, do not reveal whether the water molecules are hydrogen-bonded to each other in the way that they are bonded in ice. The second virial coefficient can be calculated using a potential function that includes no description of hydrogen bonding (except in so far as electrostatic, induction, and dispersion forces contribute to hydrogen bonding), but this does not preclude the existence of hydrogen bonds in the dimers. Attempts to gain information about the potential function from the temperature variation of the second virial coefficient have been only moderately successful owing to two factors: the second virial coefficient is relatively insensitive to the form of the assumed intermolecular potential function, and, as mentioned above, we are uncertain of the precise values of several of the terms in the potential function. The third virial coefficient is probably more sensitive to the form of the intermolecular potential, but accurate experimental values of $C(T)$ are not yet available. Moreover, taking account of forces that are not pairwise additive in calculations of the third virial coefficient is difficult.

In Chapter 3 we shall consider the potential function for interaction of water molecules from two different points of view. In Section 3.6 (b) we shall discuss semi-empirical potential functions for vibrations of H_2O molecules in ice, and in Section 3.6 (c) calculations of the energy of hydrogen bond formation will be considered.

2.2. Thermodynamic properties

The thermodynamic properties of water have probably been studied in greater detail than those of any other substance. The pressure–volume–temperature relations, the thermal energy, and the related properties of enthalpy, free energy, and entropy have been measured and computed over wide ranges of temperature and pressure: from as low as 2 °K to well over 1200 °K and, for some properties, from practically zero pressure to over 200 000 atm. We shall summarize many of these results in three different sections. In the present section we discuss the thermodynamic properties of gaseous water and the liquid–vapour and solid–vapour phase changes. In Section 3.3 we shall take up the thermodynamic properties of ice, particularly the phase relations of the polymorphs and the application of the third law of thermodynamics. The thermodynamic characteristics of liquid water will be described in Section 4.3.

(a) Pressure–volume–temperature relations

The importance of knowing the properties of steam for power generation has stimulated a number of careful studies of the pressure–volume–temperature relations. The usual procedure in these determinations has been to measure the pressure of a known amount of steam in a container of fixed volume. Several compilations of these studies are available, a recent one being the *NEL Steam Tables 1964* (Bain 1964).† This set of tables presents smoothed values for the specific volume (as well as the enthalpy and entropy) of liquid water and steam at temperatures between 0 and 800 °C and at pressures between 0 and 1000 bars.

Many of the important qualitative features of these data can be seen in Fig. 2.6. This surface shows the specific volume of water as a function of both temperature and pressure. Dashed contours of constant temperature (isotherms) are drawn on the surface. Clearly, the specific volume of water vapour decreases as the pressure is raised or as the temperature is lowered. Along any isotherm above 374·15 °C, the critical temperature, the volume is a smooth function of pressure, but below 374·15 °C the volume of the vapour decreases smoothly with increasing pressure only up to the *vapour saturation curve*. A slight increase in pressure causes condensation of the vapour, and the volume drops to the volume of the

† Keyes (1949, 1958) critically reviewed the pressure–volume–temperature data and other properties of steam. A detailed survey of pressure–volume–temperature data in the critical region was made by Nowak *et al.* (1961 *a, b*). Dorsey's book (1940) is a source of thermodynamic data available prior to 1940.

liquid along the *liquid saturation curve*. Since the liquid is comparatively incompressible, the isotherms rise sharply in the liquid region.

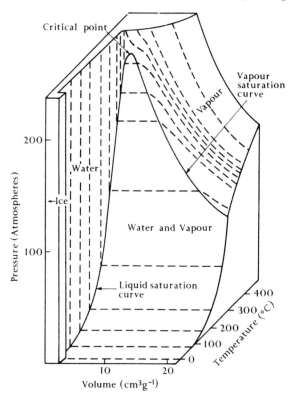

FIG. 2.6. *P–V–T* surface for H_2O. (The dashed lines are isotherms.)
Adopted with changes from Slater (1939).

Let us look more closely at the region of this surface where ice, liquid water, and water vapour are in equilibrium with each other. The details of this region are shown in the *P–T* diagram of Fig. 2.7, a projection of the *P–V–T* surface with greatly enlarged pressure and temperature scales. Equilibrium among all three phases exists only at the triple point (where the pressure is 4·58 mm Hg and the temperature is 0·01 °C). The volume of water vapour at the triple point is, of course, enormously larger than the volumes of either liquid water or ice: the volumes per gram of liquid water, ice, and water vapour at the triple point are 1·00, 1·09, and 206 100 cm³ respectively. At temperatures below the triple point, ice can be in equilibrium with the vapour; the familiar disappearance of ice on cold days takes place via this equilibrium. The pressure for which equilibrium exists at any given temperature is the *vapour pressure of ice*. According

to Washburn (Dorsey 1940, p. 598) the vapour pressure of ice is described
by the following equation:

$$\log_{10} P = \frac{A}{T} + B\log_{10} T + CT + DT^2 + E, \qquad (2.23)$$

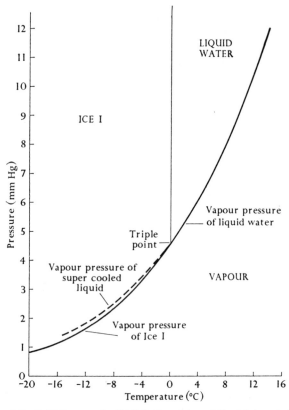

Fig. 2.7. *P–T* diagram for H_2O in the region of the triple point.

where P (in mmHg) is the vapour pressure of ice I at t °C, and

$T = t + 273 \cdot 1,$	$C = -1677 \cdot 006 \times 10^{-5},$
$A = -2445 \cdot 5646,$	$D = 120514 \times 10^{-10},$
$B = 8 \cdot 2312,$	$E = -6 \cdot 757169.$

The vapour pressure of supercooled water is slightly greater than that
of ice, as is shown by Fig. 2.7. Although difficult to see in the figure,
the vapour-pressure curve of supercooled water is smoothly continuous
with the curve of the stable liquid, but the vapour-pressure curve of ice
is not. The vapour-pressure curve of liquid water between −5 °C and

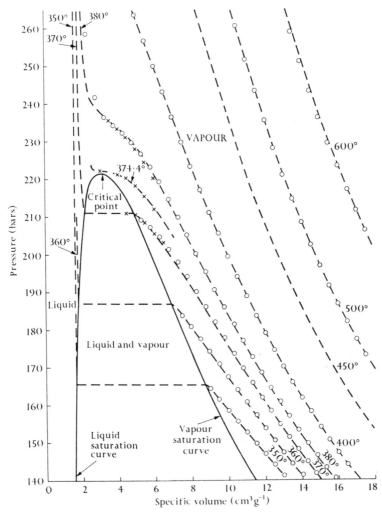

FIG. 2.8. *P–V* diagram for H_2O in the vicinity of the critical point.

— — — — experimental isotherms;
O O O O calculated from eqn (2.26);
× × × × calculated from eqn (2.27).

Experimental data from Bain (1964), except for the 374·4° C isotherm which is from Nowak *et al.* (1961 *b*).

the critical point can be represented by a formula proposed by Osborne and Meyers (Dorsey 1940, p. 574):

$$\log_{10} P = A + \frac{B}{T} + \frac{Cx}{T}(10^{Dx^2} - 1) + E \, 10^{Fy^{\frac{4}{3}}}, \qquad (2.24)$$

where P is the vapour pressure in atmospheres at t °C,

$$T = t + 273 \cdot 16, \qquad C = +1 \cdot 3869 \times 10^{-4},$$

$$x = T^2 - K, \qquad D = +1 \cdot 1965 \times 10^{-11},$$

$$y = 374 \cdot 11 - t, \qquad K = 293700,$$

$$A = +5 \cdot 4266514, \qquad E = -0 \cdot 0044,$$

$$B = -2005 \cdot 1, \qquad F = -0 \cdot 0057148.$$

Values predicted by the formula deviate from experimental measurements by less than five parts in 10 000. This formula, of course, is the equation of the projection in the P–T plane of both the vapour saturation curve and the liquid saturation curve of Fig. 2.6.

Another region of the P–V–T surface which is of special interest is the region of the critical point. Fig. 2.8 shows a projection of this part of the P–V–T surface on the P–V plane. The vapour saturation curve meets the liquid saturation curve at the critical point, where the volumes of the two phases become equal. The critical constants of H_2O are given in Table 2.5, along with those for D_2O. Note that the critical volume is only about three times larger than the volume of liquid water at the triple point. In other words, the density of the liquid decreases by a factor of 3 when it is heated from 0 to 374 °C. The density of the vapour, in contrast, increases by a factor of about 62 000 in going from the triple point to the critical point. The critical temperature of D_2O, curiously enough, is 3·2 °C lower than that of H_2O, though the melting-point, boiling-point, and all triple points of the D_2O phase diagram are several degrees higher than those of the H_2O diagram (see Tables 3.5 and 3.7).

TABLE 2.5

Critical constants for H_2O *and* D_2O

	Critical temperature, T_c (°C)	Critical pressure, P_c (atm)	Critical volume, V_c (cm³ mol⁻¹)
H_2O	374·15†	218·3†	59·1 ± 0·5†
D_2O	370·9‡	215·7‡	..

† Nowak *et al.* (1961 *a*). ‡ Oliver and Grisard (1956).

The behaviour of the isotherms can be seen in Fig. 2.8. Below the critical temperature and at small volumes they experience the discontinuity in volume and subsequent steep rise already mentioned, and far above the critical temperature they begin to assume the form of the hyperbolas predicted by the ideal gas law. In the immediate region of the critical point the pattern of the isotherms is complex and strongly temperature-dependent. Experiments have shown that at the critical point the isotherm has both zero slope and zero curvature:

$$\left(\frac{\partial P}{\partial V}\right)_{T_c} = \left(\frac{\partial^2 P}{\partial V^2}\right)_{T_c} = 0. \tag{2.25}$$

Examination of the 374·4 °C isotherm in Fig. 2.8 indicates that it very nearly obeys these conditions. A condition on isometrics—lines of constant volume—found experimentally to prevail at the critical point is

$$\left(\frac{\partial^2 P}{\partial T^2}\right)_{V_c} = 0. \tag{2.25 a}$$

An analysis of the P–V–T data for steam (Nowak and Grosh 1961) indicates that this condition is also obeyed by all isometrics up to 440 °C. That is, the pressure is a linear function of the temperature at constant volume.

Equations of state†

The derivation from first principles of the equations of state of gases is a subject of active research. One approach has been to relate the coefficients of the virial equation of state (eqn (2.14)) to molecular parameters by means of statistical mechanics. In the case of water vapour, only limited progress has been made in this direction as we have seen in Section 2.1 (*b*). Consequently the best available equations of state for steam are basically empirical, and contain numerous parameters chosen to achieve a close fit to experimental data.

A successful equation of this type was developed by Keyes (1949). It expresses pressure as a function of temperature and specific volume; for temperatures below T_c it contains five constants in addition to the gas constant, and for higher temperatures it contains an additional three. The form of the equation is

$$\log_{10}\frac{RT}{Pv} = \log_{10}\left(\frac{\omega}{v}\right) + \frac{\omega\psi}{v^2}, \tag{2.26}$$

† Over a dozen empirical equations of state for steam were reviewed by Nowak and Grosh (1961).

where

$$T = \text{temperature in } °\text{K}; \ \tau = 1/T,$$
$$v = \text{specific volume in } \text{cm}^3 \text{ g}^{-1},$$
$$P = \text{pressure in atm},$$
$$R = 4\cdot55465,$$
$$\omega = v - \delta,$$
$$\delta = 2\cdot0624 \times \exp(-0\cdot87498/v),$$
$$\psi_0 = 1260\cdot17\tau \times \exp(17\cdot09 \times 10^4\tau^2),$$
$$\psi = \psi_0(1 + \psi_1/v + \psi_2/v^2),$$

where for

$$T < T_c: \qquad \psi_1 = 305\cdot6\psi_0\,\tau \times \exp(34\cdot19 \times 10^4\tau^2),$$
$$\psi_2 = 0;$$
$$T > T_c: \qquad \psi_1 = (479\cdot76 + 141\cdot5 \times 10^3\tau)\psi_0\,\tau,$$
$$\psi_2 = (75\cdot364 - 27\cdot505\psi_0)/\psi_0^3.$$

At large volumes and high temperatures this equation becomes identical in form with Dieterici's equation. Equation (2.26) is based on data extending up to 460 °C and 367 atm. If the observed vapour densities are introduced, it represents the vapour pressure of water from 0 to 360 °C with an accuracy of better than 1 part per 1000. The computed pressures of steam for specific volumes larger than 20 cm³ g⁻¹ are within experimental error of the observed values; some computed pressures for smaller specific volumes are shown in Fig. 2.8.

The rapid change of P–V–T properties in the immediate region of the critical point makes them very difficult to represent analytically, so that it is not surprising that eqn (2.26) is not entirely satisfactory in this region. The critical isotherm computed from the $T > T_c$ equation lies 1·5 atm above the critical isotherm computed from the $T < T_c$ equation, and these calculated curves straddle the experimental isotherm. The critical isometric, moreover, does not obey the condition $(\partial^2 P/\partial T^2)_{V_c} = 0$.

An empirical equation of state for the critical region of steam was developed by Nowak and Grosh (1961). They maintain that their equation can represent the data virtually to within experimental error for volumes between V_c and $2V_c$, and for temperatures between the vapour saturation curve and 400 °C. The equation is not applicable outside this region. The form of the equation is

$$Pv - P_c v - R(T - T_c) = \sum_{n=3}^{5} a_n(v - v_c)^n, \qquad (2.27)$$

where
$$T = \text{temperature in } °K,$$
$$v = \text{specific volume in } cm^3 \text{ } g^{-1},$$
$$P = \text{pressure in bars},$$
$$R = 8 \cdot 7045,$$
$$a_3 = -4 \cdot 2201,$$
$$a_4 = 1 \cdot 0828,$$
$$a_5 = -0 \cdot 17548.$$

Values of the pressure calculated from this equation are shown in Fig. 2.8.

(b) Thermal energy

Accurate values of the enthalpy and entropy of water vapour are listed in several steam tables (e.g. Bain 1964).† Let us consider methods of determining these functions and their general dependence on temperature and pressure.

Owing to the interrelation of thermodynamic quantities, several methods for determining the enthalpy, entropy, and free energy of steam are available. Two of the most direct are:

(1) Combination of the 'ideal gas' thermodynamic functions for steam with an empirical equation of state. The ideal gas thermodynamic functions are the enthalpy, entropy, etc. that steam would exhibit in the absence of molecular interactions. They are computed from spectroscopic data, as described below. The molar Gibbs free energy $G(T, P)$, enthalpy $H(T, P)$, and entropy $S(T, P)$ of steam at temperature T and pressure P are given by

$$\left. \begin{aligned} G(T, P) &= G^0(T) + RT \ln P + \int_0^P \left(V - \frac{RT}{P'} \right) dP' \\[2mm] H(T, P) &= H^0(T) - T^2 \int_0^P \frac{\partial}{\partial T} \frac{V}{T} dP' \\[2mm] S(T, P) &= S^0(T) - R \ln P + \int_0^P \left(\frac{R}{P'} - \frac{\partial V}{\partial T} \right) dP' \end{aligned} \right\}, \quad (2.28)$$

where $G^0(T)$, $H^0(T)$, and $S^0(T)$ are the ideal gas thermodynamic functions listed in Table 2.6, V is the molar volume, and R is the gas

---

† The enthalpy, entropy, and free energy of a substance must be expressed relative to the enthalpy, entropy, and free energy of the substance in some reference state. Different reference states are chosen in the various steam tables. The *NEL Steam Tables* (Bain 1964) take liquid water at the triple point as the reference state.

constant. The variable of integration, P', has a prime to distinguish it from the final pressure P. The explicit relations between P, V, and T in the integrands are found from the empirical equations of state.

(2) Measurement of the heat capacity at constant pressure, C_P, followed by numerical integration. The relevant integrals appear in Section 3.3 (*b*) where they are discussed in connection with the third law of thermodynamics.

Keyes (1949) analysed the thermodynamic functions of steam obtained by several methods and found the consistency of the results to be generally very good. Readers interested in a detailed comparison of the methods are referred to his article.

The ideal gas thermodynamic functions mentioned in method (1) above are important not only for determining the properties of the real vapour, but also for establishing the residual entropy of ice (Section 3.3 (*b*)) and the energy of sublimation of ice (Table 3.8). The ideal gas functions are computed by the methods of statistical mechanics. A partition function is written in terms of the moments of inertia, vibrational frequencies, and other spectroscopic constants for the water molecule. A knowledge of these constants is then sufficient to evaluate the thermodynamic functions. The most elaborate computation of this sort for steam was that of Friedman and Haar (1954). They represented the partition function for water as a product of factors describing the translational, vibrational, rotational, and coupling contributions. Their partition function takes account of the centrifugal stretching of the rotating molecules, the anharmonicity of the molecular vibrations, and the coupling between rotational and vibrational motions. The required spectroscopic constants were taken from the accurate work of Benedict *et al.* (1953). Friedman and Haar computed the ideal gas thermodynamic functions for H_2O, HDO, D_2O, HTO, DTO, and T_2O for temperatures between 50 and 5000 °K; their results for H_2O between 50 and 600 °K are reproduced in Table 2.6. These authors found a negligible difference between the thermodynamic properties of $XY^{16}O$—where X and Y represent H, D, or T—and the naturally occurring mixture of $XY^{16}O$, $XY^{17}O$, and $XY^{18}O$ (see Section 1.1 (*a*)).

A few words should be said about the pressure and temperature dependence of the thermodynamic functions of steam. The entropy of steam, like the entropy of any gas, increases with temperature and decreases with pressure. This behaviour is shown in Fig. 2.9. The particular cross-section of this surface corresponding to a pressure of 1 atm is shown in Fig. 3.12.

Table 2.6

Ideal gas thermodynamic functions for H_2O†

(All entries are in dimensionless units. The zero subscript denotes 0 °K.
R is the gas constant.)

°K	$\dfrac{C_P^0}{R}$	$\dfrac{(H^0-E_0^0)}{RT}$	$\dfrac{-(G^0-E_0^0)}{RT}$	$\dfrac{S^0}{R}$
50	4·00719	3·90579	11·63213	15·53793
60	4·00634	3·92262	12·34582	16·26844
70	4·00590	3·93454	12·95144	16·88599
80	4·00573	3·94345	13·47744	17·42089
90	4·00571	3·95037	13·94232	17·89269
100	4·00581	3·95591	14·35883	18·31474
110	4·00599	3·96045	14·73609	18·69655
120	4·00622	3·96425	15·08086	19·04512
130	4·00649	3·96749	15·39830	19·36580
140	4·00680	3·97029	15·69243	19·66273
150	4·00715	3·97273	15·96644	19·93918
160	4·00755	3·97490	16·22290	20·19781
170	4·00803	3·97683	16·46394	20·44078
180	4·00860	3·97858	16·69130	20·66989
190	4·00931	3·98018	16·90646	20·88664
200	4·01020	3·98166	17·11065	21·09231
210	4·01132	3·98304	17·30495	21·28800
220	4·01272	3·98436	17·49027	21·47463
230	4·01446	3·98563	17·66741	21·65304
240	4·01658	3·98687	17·83706	21·82394
250	4·01912	3·98811	17·99984	21·98796
260	4·02214	3·98936	18·15628	22·14565
270	4·02565	3·99063	18·30687	22·29751
280	4·02970	3·99196	18·45202	22·44398
290	4·03428	3·99334	18·59213	22·58547
300	4·03942	3·99478	18·72753	22·72232
310	4·04511	3·99631	18·85855	22·85486
320	4·05136	3·99794	18·98545	22·98339
330	4·05815	3·99966	19·10850	23·10816
340	4·06547	4·00148	19·22793	23·22941
350	4·07329	4·00342	19·34395	23·34737
360	4·08160	4·00548	19·45676	23·46224
370	4·09038	4·00765	19·56653	23·57419
380	4·09958	4·00995	19·67344	23·68339
390	4·10920	4·01237	19·77763	23·79000
400	4·11919	4·01491	19·87925	23·89417
450	4·17394	4·02948	20·35295	24·38243
500	4·23453	4·04691	20·77837	24·82529
550	4·29891	4·06687	21·16500	25·23188
600	4·36590	4·08898	21·51980	25·60879

† Calculated by Friedman and Haar (1954).

The temperature dependence of the Gibbs free energy is given by
$(\partial G/\partial T)_P = -S$. We have just seen that the entropy of steam is positive
and increases with temperature. Thus the free energy must decrease
with increasing temperature, and must decrease more rapidly at higher

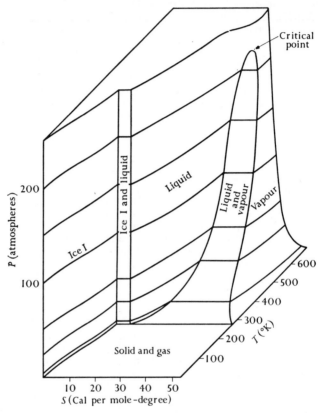

FIG. 2.9. The entropy of H_2O as a function of temperature and pressure.
Lines of constant pressure are drawn on the surface. Redrawn from Slater
(1939).

temperatures. This behaviour can be seen in Fig. 2.10. The pressure
dependence of the free energy is described by $(\partial G/\partial P)_T = V$. Thus at
low pressures, where the volume of steam is very large, the free energy
increases very rapidly with increasing pressure; but at higher pressures,
where the volume of steam is much smaller, the free energy increases
slowly with pressure. Note that the free energy, unlike the entropy,
enthalpy, and volume, is a continuous function of T and P at the phase
changes.

The behaviour of the heat capacity is complicated. The specific heat

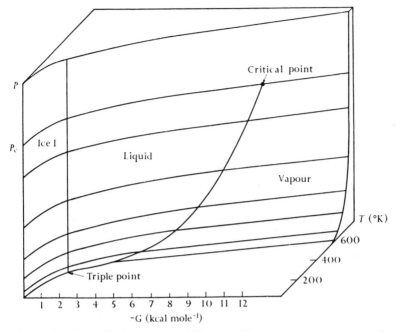

FIG. 2.10. The Gibbs free energy of H_2O as a function of temperature and pressure. The reference state is taken as ice at 0 °K. Redrawn from Slater (1939).

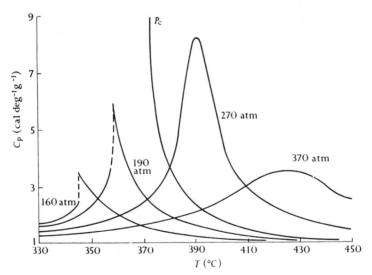

FIG. 2.11. The specific heat of H_2O at constant pressure. The specific heat of the vapour along the critical isobar approaches infinity as the temperature is lowered towards the critical temperature. From Wilson (1957).

(heat capacity per gram) of liquid water near the boiling-point and 1 atm pressure is $1 \cdot 01$ cal g^{-1} $^{\circ}$K^{-1}. Upon vaporization, the specific heat falls sharply to $0 \cdot 50$ cal g^{-1} $^{\circ}$K^{-1}. If heating is continued at 1 atm pressure, the specific heat experiences a slight minimum near 200 $^{\circ}$C, and then a gradual increase (Fig. 3.12). At somewhat larger pressures the behaviour is generally the same except that C_P is slightly greater, and the minimum occurs at higher temperatures. As the pressure approaches the critical pressure, however, marked anomalies appear in the C_P versus temperature curve (see Fig. 2.11). The specific heat of liquid water increases prior to vaporization and the specific heat of the vapour near the vapour saturation curve is very large. Close to the critical point, the value of C_P approaches infinity. At still higher pressures the C_P versus temperature curve contains a peak which becomes less pronounced as the pressure is increased.

3. Ice

Ice, unlike liquid water, is fairly well understood: most of its properties have been interpreted in terms of its crystal structure, the forces between its constituent molecules, and the energy levels of the molecules themselves. In this chapter we describe the structure of ordinary ice and what is known of the structures of its polymorphs. We then outline the thermodynamic, electrical, and spectroscopic properties of ice and, wherever possible, relate them to its crystal structure and to characteristics of the water molecule. Some properties are covered in considerable detail, not only because they are unusual or intriguing in themselves, but because they will be useful to us in Chapters 4 and 5 when we examine liquid water. The chapter closes with a discussion of hydrogen bonding and its role in determining the nature of ice.

3.1. Structure of ice I

(a) Positions of the oxygen atoms

The basic structural features of ordinary hexagonal ice (ice I) are well established. Every oxygen atom is at the centre of a tetrahedron formed by four oxygen atoms each about 2·76 Å away. Every water molecule is hydrogen-bonded to its four nearest neighbours: its O–H bonds are directed towards lone-pairs of electrons on two of these neighbours, forming two O–H⋯O hydrogen bonds; in turn, each of its lone-pairs is directed towards an O–H bond of one of the other neighbours, forming two O⋯H–O hydrogen bonds. This arrangement leads to an open lattice in which intermolecular cohesion is large. It can be seen from Fig. 3.1 that the lattice consists of puckered layers perpendicular to the c-crystal axis, containing hexagonal rings of water molecules that have the conformation of the 'chair' form of cyclohexane. There are also hexagonal rings formed by three molecules in one layer and three molecules in the adjacent layer, but these rings have the 'boat' conformation. This arrangement of oxygen atoms is isomorphous with the wurtzite form of zinc sulphide and with the silicon atoms in the

tridymite form of silicon dioxide, and consequently some authors refer
to ice I as the wurtzite or tridymite form of ice.

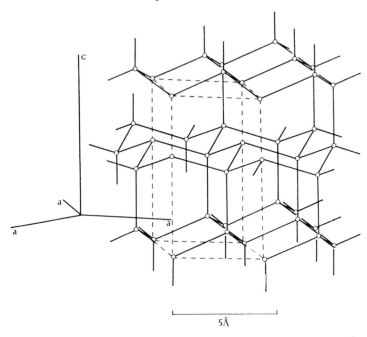

FIG. 3.1. The arrangement of the oxygen atoms in ice I. There are four
molecules per unit cell, which is outlined in the figure by dashes. Redrawn from
Owston (1958).

An important characteristic of this structure is the presence of vacant
'shafts' running both parallel and perpendicular to the c-axis; some of
these are shown in Fig. 3.2. The open structure produced by the shafts
accounts for the fact that ice I floats on its melt. This unusual property
is also exhibited by diamond, silicon, and germanium, three solids that
are structurally related to ice.†

Since W. H. Bragg (1922) first proposed the arrangement of oxygen atoms
shown in Fig. 3.1, H_2O and D_2O ice I have been studied extensively by X-ray,
electron, and neutron diffraction. No doubt exists that this arrangement is
basically correct, but some of the details are still uncertain. It is generally accepted
that the unit cell contains four oxygen atoms and has symmetry $P6_3/mmc$. The
uncertainties about the structure have to do with the precise unit cell dimensions
and their dependence on temperature.

In a critical review of this subject, Lonsdale (1958) noted that the ratio of the
unit cell dimensions, c/a, seems to be about 0·25 per cent smaller than the value

† These crystals are actually isomorphous with the oxygen atom arrangement of ice
Ic (Section 3.2 (c)).

1·633 characteristic of a crystal built from perfect tetrahedra. This non-ideal axial ratio indicates that either oxygen–oxygen separations of nearest neighbours

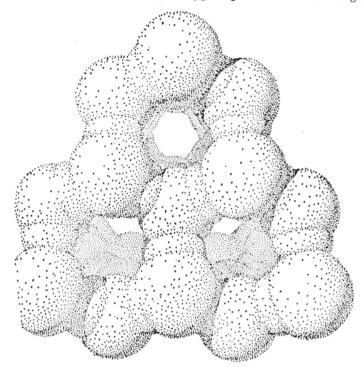

FIG. 3.2. A representation of an ice I crystal showing the van der Waals radii of the atoms. The view is down the c-axis, illustrating the open 'shafts'. Reproduced from Pimentel and McClellan (1960).

along the c-axis are slightly smaller than other oxygen–oxygen separations, or that the O ---- O ---- O angles in the crystal are not precisely equal to the tetrahedral angle, or that both these irregularities are present in ice.

Lonsdale assumed the first of these explanations. She then computed the oxygen–oxygen distances of nearest neighbours in H_2O and D_2O ice as functions of temperature, using smoothed unit cell parameters derived from X-ray and electron diffraction data.† Her results are given in Table 3.1. They indicate that the oxygen–oxygen distances for H_2O and D_2O ice do not differ significantly. They also indicate that at 0 °C all nearest-neighbour O–O distances are within 0·01 Å of 2·77 Å, but that the O–O distances in the direction of the c-axis in both ices are about 0·01 Å shorter than are the other O–O separations. This difference decreases at lower temperatures (that is, the c/a ratio approaches the ideal value of 1·633), and at −180 °C, both types of O–O separation are about 2·74 Å. In contrast to the data summarized by Lonsdale, the results of a more recent X-ray study of ice I by La Placa and Post (1960) show that the non-ideal axial ratio at

† Data of Megaw (1934), Vegard and Hillesund (1942), Truby (1955), and Blackman and Lisgarten (1957).

TABLE 3.1

Nearest-neighbour oxygen–oxygen distances in ice I at atmospheric pressure calculated by Lonsdale (1958) from diffraction data. The O–O′ distances are in the direction of the c-axis and the O–O″ distances form tetrahedral angles with the c-axis

Temp. (°C)	H$_2$O ice		D$_2$O ice	
	OH---O′ (Å)	OH---O″ (Å)	OD---O′ (Å)	OD---O″ (Å)
0	2·760	2·770	2·761	2·772
−30	2·758	2·767	2·758	2·768
−60	2·755	2·763	2·756	2·764
−90	2·752	2·759	2·754	2·760
−120	2·748	2·755	2·751	2·755
−150	2·745	2·750	2·748	2·750
−180	2·740	2·743	2·744	2·744

0 °C persists unchanged to −180°. An indication that La Placa and Post's axial ratios at low temperatures are more reliable than those suggested by Lonsdale is that coefficients of thermal expansion calculated from their data are in closer accord with directly measured values than are the corresponding coefficients computed by Lonsdale (see Section 3.3 (c)).

As mentioned above, the non-ideal axial ratios in ice may also arise from O---O---O angles which are not exactly tetrahedral. According to Brill (1962), the c/a ratio observed by La Placa and Post (1960) is consistent with departures of the angles by ±0·16° from the tetrahedral angle ($\cos^{-1}(-\frac{1}{3}) \cong 109·47°$). The negative sign applies to the O′---O---O″ angle in Fig. 3.3 on p. 76, and the positive sign to the O″---O---O‴ angle.

(b) Positions of the hydrogen atoms†

Locating the hydrogen atoms in ice has proved a difficult task, largely because hydrogen is less effective in scattering X-rays and electrons than is oxygen. Before the application of neutron diffraction to this problem, several less direct methods were used, and inasmuch as this earlier work contributed greatly to knowledge about the hydrogen positions, we will consider it before considering the neutron diffraction results.

Bernal and Fowler (1933) and Pauling (1935) reasoned that the similarity of many physical properties of ice—especially the vibrational spectrum—to those of water vapour is evidence that H$_2$O molecules in ice are intact. This ruled out suggestions (for example, Barnes 1929) that ice molecules are ionized or that the hydrogen atoms are located midway between two neighbouring oxygens. But even assuming that

† Owston (1958) reviewed this topic in detail.

each H_2O molecule is intact and that each O–H bond points toward one of the four nearest neighbouring molecules, there are six possible orientations for every H_2O molecule, and hence a vast number of possible hydrogen arrangements in an entire ice crystal. It is not immediately evident which one, or group, of these arrangements is energetically favourable.

In 1935 Pauling argued that, subject to three conditions, all arrangements are equally likely to occur. These conditions are:

(1) H_2O molecules in ice are intact, neglecting the small fraction of ionized molecules;

(2) each H_2O molecule is oriented so that its two O–H bonds are directed approximately toward two of the four nearest neighbouring oxygen atoms;

(3) the orientations of adjacent water molecules are such that only one hydrogen atom lies approximately along the axis between adjacent oxygen atoms.

The basis of Pauling's argument is that a crystal subject to only these three conditions is not completely ordered at 0 °K, and hence has a residual entropy. He showed that the value of the entropy arising from this disorder may be estimated, and that it agrees very well with the measured residual entropy at 0 °K.

Pauling's calculation of the residual entropy is as follows: there are N molecules, and thus $2N$ hydrogen atoms, in a mole of ice. Ignoring condition 1, there are 2^{2N} possible arrangements because each hydrogen atom (or rather hydrogen nucleus) has the choice of two positions, one near one oxygen atom, and the other near the neighbouring oxygen atom. Introducing condition 1 (that molecules in ice are intact), all arrangements of hydrogen nuclei around an oxygen atom producing any species other than H_2O are ruled out. Of the 2^4 ways of arranging the four hydrogen nuclei about a given oxygen atom, only six produce H_2O; the others produce H_3O^+, etc. Hence the total number of permitted configurations of the crystal is

$$W = 2^{2N} \times (\tfrac{6}{16})^N = (\tfrac{3}{2})^N.$$

The entropy arising from this disorder, S_0, is given by

$$S_0 = k \ln W = 0{\cdot}805 \text{ e.u.}$$

This value is in excellent agreement with the measured residual entropy of ice I, $0{\cdot}82 \pm 0{\cdot}15$ e.u. (Giauque and Ashley 1933, Giauque and Stout 1936). In addition, the measured residual entropy of D_2O ice I, $0{\cdot}77 \pm 0{\cdot}1$

e.u. (Long and Kemp 1936), being equal within experimental error to the H_2O value, tends to confirm Pauling's hypothesis.

Pauling's calculation of the residual entropy is not exact. This was noted by Onsager and Dupuis (1960), who showed that Pauling's result is a lower bound for the actual number. DiMarzio and Stillinger (1964) applied methods of lattice statistics to this problem, and their work was extended by Nagle (1966). Nagle proved that the correct calculated value of S_0 is 0.8145 ± 0.0002 e.u. for both ice I and ice Ic. Thus Pauling's value is within 1.2 per cent of the correct value.

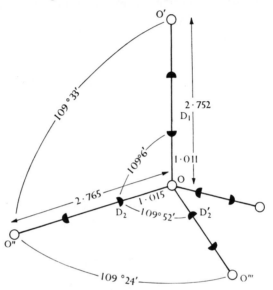

FIG. 3.3. Molecular dimensions in D_2O ice I at $-50\,°C$ as determined by Peterson and Levy (1957). Oxygen atoms are represented by open circles and deuterons by shaded half-circles. Of course, at any given time, there is only one deuteron along each O⋯O axis. The accuracy of the dimensions is probably less than the number of digits in the figure indicates (see Lonsdale 1958). Reproduced from Owston (1958).

Neutron diffraction (Peterson and Levy 1957) has confirmed that Pauling's disordered structure is essentially correct at -50 and $-150\,°C$. The diffraction pattern of D_2O ice shows four 'half-deuterons' adjacent to every oxygen atom; this is the pattern that Pauling's disordered structure would produce. Peterson and Levy believe that their data preclude a structure in which the deuterons are ordered, for example along the c-axis, by more than 20 per cent.

Peterson and Levy's neutron diffraction studies also yielded values for the dimensions of D_2O molecules in ice. These authors found that the O–D bond length is 1.01 Å (see Fig. 3.3), slightly longer than the equilibrium bond length of an isolated molecule, 0·96 Å. They also found that the D–O–D valence angle is nearly equal to the corresponding O----O----O angle, and hence about 5° larger than in an isolated molecule.

This result was questioned by Chidambaram (1961). Chidambaram argued that the O–D----O hydrogen bond is more easily bent than the D–O–D valence angle, and hence that the D–O–D angle in ice I should not increase to 109·5° during condensation. He showed that the data of Peterson and Levy are consistent with a D_2O ice structure in which water molecules are only slightly deformed from their vapour state valence angles of about 104·5°, and in which O–D----O bonds are slightly bent. In this structure, each deuteron is about 0·04 Å off the O----O axis; or in other words, the O–D----O bonds are bent by an average of 6·8°. In support of this model, Chidambaram cited the small change of frequency for the H–O–H bending mode in passing from water vapour to ice (1595 cm^{-1} to 1640 cm^{-1}), and the small deviations of H–O–H angles from 104·5° of water molecules in hydrated crystals. Some nuclear magnetic resonance studies of ice (Section 3.5(c)) give support to Chidambaram's structure.

(c) *Amplitudes of thermal vibration*

The amplitudes of the thermal vibration of atoms in ice I have been estimated from X-ray and neutron diffraction data, as well as from thermodynamic data. Peterson and Levy (1957) determined the root-mean-square vibrational amplitudes of oxygen and deuterium atoms in D_2O ice at −50 and −150 °C (Table 3.2) from their neutron diffraction data. They found that the oxygen vibrations are nearly isotropic but that the deuterium vibrations are markedly anisotropic. Owston (1958) estimated from X-ray data that the H_2O molecule in ice has a root-mean-square vibrational amplitude of about 0·25 Å at −10 °C.

Leadbetter (1965) calculated the vibrational amplitudes of atoms in H_2O and D_2O ice from thermodynamic data. He estimated the contributions to the amplitudes arising from the ν_L and ν_T intermolecular vibrational modes (Section 3.5(a)) as well as those from the zero-point vibrations of the intramolecular modes; only the total root-mean-square amplitudes are given in Table 3.2. Note that Leadbetter's results for D_2O are in good agreement with those of Peterson and Levy.

(d) *Structure of ice I: a summary*

The salient features of the structure of ice I are firmly established, but some details are not yet clear. There appear to be no appreciable

TABLE 3.2

Root-mean-square amplitudes of thermal vibrations in ice I (Å)

Authors	Experimental data	Temp. (°C)	H₂O		D₂O	
			O atoms	H atoms	O atoms	D atoms
Peterson and Levy (1957)	Neutron diffraction	−150			0·138	0·167
		−50			0·173	0·201
Owston (1958)	X-ray diffraction	−10	0·25			
Leadbetter (1965)	Thermo-dynamic	−273	0·092	0·150	0·090	0·129
		−173	0·132	0·178	..	..
		−150	..	..	0·145	0·173
		−73	0·185	0·221	..	..
		−50	..	..	0·195	0·217
		0	0·215	0·248	0·214	0·236

differences in the structures of H_2O and D_2O ice I, the separation of nearest neighbouring oxygen atoms being about 2·76 Å in both at 0 °C. Evidence exists for deviations in the arrangements of oxygen atoms from perfectly tetrahedral coordination at 0 °C, but there is no general agreement on the temperature dependence of this deviation. The deviation may arise from hydrogen bonds along the *c*-axis being somewhat shorter than the others, or from differences in the values of the two crystallographically distinct O····O···O angles, or from a combination of both effects. In any case, the origin of these deviations in terms of intermolecular forces is not known.

The dimensions of water molecules in ice I are not very different from those of isolated molecules: the O–H distance is about 1·01 Å, and the H–O–H angle is probably not much greater than the valence angle in the isolated molecule, 104·5°.

Of the many possible arrangements of hydrogen nuclei in an ice crystal, corresponding to different orientations of H_2O molecules, all those that are compatible with the conditions on p. 75 are of nearly equal energy. Other arrangements, such as those involving the defects discussed in Section 3.4 (*b*), are of greater energy and occur only rarely. Even so, the number of possible hydrogen arrangements in a mole of ice is as large as $(3/2)^{6·02 \times 10^{23}}$. The high dielectric constant of ice (Section 3.4 (*a*)) shows that at temperatures not very far below the melting point, the crystal continually changes from one of these arrangements to another.

It seems likely that some ordered arrangement of hydrogen atoms is of slightly lower internal energy than the disordered arrangement that is observed at temperatures near the melting-point, and at very low temperatures this ordered arrangement becomes the thermodynamically stable structure. The change of molecular orientations is so slow at low temperatures, however, that thermodynamic equilibrium is not attained in a finite period of time. In other words, as ice I is cooled, changes of molecular orientation become more and more sluggish, and the crystal eventually becomes 'frozen' in a disordered structure that is probably of higher energy than some ordered structure.

3.2. Structures of ice polymorphs

Ordinary ice I is one of at least nine polymorphic forms of ice. Ices II to VII are crystalline modifications formed at high pressures; they were discovered by Tammann (1900) and Bridgman (1912, 1935, 1937). Ice VIII is a low-temperature modification of ice VII, which has been recognized only recently as being distinct from ice VII. Most of these high-pressure polymorphs exist metastably at liquid-nitrogen temperature and atmospheric pressure, and hence their structures and properties can be studied without undue difficulty. These cold metastable ices are said to be *quenched*.

The regions of stability of the stable ice polymorphs are illustrated by the $P-V-T$ surface of Fig. 3.4. In addition to the phases shown on this surface, there are three modifications of ice that have been found to exist metastably within the fields of the stable ices: ice IV was found by Bridgman within the field of ice V; and both ice Ic, often called cubic ice, and so-called 'vitreous ice' have been found within the low-temperature field of ice I. Vitreous ice is not a true polymorph; it is a glass, or in other words, highly supercooled liquid water.

(a) Ices II, III, and V

Ices II, III, and V occupy the central portion of Bridgman's phase diagram. Their structures, as determined by Kamb and his co-workers, have a number of similarities. Every water molecule is hydrogen-bonded to its four nearest neighbours. The tetrahedra formed by the four nearest neighbours are much less regular than the tetrahedra in ice I, indicating that the hydrogen bonds in these polymorphs are distorted. As in ice I, the nearest neighbours to every molecule at 1 atm lie at $2\cdot8\pm0\cdot1$ Å. In contrast to ice I, where the closest approach of non-hydrogen-bonded molecules is $4\cdot5$ Å, molecules in these polymorphs have neighbours to which they are not hydrogen-bonded in the range 3·2–3·5Å. Thus the greater compactness of these polymorphs compared to ice I arises not from the presence of shorter hydrogen bonds, but from distorted hydrogen bonds that permit closer approach of non-nearest

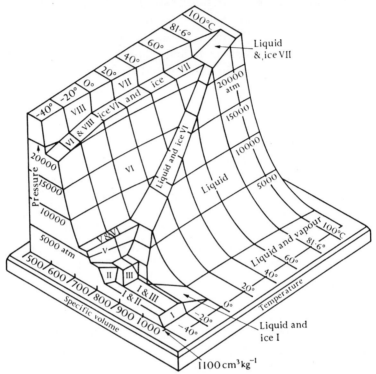

FIG. 3.4. *P–V–T* surface for H_2O. Adapted with changes from Zemansky (1957).

neighbours. The most notable difference in the structures of ices II, III, and V has to do with the ordering of hydrogen atoms. Ice V, and ice III in its field of stability, are similar to ice I in that their hydrogen atoms are disordered (that is, the orientations of the molecules are random, subject to the three conditions on p. 75). Ice II and supercooled ice III seem to have ordered arrangements of hydrogen atoms.

By means of X-ray diffraction, Kamb (1964) found that the unit cell of quenched ice II is rhombohedral and contains twelve water molecules (Table 3.3). The structure is composed of columns of puckered hexagonal rings, reminiscent of the columns in ice I, but linked more compactly (Fig. 3.5 (a)). Kamb described the relation of ice II to ice I in this way: the columns of hexagonal rings in ice I are detached, moved relatively up

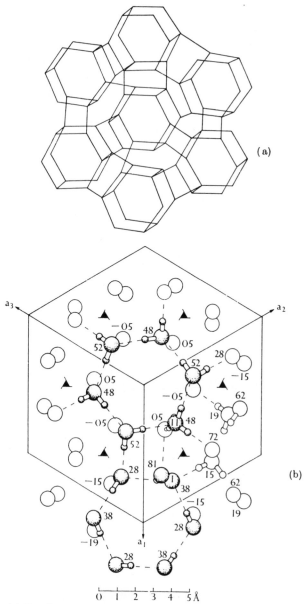

FIG. 3.5. (a) Topology of hydrogen bonding in ice II. Each line represents an O–H⋯O bond, and the junction of four lines represents an H_2O molecule. The hydrogen-bond lengths and angles are not drawn to scale here as they are in (b). Seven hexagonal columns, similar to those in ice I, are visible in the figure. Redrawn from Levine (1966). (b) Structure of ice II. Either a rhombohedral or hexagonal unit cell may be chosen for this structure. Here the rhombohedral unit cell is outlined, and the view is along the hexagonal c-axis. Heights of oxygen atoms above a hexagonal (0001) plane are given in hundredths of the c-axis ($c = 6·25$ Å). The ordered arrangement of hydrogens proposed by Kamb is shown in two rings. Hydrogen bonds are represented by dashed lines; bonds linking hexagonal rings to rings above and below are omitted to avoid confusion. Oxygen atoms O_I and O_{II} are discussed in the text. From Kamb (1964).

and down parallel to the c-axis, rotated about 30° around the c-axis, and relinked in the more compact way shown in Fig. 3.5 (a). The steric requirements of relinking cause the hexagonal rings in each column to twist relative to one another through an angle of about 15° and alternate rings to flatten considerably. Kamb believes the ordered arrangement of protons has the effect of nearly flattening the ring containing O_{II} in Fig. 3.5 (b), and of puckering the ring containing O_I more strongly than the rings in ice I.

Some characteristics of the ice II structure are summarized in Table 3.4, along with characteristics of other ice structures. The oxygen–oxygen separation of nearest neighbours in ice II varies from 2·75 to 2·84 (± 0.01) Å; slightly larger than the nearest-neighbour distance in ice I. Every molecule in ice II has a neighbour at a distance of 3·24 Å to which it is *not* hydrogen-bonded; oxygen atoms I and II in Fig. 3.5 (b) have these relative positions. Eighteen different O····O····O angles are found in ice II, ranging from 80° to 128°. Because of the ordered arrangement of hydrogens in this polymorph, not all O····O····O angles are presented to H–O–H groups for hydrogen bonding. In other words, not all O····O····O angles need serve as *donor angles*. In fact, Kamb (1964) argued that only two O····O····O angles actually serve as donor angles. If we accept his argument and further assume that all H–O–H angles are about 105°, we find that the O–H····O hydrogen bonds are bent on the average by an angle θ of 8°.

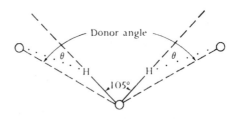

The hypothesis of an ordered arrangement of hydrogen atoms in ice II is supported by several forms of evidence.

(1) Thermodynamic: ice II has an entropy roughly $k\ln(\tfrac{3}{2})^N$ e.u. lower than that of neighbouring phases. Kamb pointed out that this difference is to be expected if ice II has ordered hydrogens and the neighbouring phases do not, and if all phases are otherwise the same in entropy.

(2) Spectroscopic: the infra-red spectrum of ice II (Section 3.5) is consistent with an ordered arrangement of hydrogens. In fact,

TABLE 3.3

Crystallographic properties of ice polymorphs†

Ice	I	Ic	II	III	V	VI	VII	VIII
Crystal system	Hexagonal	Cubic	Rhombohedral	Tetragonal	Monoclinic	Tetragonal	Cubic	Cubic
Space group‡	P6₃/mmc	F$\bar{4}$3m	R$\bar{3}$	P4₁2₁2	A2/a	P4₂/nmc	Im3m	Im3m
Unit cell dimensions (Å)§	a 4·48 c 7·31	a 6·35	a 7·78 α 113·1°	a 6·73 c 6·83	a 9·22, b 7·54 c 10·35, β 109·2°	a 6·27 c 5·79		a 3·41
No. molecules/unit cell	4	8	12	12	28	10	2	2
Density at −175 °C, 1 atm (g cm⁻³)	0·94	..	1·17	1·14	1·23	1·31	..	1·50
Density at (T °C, P kbar) in region of stability (g cm⁻³)	0·92 (0°, 1)	0·93 (−130°, 1)	1·18 (−35°, 2·1)	1·15 (−22°, 2·0)	1·26 (−5°, 5·3)	1·34 (15°, 8)	∼1·65 (25°, 25)	∼1·66 (−50°, 25)

† Data for ices I and Ic are from Lonsdale (1958); data for the high-pressure polymorphs are from Kamb (1965 *a*, *b*), Kamb (1967), and Kamb *et al.* (1967).

‡ The space groups for ices VI, VII, and VIII are not entirely certain.

§ For 1 atm and −175 °C, except for ice Ic which refers to −130° C.

Bertie and Whalley (1964 *b*) predicted ordered hydrogens on the basis of spectral data.

(3) Dielectric: the small dielectric constant and absence of dielectric relaxation in ice II (Section 3.4) are consistent with a structure in which hydrogen atoms are fixed in definite positions.

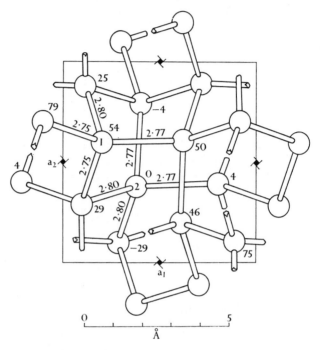

FIG. 3.6. The structure of ice III, as viewed along the *c*-axis. Oxygen atoms are represented by spheres and O–H····O bonds by rods; hydrogen atoms are not shown. Numbers adjacent to the oxygen atoms give their *z*-coordinates in hundredths of the *c*-axial length. Numbers along the bonds give their lengths in Å. O_1 and O_2 atoms are discussed in the text. From Kamb (1967).

The specific ordered arrangement of hydrogens proposed by Kamb (1964) and illustrated in Fig. 3.5 (*b*) should be regarded as being less firmly established than the presence of order *per se*. Kamb's reasons for favouring this particular arrangement are quite complex; one is that the corresponding donor angles are favourable and another is that out of several possible arrangements, the calculated X-ray structure factors for this one give the best agreement with the X-ray data.

Kamb and Datta (1960) studied quenched ice III by X-ray methods. They found that the unit cell is tetragonal and contains twelve molecules. The structure (Fig. 3.6) may be described in terms of two types of

TABLE 3.4

Structural characteristics of ice polymorphs†

Ice	I	Ic	II	III	V	VI	VII	VIII
Number of nearest neighbours	4	4	4	4	4	4	8‡	8‡
Distances of nearest neighbours (Å)	2·74	2·75§	2·75–2·84	2·76–2·80	2·76–2·87	2·81	2·86‖	2·86‖
Distance of closest non-H-bonded neighbour (Å)	4·49	4·50§	3·24	3·47	3·28, 3·46	3·51	2·86‖	2·86‖
O···O angles (deg)	109·5°±0·2°	109·5°	80°–128°	87°–141°	84°–135°	76°–128°	109·5°	109·5°
Hydrogen positions	Disordered	Disordered	Ordered	Disordered above −40 °C	Disordered	Disordered	Disordered	Ordered

† Entries, except where noted, refer to −175° C and 1 atm pressure. Data for ices I and Ic are from Lonsdale (1958); data for the high-pressure polymorphs are from Kamb and Datta (1960), Kamb (1964), Kamb (1965 a, b), Kamb (1967), and Kamb et al. (1967).

‡ At −130 °C.

§ 4 are hydrogen-bonded to central molecule.

‖ At 25 kbar. In quenched ice VII at atmospheric pressure the nearest-neighbour distance is 2·95 Å (Bertie et al. 1964).

oxygen atoms: O_1 atoms lie on a hydrogen-bonded helix having a four-fold screw axis; these helices are linked by the O_2 atoms, each of which forms hydrogen bonds with O_1 atoms in four separate helices. Nearest-neighbour separations vary from 2·76 to 2·80 Å in this polymorph (Kamb 1967). See Table 3.4.

Dielectric studies of ice III near −30 °C (Section 3.4) show that molecular orientations are constantly changing, and hence disordered. On the other hand, spectroscopic studies (Section 3.5) indicate that the orientations are ordered at liquid-nitrogen temperature. Apparently ice III undergoes a disorder–order transition as it is cooled below −30 °C. Whalley and Davidson (1965), in fact, found evidence for such a transition in the phase diagram. Diffraction studies of sufficient accuracy to confirm order in the hydrogen arrangement of quenched ice III have not yet been reported.

Ice V crystallizes in a monoclinic unit cell containing twenty-eight molecules. Kamb *et al.* (1967) described its structure as follows: two types of zig-zag chains of hydrogen-bonded molecules run parallel to the *a*-axis of the crystal. One type of chain is formed from alternating O_2 and O_3 molecules, and the other is formed wholly from O_4 molecules (see Fig. 3.7). The O_2–O_3 chains hydrogen-bond in pairs to the O_4–O_4 chains; O_2–O_3 chains are joined by O_1 atoms.

The average tetrahedral coordination of molecules is more highly distorted in ice V than in either ice II or ice III. The separations of nearest neighbours range from 2·76 to 2·87 Å, and $O\text{----}O\text{----}O$ angles range from 84 to 135°. The smallest separations of non-hydrogen-bonded molecules are 3·46 and 3·28 Å; these separations are indicated by dashed lines in Fig. 3.7.

Kamb *et al.* (1967) believe that the hydrogen atoms in quenched ice V are disordered. A Fourier synthesis, using as coefficients the difference of the observed structure factors and those calculated from the X-ray data after refinement of the oxygen positions, shows peaks that may be attributed to the hydrogens. Thirteen of the sixteen observed peaks correspond roughly to the hydrogen positions expected for a disordered structure in which the hydrogen atoms lie along the O–O axes about 1 Å from the oxygen atoms. Spectroscopic studies (Section 3.5) support a disordered structure.

Ice IV is a metastable phase which Bridgman (1935) found within the field of stability of ice V. This polymorph has been observed only by Bridgman, and only definitely in the D_2O phase diagram. Nothing is known about its structure.

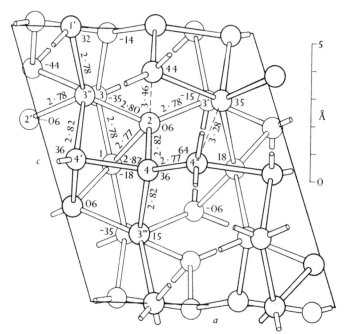

Fig. 3.7. The structure of ice V, as viewed along the *b*-axis. Oxygen atoms are represented by spheres and O–H···O bonds by rods; hydrogen atoms are not shown. Numbers adjacent to the oxygen atoms give their *y*-coordinates in hundredths of the *b*-axial length (7·54 Å). Numbers along the bonds give their lengths in Å. Numbered molecules are discussed in the text. Redrawn from Kamb *et al.* (1967).

(b) *Ices VI, VII, and VIII*

Ices VI, VII, and VIII are the densest of the known forms of ice. The relative compactness of these polymorphs is a consequence of their interpenetrating structures: in each of these ices, a fully hydrogen-bonded framework forms cavities in which molecules of a second but identical framework reside. The frameworks are interpenetrating, but not interconnecting.

Kamb (1965 *a*) used X-ray diffraction to study ice VI, and found a tetragonal unit cell containing ten molecules. As in all the other ices, each molecule is hydrogen-bonded to its four nearest neighbours. The molecules form chains that run parallel to the *c*-axis. These chains are hydrogen-bonded laterally to four neighbouring chains, thereby forming one complete framework (Fig. 3.8). Every set of four chains surrounds a shaft that is occupied by a chain of the second framework.

All three types of nearest-neighbour distances are about 2·81 Å in ice VI. Every water molecule has eight non-hydrogen-bonded neighbours

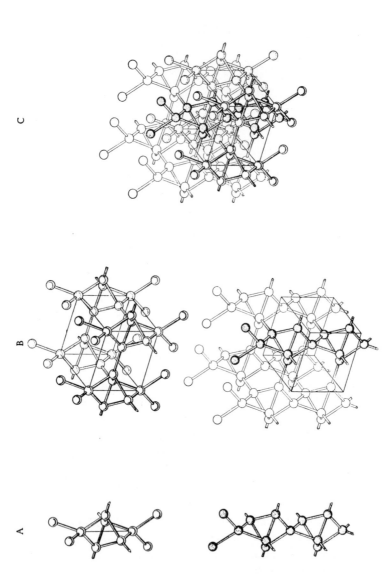

Fig. 3.8. The structure of ice VI. Water molecules are represented here in the same way they are in Fig. 3.7. Column A shows the hydrogen-bonded chains of water molecules that run parallel to the c-axis. Each chain participates in one of the component frameworks. Note that the two chains are identical except that the lower one is rotated by 90°. Column B shows four chains of each type laterally hydrogen-bonded to form each of the frameworks. The positions of the chains relative to the unit cell (outlined) are shown. Column C shows the two frameworks combined to give ice VI. Reproduced from Kamb (1965 a).

at a distance of 3·51 Å; these eight are members of the other framework. The O---O---O angles depart markedly from 109·5°, some being as large as 128° and others as small as 76°.

Bridgman (1937) discovered ice VII and mapped its phase boundaries with the liquid and with ice VI (Fig. 3.4). Careful inspection of his phase diagram led Whalley and Davidson (1965) to suggest that ice VII undergoes a disorder–order transition as it is cooled below about 5 °C. Thermodynamic and dielectric studies (Sections 3.3 and 3.4) confirmed that such a transition does occur: that, whereas the molecular orientations are constantly changing above 5°, they are fixed below this temperature; and that the entropy associated with this transition is $\sim -k\ln(\tfrac{3}{2})^N$. Thus it seems that ice VII has a disordered arrangement of hydrogens, and transforms when cooled to 5 °C to a phase having ordered hydrogens. Whalley et al. (1966) proposed that the low-temperature phase be known as ice VIII.

Kamb and Davis (1964) studied ice at 25 kbar and −50 °C (presumably ice VIII) by X-ray methods. They found that this polymorph has a body-centred cubic structure, each oxygen atom having eight nearest neighbours at a distance of about 2·86 Å. They proposed that every molecule is tetrahedrally hydrogen-bonded to four of these neighbours. This structure, shown in Fig. 3.9, can be regarded as two interpenetrating but not interconnecting lattices of the ice Ic type. Each molecule of one lattice occupies a cavity in the other lattice. The density of ice VIII (1·66 g cm^{-3} at 25 kbar) is not quite twice the density of ice Ic, owing to the longer oxygen–oxygen distances in ice VIII. The fact that this distance is greater than the 2·75 Å separation in ice Ic suggests that there are significant repulsions between each molecule and its four non-hydrogen-bonded neighbours (Kamb 1965 b).

Weir et al. (1965) reported an X-ray diffraction study of ice VII at 25 kbar and 25 °C. They also found a body-centred cubic structure. This implies that ice VII and ice VIII have identical structures, except that molecular orientations are ordered in ice VIII and disordered in ice VII.

(c) Vitreous ice and ice Ic

Vitreous ice is formed when water vapour condenses on a surface maintained below −160 °C; the X-ray and electron diffraction patterns of the product are diffuse, hence the name vitreous. This substance is almost certainly a glassy form of water, but practically nothing is known about its structure. As vitreous ice is warmed, it transforms irreversibly to ice Ic. The transformation is accompanied by a release of about 0·2 to 0·3 kcal mol^{-1} (Ghormley 1956, Dowell and Rinfret 1960). McMillan and Los (1965) believe they observed a glass transformation while warming vitreous ice at -139 °C, followed by crystallization into ice Ic at -129 °C.

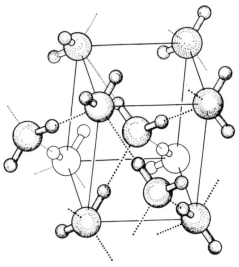

FIG. 3.9. The structure of ices VII and VIII. Hydrogen bonds are shown by dotted lines, and the unit cell is outlined by solid lines. The water molecules are shown in one of the many sets of orientations they may assume in ice VII. In ice VIII their orientations are ordered, but the nature of this order is not yet known. It seems likely that, in the ordered arrangement, molecules of one framework have favourable electrostatic interactions with molecules in the other framework. Redrawn from Kamb and Davis (1964).

Ice Ic, often called cubic ice, can be formed by warming vitreous ice, by condensing water vapour on a surface held at a temperature between -140 and -120 °C (Blackman and Lisgarten 1958), or by warming any of the quenched high-pressure ices (Bertie *et al.* 1963 and 1964). Whatever the method of preparation, ice Ic transforms irreversibly upon further warming to ice I, with a small enthalpy change.

Blackman and Lisgarten (1958) reviewed the work on vitreous ice and ice Ic up to 1958. There seems to be no well-defined temperature at which vitreous ice transforms to ice Ic. Several investigators have observed the transformation at around -160 °C, but others have observed it at temperatures as high as -120 °C. The transformation of ice Ic to ice I has also been observed over a wide range of temperatures: from about -130 °C (Dowell and Rinfret 1960) to about -70 °C (Beaumont *et al.* 1961). Bertie *et al.* (1963) found that the rate of this transformation depends on both the temperature and the thermal history of the sample.

The structure of ice Ic has been studied by X-ray and electron diffraction. The arrangement of oxygen atoms is similar to that in ice I, and is identical to the arrangement of carbon atoms in diamond (Fig. 3.10). Every water molecule is tetrahedrally hydrogen-bonded to its four nearest neighbours. The nearest-neighbour distance is 2·75 Å at −130 °C, about the same as in ice I at the same temperature. As in ice I, the oxygen atoms are arranged in puckered layers containing hexagonal rings with the 'chair' conformation. Unlike ice I, the stacking of puckered layers is such that the hexagonal rings formed by three oxygen atoms in one layer and three oxygen atoms in the adjacent layer also have the 'chair' conformation.

Honjo and Shimaoka (1957) concluded from a comparison of the observed electron diffraction intensities with those calculated from

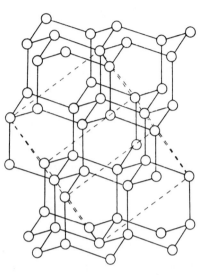

FIG. 3.10. The arrangement of oxygen atoms in ice Ic; this arrangement is isomorphous with diamond. The unit cell is outlined by dashed lines. Redrawn from Brill (1962).

various models, that the hydrogen atoms in ice Ic are disordered in the same manner as they are in ice I. From their electron diffraction studies these authors estimated that the O–H distance in ice Ic is about 0·97 Å; the difference between this value and that of the O–D distance in ice I of 1·01 Å is probably not significant.

(d) Structural characteristics of ice polymorphs: a summary

A number of structural characteristics of the ice polymorphs are summarized in Table 3.4. Some structural features are common to all polymorphs whereas others are found only in the high-pressure phases. The features that are common to all known ice polymorphs include:

(1) intact water molecules having H–O–H angles and O–H lengths not very different from the corresponding quantities for an isolated water molecule,†

† The only direct evidence regarding the positions of the hydrogen atoms in ice polymorphs is for ices I, Ic, II, and V. Nevertheless, the infra-red and Raman spectra of ices III and VI are sufficiently like those of ices I and Ic to indicate that the water molecules are intact in these ices and that the H–O–H angles and O–H lengths are

(2) water molecules that are hydrogen-bonded to four neighbours,

(3) approximately tetrahedral coordination of the four hydrogen-bonded neighbours.

Structural features found only in the high-pressure polymorphs include:

(1) non-hydrogen-bonded molecules closer than 4·5 Å to each other,

(2) equilibrium hydrogen bond angles differing by more than a few degrees from 180° (the equilibrium O----H–O angles in ices I and Ic deviate from 180° by at most 7°),

(3) equilibrium nearest neighbour O----O separations differing significantly from 2·76 Å.

One structural feature is found only in the low-temperature region of phases or in phases which exist only at low temperatures:

(1) ordered hydrogen positions.

In the following section we shall consider the relation between the structural features of a polymorph and the region of the phase diagram in which it is stable.

3.3. Thermodynamic properties

(a) Phase relations

With the exception of the metastable polymorphs, each form of ice is stable in a well-defined region of temperature and pressure. Bridgman's measurements of the pressure–volume–temperature relations of H_2O and D_2O outlined the region of stability of each polymorph. His findings, supplemented with some more recent results, are summarized in Fig. 3.11. Let us consider the structure of this phase diagram, and also of the P–V–T surface (Fig. 3.4) of which the diagram is a projection.

A point on a phase diagram where three phases meet is called a *triple point*. Eight triple points are known for water (Table 3.5) and seven of them are shown in Fig. 3.11. The eighth one is the ice I–liquid–vapour triple point, which occurs at too low a pressure to be shown on the same scale. Five of the triple points occur at junctures of the liquid with other phases, and three occur at the junctures of three solid phases. Ices II and VIII are the only stable phases that cannot be in equilibrium with the liquid. Still other phases may exist at higher pressures, but Pistorius *et al.* (1963) followed the melting curve of ice VII up to a pressure of

reasonably close to those in ices I and Ic (Bertie and Whalley 1964 b, Taylor and Whalley 1964, Marckmann and Whalley 1964). In addition, the crystal structures of ices VII and VIII imply that their H–O–H angles are not far from 105°.

about 220 000 kbar without encountering another triple point. At this
pressure, ice VII melts at 442 °C, 68° above the critical point of steam.

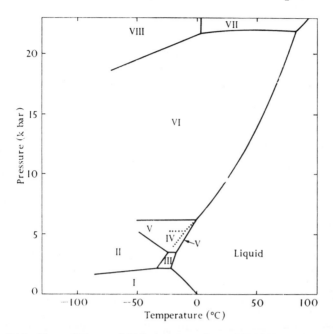

FIG. 3.11. Phase diagram of H_2O, based on data of Bridgman (1912, 1935,
1937) and Brown and Whalley (1966). The field of metastable ice IV is shown
by dashed lines; it should be noted that this field was actually mapped by
Bridgman only for D_2O. Adapted with changes from Kamb (1965 a).

TABLE 3.5

Triple points of water

Phases in equilibrium	H_2O		D_2O	
	Pressure (kbar)†	Temp. (°C)	Pressure (kbar)†	Temp. (°C)
Ice I–liquid–vapour	$6 \cdot 1 \times 10^{-6}$	0·01	..	..
Ice I–liquid–ice III	2·07	−22·0	2·20	−18·8
Ice I–ice II–ice III	2·13	−34·7	2·25	−31·0
Ice II–ice III–ice V	3·44	−24·3	3·47	−21·5
Ice III–liquid–ice V	3·46	−17·0	3·49	−14·5
Ice V–liquid–ice VI	6·26	0·16	6·28	2·6
Ice VI–liquid–ice VII	22·0	81·6	..	..
Ice VI–ice VII–ice VIII	21	∼ 5	..	..

† 1 kbar = 10^9 dyn cm^{-2} = 986·9 atm.

Bridgman used the Clapeyron equation

$$\frac{\mathrm{d}P}{\mathrm{d}T} = \frac{\Delta S}{\Delta V} \tag{3.1}$$

to determine the entropy changes for ice–ice transitions from the slopes of lines on his phase diagram and from his experimental values for the volume changes of the transitions. The enthalpy and internal energy changes for a transition are then given by

$$\Delta H = T\Delta S, \quad \text{and} \quad \Delta E = \Delta H - P\Delta V.$$

Bridgman's results are summarized in Table 3.6; we shall refer to them often in the following discussion.

Bridgman (1935) also studied the pressure–volume–temperature relations of D_2O. He found that the triple points on the D_2O diagram all occur at higher temperatures than those in the H_2O diagram (see Table 3.5) and that the transition lines, except those running approximately horizontally, all run at higher temperatures on the D_2O diagram. The differences in the triple-point temperatures for the isotopes are all about 3 °C. The enthalpy of melting of all ices in the low-pressure range is greater for the D_2O system than for the H_2O system. This difference first increases with increasing pressure and then decreases until, at the liquid–V–VI triple point, D_2O and H_2O have the same enthalpy of melting. Volume changes of melting are generally greater for the D_2O system, but the detailed behaviour of these changes is quite complicated.

Bridgman attributed the higher triple points and enthalpy of fusion of D_2O to the smaller zero-point energy of D_2O ice. Owing to its smaller zero-point energy D_2O must absorb more thermal energy than H_2O before melting. As noted by Bridgman, this explanation presupposes that zero-point energies are smaller in the liquid than in the crystal.

We are now prepared to discuss the relation of the phase diagram to the structural features of the ice polymorphs (see Section 3.2 (*d*) for a summary of these features). Let us begin with the ordered arrangement of hydrogen atoms that is found in ice II and ice VIII, phases not stable at high temperatures.

Examination of the ΔS values in Table 3.6 reveals that the transitions between ice II and its neighbouring phases, and also between ice VIII and its neighbouring phases, involve entropy changes of 0·8 to 1·2 e.u. In contrast, all other ice–ice transitions involve average entropy changes smaller by an order of magnitude. Kamb (1964) and Whalley and Davidson (1965) explained these ΔS values in terms of the ordered positions of hydrogens in ices II and VIII (Section 3.2). Their explanation is based on Pauling's calculation of the entropy in ice I associated with the disordered arrangement of hydrogen atoms. It will be recalled from Section 3.1 (*b*) that this entropy is about 0·8 e.u. Since the hydrogens

TABLE 3.6

Thermodynamics of ice–ice transitions†

Transition From	To	T (°C)	P (kbar)	ΔV (cm³ mol⁻¹)	ΔS (e.u.)	ΔH (cal mol⁻¹)	ΔE (cal mol⁻¹)	$P\Delta V$ (cal mol⁻¹)
I	II	−35	2·13	−3·92	−0·76	−180	19	−199
I	III	−22	2·08	−3·27	0·4	94	256	−162
		−35	2·13	−3·53	0·16	40	219	−179
		(−60)‡	(2·08)‡	(−3·70)‡	(−0·46)‡	(−99)‡	(83)‡	(−182)‡
II	III	−24	3·44	0·26	1·22	304	283	21
		−35	2·13	0·39	0·92	220	200	20
II	V	−24	3·44	−0·72	1·16	288	347	−59
III	V	−17	3·46	−0·98	−0·07	−17	64	−81
		−24	3·44	−0·98	−0·06	−16	65	−81
V	VI	0·16	6·26	−0·70	−0·01	−4	101	−105
VI	VII	81·6	22	−1·05	~0	~0	550	−550
VI	VIII§	~5	~21	:: 0·000	~−1·01	−282	::	::
VII	VIII§	~5	~21	±0·0005	−0·93	−260	−260	::

† Data of Bridgman (1912, 1935, 1937), except where noted. Values of ΔH, ΔE, and $P\Delta V$ have been calculated by the present authors.
‡ Supercooled ice III.
§ Data of Brown and Whalley (1966) and Whalley et al. (1966).

in ices III, V, VI, and VII are also disordered, these phases, like ice I, have an extra entropy of about 0·8 e.u. It thus seems reasonable to ascribe the entropy increase of 0·8 to 1·2 e.u. in the transition from ice II or ice VIII to other phases primarily to the entropy of hydrogen disorder.

Accepting this explanation for the ΔS values, we see that much of the complexity of the phase diagram of ice is a consequence of the ordered arrangement of hydrogen atoms in ices II and VIII. The slopes of lines on the phase diagram, as mentioned above, are described by eqn (3.1). From Table 3.6 we see that the average entropy changes for the transitions which do not involve ices II or VIII (that is, the I–III, III–V, V–VI, and VI–VII transitions) are all very small. Hence the corresponding values of dP/dT are all very small, and the lines between these phases on the phase diagram are nearly horizontal. In contrast, the ΔS values for the transitions involving ices II and VIII are much larger. Thus the boundary lines between these phases and their neighbours are distinctly non-horizontal. The precise value of each slope is determined by the ratio of ΔS to ΔV. Where ΔV is negative (as in passing from II to V) the slope is negative. Where ΔV is comparatively large (as in the I–II transition) the slope is more nearly horizontal than where ΔV is very small (as in the VII–VIII transition). In short, if hydrogen ordering did not take place and ices II and VIII were non-existent, all lines on the ice phase diagram would run nearly horizontally.

In the preceding paragraphs, we have neglected an important point: though ΔS for the I–III transition is small when averaged over all temperatures, the value actually ranges from about $-0·46$ e.u. at $-60°$ to about 0·4 e.u. at $-22°$. Whalley and Davidson (1965) noted that the change in ΔS from the lowest to highest temperature is about 0·86 e.u., roughly the entropy associated with disorder of hydrogen atoms. This led them to suggest that the hydrogen atoms of ice III are disordered near $-30\ °C$, but gradually become ordered as this polymorph is cooled to $-60°\ C$. Spectroscopic data for ice III (Section 3·5) are in accord with this suggestion.

We have not yet accounted for the fact that ordered hydrogens are found only in phases that exist at relatively low temperatures. It is well known that of all possible crystal structures for a substance, the one that is stable at a given temperature and pressure is the one with lowest free energy. The difference in free energy, ΔG, of two crystal structures is given by

$$\Delta G = \Delta E + P\Delta V - T\Delta S, \tag{3.2}$$

where ΔE is the difference in their internal energy. A large internal energy, a large volume, or a small entropy will tend to make a particular crystal form unstable. At higher temperatures, a small entropy contributes more strongly to such an instability. Now the entropy change associated with the transition from a disordered to an ordered form of ice is about -0.8 e.u., and hence such a transition increases the free energy by $0.8 \times T$ cal mol^{-1}. This is about 240 cal mol^{-1} at 300 °K, comparable in magnitude to the values of ΔE for ice–ice transitions (Table 3.6). As a disordered polymorph is cooled, this $T\Delta S$ term decreases, and the crystal may eventually transform to an ordered polymorph. For such a transformation to occur, some ordered crystal structure must exist with a smaller internal energy (and/or volume) than the disordered structure. Then during the transformation, the increase in free energy arising from the $T\Delta S$ term of eqn (3.2) is compensated by a decrease arising from the ΔE term, and perhaps also from the $P\Delta V$ term.

In Section 3.2 (d) it was noted that certain structural features are found only in the high-pressure ices. These include distorted hydrogen bonds and the close approach of non-hydrogen-bonded neighbours. Such features permit relatively high densities without necessitating the complete rupture of hydrogen bonds. The reason these features occur in the high-pressure polymorphs is apparent from eqn (3.2): at high pressures, a large volume contributes strongly to the instability of a polymorph. For example, the relatively small ΔV for the VI–VII transition, -1 cm^3 mol^{-1}, causes a decrease in $P\Delta V$ of ~ 500 cal mol^{-1}, simply because P is so large at the transition point. Thus structural features that permit smaller volumes are favoured in the high-pressure polymorphs.

Examination of Table 3.6 shows that the high-pressure polymorphs have larger internal energies than ice I. These larger internal energies undoubtedly arise from distorted hydrogen bonds and also from closely situated, non-bonded neighbours that are in repulsive contact. Highly distorted hydrogen bonds and nearby non-bonded neighbours do not occur in ice I, because the smaller volume permitted by these features does not compensate, at low pressures, for the larger internal energy that they entail.

It was also noted in Section 3.2 (d) that some structural features are common to all known ice polymorphs. In all polymorphs, for example, each molecule is hydrogen-bonded to four nearest neighbours, and these four neighbours form a tetrahedron (somewhat distorted in ices II, III, V, and VI) about the central molecule. The occurrence of this feature in all polymorphs demonstrates, of course, that this basic configuration of water molecules is particularly effective in maintaining a low free energy over a wide range of temperatures and pressures.

In closing our discussion of the phase diagram of ice it should be mentioned that no completely satisfactory explanation has been given for the stability of ordinary ice I relative to ice Ic. Bjerrum (1951, 1952) presented calculations, based on a point-charge model for the water molecule, which indicated that ice I is the more stable structure owing to electrostatic interactions of the molecules along the c-axis. His calculations also implied, however, that the hydrogen atoms in ice I are ordered to some extent, even up to the melting-point, and this implication is inconsistent with evidence mentioned in Section 3.1. Pitzer and Polissar (1956) later showed that, if more interactions are included, Bjerrum's model does not predict a strongly ordered arrangement of hydrogens. They did find, though, that if even a small amount of ordering takes place, ice I is the more stable form. As no conclusive evidence exists for any ordering in ice I, the stability of ice I relative to ice Ic should be regarded as an unexplained fact.

(b) Thermal energy

The heat capacity of ice I has been measured calorimetrically from 2 °K to the melting-point (Giauque and Stout 1936, Flubacher *et al.* 1960). At very low temperatures the heat capacity approaches zero: C_P at 2·144 °K, for example, is 0·00042 cal mol^{-1} °C^{-1}. As the temperature rises, C_P increases gradually (see Fig. 3.12), until it is about 9 cal mol^{-1} °C^{-1} at the melting-point. Upon fusion, C_P doubles. The heat capacity of the liquid is nearly constant from 0 to 100 °C, but experiences a slight minimum near 35 °C. Then upon vaporization, C_P falls back to about 9 cal mol^{-1} °C^{-1}.

It is noteworthy that Giauque and Stout (1936) found ice to be sluggish in reaching thermal equilibrium in the range 85–100 °K. The cause of this sluggishness is not known.

The enthalpy, entropy, and free energy of H_2O at any temperature T, relative to the enthalpy, entropy, and free energy of ice at 0 °K, can be found by numerical integration of C_P. The difference in enthalpy of a substance at T °K and 0 °K, $H_T - H_0$, is given by

$$H_T - H_0 = \int_0^T C_P \, dT + \Delta H_{pc}, \qquad (3.3)$$

where ΔH_{pc} represents the sum of all enthalpy changes for phase transi-

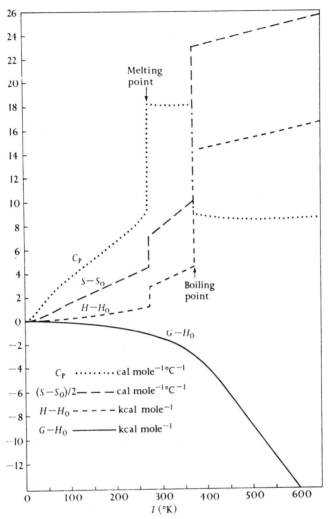

Fig. 3.12. Enthalpy, entropy, free energy, and isopiestic heat capacity of H_2O at 1 atm pressure. Enthalpy and free energy are in units of kcal mol^{-1}, heat capacity is in units of cal mol^{-1} °C^{-1}, and entropy is in units of 2 cal mol^{-1} °C^{-1}. Data are from Dorsey (1940).

tions occurring between 0 and T °K. The difference in entropy at T °K and at 0 °K, $S_T - S_0$, is given by

$$S_T - S_0 = \int_0^T \frac{C_P}{T}\, \mathrm{d}T + \Delta S_{pc} \tag{3.4}$$

where ΔS_{pc} represents the sum of entropy changes for all phase changes occurring between 0 and T° K. S_0 for a perfectly ordered crystal is conventionally equated to zero. Ice I, as discussed in Section 3.1 (b), is not perfectly ordered at 0 °K. The evidence for this rests partly on the value of S_0, which we shall derive presently.

The difference in Gibbs free energy at T and 0 °K, $G_T - G_0$, is given by

$$G_T - G_0 = H_T - H_0 - T S_T. \tag{3.5}$$

It should be noted that since $G = H - TS$, G_0 equals H_0.

Fig. 3.12 shows plots of $H_T - H_0$, $S_T - S_0$, and $G_T - G_0$ for H_2O at atmospheric pressure from 0 to about 650 °K, as determined from the foregoing equations.

TABLE 3.7

Thermodynamic constants for phase changes of water

(a) Fusion and vaporization of H_2O and D_2O at 1 atm pressure

	Fusion		Vaporization	
	H_2O	D_2O	H_2O	D_2O
Temperature (°K)	273·15	276·97[a]	373·15	374·59[a]
ΔC_P, isopiestic heat capacity change (cal mol^{-1} °C^{-1})	8·911[b]	9·48[b]	−10·021	..
ΔH, enthalpy change (kcal mol^{-1})	1·4363[b]	1·501[b]	9·7171[b]	9·927[a]
ΔS, entropy change (cal mol^{-1} °C^{-1})	5·2581[b]	5·419	26·0400[b]	26·501
ΔV, volume change (cm^3 mol^{-1})	−1·621[d]	..	$3·01 \times 10^4$	..
ΔE, internal energy change (kcal mol^{-1})	1·4363	..	8·988[c]	..

(b) Sublimation of H_2O and D_2O

	At ice I–liquid–vapour triple point		At 0° K to the ideal vapour	
	H_2O	D_2O	H_2O	D_2O
Temperature (°K)	273·16	276·98	0	0
ΔH, enthalpy change (kcal mol^{-1})	12·203[b]	12·63[f]	11·32[e]	11·92[e]
ΔS, entropy change (cal mol^{-1} °C^{-1})	44·674	45·60	0	0
ΔE, internal energy change (kcal mol^{-1})	11·661[c]	12·08[g]	11·3[e]	..

[a] Shatenshtein *et al.* (1960).
[b] Rossini *et al.* (1952).
[c] Calculated from data reported by Dorsey (1940).
[d] Dorsey (1940).
[e] See Table 3.8.
[f] Kirshenbaum (1951).
[g] Némethy and Scheraga (1964).

The changes of thermodynamic properties at the melting- and boiling-point are listed in Table 3.7. Also recorded in this table are the enthalpy and internal energy changes for sublimation at both the ice I–liquid–vapour triple point and 0 °K. The values of ΔH and ΔE for sublimation at 0 °K have been obtained by the addition of a series of enthalpies and internal energies, as illustrated in Table 3.8. The enthalpy of sublimation at 0 °K is a direct measure of the intermolecular energy in ice, and we shall make use of this quantity in our discussion of the hydrogen-bond energy in Section 3.6 (a).

TABLE 3.8

Energy and enthalpy of sublimation of ice I at 0 °K

(All entries are in units of kcal mol^{-1})

Contribution	H$_2$O	D$_2$O
Enthalpy of sublimation		
$H_{298\cdot16°}(\text{vap})\dagger - H_{298\cdot16°}(\text{liq})$	$10\cdot5196 \pm 0\cdot0031^a$	$10\cdot8505 \pm 0\cdot0086^a$
$H_{298\cdot16°}(\text{liq}) \quad - H_{\text{melt. pt.}}(\text{liq})$	$0\cdot4370 \pm 0\cdot0002^b$	$0\cdot4231 \pm 0\cdot0007^b$
$H_{\text{melt. pt.}}(\text{liq}) - H_{\text{melt. pt.}}(\text{ice})$	$1\cdot4363 \pm 0\cdot0009^c$	$1\cdot501 \pm 0\cdot004^b$
$H_{\text{melt. pt.}}(\text{ice}) - H_{0°K}(\text{ice})$	$1\cdot290 \pm 0\cdot001^b$	$1\cdot530 \pm 0\cdot003^b$
$-[H_{298\cdot16°}(\text{vap})\dagger - H_{0°K}(\text{vap})\dagger]$	$-2\cdot3669 \pm 0\cdot0007^a$	$-2\cdot3795 \pm 0\cdot0007^a$
$H_{0°K}(\text{vap})\dagger \quad - H_{0°K}(\text{ice})$	$11\cdot316 \pm 0\cdot004$	$11\cdot925 \pm 0\cdot01$
Internal energy of sublimation		
$E_{273\cdot16°}(\text{vap}) \quad - E_{273\cdot16°}(\text{ice})$	$11\cdot66^d$	
$E_{273\cdot16°}(\text{ice}) \quad - E_{0°K}(\text{ice})$		
$\cong H_{273\cdot16°}(\text{ice}) - H_{0°K}(\text{ice})$	$1\cdot29^b$	
$-[E_{273\cdot16°}(\text{vap}) \quad - E_{0°K}(\text{vap})]$	$-1\cdot61^e$	
$E_{0°K}(\text{vap}) \quad - E_{0°K}(\text{ice})$	$11\cdot3$	

† Ideal vapour.
^{a} Rossini, Knowlton, and Johnston (1940).
^{b} Whalley (1957). Whalley's values are given in units of joules, and have been converted by the present authors using the factor 1 joule $= 0\cdot239045$ cal.
^{c} Rossini *et al.* (1952).
^{d} See Table 3.7.
^{e} Bernal and Fowler (1933).

We now must consider the origin of the heat capacity of ice. This property arises from the excitation of intermolecular vibrations of water molecules, the intramolecular vibrations being hardly excited at room temperature (Section 1.1 (*f*)). Spectroscopic studies indicate (Section 3.5 (*a*)) that the intermolecular vibrations of ice are of two distinct types: hindered translations and hindered rotations (usually called *librations*).

Several authors (for example, Blue 1954, Flubacher *et al.* 1960, Lead-better 1965) have shown that the heat capacity of ice may be explained in terms of these motions. As ice is warmed from 0 °K, the hindered translations are excited first. These vibrations have smaller characteristic frequencies (average around 200 cm^{-1}) than the librations (500–800 cm^{-1}), so they require smaller quanta of thermal energy for excitation. Leadbetter's (1965) analysis indicates that below 80 °K the heat capacity arises almost entirely from excitation of the hindered transla-tions. By 150 °K, the librations also contribute significantly to the heat capacity.

The residual entropy of ice was used to establish the positions of hydrogen atoms in ice (Section 3.1 (*b*)), so it is desirable to consider how this property is determined. The residual entropy of ice can be found by comparing the values, measured by two different methods, for the entropy of a mole of ideal water vapour at 298·1 °K and 1 atm pressure. These two methods are:

(1) Calculation from statistical mechanical expressions, using spectro-scopic data. The resulting quantity, denoted S_{spec}, is given in Table 3.9 (*a*) along with the contributions to it arising from the translation, rotation, and vibration of water molecules.

(2) Calculation from calorimetric data, using eqn (3.4). The resulting quantity, denoted S_{cal}, is given in Table 3.9 (*b*) along with its various contributions.

Now it is apparent from Table 3.9 that S_{spec} exceeds S_{cal} by several times the error of determination. Since S_{spec} is the difference between the entropy of water vapour under the stated conditions and of a hypo-thetical, perfectly-ordered ice crystal at 0° K, the discrepancy of S_{spec} and S_{cal} implies that real ice I is not perfectly ordered at 0 °K. The difference of S_{spec} and S_{cal} is called the *residual entropy* and denoted S_0.

(c) *P–V–T data for ice I*

In this section we present values for the density, coefficients of thermal expansion, and coefficient of compressibility of ice I.† The density and coefficients of thermal expansion have been determined both from measurements on bulk ice and from X-ray diffraction studies of ice crystals. The values obtained from diffraction

---

† The coefficient of linear expansion, α, is a measure of the fractional change of length of a substance with temperature. It is defined by $\alpha = l_0^{-1}(\partial l/\partial T)_P$ where l_0 is the length of the sample. The linear expansion of ice I is not necessarily the same in the *c*-axis direction as in directions perpendicular to the *c*-axis. The coefficient of cubical expansion is defined by $\beta = V_0^{-1}(\partial V/\partial T)_P$, where V_0 is the volume of the sample. The coefficient of adiabatic compressibility, γ_S, is defined by

$$\gamma_S = -V_0^{-1}(\partial V/\partial P)_S.$$

studies may be more significant because they depend only on the lattice dimensions, whereas values based on bulk measurements may also depend on the texture of the sample.

TABLE 3.9

The residual entropy of ice I

(All entries in e.u.)

(a) Contributions to the spectroscopic entropy (S_{spec}) of H_2O at 298·1 °K and 1 atm pressure (calculations of Rushbrooke 1962)

S_{trans}	from Sackur–Tetrode equation	34·61
S_{rot}	from classical partition function	10·48
S_{vib}	taking $\nu = 3652, 1592, 3756$ cm^{-1}	0·00
		45·09

(b) Contributions to the calorimetric entropy (S_{cal}) of H_2O at 298·1 °K and 1 atm pressure (calculations of Giauque and Stout 1936)

0–10 °K: Debye extrapolation with $h\nu/k = 192°$	0·022†
10–273·1 °K: graphical integration of C_P/T	9·081
Fusion at 273·1 °K	5·257
273·1–298·1 °K: graphical integration of C_P/T	1·580
Vaporization at 298·1 °K	35·220
Correction for gas imperfection	0·002
Compression to 1 atmosphere	−6·886
	44·28±0·05

(c) Residual entropy of ice

S_{spec}	45·09
S_{cal}	44·28
S_0 (residual entropy)‡	0·81

† The contribution to S_{cal} below 10 °K calculated by the Debye extrapolation is the same to this accuracy as the directly measured value of Flubacher et al. (1960).

‡ This value is 0·01 cal mol^{-1} °C^{-1} smaller than the value reported by Giauque and Stout owing to a different value of S_{spec}.

The coefficients of expansion determined by La Placa and Post (1960) from an X-ray diffraction study (Table 3.10 (a)) are in fair agreement with the bulk measurements recorded in Table 3.10(b). These bulk measurements were obtained by Leadbetter (1965), who averaged and smoothed the results of Powell (1958) and Dantl (1962). Leadbetter believes that these values are accurate to better than 5 per cent above −173 °C. Lonsdale (1958) obtained a set of thermal expansion coefficients by smoothing the results of several diffraction studies; but her results indicate that β increases at lower temperatures, and are hence not in accord with the other studies. Nevertheless, it should be noted that Lonsdale's value for the density of ice I at 0 °C (0·9164 g ml^{-1}) is close to the precise bulk value of Ginnings and Corruccini (1947; see Table 3.10 (a)).

Dantl's (1962) dilatometric study of single ice crystals indicates that β becomes negative as ice is cooled below 63 °K and then passes through a minimum near 35 °K. Many other substances with tetrahedral structures (for example, diamond,

TABLE 3.10

P–V–T data for ice I at atmospheric pressure

(a) From measurements on bulk ice

Property	Temp. (°C)	Value	Reference
Density, ρ_0 (g ml^{-1})	0	0.91671 ± 0.00005	[a]
Coefficient of cubical expansion, β (units of 10^{-6} °C^{-1})	-13	152	[b]
	-53	125	
	-93	96	
	-133	69	
	-173	39	
	-213	-3	
	-253	-9	
Coefficient of adiabatic compressibility, γ_S (units of 10^{-12} cm^2 dyn^{-1})	-13	12·8	[c]
	-53	12·2	
	-93	11·7	
	-133	11·3	
	-173	11·1	
	-213	10·9	
	-253	10·9	

(b) From X-ray diffraction of ice[d]

Temp. (°C)	Density, ρ_0 (g cm^{-3})	Coefficient of linear expansion, α (10^{-6} °C^{-1})		Coefficient of cubical expansion, β (10^{-6} °C^{-1})
		$\perp c$-axis	$\|c$-axis	
-10	0·9187			
		46	63	156
-20	0·9203			
		45	48	138
-40	0·9228			
		44	41	129
-60	0·9252			
		40	35	115
-80	0·9274			
		34	30	99
-100	0·9292			
		22	27	71
-120	0·9305			
		12	25	50
-140	0·9314			
		32	23	88
-160	0·9331			
		14	22	51
-180	0·9340			

[a] Ginnings and Corruccini (1947).

[b] Calculated by Leadbetter (1965) from data of Powell (1958) and Dantl (1962).

[c] Calculated by Leadbetter (1965) from data of Bass *et al.* (1957) and Zarembovitch and Kahane (1964).

[d] Data of La Placa and Post (1960). The present authors have computed values of ρ_0 and β from these data, taking the molecular weight of H_2O as 18·01534 and Avogadro's number as 6.02380×10^{23}.

silicon, germanium, vitreous silica, and InSb) also exhibit negative thermal expansion at low temperatures (Collins and White 1964). This phenomenon is presumably associated in some way with the excitation of hindered translational vibrations that occurs in this temperature region. Dantl could detect no anisotropy in the thermal expansion of ice, and found the thermal expansion of D_2O to differ only slightly from that of H_2O.

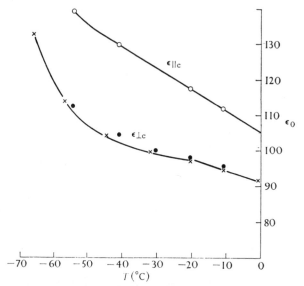

FIG. 3.13. The static dielectric constant of ice I, ϵ_0, as a function of temperature.

$\times$ $\times$ Polycrystalline sample (Autry and Cole 1952).
$\bigcirc$ $\bigcirc$ Single crystal; electric field parallel to c-axis   } (Humbel *et al.*
●   ●   Single crystal; electric field perpendicular to c-axis }   1953).

The values for the coefficient of adiabatic compressibility in Table 3.10 (*a*) were derived by Leadbetter (1965) from elastic constants. Leadbetter believes that the uncertainty in these coefficients is not greater than 10 per cent. Readers interested in the mechanical and elastic properties of ice are referred to the reviews by Glen (1958) and Stephens (1958).

3.4. Electrical properties and self-diffusion

(a) Dielectric constant and dipole moment

The static dielectric constants, ϵ_0, of both polycrystalline and single crystals of ice I have been carefully determined (Auty and Cole 1952, Humbel *et al.* 1953). Fig. 3.13 shows that ϵ_0 increases with decreasing temperature and that ϵ_0 parallel to the c-axis is slightly larger than ϵ_0 perpendicular to the c-axis. The dielectric constant of polycrystalline ice is higher at 0 °C than that of water, even though the decrease in the volume of water on melting would be expected to cause a change in the opposite direction. The application of pressure to ice I increases ϵ_0, as is shown in Fig. 3.14.

The dielectric properties of the high-pressure polymorphs were investigated by Wilson *et al.* (1965) and Whalley *et al.* (1966). Wilson *et al.* measured values of ϵ_0 for ices II, III, V, and VI over a range of temperatures and pressures; their results for a constant temperature of $-30\ °C$ are shown in Fig. 3.15. They found that, with the exception of ice II, each of these polymorphs has a larger value of ϵ_0 than all polymorphs stable at lower pressures. Ice II has a low value of ϵ_0 (4·2), which is independent of temperature and pressure. Whalley *et al.* (1966) found that ϵ_0 for ice VII at 22 °C and 21 kbars is roughly 150; this is somewhat smaller than ϵ_0 of ice VI extrapolated to the same temperature and pressure (about 185). These authors also found that ice VIII, like ice II, has a very small value of ϵ_0.

The large dielectric constants of ices I, III, V, VI, and VII tell us that water molecules in these polymorphs are constantly changing their orientations as a result of thermal agitation. In the following section we shall consider the rate and the mechanism of these changes; here we use Kirkwood's theory (Kirkwood 1939) to interpret the observed ϵ_0 values in terms of the polarity and local correlation of H_2O molecules in ice.

Though Kirkwood's theory is strictly applicable only to isotropic substances composed of non-polarizable dipoles (e.g. see Buckingham 1956), it can be used to give a semi-quantitative description of the dielectric properties of ice. For highly polar substances Kirkwood's equation assumes the form†

$$\epsilon_0 = 2\pi N^* \frac{\mathbf{m} \cdot \mathbf{m}^*}{kT} \tag{3.6}$$

where N^* is the number of molecules per unit volume, kT is the product of Boltzmann's constant and the absolute temperature, and $\mathbf{m}$ and $\mathbf{m}^*$ are quantities related to the molecular dipole moment as follows:

1. $\mathbf{m}$ is the average dipole moment of an H_2O molecule surrounded by its neighbours. Its magnitude is greater than that of $\mathbf{\mu}$, the dipole moment of an isolated molecule, because in ice each molecule is further polarized by the electrostatic fields of its strongly polar neighbours (see Fig. 3.16). If $\mathbf{F}$ is the uniform electrostatic field arising from neighbouring molecules, and α is the polarizability of the central molecule, then $\mathbf{m} = \mathbf{\mu} + \alpha\mathbf{F}$. We shall discuss the probable magnitude of $\mathbf{m}$ below.

† See Edsall and Wyman (1958) for a discussion and simplified derivation of this equation.

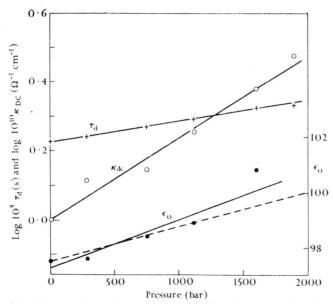

FIG. 3.14. Pressure dependence of the static dielectric constant (ϵ_0), dielectric relaxation time (τ_d), and logarithm of the direct current conductivity (κ_{DC}) of ice I at $-23 \cdot 4$ °C. Data of Chan et al. (1965). The dashed line is discussed in the text. Adapted with changes from Chan et al. (1965).

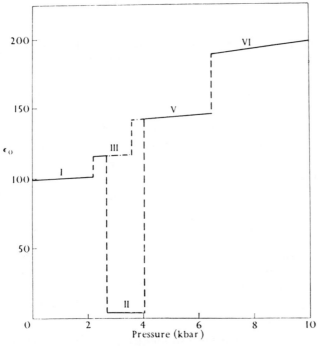

FIG. 3.15. Pressure dependence of the static dielectric constant, ϵ_0, of ices I, II, III, V, and VI at -30 °C. Redrawn from Wilson et al. (1965).

2. **m*** is the vector sum of the dipole moment of an arbitrary 'central' molecule and the dipole moments of the neighbouring molecules. As can be seen from Fig. 3.16, the network of tetrahedral hydrogen bonding in ice causes neighbours to be aligned in such a way that components of

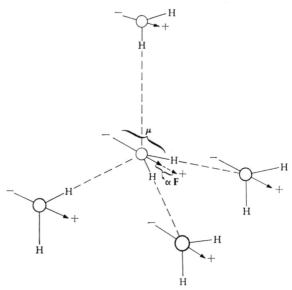

FIG. 3.16. The magnitude of the dipole moment, m, of an H_2O molecule in ice is greater than the corresponding quantity for an isolated water molecule, μ, because of the electrostatic fields arising from dipolar neighbouring molecules. Here an arbitrary central molecule is shown with its four nearest neighbours. The electrostatic field, **F**, arising from the neighbours induces an additional moment αF (where α is the molecular polarizability) in the central molecule.

their dipole moments lie in the direction of the dipole moment of the central molecule. Clearly **m*** depends both on the magnitude of **m** and on the relative orientations of neighbouring molecules. A function of **m** and **m*** that depends only on the relative orientations of neighbouring molecules is g, the *Kirkwood correlation parameter*, given by

$$g = \frac{\mathbf{m^*} \cdot \mathbf{m}}{m^2} = 1 + \sum_{i=1} N_i \langle \cos \gamma_i \rangle, \qquad (3.7)$$

where $m = |\mathbf{m}|$, N_i is the number of neighbouring molecules in the ith coordination shell, and $\langle \cos \gamma_i \rangle$ is the average cosine of angles formed by the dipole moments of molecules in the ith shell with the dipole moment of the central molecule. We shall discuss the probable magnitude and significance of g below.

It should be noted that both **m** and **m*** refer to the substance in the absence of an external electric field.

By combining eqns (3.6) and (3.7), we can write Kirkwood's equation in the form

$$\epsilon_0 = 2\pi N * \frac{m^2 g}{kT}. \tag{3.6a}$$

The physical meaning of this expression is that the dielectric constant of a substance depends not only on the magnitude of the permanent dipole moment of its molecules and the number of dipoles per unit volume, but also on the extent to which the molecules induce additional moments in each other, and the extent to which the directions of their dipoles are correlated. A strong correlation of dipole directions (that is, a large value of g) means that when one molecule is aligned with the external field, its neighbours tend to be aligned also. Ice has a large dielectric constant because its tetrahedral structure leads to both a large dipole moment in each molecule (large m) and a strong angular correlation between the dipole moments of its molecules (large g). The inverse relationship between dielectric constant and temperature in eqn (3.6a) arises, of course, from the opposition of thermal agitation to alignment of dipole moments in the direction of the applied field.

Let us consider the magnitude of **m** in ice I. In contrast to μ, m is not accessible to direct measurement. Onsager and others have estimated m from the dielectric properties of ice, and some investigators have made direct calculations of m. According to Onsager's theory of dielectrics (1936; Böttcher 1952, p. 70), the magnitude of **m** in strongly polar dielectrics is related to the magnitude of μ by

$$m \cong \left(\frac{n^2+2}{3}\right)\mu, \tag{3.8}$$

where n is the refractive index of the medium. For ice I this equation predicts a value for m of 2·3 D. It should be noted that Onsager's theory depicts the central molecule as a point-dipole at the centre of a spherical cavity about the size of the molecule, in a continuous dielectric medium. This model is almost certainly a poor one for an open, hydrogen-bonded structure such as ice, so it is doubtful that eqn (3.8) gives an accurate value for m. A larger estimate of m (3·8 D) was made by Onsager and Dupuis (1962) from a consideration of the temperature dependence of ϵ_0. This value is twice as large as μ (1·83 D) and indicates that the electrostatic field arising from neighbouring molecules is very large.

A direct calculation of **m** based on a multipole-moment model of the water molecule predicts a magnitude of 2·6 D (Coulson and Eisenberg

1966 a). In this work the electric field acting on the central molecule was found to be about 0.52×10^6 e.s.u. cm^{-2} (roughly 150 000 000 V cm^{-1}), and to have the same direction as the permanent dipole moment of the central molecule. This means that ice molecules are oriented so that the energy of interaction of their dipole moments with the electric field produced by their neighbours is a minimum—that is, binding energy a maximum. Of the total field acting on the central molecule, nearly 20 per cent arises from the quadrupole and octupole moments of the neighbours, and about 20 per cent arises from second and further neighbours.

Now let us consider the magnitude of g for ice I. From eqn (3.7), it is evident that g would equal unity if neighbouring molecules were randomly oriented with respect to the central molecule. Owing to the pattern of hydrogen bonding in ice, however, neighbouring molecules tend to have their dipole moments pointing in the same direction as the central molecule (Fig. 3.16); hence $\langle \cos \gamma_i \rangle$ of eqn (3.7) is large and positive, and hence g is greater than unity. Progress in computing g from the known structure of ice I was reviewed by Hollins (1964); he concluded that, to a first approximation, this quantity is 3. According to Hollins, the 4 nearest neighbours contribute 1.333 to g, the 12 next-nearest neighbours contribute 0.44, and the 25 third-nearest neighbours contribute about 0.48.

Given the values of m and g we can calculate the temperature dependence of ϵ_0 from Kirkwood's theory, using eqn (3.6 a). Taking $m = 2.6$ D and $g = 3$ we find $\epsilon_0 \simeq 2.8 \times 10^4/T$. Hollins (1964) found that the best fit to the data of Auty and Cole (1952), assuming a $1/T$ temperature dependence of the data, is $\epsilon_0 \simeq 2.50 \times 10^4/T$.

Kirkwood's theory is also helpful in interpreting the pressure dependence of ϵ_0. The observed increase of ϵ_0 with pressure (Fig. 3.14) may arise from an increase in density (more dipoles per unit volume), an increase in m, or an increase in g. The effect of increased density on ϵ_0 is given approximately by the dashed line in Fig. 3.14. In drawing this line we have assumed that the isothermal compressibility of ice I is 11.1×10^{-12} cm^2 dyn^{-1}. The dielectric constant would follow this line if the increase in number of dipoles were the only consequence of applied pressure. It appears that the rate of increase of ϵ_0 with pressure is somewhat greater than that indicated by this line, so that m or g may also increase during compression. An increase in m is to be expected since the field acting on a molecule grows as its neighbours move closer.

A more quantitative interpretation of the pressure dependence of ϵ_0 was given by Chan et al. (1965). They assumed that m is given by eqn (3.8); then they differentiated eqn (3.6 a) with respect to pressure. They simplified the resulting expression by assuming that the refractive index, n, is related to the molecular polarizability by the Lorenz–Lorentz equation. The pressure dependence of ϵ_0 may then be written

$$\left(\frac{\partial \ln \epsilon_0}{\partial P}\right)_T = \frac{2n^2+1}{3}\gamma_T + \frac{2(n^2-1)}{3}\left(\frac{\partial \ln \bar{\alpha}}{\partial P}\right)_T + 2\left(\frac{\partial \ln \mu}{\partial P}\right)_T + \left(\frac{\partial \ln g}{\partial P}\right)_T,$$

$$(3.9)\dagger$$

where γ_T is the coefficient of isothermal compressibility. The first term on the right in this equation represents the increase of ϵ_0 with pressure that arises from the combined effects of more dipoles per unit volume and of larger induced dipole moments. The next three terms describe the effect on ϵ_0 of the changes of $\bar{\alpha}$, μ, and g with pressure.

The experimental results of Chan et al. (1965) indicate that $(\partial \ln \epsilon_0/\partial P)_T$ is $14(\pm 3)\times 10^{-6}$ bar^{-1} at $-23{\cdot}4$ °C over the pressure range 0–2 kbar. Now if we take $\gamma_T = 11{\cdot}1\times 10^{-12}$ cm^2 dyn^{-1} and $n^2 = 1{\cdot}77$, we find that the first term on the right in eqn (3.9) is 17×10^{-6} bar^{-1}. Thus it seems that the other three terms are small or nearly cancel one another.

Among the high-pressure polymorphs, ices II and VIII are the only ones with small values of ϵ_0. Apparently the H_2O molecules in these polymorphs are 'frozen in', that is, they are unable to change their orientations in the presence of an applied field. This conclusion is consistent with other data, which indicate that orientations of molecules in these ices are ordered (Section 3.2).

The ϵ_0s of the other high-pressure polymorphs exceed that of ice I. The greater density of these polymorphs results in more dipoles per unit volume and in larger values of m; both these factors tend to increase ϵ_0. Wilson et al. (1965) and Whalley et al. (1966) argued that the g values for these polymorphs are not very different from the g value for ice I. They estimated g for each polymorph from eqn (3.6 a), after first estimating m from eqn (3.8). This procedure gave g values between $2{\cdot}4$ and $3{\cdot}4$ for ices I, III, V, VI, and VII. Wilson et al. (1965) believe that this narrow range of g values constitutes evidence that ices III, V, and VI, like ice I, are four-coordinated. Other arrangements of neighbouring molecules would entail different degrees of correlation and consequently different g values.

† Chan et al. (1965) assumed that the last term of this equation is zero.

(b) Dielectric polarization and relaxation

The large static dielectric constants of most ice polymorphs indicate that the molecules in these crystals are able to change their orientations. Studies of the frequency dependence of the dielectric constant, ϵ, have yielded information on the rate and mechanism of these reorientations. Let us consider the general behaviour of ϵ as a function of the frequency of an applied electric field, and then the data on the frequency dependence of ϵ in ice. We shall discuss the probable mechanism of reorientation of the molecules at the end of the section.

The frequency dependence of ϵ

At relatively low frequencies of the applied field, over 95 per cent of the dielectric constant ϵ arises from reorientations of H_2O molecules. As the frequency is increased, molecules do not reorient fast enough to come into equilibrium with the field, and the dielectric constant falls to a much smaller value, ϵ_∞. This phenomenon is called *dielectric dispersion*, and can be described for many substances (including water and ice I) by a simple equation (e.g. Smyth 1955):

$$\epsilon = \epsilon_\infty + \frac{\epsilon_0 - \epsilon_\infty}{1 + (\omega\tau_d)^2}, \tag{3.10}$$

where τ_d is the *dielectric relaxation time*, and ω is 2π times the frequency of the applied field in cycles per second. The quantity τ_d reflects the time for decay of macroscopic polarization of the substance when the external field is removed. It is somewhat larger than the molecular rotational correlation time, τ_{rd}, which is the average interval between reorientations of a given molecule. Theoretical work of Glarum (1960) and Powles (1953; see eqn (4.21)) suggests that $\tau_{rd} \cong 0.7\tau_d$ for ice and water. The value of τ_d for ice I at 0 °C is about 2×10^{-5} s, so that an average H_2O molecule experiences roughly 10^5 reorientations every second.

It is important to realize that the reorientation of molecules is caused by thermal agitation, and takes place whether or not an alternating electric field is applied to the system. The applied electric field, in fact, biases the orientation of molecules to only a very small extent. This was noted for the case of ice by Debye (1929), who based his argument on the fundamental equation of electric polarization

$$\epsilon_0 - 1 = \frac{4\pi \mathbf{P}}{\mathbf{E}}. \tag{3.11}$$

Here $\mathbf{P}$ is the electric dipole moment per unit volume induced by the applied field **E**. Debye used this equation to show that if ice at 0° C is placed in an electric field of 1 V cm⁻¹, the net degree of orientation of the water dipoles is equivalent to the rotation by 180° of only one molecule in 10^6.

The high-frequency dielectric constant, ϵ_∞, is temperature-independent. We shall discuss this quantity below.

Frequency dependence of ϵ of ice polymorphs

The dielectric relaxation times of the ice polymorphs in which molecules are free to rotate may be expressed in the form

$$\tau_d = A \exp\left\{\frac{E_A}{RT} + \frac{\Delta V^\ddagger(P-P_0)}{RT}\right\}, \qquad (3.12)$$

where P_0 is a reference pressure, and A, E_A, and $\Delta V^\ddagger$ are the experimentally determined parameters that are listed in Table 3.11. The quantities E_A and $\Delta V^\ddagger$ are called the energy and volume of activation for dielectric relaxation.

The dielectric relaxation time of ice I at 0 °C is 2×10^{-5} s; as the temperature is lowered it increases rapidly and by -65 °C it is about 4×10^{-2} s. Pressure increases τ_d (that is, $\Delta V^\ddagger$ is positive), as shown by Fig. 3.14. The relaxation rates of ices III, V, and VI are about 100 times faster than that of ice I near -40 °C (Wilson *et al.* 1965). In other words, H_2O molecules in these ices change their orientations 100 times faster than ice I molecules. At 22 °C and 21·4 kbar ice VII relaxes about three times faster than ice VI (Whalley *et al.* 1966).

Wilson *et al.* (1965) found that the relaxations of the high-pressure ices cannot be precisely described by a single relaxation time for each ice. The parameter α in Table 3.11 indicates the deviation of the frequency dependence of each ice from that given by eqn (3.10). This parameter can assume values from 0 (for a single τ_d) to 1; the largest α among the ices is 0·05 for ice VI.

The high-frequency dielectric constant, ϵ_∞, for each ice is also given in Table 3.11. For ice I, ϵ_∞ is 3.1. As we shall see presently, about 1·7 units of ϵ_∞ represent electronic polarization, so the difference $3\cdot1 - 1\cdot7$ must arise from atomic movements. This difference is much greater than that observed for most substances (Smyth 1955). Such differences are usually ascribed to the relative displacements of the atoms of each molecule by the field, but in the case of ice these displacements can account for only a fraction of the difference. The greater part of the difference arises from the bias of intermolecular vibrations of

TABLE 3.11

Parameters for the dielectric relaxation of ice polymorphs. P_0 and T_0 are the pressure and temperature at the centre of the region to which the parameters apply

Ice	P_0 (kbar)†	T_0 (°C)	ϵ_∞	E_A (kcal mol^{-1})	A (s)	$\Delta S^{\ddagger}$ (e.u.)§	$\Delta V^{\ddagger}$ (cm^3 mol^{-1})	α (at -30 °C)	Distinct lattice sites	References
I (H$_2$O)	0	-23.4	3.1	13.25	5.3×10^{-16}	9.8	2.9	0	1	a, b
I (D$_2$O)	0	..	..	13.4	7.7×10^{-16}	..	..	0	1	a
III	3	-30	3.5	11.6	9.5×10^{-17}	13.1	4.5	0.04	2	c, d
V	5	-30	4.6	11.5	2.5×10^{-16}	11.3	4.8	0.015	4	c, d
VI	8	-30	5.1	11.0	7.0×10^{-16}	9.2	4.4	0.05	2	c, d
VI	19	22	..	13.6	4.0×10^{-17}	15	..	..	2	e
VII	22	22	..	11.6	6.4×10^{-16}	9.2	2.5	> 0	1	e

† These values apply to eqn (3.12).

§ Calculated by Whalley et al. (1966) from the relation $\Delta S^{\ddagger} = -R \ln(AekT/h)$.

a Auty and Cole (1952).

b Chan et al. (1965).

c Wilson et al. (1965).

d Davidson (1966).

e Whalley et al. (1966).

H_2O molecules by the external field. From absolute intensities of infra-red absorption, Whalley (1967) found that the ν_T band associated with hindered translations of molecules (Section 3.5) accounts for most of the difference, and that the ν_L band associated with librations also accounts for some. Since these vibrations are very rapid compared to molecular reorientations, the polarization associated with them persists at frequencies higher than the dielectric dispersion.

For applied fields of optical frequencies, ϵ is equal to the square of the refractive index, about 1·7. Ice I, being an uniaxial crystal, is birefringent. The birefringence, however, is very small: at $-3\,°C$ the index of refraction of the sodium D-line for the ordinary ray (directed along the c-axis) is 1·3090 and that for the extraordinary ray (directed perpendicular to the c-axis) is 1·3104 (Merwin 1930). Dorsey (1940, p. 484) pointed out that the specific refraction

$$\frac{n^2-1}{n^2+2} \times \frac{1}{\rho_0},$$

where ρ_0 is the density, is remarkably constant for all three phases of H_2O stable at atmospheric pressure. The values of the specific refraction for sodium D-line radiation are:

Ice I	$-3\,°C$	ordinary ray	$0·2097\ cm^3\ g^{-1}$
		extraordinary ray	$0·2105$
Liquid	$20\,°C$		$0·2061$
Vapour	$110\,°C$		$0·2088$

The small spread of these numbers indicates that the mean electronic polarizability of H_2O does not change with phase.

Mechanism of molecular reorientation in ice

We are now ready to ask how H_2O molecules reorient in ice. An answer now widely accepted was proposed by Bjerrum in 1951. Bjerrum postulated the existence of a small concentration of orientational defects in ice to account for the reorientations. According to this idea, a pair of D- and L-orientational defects is formed when thermal agitation forces an H_2O molecule to rotate through 120° around one of its O–H····O axes, thus leaving one pair of neighbouring O····O atoms with no intervening hydrogen (L-defect), and another pair of neighbours O–H H–O with two hydrogens (D-defect). A subsequent similar rotation of one of the adjacent molecules separates these two defects. This process is depicted schematically in Fig. 3.17. The reorientation of H_2O molecules is supposed to occur at these defect sites, each reorientation causing the defect site to move one lattice position.

The actual molecular configuration in the neighbourhood of a defect is not known, but it is certainly not exactly as shown in Fig. 3.17. The non-bonded hydrogen atoms facing each other in a D-defect must push their respective H_2O molecules apart. A simple calculation (Eisenberg and Coulson 1963) indicates that a balance between the repulsion of these

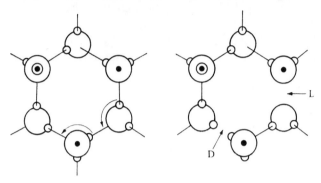

FIG. 3.17. Schematic representation of the formation of a pair of D- and L-defects in ice I. The c-axis is perpendicular to the page.

hydrogens and the strain energy of bent hydrogen bonds in the region of the two H_2O molecules is achieved when each H_2O molecule has moved about 0·5 Å away from the other. Other investigators have considered the possibility that one (Dunitz 1963) or both (Cohan et al. 1962) of the molecules forming a D-defect are rotated away from the positions shown in Fig. 3.17. Still other investigators have suggested that the orientational defects form associations with the ionic defects that we shall discuss in the next section (Eigen and De Maeyer 1958, Onsager and Dupuis 1962), or with interstitial molecules (Haas 1962).

Direct evidence for D- and L-defects has not been found. Nevertheless, there are several reasons for believing that they do exist.

(1) There is good a *posteriori* agreement of the defect theory with the observed dielectric properties and conductivity of ice, as well as with the same properties of solid solutions of HF in ice. The development of the kinetic theory and interpretation of experiments in terms of the defects was carried out by Gränicher et al. (1957), Jaccard (1959), Onsager and Dupuis (1962), and others. Gränicher (1963) and Jaccard (1965) have given brief summaries of this work.

(2) Calculated values of E_A (Bjerrum 1951) and $\Delta V^{\ddagger}$ (Chan et al. 1965) for dielectric relaxation, based on models of the defect, are in accord with the experimental values.

(3) There is no other plausible mechanism for reorientation of ice

molecules. Bjerrum (1951) and Gränicher (1958) considered and rejected many alternate mechanisms. Mechanisms involving only ionic defects, once believed to account for the polarization of ice crystals in an electric field, were shown by Bjerrum (1951) to lead to polarization of the wrong sign. Another mechanism, proposed by Frank (1958) and involving a local 'melting' of the crystal, would be expected to have a negative $\Delta V^{\ddagger}$ instead of the positive value actually observed (Chan et al. 1965).

Bjerrum (1951), Jaccard (1959), and others have deduced some of the properties of orientational defects in ice I. Bjerrum noted that n, the mean number of reorientations per molecule per second, is roughly equal to $1/\tau_d$ at -10 °C, or about 2×10^4. He then expressed n as

$$n = c \times n', \tag{3.13a}$$

where c is the concentration of orientational defects (in units of number of defects per molecule) and n' is the number of reorientations per defect per second. The concentration of defects at -10 °C is only about 2×10^{-7} (Table 3.12), so that the rate of turns of molecules at the defects must be very large, about 10^{11} s^{-1}. Apparently a molecule waits a relatively long time (about 5×10^{-5} s) for a defect to migrate to its lattice site, but when one arrives, it reorients very rapidly (in about 10^{-11} s).

Bjerrum (1951) pointed out that E_A, the experimental energy of activation for dielectric relaxation, is related to both the energy required to form a pair of orientational defects, E_{DL}, and the energy required to produce a reorientation at a defect, E'. Since both c and n' increase exponentially with temperature, E_A is given by

$$E_A = \tfrac{1}{2}E_{DL} + E'. \tag{3.13b}$$

Jaccard (1959) inferred values of E_{DL} and E' from experiments on ice and solid solutions of HF in ice; these values are given in Table 3.12. Bjerrum further noted that the formation of a pair of D- and L-defects corresponds to the reaction $2N \rightarrow D + L$, where N represents a normal hydrogen bond. If we let E_N, E_D, and E_L represent the energies of formation of, respectively, a hydrogen bond, a D-defect, and an L-defect from separated H_2O molecules, we can write

$$E_{DL} = E_D + E_L - 2E_N. \tag{3.13c}$$

Various authors (including Bjerrum (1951), Cohan et al. (1962), Dunitz (1963), and Eisenberg and Coulson (1963)) have estimated E_D and E_L from models for the defects.

The mechanism of dielectric relaxation in the high-pressure polymorphs is probably similar to that in ice I. The values of E_A, $\Delta S^{\ddagger}$, and $\Delta V^{\ddagger}$ for ices III, V, VI, and VII are near enough to the corresponding values for ice I to indicate that orientational defects are of central importance in their relaxation processes. Wilson et al. (1965) suggested that the lower values of E_A for ices III, V, and VI indicate weaker hydrogen bonds in these phases. Weaker hydrogen bonds would result in smaller values of E_{DL} or E', or both, and therefore in a smaller E_A.

Davidson (1966) and Wilson *et al.* (1965) suggested that a correlation exists between the dispersion parameter α and the number of different types of crystal site in a polymorph (Table 3.11). They reasoned that the molecules having different environments are likely to have different relaxation times, and hence have dielectric relaxations that can be described only with a value of α greater than zero.

TABLE 3.12

Derived properties of orientational and ionic defects in ice I at $-10\ °C$.

(Compiled by Gränicher 1963)

Property	Orientational defect	Ionic defect
Reaction equation	$2N \rightleftharpoons D+L$	$2H_2O \rightleftharpoons H_3O^+ + OH^-$
Energy of formation (kcal/mol-of-defect pair)	$E_{DL} = 15\cdot7 \pm 0\cdot9$	$E_\pm = 22 \pm 3$
Concentration of defects (mol-of-defect/mol-of-ice)	$c = 2 \times 10^{-7}$	$\sim 3 \times 10^{-12}$
Activation energy of diffusion (kcal/mol)	$E' = 5\cdot4 \pm 0\cdot2$	~ 0
Mobility ($cm^3\ V^{-1}\ s^{-1}$)	$\mu^L = 2 \times 10^{-4}$	$\mu^+ = 8 \times 10^{-2}$
Mobility ratio	$\mu^L/\mu^D > 1$	$\mu^+/\mu^- \sim 10$ to 100

(c) Electrical conductivity

Ice I exhibits a time-independent direct-current conductivity κ. The value of κ for H_2O ice I at $-10\ °C$ is about $10^{-9}\ \Omega^{-1}\ cm^{-1}$, an order of magnitude smaller than κ for liquid water at the melting-point. Electrolysis experiments (Workman *et al.* 1954, Gränicher *et al.* 1957) indicate that ions (presumably protons) are the sole charge carriers: hydrogen gas is formed at the negative electrode and oxygen gas at the positive electrode in amounts predicted by Faraday's law. Thus the conductivity is intimately related to the ionic dissociation of H_2O molecules. This dissociation may be represented by the equation

$$2H_2O \underset{k_R}{\overset{k_D}{\rightleftharpoons}} H_3O^+ + OH^-, \qquad (3.14)$$

where k_D is the rate constant for dissociation and k_R is the rate constant for recombination. The ratio of these constants, K_{H_2O}, is the equilibrium constant for the dissociation reaction.

Eigen and De Maeyer (1958, 1959) and Eigen *et al.* (1964) studied the dissociation reaction in ice by a series of elegant experiments. Let us consider the results of their experiments and the implications of the results for the mechanism of charge transport in ice. For a full description of these experiments, and for a detailed and lucid discussion of charge transport in ice and water, the reader is referred to their original papers. These papers also include a review of earlier work.

Eigen and his colleagues first noted that the electrical conductivity is related to the product of the concentration and the mobility of the charge carriers, and thus that conductivity measurements alone cannot provide such details of reaction (3.14) as k_D, k_R, and K_{H_2O}. They then determined k_D from the 'saturation current' at high field strengths. In this experiment, a strong electric field is applied to a thin layer of ice; the resulting current is determined solely by the dissociation of water molecules, and is thus related directly to k_D. They determined k_R by relaxation methods, and combining this quantity with k_D they found K_{H_2O} and consequently the concentration of protonic charge carriers in ice. By combining other information from their saturation-current studies with the conductivity measurements they were able to determine the mobility of the protonic charge carriers. Their results are summarized in Table 3.13 and in the right-hand column of Table 3.12.

TABLE 3.13

Ionic dissociation and migration in ice I according to Eigen et al. (1964)

(All entries are for $-10\,°C$.)

Property	H_2O ice I	D_2O ice I
Direct current conductivity κ (Ω^{-1} cm^{-1})	$1\cdot0 \times 10^{-9}$	$3\cdot6 \times 10^{-11}$
Activation energy for conductivity (kcal mol^{-1})	11	13
Rate constant for dissociation of H_2O (D_2O), k_D (s^{-1})	$3\cdot2 \times 10^{-9}$	$2\cdot7 \times 10^{-11}$
Rate constant for recombination of H_2O (D_2O), k_R (mol^{-1} l s^{-1})	$0\cdot86 \times 10^{13}$	$0\cdot13 \times 10^{13}$
Equilibrium constant for dissociation reaction, K_{H_2O} (mol l^{-1})	$3\cdot8 \times 10^{-22}$	$0\cdot2 \times 10^{-22}$
Mobility of proton (deuteron) μ (cm^2 V^{-1} s^{-1})	$\sim 0\cdot08$	$\sim 0\cdot01$

The molecular mechanism for conductivity in ice I almost certainly involves ionic defects (Bjerrum 1951, Eigen and De Maeyer 1958) that are formed when an H_2O molecule in the lattice dissociates and one of its protons jumps to an adjacent molecule (Fig. 3.18). Subsequent proton jumps result in the migration of the ionic defects throughout the crystal. It is clear from Fig. 3.18, though, that once a proton has followed a given path through the crystal toward the negative electrode, no other proton may follow the same path until H_2O molecules along the path have reoriented. This does not cause interruption of conduction, because reorientations are much more frequent at a given molecule than are proton jumps. We noted in the preceding section that each molecule experiences about 2×10^4 reorientations per second at $-10\ °C$. We can estimate the number of proton jumps per second at a given molecule from Eigen's (1964) estimate of the mean time of residence of a proton with a given H_2O molecule in ice ($\sim 10^{-13}$ s) and from the concentration of ionic defects ($\sim 3 \times 10^{-12}$ molecule^{-1} at $-10\ °C$; see Table 3.12).

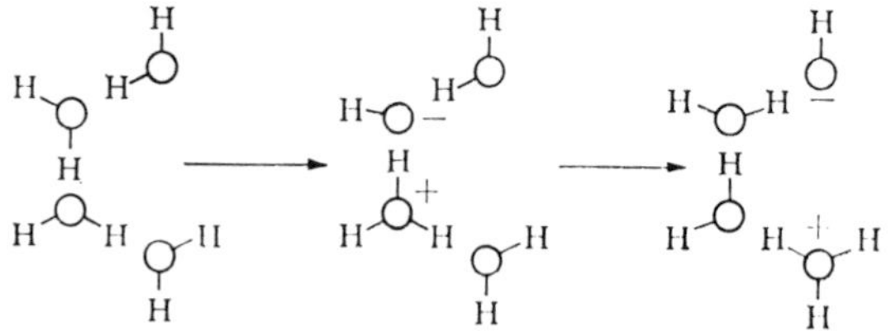

FIG. 3.18. Schematic representation of the formation and migration of ionic defects in ice I.

The quotient of these numbers (~ 30) is a rough estimate of the mean number of jumping protons that arrive each second at an ice molecule at $-10\ °C$. Thus, although the rate of proton jumps is very rapid, the concentration of jumping protons is so small that the frequency of jumps at each molecule is small. The arrival of a jumping proton at a molecule is a rare event compared to the arrival of an orientational defect.

Eigen and De Maeyer (1958) and Onsager and Dupuis (1962) noted that some of the ionic defects in ice may be 'trapped' and may thus make no contribution to the conductivity. A possible example of a trapped H_3O^+ ion would be one which is situated next to an L-defect. The attraction of a lone-pair of electrons on the H_2O molecule in the L-defect for the positive charge on the adjacent H_3O^+ ion would immobilize both the ionic defect and the orientational defect.

(d) Self-diffusion†

Kuhn and Thürkauf reported in 1958 that deuterium (^2H) and ^{18}O tracers diffuse in ice I at the same rate. Soon afterwards Dengel and Riehl (1963) and Itagaki (1964) discovered that tritium (^3H) diffuses at about the same rate as the other tracers. These findings suggest that intact water molecules are able to migrate through the ice lattice in some fashion. Since this self-diffusion must involve defects in the lattice, it is convenient to consider this property along with dielectric relaxation and direct current conductivity, phenomena which also proceed by

† Data on the self-diffusion in ice were summarized briefly by Kopp et al. (1965), who also discussed diffusion of HF in ice.

lattice defects. The self-diffusion coefficients measured by means of the three tracers, and the activation energy for diffusion of tritium, are given in Table 3.14.

TABLE 3.14

Self-diffusion in ice I

Authors	Tracer	Temperature (°C)	Coefficient of self-diffusion (cm² s⁻¹)	Activation energy, E_A (kcal mol⁻¹)
Kuhn and Thürkauf (1958)	^{18}O, ^2H	-2	10×10^{-11}	
Dengel and Riehl (1963)	^3H	0 to -33	2×10^{-11} at -7 °C	$13 \cdot 5 \pm 1$
Itagaki (1964)	^3H	-10 to -35	$2 \cdot 8 \times 10^{-11}$ at -10 °C	$15 \cdot 7 \pm 2$

The molecular mechanism of self-diffusion in ice is not known for certain. Haas (1962) proposed that self-diffusion takes place via inter-stitial molecules that are associated with the D- and L-orientational defects described in Section 3.4 (b). In support of his proposal, Haas noted that the activation energies for self-diffusion and dielectric relaxa-tion are nearly equal. From the magnitude of the self-diffusion coefficient he inferred that, if a migrating interstitial molecule moves by jumps of one lattice position, its rate of migration would be about equal to the rate of migration of orientational defects. Onsager and Runnels (1963) extended calculations of the sort made by Haas and came to a contrary conclusion: migration of the diffusing molecules is an order of magnitude faster than the migration of orientational defects. They thus rejected Haas's proposal that most interstitial molecules migrate in association with orientational defects. They suggested instead that a water molecule diffuses several lattice positions 'in the interstitial space' and then occupies a normal lattice position. They based this proposal on nuclear magnetic resonance spin-lattice relaxation times, but did not publish their detailed arguments. They believe that the average length of a diffusional jump is about three lattice positions.

3.5. Spectroscopic properties

(a) Vibrational spectrum of ice I

The vibrations of ice crystals may be studied by means of any radiation or particle that exchanges energy with the crystal. Electromagnetic radiation in the form of infra-red and Raman spectroscopy has been extensively used for this purpose. Other techniques, such as scattering of cold neutrons and analysis of heat capacity curves, have recently yielded some information on vibrations of ice, but infra-red and Raman spectroscopy remain the most useful methods.† In this section we describe the general appearance of the infra-red spectrum of ice and the interpretation of the spectrum in terms of crystal structure and atomic motions. Much less attention is devoted to the other techniques because to date they have provided very little additional information.

Table 3.15 lists the prominent bands of the vibrational spectrum of ice; most of these can be identified in the infra-red spectra shown in Fig. 3.20 on p. 128. Three broad and intense bands are found at frequencies between 50 and 1200 cm^{-1}, a spectral region in which water vapour exhibits no absorption other than the fine lines indicative of transitions between rotational states. Hence these three bands must be due to intermolecular vibrations. The frequency region 1200–4000 cm^{-1}, containing the absorptions of the fundamental modes of water vapour, shows bands in ice with maxima at about 1650 and 3220 cm^{-1}; the former lies at somewhat higher frequencies than the ν_2 mode in the vapour, and the latter at considerably lower frequencies than the ν_1 and ν_3 vapour modes. There is in addition a band near 2270 cm^{-1}, often called the 'association band', which does not correspond to any mode in the vapour spectrum.

The vibrational spectrum of ice is not easily interpreted despite the simplicity of the constituent water molecules and the abundance of information on their relative positions in the crystal. The reason for this is that the normal modes of vibration of an ice crystal are unknown and, as a result, one cannot rigorously assign each absorption band to a particular set of atomic motions. The progress that has been made in assigning bands has come largely by comparing the vibrational spectrum of ice to that of water vapour. To discuss these developments, we must first outline the theory of vibrations of molecular crystals. The theory may seem abstract, but when we apply it to the interpretation of the spectrum of ice below, its physical significance ought to become quite clear.

† Ockman (1958) compiled a comprehensive review of the infra-red and Raman spectroscopy of ice up to October 1957. Important work since 1957 includes the far infra-red spectra by Zimmermann and Pimentel (1962) and Bertie and Whalley (1967); the H_2O–D_2O mixed crystal spectra by Hornig et al. (1958), Haas and Hornig (1960), and Bertie and Whalley (1964 a); and the infra-red and Raman spectra of the high-pressure ices by Bertie and Whalley (1964 b), Taylor and Whalley (1964), and Marckmann and Whalley (1964).

TABLE 3.15

Salient features of the vibrational spectrum of ice I contrasted with the spectrum of water vapour

(Cited frequencies are in cm⁻¹ and refer to the infra-red spectrum. Frequencies for D_2O are in parentheses.)

Frequency region (cm⁻¹)	Water vapour	Ice I	Notation for band	Detected by†
50–1200	Line spectrum arising from molecular rotation. Most intense near 200 cm⁻¹ at room temperature.	Intense band‡ at ∼ 60 (∼ 60) arising from hindered translations.	ν_{T_2}	Raman, neutron, heat capacity
		Intense, broad band at 229 (222) arising from hindered translations. Some structure evident.	ν_T	Infra-red, Raman, neutron, heat capacity
		Intense, broad band§ at 840 (640) arising from librations. Structure evident.	ν_L	Infra-red, Raman, neutron, heat capacity
1200–4000	Four vibration–rotation bands arising from the three fundamental modes and the first overtone of ν_2: $\nu_1 = 3657$ (2671) $\nu_2 = 1595$ (1178) $\nu_3 = 3756$ (2788) $2\nu_2 = 3151$	Broad, weak band at 1650 (1210) probably associated with ν_2.	ν_2	Infra-red, Raman
		Broad, weak band at 2270 (1650). Possibly associated with overtones of ν_L and ν_T or combinations of them with ν_2. Called 'association band'.	ν_A	Infra-red, Raman
		Very intense, broad band around 3220 (2420) arising from O–H stretching modes. Some structure evident.	ν_s	Infra-red, Raman
Above 4000	Many vibration–rotation bands arising from overtones and combinations of the three fundamental modes. See Table 1.3.	Many relatively weak bands arising from over-tones and combinations of the three fundamental modes with each other and with the lattice modes. Few, if any, assigned with certainty.		Infra-red, Raman

† Details of the infra-red and Raman spectra are given in Table 3.16. The cold neutron spectroscopy is the work of Larsson and Dahlborg (1962) and the heat capacity curve analysis the work of Leadbetter (1965).

‡ This band does not appear in the direct infra-red spectrum but is evident in a plot of (optical density)/ν^2 (see Bertie and Whalley 1967).

§ In the cold neutron spectrum (Larsson and Dahlborg 1962) the counterpart of this band has its maximum at a lower frequency. This is also found in the analysis of the heat capacity (Leadbetter 1965).

Vibrations of molecular crystals

The spectra of ice and water vapour differ because for the same displacements, H_2O molecules in the two phases experience different changes in potential energy. These differences can be expressed mathematically as follows. First we denote the potential energy function describing the vibrations of an isolated water molecule by U^0 (Section 1.1 (*d*)). Now the potential energy of an ice crystal, U, is not merely the sum of many such functions, but may be written within the harmonic approximation in the form (Hornig 1950, Vedder and Hornig 1961):

$$U = \sum_j (U_j^0 + U_j') + \sum_j \sum_k U_{jk} + U_L + U_{Lj}. \qquad (3.15)$$

Here U_j^0 is the potential function of the jth molecule in the absence of its neighbours. All other terms describe the perturbations of neighbouring molecules that account for the spectroscopic differences of crystal and vapour.

The term U_j' describes the change in U_j^0 owing to the neighbouring molecules fixed in their equilibrium positions, and depends on the equilibrium positions and orientations of the neighbours. It accounts for the shifts in spectral frequencies that are due to the electrostatic forces, hydrogen bonds, and other forces that would act on the jth molecule if the atoms in all of the other molecules in the crystal were motionless. For this reason, the physical effect produced by U_j' is called the *static field effect*. In ice, hydrogen bonds to neighbouring molecules account for most of the static field effect. A point of importance is that the perturbation U_j' is not necessarily the same for each molecule in the crystal. Since it depends on the environment of the jth molecule, the existence of different molecular environments in the crystal can produce different shifts of the vapour-molecule frequencies. Because of this, the crystal spectrum may contain information about the variety of molecular environments in the crystal.

The term U_L is the potential function for intermolecular or *lattice* modes of vibration; it is a function of the positions and orientations of neighbouring molecules. In a lattice mode, the vibrating species is to a first approximation a rigid molecule. The molecule may execute a hindered translation, a hindered rotation (usually called a libration), or some combination of the two. A spectral band caused by a hindered translational motion can be distinguished experimentally from one caused by a librational motion by the effect of isotopic substitution on the band frequencies. In the case of ice, the ratio of frequencies of a hindered translational band in the spectra of H_2O and D_2O ices is

$\sqrt{(20/18)} = 1\cdot05$, whereas the same ratio for a librational band is about $\sqrt{2}$.† In both H_2O and D_2O ices, the frequencies of the lattice modes are considerably lower than the frequencies of modes associated with internal motions of water molecules. The reason is that an atom vibrating within a molecule has both a smaller mass, and a larger restoring force acting on it, than an entire molecule vibrating within the lattice. Both factors contribute to the relatively low frequencies of the lattice modes.

The U_{jk} term of eqn (3.15) describes the coupling of intramolecular modes of the jth molecule with those of the kth molecule. Whereas U_j^0 depends only on the displacement of atoms in the jth molecule from their equilibrium positions, U_{jk} depends on displacements of atoms in both the jth and kth molecules. When an intramolecular mode of one molecule is coupled with the same intramolecular mode of N neighbouring molecules, the spectral band associated with the mode is split into $N+1$ components, thus complicating the interpretation of the spectrum. Fortunately this complication can often be circumvented by studying small amounts of the given compound dissolved in a crystal of isotopic molecules. For example, we shall presently summarize data indicating that the O–H stretching vibrations in ice are coupled to the O–H stretching vibrations of neighbouring molecules; but in a D_2O crystal containing small amounts of HDO, the O–H stretching vibrations are not strongly coupled to other vibrations. Hence the effect of coupling, that is, the effect of the U_{jk} term on the frequency of the intramolecular vibrations, can be largely eliminated by using a dilute solution in an isotopic crystal.

The physical basis for coupling and uncoupling is as follows: the oscillations of weakly connected vibrators having nearly the same characteristic frequency are said to be coupled. Neighbouring molecules in a crystal, and two pendulums suspended from a taut string, are examples of such a coupled system (Fig. 3.19), since displacements in one vibrator produce forces in the other vibrator. If the frequencies of the uncoupled vibrators are nearly the same, then the introduction of a physical connection between them will produce a much larger shift in the frequencies of the system than if the frequencies of the uncoupled vibrators are quite different. The frequency changes produced by connecting two pendulums of very different length are therefore small,

† The frequency of a vibration is inversely proportional to the square root of the mass of the vibrating species. Since it is the hydrogens that move during a libration, the frequency ratio of the libration bands in H_2O and D_2O ices should be $1/\sqrt{\frac{1}{2}} = \sqrt{2}$. In contrast, entire water molecules move during a hindered translation, so that the frequency ratios of hindered translational modes in H_2O and D_2O ices should be $\sqrt{(20/18)}$.

and we can say that two pendulums can be uncoupled by making one of the pendulums much longer than the other. Similarly the O–H bond in a particular water molecule is said to be strongly coupled with the other O–H bonds in a crystal of ordinary H_2O ice, but if all of the other protons

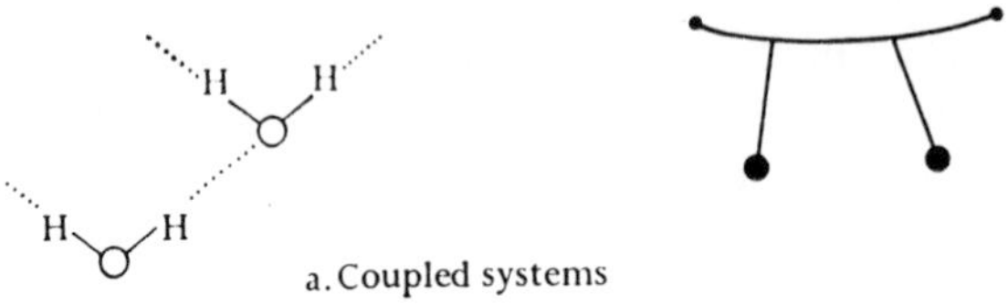

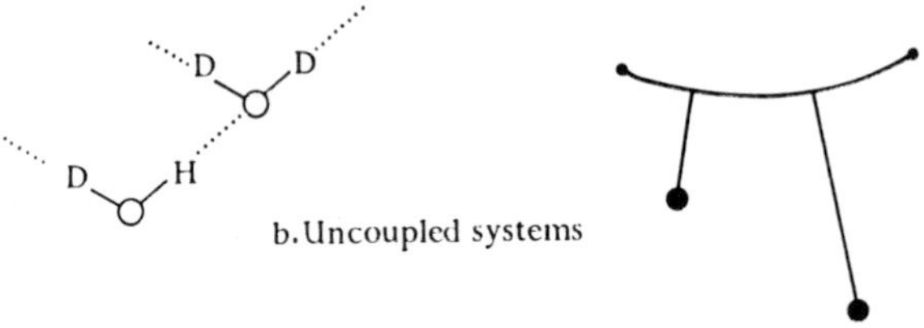

a. Coupled systems

b. Uncoupled systems

FIG. 3.19. Coupled and uncoupled vibrating systems.

in the crystal except that in the particular O–H bond are replaced by deuterons (producing an HDO molecule in a D_2O lattice), then this O–H bond is said to have been uncoupled from the lattice. By the same principle, the O–H and O–D stretching motions of an HDO molecule are not *intramolecularly* coupled. That is, the two stretching modes of HDO are nearly pure O–H and O–D bond elongations.

The last term in eqn (3.15), U_{Lj}, describes the coupling of lattice motion with intramolecular displacements. In ice, where the frequencies of lattice and intramolecular modes are widely separated, this form of coupling is probably not important. We shall not consider this term further.

The O–H stretching band, ν_s

We are now prepared to interpret the observed spectrum of ice in terms of atomic motions. Let us begin with the broad band around 3220 cm^{-1}. This is the only strong absorption band of ice anywhere near the frequencies of the ν_1 and ν_3 O–H stretching modes of water vapour (at 3657 and 3756 cm^{-1} respectively; see Table 3.15). This band is therefore undoubtedly associated with O–H stretching motions. It is not immediately clear, however, why this band is centred at a frequency roughly 10 per cent lower than the vapour stretching modes; nor is it immediately clear why one broad band is found in ice in place of the two sharp ones in the vapour.

On further study it seems certain that the 10 per cent reduction in O–H stretching frequencies is due largely to the static field effect (the U'_j term in eqn (3.15)) of hydrogen bonds. A survey of spectroscopic studies of hydrogen bonding (Pimentel and McClellan 1960) shows that in many systems the stretching frequencies of O–H groups are reduced by an amount of the order of 10 per cent during hydrogen-bond formation. Reasoning qualitatively, one can explain the decreased frequencies by the attraction of O_B for H_A in the O_A–$H_A$$\cdots$$O_B$ hydrogen bond. This facilitates O_A–H_A stretching and therefore diminishes the stretching frequencies. A quantitative description of this effect, based on the Hellmann–Feynman theorem, was developed by Bader (1964 b).

We must now account for the presence of one very broad O–H stretching band in ice instead of the two sharp bands of the vapour. Spectroscopic studies of dilute solutions of HDO in H_2O and D_2O ices (Hornig et al. 1958, Bertie and Whalley 1964 a, b) indicate that the observed band in ice is actually an unresolved superposition of a number of bands. This multiplicity of bands is apparently caused by two effects:†

(1) The ν_1 and ν_3 intramolecular stretching modes of one molecule couple with the corresponding modes of neighbouring molecules, because of the U_{jk} term of eqn (3.15). The well-defined stretching frequencies of the isolated molecule are in this way replaced by broad bands of coupled frequencies.

(2) The perturbation U'_j varies slightly from molecule to molecule, and hence the stretching frequencies are different for different molecules. In other words, since molecules in the ice crystal do not have identical environments they experience different static field effects.

Evidence for the first effect is shown in Fig. 3.20. From the lower panel it can be seen that the O–H stretching band (at 3277 cm^{-1}) of a dilute solution of HDO in D_2O ice is very narrow compared to the band in pure H_2O. Now the O–H stretch of HDO is largely uncoupled from vibrations of neighbouring molecules. Hence the relative narrowness of the O–H stretching band of HDO in D_2O, compared to the stretching band in pure H_2O ice, suggests that the breadth of the latter band results partly from coupling of vibrations (Hornig et al. 1958, Bertie and Whalley

† A third effect, Fermi resonance, will be considered below.

1964 *a*). Similarly, the relatively narrow O–D stretching band of HDO in H_2O (at 2421 cm^{-1} in curve (*b*) of the upper panel of Fig. 3.20) compared to the stretching band in pure D_2O ice, suggests that the latter owes its breadth in part to coupling of vibrations.

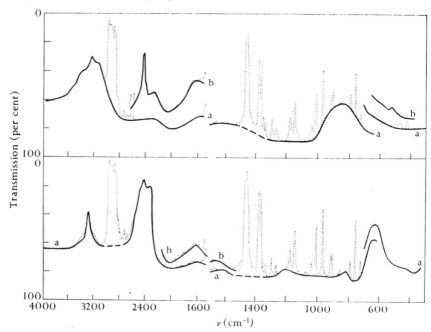

FIG. 3.20. Infra-red spectra of ice I at ∼ 110 °K reported by Bertie and Whalley (1964 *a*). Solid lines indicate absorption due to ice, the dotted lines indicate absorption due to a mulling agent (isopentane) used to coalesce the powdered ice, and the dashed lines indicate regions where the absorption of ice is uncertain owing to the mulling agent. Some of these spectra were actually obtained from ice Ic but spectra of ice I under the same conditions were found to be identical (see following section).

Upper panel:
    curve (*a*): 100% H_2O.
    curve (*b*): 95% H_2O, 5% D_2O†; a thicker sample than curve (*a*).
Lower panel:
    curve (*a*): 5% H_2O, 95% D_2O.†
    curve (*b*): 0·2% H_2O, 99·8% D_2O.†

Adapted with changes from Bertie and Whalley (1964 *a*).

† Initial composition. Proton jumps soon produce a mixture of HDO and the more abundant isotope of water initially present. Only small amounts of the less abundant isotope are in the equilibrium mixture.

We must still account for the breadths of the uncoupled stretching bands of HDO, which are wider than the narrow stretching bands of water vapour. Variations in the static field perturbation U'_j for different molecules (the second effect mentioned above) probably account for most of the residual width of the uncoupled bands. The evidence for this comes from the difference of the O–D stretching bands of HDO in dilute solutions in ices I and II (Bertie and Whalley 1964 a, b).

When HDO is dissolved in H_2O ice I, it is found that the O–D stretching band consists of a single line with a half-width of 30 cm^{-1}. The corresponding band in ice II, however, is split into four fine peaks, each with a half-width of about 5 cm^{-1} (Table 3.16). This difference is not due to coupling, since coupling has been largely eliminated in these dilute isotopic solutions. In fact the difference probably arises from variations in the U_j' terms as follows: ice II has an ordered arrangement of hydrogens that gives rise to four equilibrium oxygen–oxygen separations (Section 3.2 (a)). Each of these four presents a distinct static field perturbation, U_j', to the vibrating O–D group, and this results in four narrow stretching bands. Ice I, in contrast, is characterized by a disordered arrangement of hydrogens that must result in a distribution of equilibrium oxygen–oxygen distances. These in turn give rise to a distribution of U_j' terms, which account for a single relatively broad O–D stretching band.

Several facts mentioned above should be emphasized because they will be useful to us later in interpreting the spectrum of liquid water (Section 4.7). They are:

(1) The half-width of the absorption band associated with a single O–D stretching vibration is no more than 5 cm^{-1}. The half-width of the absorption band associated with a single O–H stretching vibration is no more than 18 cm^{-1} and is probably less (Bertie and Whalley 1964 b).

(2) When different molecular environments are present in the sample, the variation in U_j' terms results in several stretching bands. These bands may be superimposed to form one broader band as in ice I or they may be distinct as in ice II, depending on the distribution of molecular environments.

(3) When the stretching vibrations of neighbouring molecules are coupled, the observed band is very broad.

One other effect may impede interpretation of the stretching band of ice. The first overtone of the H–O–H bending vibration (see below) falls at about the same frequency as the O–H stretching band. The absorption intensity of this overtone by itself would be negligible compared to the intensity of the O–H stretching mode. But because these bands overlap, the bending overtone may 'borrow' intensity from the stretching band, and consequently may contribute substantially to the breadth of the observed band near 3200 cm^{-1}. This borrowing of intensity by one band from an overlapping band is called *Fermi resonance*. The frequencies of both modes involved in Fermi resonance are shifted from their frequencies in the absence of resonance. Fermi resonance does not, however, cloud the interpretation of the stretching bands of dilute solutions of HDO, because the overtone of the bending mode does not overlap these modes.

The detailed shape of the stretching band in ice is still not thoroughly understood. Several interpretations have been given. Haas and Hornig (1960) assigned the main maximum of the band to the ν_3 modes of water molecules (which are presumably coupled). They believe that two subsidiary bands are located at 3125 and 3360 cm^{-1} and that both contain nearly equal admixtures of ν_1 and $2\nu_2$ in Fermi resonance. According to Bertie and Whalley (1964 a), coupled ν_3 vibrations contribute strongly to the main maximum, but the observed band is a superposition of more than three component bands. The component bands arise through complex coupling of all normal modes.

The H–O–H bending band, ν_2, and the association band, ν_A

The H–O–H bending mode of the vapour, ν_2, is at 1595 cm^{-1}. A broad, weak band with a maximum near 1650 cm^{-1} appears in the ice spectrum. Since the formation of hydrogen bonds is found to increase bending frequencies slightly (Pimentel and McClellan 1960), this band is probably associated with H–O–H bending vibrations. The temperature dependence of the frequency of the band maximum corroborates this assignment. Zimmermann and Pimentel (1962) found that the frequency of the maximum decreases with temperature (~ 0.3 cm^{-1} °C^{-1}), whereas the frequencies of lattice vibrations simultaneously increase. This seems to rule out the suggestion that the 1650 cm^{-1} band is primarily associated with overtones of the lattice modes. The effect of coupling on the 1650 cm^{-1} band is uncertain. Zimmermann and Pimentel (1962) did not find evidence for coupling from the spectra of dilute isotopic crystals, and they concluded that H–O–H bending vibrations of molecules are not coupled in ice. This conclusion has not been universally accepted (Bertie and Whalley 1964 a).

The ν_A band at 2270 cm^{-1} has no counterpart in the spectrum of water vapour. The temperature dependence of the band maximum is similar to the temperature dependence of the bands associated with lattice modes, and thus it is probably an overtone or combination of lattice modes (Zimmermann and Pimentel 1962). Bertie and Whalley (1964 a) assigned it to both $3\nu_L$ and $\nu_2 + \nu_L$.

Lattice modes

The three prominent bands in the 50–1200 cm^{-1} region arise from intermolecular modes of vibration. The ratio of frequencies in H_2O and D_2O ice shows whether a band is associated with hindered translations or librations. From Table 3.15 we see that the H_2O/D_2O frequency ratio of the band near 800 cm^{-1} is $840/640 = 1\cdot3$, so this band may be assigned to librational motions (e.g. Ockman 1958). The H_2O/D_2O frequency ratio of the band near 229 cm^{-1} is $229/222 = 1\cdot03$ and so may be ascribed to hindered translational motions. The band near 60 cm^{-1} in the neutron scattering and Raman spectra also appears to arise from a hindered translation (Ockman 1958, Larsson and Dahlborg 1962).

Bertie and Whalley (1967) investigated in detail the region of the infra-red spectrum from 50 to 360 cm^{-1}, which is associated with hindered translations. In addition to the main maximum at 229 cm^{-1}, they found a less intense maximum at 164 cm^{-1} and a shoulder near 190 cm^{-1}. They assigned the peaks at 229 and 164 cm^{-1} to maxima in the density of vibrational states owing to transverse optic and longitudinal acoustic vibrations respectively, and they assigned the shoulder at 190 cm^{-1} to the maximum in the longitudinal optic vibrations. They believe that the peak which appears near 65 cm^{-1} in the spectrum of optical density$/\nu^2$ is due to the maximum in the transverse acoustic vibrations.

Bertie and Whalley (1967) found that the main maximum of the band near 229 cm^{-1} shifts to lower frequencies and decreases in intensity as ice is heated from 100 to 168° K. They attributed these changes to hot bands, that is to transitions from excited vibrational levels to even higher levels.

Several investigators have analysed the normal modes of vibration of small groups of water molecules arranged as in ice, and have assigned bands in the lattice region of the observed spectrum to various of these normal modes. This procedure gives a qualitative idea of the molecular motions that are associated with particular bands in the spectrum, and can lead to approximate potential energy functions for the system (Section 3.6(b)). In one such study, Zimmermann and Pimentel (1962) considered a five-atom system, consisting of a central water molecule and the two neighbouring oxygen atoms that are hydrogen-bonded to its hydrogen atoms. Kyogoku (1960), in a more elaborate study, analysed the nine-atom system comprised by a central oxygen atom, the four surrounding hydrogen atoms, and the four neighbouring oxygen atoms. Walrafen (1964) considered the normal modes of a five-molecule system (see Section 4.7 (c)). In these three studies, the ν_L band of the spectrum was assigned to hindered rotational motions and the ν_T band was assigned to hindered translational motions.

Summary

Let us summarize this section by imagining the infra-red spectrum of a hypothetical ice crystal whose potential energy we can alter at will.

Initially, the potential energy function of every molecule is equal to U^0, and the motion of molecular centres of mass is forbidden. The only infra-red absorption of the crystal would then be caused by the ν_1, ν_2, and ν_3 vibrational modes (plus their overtones and combinations) of individual molecules, and would appear as sharp lines at the vapour frequencies. Now we introduce the static field effect described by U'_j, but not the coupling of intramolecular modes described by U_{jk}. This means that we allow the equilibrium electric fields of neighbouring molecules to act on each other, thus forming hydrogen bonds, but we do not allow the internal vibrations of one molecule to influence its neighbours' vibrations. For the moment we assume that our ice crystal is perfectly ordered, with only a single oxygen–oxygen separation and hence a single function U'_j. The inclusion of U'_j shifts the frequency of each line: the ν_1 and ν_3 modes, originally at 3657 and 3756 cm^{-1}, shift to about 3200 cm^{-1}. The ν_2 bending mode shifts from 1595 cm^{-1} to about 1650 cm^{-1}. If we now suppose that the hydrogen arrangement of the crystal is disordered, the absorptions take on finite widths owing to the variation of U'_j from molecule to molecule. Even so, the half-widths of the O–H stretching bands are still no greater than 50 cm^{-1}.

Up to this point we have held the molecular centres of mass motionless. Now we ease this restriction by adding the lattice potential U_L: the molecules execute hindered translations and librations, and absorption bands appear near 60, 229, 840 and 2270 cm^{-1}. Finally we introduce the U_{jk} perturbation, thus interacting the ν_1, ν_2, and ν_3 modes of each molecule with those of its neighbours. This step radically alters the spectrum in the region of 3200 cm^{-1}. The ν_1 and ν_3 modes are split into many vibrations; these may interact with the first overtone of the ν_2 mode, and all the resulting bands are superimposed, producing a band like the one that is actually observed.

(b) Vibrational spectra of ice polymorphs

Portions of the infra-red and Raman spectra of ice Ic and of the quenched high-pressure ices have been recorded in recent years. These studies are summarized in Table 3.16. The most striking feature of these spectra is their similarity to one another and to the spectrum of ice I. These similarities include:

(1) Strong bands in the infra-red spectra of ices I, Ic, II, III, and V near 3200 cm^{-1} (2400 cm^{-1} for D_2O) undoubtedly arising from O–H stretching vibrations. None of the polymorphs shows sharp absorption bands near the frequencies of H_2O vapour; hence it may be concluded

that all molecules are fully hydrogen-bonded. The infra-red spectra of ices VI and VII have not been recorded in this region, although their Raman spectra have. Molecules in both these polymorphs seem to be fully hydrogen-bonded, though the shift of absorption of ice VII towards the vapour frequencies indicates that hydrogen bonding in this polymorph may be weaker than in the others (Marckmann and Whalley 1964). These conclusions are in accord with available crystallographic evidence (Section 3.2): water molecules in all polymorphs are found to be fully hydrogen-bonded, but the hydrogen-bond length in ice VII at atmospheric pressure ($\sim 2 \cdot 95$ Å) is considerably longer than hydrogen-bond lengths in the other polymorphs.

(2) Strong, broad bands around 800 cm^{-1} (600 cm^{-1} for D_2O) in the infra-red spectra of ices Ic, II, III, and V. These may be assigned, as in ice I, to molecular librations. In addition, the Raman spectra of ices Ic, II, III, and V show a broad band around 200 cm^{-1}, similar to the one in ice I that arises from hindered translations of molecules. The similarity of the bands in ices II, III, and V to the corresponding bands in ice I indicates that forces between neighbouring water molecules in these polymorphs are nearly the same as the forces in ice I. In other words, hydrogen bonding in these polymorphs is not qualitatively different from that in ice I.

(3) Bands with maxima in the 1650–1700 cm^{-1} range (1200–1250 cm^{-1} for D_2O) of the infra-red spectra of ices Ic, II, III, and V. These bands are probably associated with the ν_2 modes of water molecules. In ices II, III, and V this band is more intense, relative to the stretching band, than is the corresponding band in ice I. Bertie and Whalley (1964 b) suggested that these stronger intensities may be due to the more pronounced bending of hydrogen bonds in these ices.

(4) Virtually identical infra-red spectra of ice I and ice Ic (Hornig et al. 1958, Bertie and Whalley 1964 a). The strong resemblance of their structures (Section 3.2 (c)) makes this identity understandable.

There are a number of small differences in the spectra of the ice polymorphs. Perhaps the most interesting are in the stretching bands of HDO in a dilute solution in D_2O and H_2O crystals. Briefly, HDO molecules may be used as 'probes' to test for variation of molecular environments in an H_2O or D_2O crystal. Their O–D (or O–H) stretching modes are only weakly coupled through the U_{jk} term of eqn (3.15) to the stretching modes of the H_2O (or D_2O) molecules around them. As a result, any variations in the O–D (or O–H) stretching frequencies of different HDO molecules are determined largely by variations in the static perturbations, U'_j, which they experience. Hence the observed shapes of O–D (or O–H) stretching bands of HDO in dilute solution in H_2O (or D_2O) crystals contain information about environments of the HDO molecules.

It has already been mentioned that the O–D stretching band of a dilute solution of HDO in H_2O ice II has four distinct narrow peaks. The same band for ice III has two peaks, whereas the corresponding bands for ices I and V are relatively broad and have no fine structure at all (Table 3.16; Bertie and Whalley 1964 a, b). We have also mentioned that, as a consequence of this observation, it seems likely that each O–D group in ice II experiences one of four different static perturbations U'_j, and that Bertie and Whalley (1964 b) attributed the different U'_j values to the presence of four equilibrium oxygen–oxygen separations in ice II. To explain distinct oxygen-oxygen separations, Bertie and Whalley predicted that the hydrogen atoms in ice II have fixed, ordered positions. This prediction has been borne out by crystallographic, thermodynamic, and dielectric data (Sections 3.2, 3.3 (a), and 3.4 (a)). By similar reasoning, the two peaks of the corresponding band in ice III may be explained by the presence of at least two oxygen–oxygen separations in the crystal lattice of quenched ice III. The corresponding bands for ices I and V have a breadth comparable to the total spread of peaks in ices II and III, but no fine structure, indicating the existence of many slightly different static perturbations U'_j. The slight variations of U'_j in ices I and V probably arise from a distribution of oxygen–oxygen separations. The half-widths of the bands are consistent with a distribution of O----O distances of several hundredths of an ångstrom (Bertie and Whalley 1964 a, b). Such a distribution of separations could result from the disordered arrangement of hydrogen atoms known to occur in both these polymorphs. Infra-red spectra of dilute isotopic crystals of ices VI and VII have not been reported.

A second difference in the spectra of the ice polymorphs is the degree of fine structure in the band around 800 cm^{-1}, associated with the molecular librations, ν_L. The ν_L band in both ices II and III is rich in detail, but in ice V, and especially ice I, practically no fine structure can be found. Bertie and Whalley (1964 b) attributed the fine structure of this band in ices II and III to strict selection rules which are the consequence of ordered hydrogen arrangements in these polymorphs.

Small differences in band frequencies of the ices suggest that hydrogen bonds in the high-pressure polymorphs are more easily bent and stretched, and are probably slightly weaker, than those of ice I. For example, the

infra-red frequencies of O–H stretching vibrations of HDO in ice polymorphs increase in the order (see Table 3.16 for greater detail):

Polymorph:	I	III	V	II
ν (O–H stretch) in cm^{-1}:	3277	3318	3350	~ 3350

Raman frequencies for O–H stretching in pure H_2O ices show a similar
trend:

Polymorph:	I	III	V	II	VI	VII
ν (O–H stretch) in cm^{-1}:	3085	3159	3181	3194	3204	3350

It has been found that relatively high stretching frequencies of O–H
groups in hydrogen bonds are indicative of relatively weak hydrogen
bonds (Pimentel and McClellan 1960). Thus the higher stretching
frequencies of the polymorphs to the right of these series indicate that
hydrogen bonds in these polymorphs are weaker than hydrogen bonds
in the polymorphs to the left.

The relative resistance to bending and stretching of hydrogen bonds
in the polymorphs may be estimated from the sequence of frequencies
of the intermolecular modes. Infra-red frequencies of the ν_L bands of
HDO in ice polymorphs decrease in the order:

Polymorph:	I	III	V	II
ν_L (HDO in D_2O) in cm^{-1}:	~ 822	~ 786	~ 780	~ 770

Raman frequencies of the ν_T mode in D_2O polymorphs decrease in the
order:

Polymorph:	I	III	V	II
ν_T in cm^{-1}:	217	166	159	146

Since lower frequencies for the ν_L and ν_T modes imply that hydrogen
bonds are more easily bent and stretched, the hydrogen bonds of the
high-pressure polymorphs must be more easily distorted from their
equilibrium angles and lengths than are the hydrogen bonds of ice I.

(c) *Nuclear magnetic resonance*

Nuclear magnetic resonance (NMR) is a useful tool for studying the
location of protons in ice crystals. This method depends on the fact that
the degree of broadening of the proton resonance band is inversely
proportional to the cube of the equilibrium proton–proton separation of
the two protons of an ice molecule. Of course, the proton–proton separation is not sufficient to determine the dimensions of an H_2O molecule in
the crystal. Once the equilibrium bond length is known, however, the
equilibrium H–O–H angle can be determined, or vice versa. Fig. 3.21

Table 3.16

TABLE 3.16

Comparison of the vibrational spectra of the ices in the fundamental and lattice mode regions

(All entries are for infra-red spectra unless noted. All entries except those in parentheses give frequencies of band maxima in cm^{-1}; numbers in parentheses are band widths in cm^{-1} at half-maximum intensity.)[†]

Vibrational band	Ice I				Ice II			
	H$_2$O	H–OD in D$_2$O	D$_2$O	D–OH in H$_2$O	H$_2$O	H–OD in D$_2$O	D$_2$O	D–OH in H$_2$O
O–X stretching band: ν_S						3373		2493
Infra-red spectrum	3220‡	3277	2425‡	2421§	3225‡	3357	~ 2380‡	2481
	(~ 500)	(~ 50)	(~ 300)	(~ 30)	(~ 500)	3323		2460
								2455
								(each ~
Raman spectrum	3085‡		2283‡		3194‡		2353‡	
	(~ 40)		(~ 25)		3314		2489	
	3210		2416					
Association band: ν_A	2270		1650		2220		1620	
X–O–X' bending band: ν_2	1650	1490‖	1210		1690		1220	
Librational band: ν_L	~ 840§	~ 822	~ 640‡	~ 515	~ 800‡	~ 770	~ 593‡	~ 464§
	(~ 200)		(~ 150)		~ 642§		~ 507	
Hindered translational band: ν_T								
Infra-red spectrum	229‡		222‡					
Raman spectrum	225		217		~ 151‡		~ 146	

† The infra-red data, except where noted, are from the work of Bertie and Whalley (1964 *a*, *b*, 1967) and refer to sample temperatures of −160±20 °C. The Raman data are from the work of Taylor and Whalley (1964; ices I, II, III, V) and Marckmann and Whalley (1964; ices VI, VII), and refer to sample temperatures of −196 °C. All spectra were taken at atmospheric pressure.

‡ Two or more maxima are visible.

§ Shoulders are visible on the main peak.

‖ Haas and Hornig (1960).

Ice III				Ice V				Ice VI		Ice VII	
₂O	H–OD in D₂O	D₂O	D–OH in H₂O	H₂O	H–OD in D₂O	D₂O	D–OH in H₂O	H₂O	D₂O	H₂O	D₂O
250§	3318§	~2450‡	2461§ 2450	3250§	3350	~2390‡	2461§				
59‡ 281		2327‡ 2457		3181‡ 3312		2344‡ 2485		3204 (~50)	2370 (~35)	3348 3440 3470	2462 2563 2546
225§		1615		2210		1610					
390		1240		1680		1225					
~812‡ ~734	~786	~600‡	~473	~730	~780	~490	~445				
		166		169		159					

shows the combinations of H–O–H angles and O–H bond lengths that
are consistent with Kume's (1960) NMR study of ice. The width of the
strip is an indication of experimental uncertainty in the proton–proton
separation. An ice molecule with bond length of 1·01 Å and H–O–H

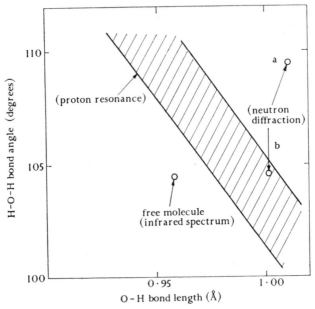

Fig. 3.21.† Equilibrium dimensions of the water molecule in ice I. The
shaded strip shows values consistent with the NMR spectrum of ice I
reported by Kume (1960). The values (a) and (b) are those proposed by
Peterson and Levy (1957) and Chidambaram (1961) respectively from
neutron diffraction of D_2O ice I.

† Adapted with changes from Kume (1960).

angle of 109·5°, originally proposed on the basis of neutron diffraction
data (Peterson and Levy 1957), is not consistent with the NMR results.
On the other hand, a molecule with a bond length of 1·0 Å and a bond
angle near to that of an isolated molecule is consistent with both neutron
diffraction (Chidambaram 1961) and NMR data.

NMR studies also provide some information about the redistribution
of charge during hydrogen-bond formation. Components of the electrostatic field gradients at the deuterons in D_2O ice can be evaluated from
splittings of the NMR spectrum that arise from the interaction of the
quadrupole moments of the deuterons with the field gradients of the ice
crystal. The field-gradient components are found to be about 30 per cent
less in ice I (Waldstein et al. 1964) than in the free molecule (Table 1.5).

Let us consider why this should be the case for the largest component of the field gradient, the one which lies nearly along the O–D axis. If we denote this axis by z', and the electrostatic potential at the deuteron by $\mathscr{V}$, then this component of the field gradient at the deuteron is $\partial^2 \mathscr{V}/\partial z'^2$. Experiments show that $\partial^2 \mathscr{V}/\partial z'^2$ is positive at the deuteron in ice (Waldstein *et al.* 1964), as in the isolated water molecule (Posener 1960), indicating that the contribution to this quantity from the positive oxygen nucleus O_A outweighs the negative contribution from the electrons in the O_A–D bond. Now the observed decrease of some 30 per cent in $\partial^2 \mathscr{V}/\partial z'^2$ during the formation of the O_A–D···O_B hydrogen bond could be due to (1) the longer O_A–D distance in ice, and hence smaller positive field gradient at the deuteron arising from the O_A nucleus, or to (2) the electric field gradient produced by O_B at the deuteron, or to both effects. Quantum-mechanical calculations (Weissmann 1966) indicate that if the O–D bond length were maintained at its vapour-state value of about 0·96 Å in the hydrogen bond, the approach of O_B would decrease $\partial^2 \mathscr{V}/\partial z'^2$ by only 10 per cent. Apparently it is effect (1), the increase in the O_A–D bond length during hydrogen-bond formation, which is the major factor in lowering the field gradient at the deuteron. The calculations by Weissmann (1966) of $\partial^2 \mathscr{V}/\partial z'^2$ in both the isolated molecule and in ice I agree remarkably well with experiment, although the SCF-m.o. wave functions employed by her were approximate and the three-centre integrals arising in the calculation were evaluated approximately.

3.6. Hydrogen bonding

(a) *Experimental energy of hydrogen bonding*

An experimental value for the energy of the hydrogen bond in ice is often useful for comparison with calculations, or for the interpretation of experiments. Examination of the literature on this subject shows that a wide range of values has been reported. Each of these values corresponds to one possible definition of 'hydrogen-bond energy', and which definition is the appropriate one depends on the experiment or calculation being considered. Let us discuss several definitions and the values of the hydrogen-bond energy, $E_{\text{H-bond}}$, to which they lead.

The experimental *lattice energy* of ice is the energy that would correspond to the result of a rigorous quantum-mechanical calculation of the intermolecular energy. It may be defined as the difference in energy between a mole of isolated water molecules at 0 °K with atoms motionless, and a mole of ice at 0 °K with atoms motionless. The term 'atoms motionless' means that the zero-point energy of isolated water molecules is zero ($Z_{\text{intra-vap}} = 0$), and that both the intramolecular and intermolecular zero-point energies of the water molecules in ice are zero ($Z_{\text{intra-ice}} = Z_{\text{inter}} = 0$). The intramolecular zero-point energy is the

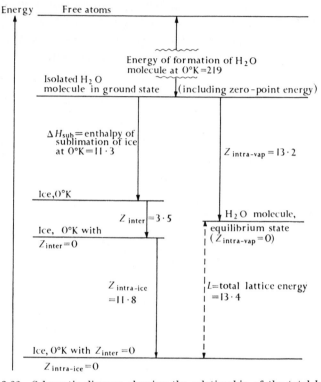

Fig. 3.22. Schematic diagram showing the relationship of the total lattice energy of ice to the enthalpy of sublimation and zero-point energies. The horizontal lines define states of H_2O; the vertical arrows give the energies of transition between the states. All energies are given in kcal mol^{-1}.

zero-point energy associated with internal modes of vibration; its value for an isolated molecule differs from its value for a molecule in ice because the frequencies of the internal modes differ. The intermolecular zero-point energy is associated with the intermolecular modes of vibration in ice. From Fig. 3.22 it is clear that the lattice energy L so defined is given by

$$L = \Delta H_{\text{sub}} + Z_{\text{inter}} + Z_{\text{intra-ice}} - Z_{\text{intra-vap}}, \qquad (3.16)$$

where ΔH_{sub} is the enthalpy of sublimation of ice at 0 °K.

We can evaluate L from the experimental enthalpy of sublimation of ice at 0 °K (11·3 kcal mol^{-1}; see Table 3.7) and from values of the zero-point energies determined from spectroscopic data. According to Whalley

(1957, 1958), $Z_{inter} = 3.5$ kcal mol^{-1} and $Z_{intra\text{-}ice} - Z_{intra\text{-}vap} = -1.4$ kcal mol^{-1}. Hence the total lattice energy of ice at 0 °K is

$$11.3 + 3.5 - 1.4 = 13.4 \text{ kcal mol}^{-1}.$$

Definition 1. The first definition of the hydrogen-bond energy will be formulated in terms of the lattice energy: $E_{H\text{-bond}}$ equals the lattice energy of a mole of ice divided by the number of hydrogen bonds in a mole. Since each mole of water molecules contains two moles of hydrogen atoms, and since each hydrogen atom participates in one hydrogen bond (excluding the small fraction on the surface of the crystal),

$$E_{H\text{-bond}} = \frac{L}{2} = \frac{13.4}{2} = 6.7 \text{ kcal/mol-of-hydrogen-bond.} \quad (3.16\,a)$$

A rigorous quantum-mechanical calculation of the hydrogen-bond energy in ice would presumably yield this value.

Definition 2. A similar definition of $E_{H\text{-bond}}$ can be formulated in terms of the enthalpy of sublimation, ΔH_{sub}:

$$E_{H\text{-bond}} = \frac{\Delta H_{sub}}{2} = \frac{11.32}{2} = 5.66 \text{ kcal/mol-of-hydrogen-bond at 0 °K.}$$
$$(3.17)$$

Since ΔH_{sub} is a function of temperature, $E_{H\text{-bond}}$ as defined here depends on the temperature. This definition gives a slightly larger value for the energy of the deuterium bond in D_2O at 0 °K, 5.96 kcal/mol-of-deuterium-bond.

The hydrogen-bond energy defined by eqn (3.17) is clearly more appropriate than that defined by eqn (3.16 a) for considering such properties as the vapour pressure of ice.

Definition 3. If we adopt either of the above definitions, we ascribe the entire intermolecular energy to hydrogen bonding. In so doing we include in $E_{H\text{-bond}}$ the effects of dispersion and repulsive forces, which are present not only in ice but also in crystals of non-hydrogen-bonded substances. A definition may be based on the premise that the contributions to ΔH_{sub} from hydrogen bonds and from other forces are distinct:

$$E_{H\text{-bond}} = \frac{\Delta H_{sub} - E_{other}}{2}, \quad (3.18)$$

where E_{other} represents the intermolecular energy associated with the other forces.

This definition suffers from the ambiguity involved in estimating

E_{other}. This term is not an observable quantity nor is it subject at present to accurate calculation. Each method of evaluating E_{other} (see below) constitutes an operational definition of $E_{\text{H-bond}}$; thus Definition 3 actually encompasses a class of many different definitions.

Pauling (1960) and Taft and Sisler (1947) assumed that E_{other} is the enthalpy of sublimation that ice would have if it were not hydrogen-bonded, and they estimated its value from the thermodynamic properties of related compounds. Pauling concluded that $E_{\text{H-bond}}$ is about 5 kcal/mol-of-hydrogen-bond, and Taft and Sisler concluded that it is 4·25 kcal/mol-of-hydrogen-bond. Searcy (1949) modified these estimates by taking into account the increased density that a hypothetical non-hydrogen-bonded ice would have over real ice, and he concluded that $E_{\text{H-bond}}$ is 6·4 kcal/mol-of-hydrogen-bond. Searcy's value of $E_{\text{H-bond}}$ is larger that $\Delta H_{\text{sub}}/2$ because he believes that the repulsive energy between molecules in the non-hydrogen-bonded ice outweighs the attractive dispersion energy, and thus that E_{other} is negative. Harris and O'Konski (1957) adopted an even larger value for the repulsive energy and concluded that $E_{\text{H-bond}}$ is about 7·7 kcal/mol-of-hydrogen-bond.

Apparently different methods of estimating E_{other} lead to quite different values of $E_{\text{H-bond}}$. Which, if any, of these values correspond to the energy changes associated with given physical processes (such as dielectric relaxation or self-diffusion) is not immediately clear.

Definition 4. A number of interesting and important processes occur in the ices and in liquid water whose molecular description involves the concept of breaking hydrogen bonds between neighbouring H_2O molecules that remain close together after the bond is broken (for example, the production of D- and L-defects in ice and the changing structure of liquid water when the pressure and temperature are changed). The energies of hydrogen bonds obtained from Definitions 1, 2, and 3 are not appropriate for such situations. For instance, the interaction of non-adjacent molecules contributes an energy, $E_{\text{non-adj}}$, to the lattice energy and sublimation energy of ice which is included in the term E_{other} in eqn (3.18) (calculations described in Section 3.6 (c) suggest that $E_{\text{non-adj}}$ is somewhat greater than 0·8 kcal/mol-of-ice). This contribution will be slightly altered when a hydrogen bond between neighbouring molecules is broken. Furthermore, the electrostatic, dispersion, and repulsion energies between neighbouring H_2O molecules in ice or liquid water will surely be altered when the hydrogen bond between them is broken, if only because the distance between the molecules is changed. The energy of a hydrogen bond between two H_2O molecules might therefore be defined as

$$E_{\text{H-bond}} = \frac{\Delta H_{\text{sub}} - E_{\text{other}}}{2} + \Delta E_{\text{other}}, \qquad (3.19)$$

where ΔE_{other} is the change in electrostatic, dispersion, and repulsion energies (also including a possible small change in $E_{\text{non-adj}}$) on breaking a hydrogen bond between neighbours. Unfortunately the value of ΔE_{other} is not only unobtainable by any direct measurement, but its evaluation depends very much on exactly what one means by a 'broken' hydrogen bond in ice or liquid water. Indeed, its value will probably be different for different physical processes. Thus the estimation of a hydrogen-bond energy in terms of this definition is particularly difficult.

In summary, the 'experimental energy of the hydrogen bond in ice' is not a precisely definable term. The particular value of $E_{\text{H-bond}}$ that is chosen should depend on the context in which it is to be used. The appropriate value for interpreting physical processes such as dielectric relaxation and self-diffusion will probably not be evident until both the processes and the potential energy surface for the interaction of water molecules are better understood.

(b) Potential functions for hydrogen-bonded molecules

Though potential functions were mentioned frequently in Section 3.5, no explicit expressions were given for the potential energy of ice in terms of internuclear separations. Such expressions have been developed by assuming a potential function of reasonable form containing one or more undetermined force constants; the constants are then chosen to reproduce spectral frequencies or other experimental data. It is unlikely that these functions accurately describe intermolecular forces in ice, but they provide some insight into spectroscopic results, and they can be used for rough calculations.

Zimmermann and Pimentel (1962) determined approximate force constants for hydrogen-bonded water molecules by analysing the vibrations of the five-atom system $O \cdots H-O-H \cdots O$. The values of the force constants for $O-H \cdots O$ stretching $(k_{\bar{R}})$, $O-H \cdots O$ bending (k_{θ}), and $H-O-H$ bending (k_{α}) were found from the frequencies of the ν_T, ν_L, and ν_2 bands; these values are listed in Table 3.17. The force constant k_{θ} is roughly half of $k_{\bar{R}}$, and both decrease with increasing temperature. Zimmermann and Pimentel attributed these decreases to weakening of the hydrogen bonds owing to increases in the $O-H \cdots O$ distance during thermal expansion of the crystal. Values of $k_{\bar{R}}$ determined by other workers from spectroscopic frequencies and by Haas (1960) from elastic constants (Table 3.17) are in good agreement with Zimmermann and Pimentel's values. The constant $k_{\bar{R}}$ is only about 2 per cent of the constant $k_{\bar{r}}$ for O–H stretching (Section 1.1 (d)).

The value of k_α found by Zimmermann and Pimentel is over five times larger than k_θ, and increases slightly with increasing temperature. Note that their value of k_α at 0 °C is about 25 per cent smaller than k_α for an isolated water molecule $(0{\cdot}76 \times 10^5$ dyn cm^{-1}; Section 1.1 (d)). Though bending the H–O–H valence angle requires less energy in ice than in an isolated molecule, it requires much more energy than bending the O–H $\cdots$ O hydrogen-bond angle.

Assuming that we have accurate values for these force constants, we can express the change in potential energy for moderate stretching of a hydrogen bond by

$$\Delta U = \tfrac{1}{2}k_{\bar{R}}(\Delta \bar{R})^2 \qquad (3.20)$$

and the change in potential energy for moderate bending by

$$\Delta U = \tfrac{1}{2}k_\theta(\bar{R}-\bar{r})\bar{r}(\Delta\theta)^2. \qquad (3.21)$$

The quantities $\Delta \bar{R}$ and $\Delta \theta$ in these equations represent the changes in O $\cdots$ O distance and O–H $\cdots$ O angle from their equilibrium values; $\bar{r}$ is the O–H bond length. To the same level of approximation the change in potential energy for moderate distortion of the H–O–H bond angle

TABLE 3.17

Force constants for vibrations in ice I

(All ks are in units of 10^5 dyn cm^{-1}.)

Authors	Experimental data	Temp. (°C)	$k_{\bar{R}}$ (O–H$\cdots$O stretching)	k_α (H–O–H bending)	k_θ (O–H$\cdots$O bending)
Haas (1960)	Elastic constants		0·17		
Kyogoku (1960)	Spectroscopic frequencies		0·19		
Zimmermann and Pimentel (1962)	Far i.r. frequencies	0	(0·155)†	(0·56)†	(0·085)†
		−20	0·158	0·545	0·088
		−50	0·162	0·525	0·090
		−95	0·168	0·505	0·092
		−130	0·173	0·495	0·094
		−180	0·178	0·49	0·095
Tsuboi (1964)	Raman frequency		0·18		
Bertie and Whalley (1967)	Far i.r. frequencies	−173	0·17–0·19		

† Determined by extrapolation.

from its equilibrium value of 2α is given by

$$\Delta U = \tfrac{1}{2}k_\alpha \bar{r}^2 \{\Delta(2\alpha)\}^2. \tag{3.22}$$

The units of ΔU in these equations are ergs per molecule if the distances are in centimetres and the angles are in radians and if the constants of Table 3.17 are employed.

It should be emphasized that these expressions are almost certainly inaccurate for all but small deviations of bond lengths and angles from their equilibrium values because the expressions take no account of the anharmonicity of the potential energy. An expression that may give a more accurate description of hydrogen-bond stretching for larger deviations was developed by Kamb (1965 b) from the compressibility and coefficient of thermal expansion of ice I. It has the form

$$\Delta U = 3{\cdot}0\left(\frac{\Delta\bar{R}}{2{\cdot}76}\right) + 162\left(\frac{\Delta\bar{R}}{2{\cdot}76}\right)^2 - 195\left(\frac{\Delta\bar{R}}{2{\cdot}76}\right)^3 \tag{3.23}\dagger$$

where ΔU is in kcal mol^{-1} and $\Delta\bar{R}$ is the change in hydrogen-bond length in Å.

Several authors have devised semi-empirical potential functions to describe the O–H stretching vibration in an O–H····O hydrogen bond. The chief interest of such functions lies in their ability to correlate spectroscopic data from different O–H····O systems. Readers interested in this topic are referred to articles by Lippincott and Schroeder (1955) and Reid (1959).

(c) Theoretical description of the hydrogen bond in ice

An accurate calculation of the energy and other properties of a hydrogen bond in ice from first principles entails difficult problems. A calculation of the energy, for example, must be very accurate indeed, since the formation of a hydrogen bond alters the total energy of a water molecule by only about 1 part in 7000. An accurate description of a single hydrogen bond in ice, moreover, should include the effects of at least several neighbouring molecules, since they influence the electronic distribution of the hydrogen bond under question.

To date most investigators have bypassed these difficulties by regarding the hydrogen-bond energy as the sum of several component energies, and then evaluating each component by approximate methods. The

---

† The coefficient 3·0 of the first term should replace the coefficient 2·2 in the original article (private communication from Dr. Kamb).

component energies are generally considered to be of four types (see Coulson 1957 and 1959 *b* for a detailed discussion of these energies):

(1) *Electrostatic.* Coulson (1959 *b*) defined the electrostatic energy as that which 'would arise if, in some hypothetical fashion, we could bring the interacting species together, without any deformation of either charge cloud, or any electron exchange'. This corresponds to a picture of a hydrogen bond as a classical electrostatic attraction between one of the lone-pairs of electrons on one H_2O molecule and one of the hydrogen atoms or O–H bonds on the neighbouring molecule. The tendency of many hydrogen bonds to be linear, a configuration that results in the maximum *electrostatic* binding energy, suggests that the electrostatic contribution is large.

(2) *Delocalization (or distortion).* The increase in binding energy arising from the deformation of the charge clouds and exchange of electrons that takes place when the O_A–H_A and O_B groups are brought together is the delocalization energy. The delocalization of electrons during this process probably consists of both a polarization of O_A–H_A and O_B by each other, and also a migration of electrostatic charge from the region of O_B to the region of O_A and H_A.

(3) *Repulsive.* Repulsive forces arise from the overlap of the charge clouds of non-covalently bonded atoms. There is undoubtedly considerable repulsion between H_A and O_B in an O_A–H_A⋯O_B hydrogen bond in ice. This is because the sum of the van der Waals radii of a hydrogen and oxygen atom is 2·6 Å (Pauling 1960, p. 260), whereas H_A and O_B are separated by only 1·8 Å. Moreover, O_A and O_B, separated by 2·76 Å in ice I, are also a bit closer than the sum of their van der Waals radii. Hence interactions of O_B with both H_A and O_A give rise to repulsive forces. The repulsive contribution to the energy tends to oppose bonding whereas the other three contributions favour bonding.

(4) *Dispersion.* The energy arising from dispersion forces between H_2O molecules makes a small but significant contribution to the total hydrogen-bond energy.

Probably the earliest calculation of the hydrogen-bond energy of ice in terms of constituent energies was by Bernal and Fowler (1933). They calculated an electrostatic contribution of 7·1 kcal/mol-of-hydrogen-bond using a point-charge model of an H_2O molecule similar to those described in Section 1.2 (*a*). They estimated the dispersion-force contribution from a modified London formula, and the repulsive energy from the condition that the net force on a molecule must vanish. Their total

TABLE 3.18

Results of several calculations of the hydrogen-bond energy in ice I

(All entries are in units of kcal/mol-of-hydrogen-bond.)

Authors	Model of H₂O	Electrostatic	Distortion or delocalization	Repulsive	Dispersion	Total
Bernal and Fowler (1933)	Point charge	7·1[a]	..	−3·4	2·0	5·7
Verwey (1941)	Point charge	6·2[b]	..	−4·2	2·7	4·7
Bjerrum (1951)	Point charge	7·2	..	−3·4[c]	2·0[c]	5·8
Rowlinson (1951 a)	Point charge and multipole expansion	4·7[a]	0·2	0·9[d]		5·8
Pauling (1960)	Thermodynamic data	..	..	..	1·2	..
Taft and Sisler (1947)	Thermodynamic data	..	..	..	1·8	..
Searcy (1949)		..	..	−2·2	1·3	..
Coulson and Danielsson (1954)	Wave-mechanical	..	8·0	..	..	..
Tsubomura (1954)	Wave-mechanical	..	..	..	..	..
Weissmann and Cohan (1965)	Wave-mechanical	10·6[e]	9·6	..	..	8·2[e]
Coulson and Eisenberg (1966 b)	Multipole expansion	3·3[f]	1·0[f]	..	..	..
Campbell et al. (1967)	Multipole expansion	4·4–4·5	..	..	..	..
Experimental value						6·7[g]

[a] Includes 2nd neighbours. Neither Bernal and Fowler's nor Verwey's calculation is for the observed disordered proton structure.
[b] Includes some distortion.
[c] Taken from Bernal and Fowler (1933).
[d] Includes 1st, 2nd, and 6 3rd neighbours.
[e] SCF calculation including only 4 electrons and 3 nuclei; some integrals approximated.
[f] Includes 1st, 2nd, 3rd, and 16 4th neighbours, in the observed disordered proton structure. May not include all delocalization.
[g] From Definition 1, Section 3.6 (a).

hydrogen-bond energy is 5·7 kcal mol^{-1}. Table 3.18 shows the results of this calculation and several others (Verwey (1941), Bjerrum (1951), and Rowlinson (1951 a)) based on similar models of the water molecule. The hydrogen-bond energies predicted by these calculations are surprisingly close to the experimental value considering the simplicity of the models.

The multipole-expansion model for the water molecule (Section 1.2 (a)) has also been used to estimate the electrostatic energy (Coulson and Eisenberg 1966 b). A conclusion from this calculation was that the electrostatic energy between a water molecule and non-adjacent molecules adds somewhat to the average electrostatic energy per hydrogen bond. The 12 second neighbours of an H_2O molecule in ice I—that is, the 12 neighbours adjacent to the four nearest neighbours—add 0·28 kcal/mol-of-hydrogen-bond to the electrostatic energy. The 25 third neighbours and 16 nearest fourth neighbours add another 0·14 kcal/mol-of-hydrogen-bond.

Campbell et $al.$ (1967) carried out an extensive series of calculations of the electrostatic energy, using various multipole-moment models for the water molecule. They found values for the electrostatic energy in the range 4 to 4·5 kcal/mol-of-hydrogen-bond.

Most calculations of the hydrogen-bond energy based on point-charge models have not included any estimate of distortion or delocalization. Both experiments and calculations indicate, however, that this contribution is significant (Coulson 1957 and 1959 b). For example, both direct calculations and consideration of the dielectric constant of ice suggest that the dipole moment of an H_2O molecule in ice is at least 40 per cent greater than that of an isolated water molecule (Section 3.4 (a)). Such a large enhancement of the dipole moment requires considerable distortion of the charge cloud of a water molecule. The observed change of electrostatic field gradient at the deuteron of D_2O during hydrogen-bond formation (Section 3.5 (c)) is another indication that the electronic charge in the vicinity of the hydrogen atom is distorted. Several estimates of the increase in the hydrogen-bond energy of ice owing to delocalization are shown in Table 3.18; none of these estimates is likely to be very accurate.

Calculations with the multipole moment model indicate that non-adjacent neighbours also contribute to the distortion effect (Coulson and Eisenberg 1966 b). This means that the presence of non-adjacent neighbours increases the attraction between a molecule and adjacent molecules; or, conversely, that removal of the non-adjacent neighbours decreases this attraction. In other words, breaking some hydrogen bonds may weaken others.

Table 3.18 also contains several estimates of the dispersion and repulsive contributions to the hydrogen-bond energy. The contribution of dispersion energy has been estimated by London-type formulas, as in the calculations of Bernal and Fowler (1933) and Verwey (1941). It has also been estimated from the thermodynamic properties of non-hydrogen-bonded molecules similar in other respects to H_2O, as in the calculations of Pauling (1960), Taft and Sisler (1947), and Searcy (1949). Both methods predict about the same magnitude for this energy contribution, $\sim 1\cdot5$ kcal/mol-of-hydrogen-bond. The repulsive energy is not known with the same accuracy. As noted by Coulson (1959 b), the values of the delocalization and repulsive energies computed from a given model are intimately related, because the delocalization, which consists of a migration of electronic charge from one oxygen towards the neighbouring water molecule, will also give rise to a repulsion between the delocalized charge and the electrons of the neighbouring molecule.

A step in the direction of *ab initio* calculations of the hydrogen-bond energy in ice has been made by Weissmann and Cohan (1965). They computed the energy of the system O_A–$H \cdots O_B$ using the SCF molecular orbital technique. Although their model includes only four electrons and can hardly be an accurate description of ice, their calculated hydrogen-bond energy is encouragingly close to the experimental value (Table 3.18). Their value of the electrostatic energy, like that calculated from most of the point-charge models, is larger than the calculated total hydrogen-bond energy. The three-centre integrals in their calculation were evaluated by approximate methods.

In summary, a qualitative theoretical description of hydrogen bonding in ice has been developed in terms of the four component effects, but a description based on first principles is not yet available. Of the component energies, only the dispersion energy and perhaps the electrostatic energy are known with any confidence. Since the electrostatic attraction seems to be greater than the total hydrogen-bond energy, the combined effect of electron exchange and distortion of charge clouds during hydrogen-bond formation must oppose bonding. Dispersion and delocalization energies, like the electrostatic energy, favour hydrogen bonding, so that repulsive energy may be large. Thus the picture of a hydrogen bond that emerges from the approximation of the component effects is a small net attractive energy that is the sum of several larger attractive and repulsive energies.

(d) *The properties of ice as determined by hydrogen bonds: a summary*

In closing this chapter it may be helpful to consider the properties of ice in relation to two characteristics of hydrogen bonds: (1) the dissociation energy of these bonds, which in order of magnitude is intermediate between energies of typical covalent bonds and of dispersion attractions of molecules, and (2) the tendency of these bonds to be linear.

The relative magnitudes of hydrogen-bond and dispersion energies account for the fact that ice has a larger energy of sublimation and a higher melting-point than compounds like methane, in which cohesive forces are largely of the dispersive type. On the other hand, ice has a smaller energy of sublimation and a lower melting-point than covalent crystals such as diamond. The relative values of hydrogen bonds and dispersion forces also help to explain the open structure of ice. The presence of two hydrogen bonds per molecule is energetically more favourable than the increase in dispersion attractions that might result if ice had no hydrogen bonds and were more closely packed.

The frequencies of the internal vibrational modes of H_2O are altered much more during condensation than are those of non-hydrogen-bond-forming molecules. These large shifts, and also the strong coupling of one molecule's vibrations with those of its neighbours, result from the relatively strong forces between water molecules. Indeed, if the forces were much stronger, it would be impossible to regard the vibrational modes of ice as being simply derived from the vibrational modes of isolated water molecules.

Near the melting-point thermal agitation becomes vigorous enough to break a small number of hydrogen bonds, and consequently water molecules are able to reorient and to move through the lattice with increasing frequency as the temperature is raised. These motions give rise to the phenomena of dielectric relaxation and self-diffusion.

Hydrogen bonds in ice tend to be linear. This tendency, coupled with the tetrahedral character of the water molecule, accounts for the structures of ices I, Ic, VII, and VIII. In these polymorphs each water molecule is tetrahedrally coordinated to four molecules, and forms a nearly linear hydrogen bond with each of them. Thus both the open framework and low density of ices I and Ic, and the denser interpenetrating structures of ices VII and VIII, may be regarded as consequences of linear hydrogen bonds. The tendency of hydrogen bonds to be linear also contributes to the large dielectric constants of the ices: it is responsible for the strong angular correlation between neighbouring H_2O molecules, and accordingly for the magnitude of the dielectric constant.

The rise in density and drop in dielectric constant that accompany melting of ice I are both indicative of increased bending and perhaps breaking of hydrogen bonds in liquid water.

The tendency for linear hydrogen bonding is not so strong that it cannot be overwhelmed by other forces under certain conditions. For example, ices II, III, V, and VI all contain distinctly bent hydrogen bonds. At the pressures under which these polymorphs are stable, the decrease in free energy arising from the smaller volume permitted by bent hydrogen bonds outweighs the increase associated with the energy of bending. Even in ices I and Ic the hydrogen bonds are probably not precisely linear. This is not surprising, for if they were linear, the equilibrium bond angles of individual H_2O molecules would have to be 109·5°, several degrees larger than the valence angles of the isolated molecules. Since bending of O–H···O angles requires much less energy than bending of H–O–H angles, the former type of bending most likely predominates.

The resistance of hydrogen bonds to bending is not strong enough to prevent bending by thermal agitation. The contribution of librational modes to the heat capacity of ice shows that vibrations cause changes in hydrogen-bond angles at temperatures above 80 °K. The infra-red frequencies of librational modes of ice polymorphs indicate that resistance to hydrogen-bond bending is weaker in the high-pressure polymorphs than in ice I, and becomes weaker in ice I as the temperature increases.

4. Properties of Liquid Water

4.1. Introduction

THE purpose of this chapter and the one that follows is to develop a description of water in molecular terms. We shall be particularly interested in the relative positions and motions of the molecules, often called the 'structure' of the liquid, and the forces acting between the molecules.

Scientists, at least since the time of Roentgen (1892), have put forward hypotheses about the structure of liquid water, but efforts to verify or invalidate these hypotheses have been hampered by the lack of a general theory of the liquid state. In the absence of such a theory, conclusions about the structure of water have been based on two approaches, neither of them rigorous. The first approach consists in formulating a model for liquid water, treating the model in some fashion—usually involving massive approximations—by the methods of statistical mechanics, and comparing the calculated values of macroscopic properties with those that are observed. The fit of the computed properties to experiment is taken as an index of the correspondence of the model to reality. We shall discuss this approach in the next chapter. The second approach, which is adopted in this chapter, is to deduce aspects of the structure of the liquid from the macroscopic properties of water. The properties of water have been investigated in such great detail that even though each macroscopic property can be related only qualitatively or semi-quantitatively to some feature of the liquid structure, a useful picture of water emerges when many properties are considered.

(a) Meaning of the term 'structure' as applied to liquid water†

Before setting out to deduce details of the structure of liquid water from macroscopic properties we must have a precise idea of what we mean by 'structure'. A clear understanding of this term is especially helpful in determining which microscopic details of a liquid are reflected

† The discussion of this section is based in part on the theories of Frenkel (1946) and Fisher (1964).

in a given macroscopic property. Let us start with the relatively simple question of what is meant by the 'structure' of a crystalline solid such as ice.

The molecules in a crystal oscillate about mean positions and the array of mean positions constitutes a lattice, having a geometrical long-range order. If the average frequency of oscillation is denoted by $1/\tau_V$, then the characteristic time τ_V may be considered the average period of vibration of the molecule about its mean position. In the case of ice, as discussed in Section 3.5, there are actually many modes of oscillation of the molecules about their equilibrium positions. For the purposes of the present discussion, let us regard τ_V as the average period of the ν_T mode. This is the hindered translational mode associated with the absorption band near 200 cm^{-1}; accordingly the characteristic time τ_V is roughly 2×10^{-13} s in ice.

The molecules in a crystal also undergo rotational and translational displacements, but these are much less frequent than the oscillations. In ice I, as discussed in Section 3.4, each molecule experiences about 10^5 reorientations per second at 0 °C, and probably a somewhat greater number of translational displacements. Let us denote the average time between two displacements by τ_D. Then for ice I at 0 °C, $\tau_D \cong 10^{-5}$ s and thus $\tau_D \gg \tau_V$.

It follows naturally from this division of thermal motions into rapid oscillations and slower displacements that the term 'structure' can have three different meanings when applied to a crystal such as ice. The meaning depends on whether one considers a time interval short compared to the period for an oscillation (τ_V), or an interval longer than the period of an oscillation but less than the time for a displacement (τ_D), or an interval considerably longer than the displacement time. This can be illustrated as follows. Suppose that we take a snapshot of a crystal using a camera with a lens capable of resolving individual molecules and a shutter permitting any desired period of exposure. An exposure time short compared to τ_V would catch the molecules during the course of a single oscillation, and for ice I would result in a picture similar to Fig. 4.1 (a). The molecular images would be relatively sharp, and the lattice would appear slightly disordered because molecules would not necessarily be in their mean positions. Since the equilibrium nearest-neighbour distance in ice is about 2·8 Å, and since the root-mean-square amplitudes of ice molecules are roughly 0·2 Å near the melting-point (Section 3.1 (c)), any given nearest-neighbour distance in the snapshot might differ by as much as 15 per cent from the equilibrium distance.

Let us call the structure shown by this snapshot the *instantaneous structure*, or *I-structure*, of the crystal.

Suppose we take a second snapshot with exposure time long compared to τ_V but still short compared to τ_D. This picture would show blurred molecules centred at the points of a regular lattice, since each molecule

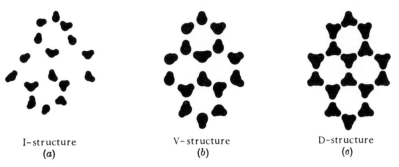

I-structure   V-structure   D-structure
(*a*)   (*b*)   (*c*)

Fig. 4.1. Schematic representations of the I-structure, V-structure, and D-structure of ice I for a small region of the crystal.

completes many oscillations while the shutter is open. The orientations of the molecules would not be averaged, however, because the exposure time is shorter than τ_D. Let us call the structure revealed by this snapshot the *vibrationally-averaged structure*, or *V-structure* for short. Fig. 4.1 (*b*) is a schematic representation of the V-structure of ice I.

A third snapshot, taken with an exposure time long compared to τ_D, would show an average of all molecular orientations, since each molecule experiences many reorientations while the shutter is open. This structure can be called the *diffusionally-averaged structure*, or *D-structure*. The D-structure of ice I is depicted schematically in Fig. 4.1 (*c*); this is essentially the structure of ice as revealed by neutron diffraction.

Let us now consider the meaning of the word 'structure' as applied to liquid water. In water, just as in ice, molecular motions may be divided into rapid oscillations and slower diffusional motions. The evidence for this is described in detail later in this chapter, but can be summarized as follows.

(1) Spectroscopic studies (Section 4.7) show that molecules in liquid water oscillate about (temporary) equilibrium positions. The frequencies of the oscillations are nearly the same as those for molecules in ice. If we regard the average period of time for an oscillation, τ_V, as the average period of the ν_T mode, we find that τ_V for water is slightly smaller than τ_V for ice ($\sim 2 \times 10^{-13}$ s).

(2) The self-diffusion, viscosity, dielectric relaxation, and NMR relaxation of water (Section 4.6) all show that the equilibrium positions and orientations of water molecules experience frequent changes in the liquid. The dielectric relaxation time of water indicates that a molecule experiences a displacement on the average about once every 10^{-11} s near the melting-point; accordingly τ_D for the liquid near 0 °C is roughly 10^{-11} s.

Thus the thermal motions in the liquid may be regarded as being of two types: rapid oscillations about temporary equilibrium positions, and slower displacements of the equilibrium positions. This division leads again to the idea of three meanings of the term 'structure'. A snapshot of the liquid with exposure time less than τ_V would catch the molecules in the course of an oscillation and would thus show the I-structure of the liquid. A second snapshot with exposure time between τ_V and τ_D would be blurred by the oscillations of molecules, but would not be blurred further by displacements of molecules. This picture would be of the V-structure. A third picture, with exposure time long compared to τ_D, and taken from a camera fixed at a point in space within the liquid, would be completely blurred. A more informative picture would be obtained by placing the camera on a given water molecule and recording the view as the molecule moves through space. This picture would not be a complete blur because there is some structure in the mutual arrangement of molecules in a liquid even over a long period of time. Let us call the relative molecular positions revealed by this last picture the D-structure of the liquid.

Several comments should be made about the distinctions among I-, V-, and D-structures. As we shall discuss throughout this chapter, various experimental techniques have provided extensive information about the D- and V-structures of water. In contrast, no experimental technique has yet given information about the I-structure of the liquid. Thus the concept of the I-structure, though useful as a heuristic device, is not helpful in interpreting experimental data, and we shall not consider it further.

A second comment has to do with the lifetime of the V-structure. The value of τ_D, and hence the average duration of the V-structure, depends strongly on temperature. At lower temperatures τ_D is larger, and the V-structure persists longer. At very low temperatures τ_D is of the order of days or weeks and we call the substance a glass. The structure of vitreous ice (Section 3.2 (c)) is undoubtedly similar to the V-structure of liquid water. At higher temperatures molecular displacements become more rapid, and ultimately approach the frequency of the oscillations. At this point the distinction between the D- and V-structures disappears.

Another point of importance is that we may think of the D-structure as either the time-average or the space-average of different V-structures. Consider an ice crystal at equilibrium. The D-structure found in one local region of the crystal is identical to the D-structure in any other region; but the V-structure in the neighbourhood of a given molecule is generally different from the V-structure about any other molecule (see Fig. 4.1). Now we may regard the D-structure in either of two ways: either as the average over time of the progression of V-structures that appear around a given molecule owing to displacements of neighbouring molecules, or alternatively, as the average over space of all V-structures simultaneously present in different regions of the crystal. The equivalence of these two points of view is the substance of the ergotic assumption of statistical mechanics.

(b) Liquid structure and experimental techniques

The bulk of this chapter is an attempt to infer from macroscopic properties details of the structure of water, and the nature of the forces responsible for the structure. Information on the V-structure of the liquid can be extracted from the study of some properties but not from many others, which contain information only on the D-structure. For example, the thermodynamic properties of water—its volume, heat capacity, compressibility, and so forth—are characteristic of the D-structure of the liquid. Taken by themselves, these properties can give no information on the V-structure. The same is true of the static dielectric constant, the X-ray diffraction pattern, the angular distribution of scattered light, the refractive index, and the nuclear magnetic resonance chemical shift of the liquid.

Techniques that do give information about the V-structure are those that employ radiation or particles that both interact with the liquid for only a short period of time and exchange a detectable fraction of their energy with molecules in the liquid. Infra-red and Raman spectroscopy as well as inelastic neutron scattering fulfil these requirements. These techniques are the main source of information on the V-structure of the liquid. The approximate time intervals that are reflected by these and other measurements are shown in Fig. 4.2. Neutron scattering provides information about time intervals as long as 10^{-11} s. This is about the same period as τ_D, so that neutron scattering is useful for studying the nature of the displacement of the positions of temporary equilibrium. Studies of the relaxation of dielectric polarization and of nuclear magnetic resonance are helpful in establishing the average time between displacements.

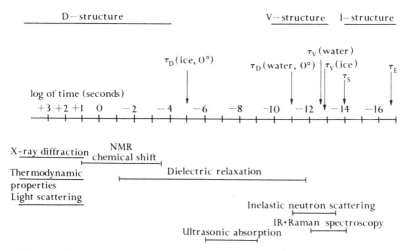

Fig. 4.2. Time scale of molecular processes in ice and liquid water. The vertical arrows indicate the periods associated with various molecular processes: τ_D and τ_V are the periods for molecular displacement and oscillation, as discussed in the text; τ_S is the period for an O–H stretching vibration and τ_E is the time required for an electron to complete one circuit in the innermost Bohr orbit.

The horizontal lines below the time scale show the time intervals for which various experimental techniques have yielded information on ice and water.

The order in which the properties of water are considered below is based on the time-scale about which they give information. Properties that refer only to the D-structure of the liquid are considered first. Then we take up properties that yield information on the molecular displacements and the lifetime of the V-structure. Finally we discuss the properties that reveal details of the V-structure.

4.2. X-ray diffraction

(a) Radial distribution functions

The diffraction pattern formed by a beam of X-rays that has passed through a sample of liquid water contains detailed information on the D-structure of the liquid. To obtain this information, the intensity of the scattered X-rays is first measured as a function of the angle between the scattered radiation and the incident beam. A modified Fourier integral of the intensity then gives $\rho(\bar{R})$, the average number of water molecules in an element of volume at a distance $\bar{R}$ from any molecule.† Let us call the arbitrary molecule from which $\bar{R}$ is measured the 'central molecule'. We may think of $\rho(\bar{R})$ as a description of the local density of molecules, averaged over a long period of time, at any point distance $\bar{R}$ from the central molecule. This is the density of molecules that would be seen in a time exposure taken by a camera placed on the central molecule.

The average distribution of molecules in a liquid is usually represented by either of two functions of $\rho(\bar{R})$, both called radial distribution functions, rather than by $\rho(\bar{R})$ itself. We must define these functions before discussing their behaviour for water:

(1) $g(\bar{R})$: the function $g(\bar{R})$ may be defined by

$$g(\bar{R}) = \rho(\bar{R})/\rho_0, \tag{4.1}$$

where ρ_0 is the bulk density of the liquid expressed as number of molecules per unit volume. Thus $g(\bar{R})$ may be considered the factor by which the average local density $\rho(\bar{R})$ at $\bar{R}$ differs from the bulk density of the liquid. At large distances from the central molecule $g(\bar{R})$ must equal unity, for at large $\bar{R}$ the average local density is equivalent to the bulk density. In the vicinity of the central molecule, however, the local density differs from the bulk density, because the forces acting between the central molecule and its neighbours affect their relative positions. In a plot of $g(\bar{R})$ against $\bar{R}$ (Fig. 4.3), $g(\bar{R})$ exceeds unity where the local density exceeds the bulk density. The oscillations in $g(\bar{R})$ near the central molecule are indicative of short-range order in the liquid; and the constant value of $g(\bar{R})$ equal to unity at large $\bar{R}$ is indicative of long-range disorder.

(2) $4\pi\bar{R}^2\rho(\bar{R})$: the quantity $4\pi\bar{R}^2\rho(\bar{R})\mathrm{d}\bar{R}$ is the average number of molecules in a spherical shell of thickness $\mathrm{d}\bar{R}$, at a distance $\bar{R}$ from the central molecule. When $4\pi\bar{R}^2\rho(\bar{R})$ is plotted against $\bar{R}$, as in Fig. 4.4, relative maxima appear at the values of $\bar{R}$ where neighbouring molecules are most likely to be found. These maxima occur at slightly larger $\bar{R}$ values than the maxima in $g(\bar{R})$. A plot of $4\pi\bar{R}^2\rho(\bar{R})$ is particularly informative because the area under the curve between any two values of $\bar{R}$ is equal to the number of neighbouring molecules within that range of distance.

† See Morgan and Warren (1938) for the function of scattered intensity that gives $\rho(\bar{R})$.

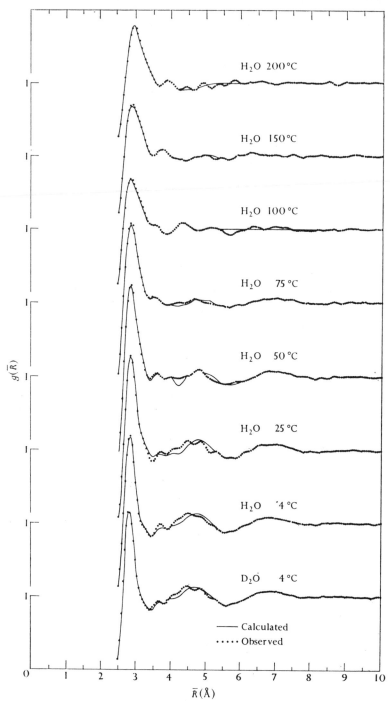

FIG. 4.3. Radial distribution functions, $g(\bar{R})$, for liquid H_2O at various temperatures and for liquid D_2O at 4 °C, as determined by Narten *et al.* (1967). Note that the base line of each curve is one unit above that for the curve below. The points were determined from experiments. The solid curves were calculated from a model which is described in Section 4.2 (*b*). The experiments at and below 100° C were carried out at atmospheric pressure; those above 100 °C were at the vapour pressure of the sample. From Narten *et al.* (1967).

Diffraction patterns and distribution functions

By examining X-ray diffraction patterns of water, Bernal and Fowler (1933) inferred that tetrahedral groupings of molecules occur frequently in the liquid. (This fundamental discovery was, however, made without determining the distribution functions; Bernal and Fowler calculated the diffraction patterns expected for various models of the D-structure of water, and compared the results with the observed patterns.)

From the structure of ice and the density of water (Section 4.3 (*b*)), Bernal and Fowler suspected that liquid water has a more open structure than do nearly close-packed simple liquids such as argon and neon. Indeed they found that the calculated X-ray diffraction pattern for a disordered, close-packed arrangement of molecules is very different from the observed diffraction pattern of water. Calculated patterns for various tetrahedral arrangements of water molecules—arrangements isomorphous with ice I and the silicon atoms of quartz—resembled the experimental pattern of water near the melting-point much more closely. On the basis of the experimental diffraction pattern for 2 °C, they suggested that the tetrahedral coordination might bear some resemblance to ice I, and that the contraction of water during warming to 4 °C might represent the completion of a transition to a more compact form of tetrahedral coordination. At higher temperatures, calculated patterns for a mixture of quartz and close-packed structures matched the experimental pattern. Their over-all conclusion was that water molecules are predominantly coordinated to four neighbouring molecules at room temperature and below, thus forming an extended, three-dimensional network of molecules, but that this four-coordination breaks down as the temperature rises.

We should note in passing that Bernal and Fowler attributed the tendency of water molecules towards four-coordination to the tetrahedral character of the water molecule (Section 1.2 (*b*)). They noted that the charge distribution of a water molecule resembles a tetrahedron with two positive and two negative corners. Extensive four-coordination, they emphasized, is a consequence of both the attraction of a positive corner (a hydrogen atom) to a negative corner (a lone-pair of electrons) and the presence of two positive and two negative corners in each molecule.

The experimental radial distribution functions for water substantiate Bernal and Fowler's conclusions about the four-coordination of water molecules and provide details on the average separation of the molecules in the liquid. The most accurate X-ray diffraction measurements of water to date are those of Narten, Danford, and Levy (1966, 1967). The radial distribution functions derived from these measurements (Figs. 4.3 and 4.4) are in fair agreement with the earlier work of Morgan and Warren (1938). Narten et al. (1966) believe that differences between their results† and those of previous investigators† are due primarily to neglect in the previous work of data for large scattering angles.

The $g(\bar{R})$ curves from the study of Narten et al. (1967) are shown in Fig. 4.3. Note that $g(\bar{R})$ vanishes for all values of $\bar{R}$ less than 2·5 Å, indicating that water molecules do not approach within 2·5 Å of the central molecule. This result is expected in view of the rapid increase of overlap repulsive forces for intermolecular separations less than 2·8 Å (Section 2.1 (a)). At 4 °C, $g(\bar{R})$ is nearly equal to unity for all $\bar{R}$ greater than 8 Å, showing that the average density of neighbouring molecules at these distances is equal to the bulk density. This means, of course, that the order imposed by the central molecule on the average positions of its neighbours does not extend beyond 8 Å. As water is heated, this short-range order extends even less far; it does not go beyond 6 Å at 200 °C. The well-resolved peak centred near 2·9 Å is due primarily to the nearest neighbours of the central molecule, and the maximum of the peak gives an approximate value for the average separation of nearest neighbours in the liquid.

In the $4\pi\bar{R}^2\rho(\bar{R})$ functions of Narten et al. (Fig. 4.4), the maximum of the first peak shifts gradually from 2·82 Å to 2·94 Å as the temperature is increased from 4 to 200 °C. At 4 °C peaks are also visible near 4·5 Å and 7 Å, but these become less sharply defined as the temperature increases. A relative maximum near 3·5 Å is present at 4 °C and persists until at least 50 °C. All changes in the radial distribution function with temperature seem to be gradual. The radial distribution functions for H_2O and D_2O at 4 °C are nearly identical.

Both Morgan and Warren (1938) and Narten et al. (1966) estimated the average number of nearest neighbours from the area under the first peak of their radial distribution curves. Such calculations are not without ambiguity, since the right-hand side of the peak is not fully resolved. Narten et al. found that the average number of nearest neighbours is about 4·4 at all temperatures from 4 to 200 °C; Morgan and Warren (1938) found that the number increases from 4·4 at 1·5 °C to 4·9 at 83 °C. From these results it is clear that molecules in liquid

---

† Previous investigations include, among others, those of Katzoff (1934), Morgan and Warren (1938), Brady and Romanow (1960), and Heemskerk (1962).

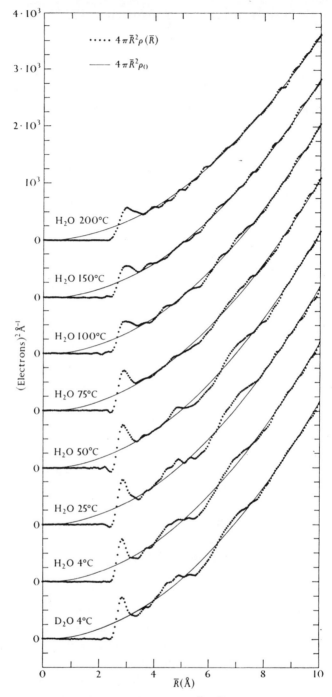

FIG. 4.4. Radial distribution functions, $4\pi\bar{R}^2\rho(\bar{R})$, for liquid H_2O at various temperatures and for liquid D_2O at 4 °C, as determined by Narten *et al.* (1966). The solid line is $4\pi\bar{R}^2\rho_0$, where ρ_0 is the bulk density of water. From Narten *et al.* (1966).

water have on the average approximately four nearest neighbours. Similar techniques give very different figures for the number of nearest neighbours in simple liquids: neon and argon, for example, are found to have an average of 8·6 and 10·5 nearest neighbours respectively (Fisher 1964).

Further evidence for four-coordination of molecules in liquid water comes from the sequence of positions of peaks and troughs in the radial distribution function. In ice I, where each water molecule is surrounded by four others and where all $H_2O \cdots H_2O \cdots H_2O$ angles are almost exactly tetrahedral (that is, equal to $\cos^{-1}(-1/3)$; see Section 3.1 (a)), each molecule has a high concentration of neighbours at distances of 2·76 Å, 4·5–5·3 Å, and 6·4–7·8 Å; but no neighbours between 2·76 and 4·5 Å or between 5·3 Å and 6·4 Å (Table 4.1). Now the peaks of the radial distribution functions for water shown in Figs. 4.3 and 4.4 roughly coincide with the distances of high concentration in ice I. Moreover, a trough is evident in the radial distribution in the 5·3–6·4 Å region where no neighbours exist in ice I. Hence most features of the radial distribution function for water are consistent with tetrahedral co-ordination of molecules. Morgan and Warren (1938) noted a gradual disappearance with rising temperature of the peak near 4·5 Å in their radial distribution functions and took this as an indication that the tetrahedral coordination in water is less sharply defined or less frequent at higher temperatures.

One feature of the radial distribution functions of Fig. 4.3 that is not consistent with strict tetrahedral coordination is the distinct peak near 3·5 Å. We shall consider several explanations for the origin of this feature in the following section.

The information about structure that has come from X-ray diffraction studies of water may be summarized as follows.

(1) Averaged over a long period of time (say $\sim 10^{-8}$ s or more), the distribution of distances of neighbouring molecules from any given molecule in the liquid is not random. Near the melting-point, the distribution of distances is strongly non-random within about 3 Å of the given molecule, more random within the range 3–8 Å from the molecule, and completely random beyond 8 Å. In other words, beyond 8 Å from the given molecule, other molecules are to be found at all distances with equal likelihood. At 200 °C, the distribution of distances is random beyond 6 Å.

(2) Averaged over a long period of time, relatively large concentrations of molecules exist at about 2·9 Å, 4·5–5·3 Å, and 6·4–7·8 Å from each

TABLE 4.1

X-ray diffraction studies of liquid water and intermolecular separations in ice polymorphs

Investigators	Temperature (°C)	Apparent number of neighbours in first coordination shell	Location of maxima in $4\pi R^2\rho(R)$ vs. R (Å)			
Narten et al. (1966)	4	4·4	2·82	3·7†	4·5†	7†
	200	4·4	2·94			
Morgan and Warren (1938)	1·5	4·4	2·90		4·5†	6·9†
	83	4·9	3·05			
Number and distance of neighbours to an arbitrary central molecule in ices I and II:‡						
Ice I			at 2·76		22 at 4·51-5·28	41 at 6·44-7·80
Ice II			4 at 2·75-2·84	8 at 3·24-3·89	9 at 4·22-5·05	

† These maxima become less sharply defined with increasing temperature.
‡ Values for ice II calculated by Levine (1966) from data of Kamb (1964).

molecule. This sequence is consistent with tetrahedral coordination of molecules in the liquid. The substantial concentration of molecules near 3·5 Å cannot be explained by strict tetrahedral coordination.

(3) Averaged over a long period of time, each molecule has four, or perhaps slightly more, nearest neighbours.

(b) *Interpretation of the radial distribution function in terms of V-structures*

The radial distribution function gives the average local density of molecules at distance $\bar{R}$ from the central molecule, and is thus indicative of the D-structure of the liquid. We cannot deduce all that we want to know about the structure of liquid water with this information alone. In the first place, the radial distribution function by itself tells nothing about the angular distribution of neighbouring molecules. Fortunately, this is not crucial, because supplementing the radial distribution function with knowledge about the structure of ice and the density of water suggests that tetrahedral coordination is a frequent configuration in the liquid. A more serious limitation of the radial distribution function is that it reveals nothing about the distributions of molecules around the central molecule during short periods of time (that is, nothing about the V-structures), other than the average of them all.

Since the D-structure is the space average of all local V-structures that are simultaneously present in the liquid (Section 4.1 (a)), many authors have attempted to interpret the radial distribution functions for water as an average of radial distribution functions for several V-structures. In this section we shall consider four schemes for decomposing the observed radial distribution function into contributions from local V-structures. Each of these schemes corresponds to one of the models for liquid water that we shall discuss later in this chapter and in Chapter 5, so that this section will also serve as an introduction to the more popular models for water. It should be emphasized from the start that all four of these models (and many others besides) are on the whole consistent with the X-ray diffraction pattern of water. Other experimental data, of the sort presented in subsequent sections of this chapter, must be used to decide which, if any, corresponds to the structure of the real liquid.

Mixture models

A 'mixture model' depicts the structure of water at any instant as a mixture of a small number of distinguishable species of water molecules. A species, in the terminology we have been using, is a local V-structure. In one type of mixture model two species of water molecules are supposed to be present at any given instant: molecules in 'clusters' and monomeric, non-hydrogen-bonded molecules. The molecules in clusters are hydrogen-bonded to four neighbouring molecules. The clusters are constantly breaking up and re-forming, so that over a long period of time every water molecule has the same average environment.

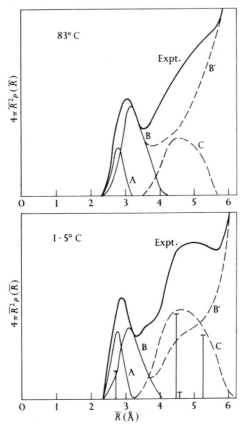

FIG. 4.5. Interpretation of the radial distribution curves of water in terms of the mixture model of Némethy and Scheraga (1962). The experimental curves are from the work of Morgan and Warren (1938). Peaks A and B show the contributions of, respectively, hydrogen-bonded and non-hydrogen-bonded first neighbours. Peak C and curve B′ show, respectively, the contributions of hydrogen-bonded and non-hydrogen-bonded second neighbours. The vertical lines in the 1·5 °C curve represent the position and relative number of neighbours in ice I. From Némethy and Scheraga (1962).

Némethy and Scheraga (1962) interpreted the radial distribution curves found by Morgan and Warren (1938) in terms of a mixture model. They considered the first peak of the experimental curves to be the sum of two peaks (see Fig. 4.5): one (peak A) centred at $\bar{R} = 2 \cdot 76$ Å was attributed to hydrogen-bonded nearest neighbours; the other (peak B) centred near 3·2 Å was attributed to non-hydrogen-bonded nearest neighbours. They centred another peak (C) near 5 Å, and assigned it to the contribution of hydrogen-bonded second neighbours. Némethy and Scheraga attributed the residual area (curve B'), once curves A, B, and C are subtracted from the experimental curves, to non-hydrogen-bonded second neighbours. They determined the area of peak A from the concentration of hydrogen-bonded molecules predicted by their theory and centred this peak at the nearest-neighbour separation of ice I. Peak B was determined by subtracting peak A from the first peak of the experimental curve. They also calculated the area of peak B from the concentration of non-hydrogen-bonded molecules predicted by their theory, and the results of the two methods were in close agreement. Peak C is a qualitative representation.

Rising temperature, according to Némethy and Scheraga's ideas, increases the concentration of non-hydrogen-bonded molecules. This causes a broadening of the first peak of the experimental distribution curve, and loss of structure at higher $\bar{R}$ values (see Fig. 4.5). In applying their theory to D_2O, Némethy and Scheraga (1964) predicted that the radial distribution function for D_2O would be nearly identical to the one for H_2O. This prediction was subsequently confirmed (see Fig. 4.4).

Interstitial models

Interstitial models are a special class of mixture models: one species of water molecule is supposed to form a hydrogen-bonded framework containing cavities in which the other species, single, non-hydrogen-bonded water molecules, reside.

Samoilov (1965) interpreted the radial distribution function in terms of an interstitial model. His reasons for favouring an interstitial model included the comparison, shown in Fig. 4.6, of the observed radial distribution function with a calculated distribution function for a 'smoothed out' ice crystal. From this figure it is evident that water has a higher density of neighbours than ice at about 3·5 Å. Samoilov also noted that each molecule in ice I is 3·47 Å distant from six 'cavity centres'. These cavities can be seen in Fig. 3.1; they join one another along the c-axis to form the open shafts shown in Fig. 3.2. The existence both of cavities in ice at about 3·5 Å from each molecule and a higher density in water than ice at about 3·5 Å, suggested to Samoilov that liquid water is similar to ice but has molecules in the cavities. As ice melts, according to Samoilov, some of the molecules break their hydrogen bonds with the lattice and move into neighbouring cavities. These interstitial molecules account for the increased radial density around 3·5 Å. Since the cavity centres are also 2·94 Å from six framework molecules, the interstitial molecules contribute substantially to the first peak of the radial distribution curve. Samoilov believes this accounts for the observation of Morgan

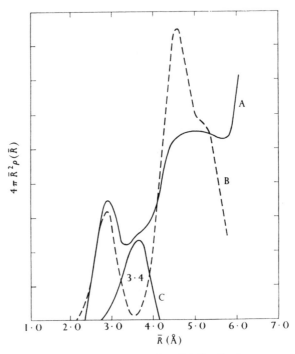

FIG. 4.6. Comparison of the experimental radial distribution curve, $4\pi\bar{R}^2\rho(\bar{R})$, for water at 1·5 °C (curve A), and the calculated radial distribution of an 'ice-like' distribution (curve B). Curve C is the difference of A and B. Curve B is for 4 neighbouring molecules at an average distance of 2·85 Å, 13 at 4·50 Å, and 9 at 5·3 Å. This distribution of neighbours is similar to that in ice I (see Table 4.1) except the first-neighbour distance is taken here as 2·85 Å rather than 2·76 Å. Each group of neighbours is distributed about its average distance in a Gaussian band to simulate vibrations of molecules about their mean positions. From Morgan and Warren (1938).

and Warren that the apparent number of nearest neighbours exceeds four even though tetrahedral coordination is partially broken down in the liquid.

Danford and Levy (1962) and Narten *et al.* (1967) made extensive calculations of radial distribution functions for an interstitial model similar in some respects to Samoilov's model. The framework in this model is an ice I lattice that is permitted to expand anisotropically with increasing temperature. The interstitial molecules are located in the cavities, but, in contrast to Samoilov's model, they are restricted to the triad axis. The ratio of interstitial to framework molecules is constrained to reproduce the experimental density. By treating three model distances, the root-mean-square displacements of the model distances, and the occupancy of framework and cavity sites as variable parameters, the authors were able to calculate radial distribution functions in close agreement with experiment. The agreement can be seen in Fig. 4.3. The authors found that the occupancy of cavity sites increases from 45 per cent at 4 °C to 57 per cent at 200 °C.

An interstitial model apparently inconsistent with the observed radial distribution for water is Pauling's (1959) 'water hydrate' model (Section 5.2 (b)). Danford and Levy (1962) showed that the radial density predicted by this model is smaller than the experimental density in the range $\bar{R} = 2\cdot8-3\cdot6$ Å, and much larger in the range $\bar{R} = 3\cdot6-4\cdot9$ Å. This work seems to be the only one in which a proposed model for water has been shown by quantitative methods to be inconsistent with the experimental radial distribution function. We should note that although the calculation indicates that Pauling's model does not accurately represent the D-structure of water, the model may still represent one of several local V-structures that exist in the liquid.

Distorted hydrogen-bond model

Pople (1951) developed a model for liquid water in which the majority of hydrogen bonds are regarded as distorted rather than broken. To facilitate interpretation of the observed radial distribution in terms of the bending of hydrogen bonds, he assumed that all molecules in liquid water are hydrogen-bonded to four neighbours, each at a fixed distance of $\bar{R}_0$. Accordingly, nearest neighbours are constrained to be $\bar{R}_0$ distant from the central molecule, but the distances from the central molecule to the second (next-nearest), third, and further neighbours will depend on the extent of hydrogen-bond bending. This situation is illustrated in Fig. 4.7. Pople further assumed that each water molecule is exactly tetrahedral, so that angles between O–H bond directions and lone-pair directions are all $\cos^{-1}(-1/3)$. A hydrogen bond is considered undistorted in Pople's model when both the O–H of a donor water molecule and the lone-pair to which it is hydrogen-bonded lie along the oxygen–oxygen line of the two molecules. In other words, the energy of hydrogen-bond bending vanishes when all $H_2O \cdots H_2O \cdots H_2O$ angles are tetrahedral, as is the case in ice I. When either the lone-pair direction or the O–H bond direction depart from the oxygen–oxygen line by an angle ϕ, the hydrogen bond is distorted, and the energy of the system is increased by

$$\Delta U = k_\phi(1 - \cos \phi). \qquad (4.2)$$

The quantity k_ϕ in this equation is called the 'hydrogen-bond bending-force constant' by Pople; it will be discussed further in section 5.3.

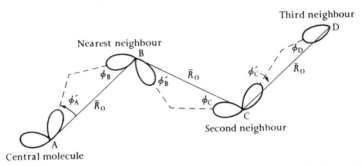

FIG. 4.7. Hydrogen-bond bending in water according to Pople (1951). Molecule A is the central molecule and B, C, and D are neighbours. Each lobe represents either an O–H bond or a lone-pair of electrons, and the angles ϕ_i show the amount of bond bending. The nearest-neighbour distance, $\bar{R}_0$, is fixed.

Pople regarded the observed radial distribution function in the range $\bar{R} = 0$–6 Å as the sum of contributions from the nearest, second, and third neighbours. He formulated expressions for these contributions and then fitted the sum of the contributions to the experimental distribution curves of Morgan and Warren (1938). The four nearest neighbours were assumed to be distributed in a Gaussian band about $\bar{R} = \bar{R}_0$, and the expression for their contribution contains two parameters determining the position and width of the distribution. Pople employed classical statistical mechanics and rather involved analytical geometry to derive expressions for the contributions of the second and third neighbours. These contributions depend on the ratio of the hydrogen-bond bending-force constant to the temperature and on the number of second and third neighbours, in addition to the positions of the nearest neighbours. By varying the number of neighbours, the hydrogen-bond bending-force constant, and the parameters of the Gaussian distribution of the first neighbours, Pople achieved a good fit to Morgan and Warren's experimental distribution functions. The best fit was obtained with the following values for parameters: a hydrogen-bond bending constant of 3.78×10^{-13} erg radian^{-2}, 11 second neighbours and 22 third neighbours, and an average distance for the nearest neighbours of 2.80 Å at 1.5 °C and 2.95 Å at 83 °C.

The calculated contribution to the radial distribution curve of each

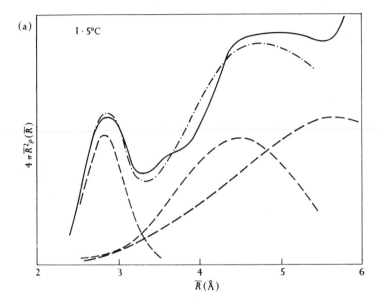

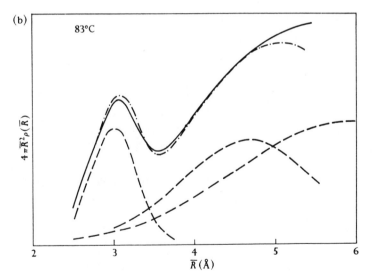

FIG. 4.8. Contributions to the radial distribution function of water as calculated by Pople (1951). (a) 1·5 °C. (b) 83 °C. Experimental results of Morgan and Warren (———). Calculated contributions of separate shells of neighbours (– – – –). Calculated total (– · – · – ·). From Pople (1951).

of the first three shells is shown in Fig. 4.8. From these it is seen that the bending of hydrogen bonds causes the second- and third-neighbour contributions to be more diffuse than the nearest-neighbour contributions. This means that the variety of possible local V-structures in liquid water is far greater than the number in ice. Note especially that hydrogen-bond bending permits some of the second and third neighbours to penetrate into regions near the central molecule. In some local V-structures second or third neighbours are within 3·0 Å of the central molecule. This offers an explanation for two features of the observed radial distribution functions:

(1) Apparent numbers of nearest neighbours greater than four (Table 4.1) can arise from the superposition of the tails of the distributions of the second and third neighbours with the distribution of nearest neighbours. At higher temperatures (Fig. 4.8 (b)) the tails become more pronounced and the apparent number of nearest neighbours increases.

(2) The high density of water around 3·5 Å relative to ice (Fig. 4.6) is also caused by the penetration of non-nearest neighbours into regions closer than 4·0 Å from the central molecule.

Finally, we should note that Pople's model does not account for the small peak which appears at about 3·5 Å in the recent radial distribution functions of Narten *et al.* (1966). This peak can be explained by the model which we consider next.

Random network model

A model for the V-structure of water suggested by Bernal (1964) may be considered an extension of the distorted hydrogen-bond model. Each water molecule is hydrogen-bonded to four other molecules, although the bonds may be considerably distorted. The linked, four-coordinated molecules form, instead of an ordered lattice as in the ices, an irregular network of rings. Many rings contain five molecules, because the H–O–H angle of a water molecule is near to the 108° angle of a five-membered ring, but others contain four, six, seven, and more molecules.

The radial distribution function for a random network of rings would be generally similar to that for Pople's bent hydrogen-bond model but would differ in one respect: the random network would produce one or possibly several small peaks in the function between the larger peaks near 2·9 and 4·5 Å. These small peaks would arise from at least two types of configurations:

(1) Four-membered rings: rings formed by four hydrogen-bonded water molecules are found in ice VI (Fig. 3.8). The oxygen–oxygen distance of hydrogen-bonded molecules in these rings is 2·81 Å and the separation of non-hydrogen-bonded molecules is about 3·5 Å.

(2) Juxtaposition of two six-membered rings by means of bent hydrogen bonds in such a way that non-hydrogen-bonded molecules are held closely together. Such a configuration is found in ice II, where every molecule has a non-hydrogen-bonded neighbour at a distance of 3·24 Å. In addition, each molecule has seven other neighbours in the range 3·52–3·89 Å (Table 4.1).

Bernal (1964) reported that a rough calculation of the radial distribution function for a random network of rings was in general agreement with experiment. No extensive calculations have been reported which would determine if this model can account for the peak near 3·5 Å in the experimental distribution functions.

4.3. Thermodynamic properties†

In this section we summarize some of the most important thermodynamic properties of liquid water, and discuss the molecular motions and interactions that account for them. We consider the thermal energy first and then the P–V–T properties; in both cases we discuss interpretations of the experimental data in terms of models that have been proposed for the structure of water.

It is impossible, of course, to infer details of the V-structure of a liquid from thermodynamic measurements alone. This is because the time elapsed during a typical thermodynamic measurement is much longer than the interval between diffusive motions of molecules. Once a structural model has been proposed on the basis of other data, however, the thermodynamic properties associated with the model can be computed by statistical mechanical methods. If a model accurately describes a liquid and if the computations are carried out rigorously, then the calculated properties must agree with experiment. Unfortunately, truly rigorous calculations for water are not yet possible and consequently the thermodynamic properties cannot be used at present to confirm any particular model of the liquid structure (see Chapter 5).

† Dorsey (1940) compiled a wealth of thermodynamic data on water. More recently, Stimson (1955) assembled accurate C_P data for atmospheric pressure; Owen et al. (1956), Kennedy et al. (1958), and Kell and Whalley (1965) reported additional P–V–T measurements; Sharp (1962) tabulated P–V–T data and thermal energy functions for the range −10–1000 °C and 1–250 000 bars; and Kell (1967) gave expressions for the accurate representation of P–V–T properties at atmospheric pressure.

(a) Thermal energy

The temperature dependence of the heat capacity, enthalpy, entropy, and Gibbs free energy of water under 1 atm pressure are shown in Fig. 3.12. The heat capacity was determined by direct measurement and the

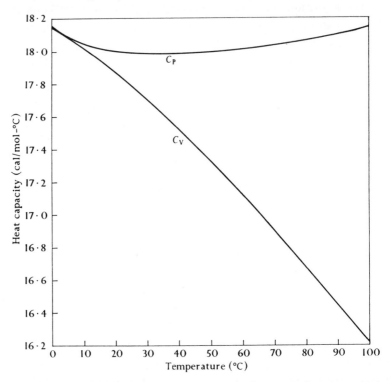

FIG. 4.9. The temperature dependences of the heat capacity at constant volume, C_V, and the heat capacity at constant pressure, C_P, of water at 1 atm pressure. Values of C_P were converted from the values reported by Stimson (1955), assuming that the molecular weight of water is 18·01534 and 1 joule = 0·23895 cal. Values of C_V were calculated from the thermodynamic relationship $C_V = C_P - TV\beta^2/\gamma_T$, using the C_P values of this figure along with data of Figs. 4.13, 4.14, and 4.15.

other quantities by integration of the proper functions of the heat capacity. Because the value of PV for liquid water at 1 atm pressure is less than 0·0005 kcal mol^{-1}, the internal energy and Helmholtz free energy of this phase are virtually equal, respectively, to the enthalpy and Gibbs free energy. The heat capacity of liquid water, as noted in Section 3.3(b), is nearly twice that of ice at the melting-point, and more than twice that of steam at the boiling-point. The heat capacity at constant volume decreases by about 11 per cent as water is heated from 0 to 100 °C, whereas the heat capacity at constant pressure changes by less than 1 per cent over the same range, passing through a minimum near 35 °C. This behaviour is shown in Fig. 4.9.

The sharp increases in the enthalpy at the melting- and boiling-points represent the latent heats of fusion and vaporization. Accurate values for these enthalpy changes are listed in Table 3.7, along with other thermodynamic constants for phase changes of H_2O and D_2O. Note that the internal energy of fusion is almost exactly equal to the enthalpy of fusion; but the internal energy of vaporization is some 0·7 kcal mol^{-1} less than the enthalpy of vaporization owing to the large volume change on vaporization.

Molecular basis of thermal energy

Comparison of the thermodynamic properties of water with those of other liquids suggests that hydrogen bonds greatly affect the properties of water. Consider the heat of vaporization as an example. The molal heats of vaporization for the related sequence of compounds H_2Te, H_2Se, H_2S decrease with decreasing molecular weight. This might lead one to expect that H_2O, the next compound in the sequence, would have an even smaller heat of vaporization; but H_2O has a heat of vaporization more than twice that of H_2S. This shows, of course, that the cohesive forces between water molecules are extraordinarily strong. The most likely origin of the extra cohesive energy of water is hydrogen bonding between molecules in the liquid. The presence of hydrogen bonding in water also provides a qualitative explanation for the unusual values of other thermodynamic properties, including the melting-point, boiling-point, and heat capacity. See Edsall and Wyman (1958) and Pauling (1960) for discussions of the effect of hydrogen bonding on these and other properties.

Some progress towards a more quantitative understanding of the thermodynamic properties of water—particularly the heat capacity and the related thermal energy functions—has been made in recent years. Basic to this understanding is the concept of *configurational* contributions to the thermodynamic properties.† These contributions arise when the structure of a phase changes with temperature or pressure; for instance, each molecule in a phase may be able to exist with two coordination numbers, one of which predominates at low temperature,

† The concept of configurational contributions to thermodynamic properties has been discussed by Bernal (1937) and Kauzmann (1948) among others. Davis and Litovitz (1965) considered possible values for the configurational contributions (called 'relaxational' contributions by them) to the thermodynamic properties of water.

the other at high temperature. Such structural changes are accompanied by changes in energy that produce contributions to the heat capacity and compressibility. Since the crystal structure of ice does not change with the temperature, there is no configurational contribution to its heat capacity in the sense defined here; raising the temperature of ice increases its energy solely through the excitation of intermolecular vibrations. When liquid water is heated there is a similar excitation of vibrations, but this can account for only about half of the heat capacity of water. The rest of the thermal energy required to heat water must be utilized in changing the structure of the liquid—by breaking and deforming hydrogen bonds, by changing coordination numbers, etc. Indeed, we know from the radial distribution function (Section 4.2 (a)) that such changes do occur as water is heated; this function changes with temperature, showing that the average relative positions of water molecules are altered during heating; and this means, of course, that the potential energy associated with the interactions of water molecules changes with temperature.

Let us call the contribution to the heat capacity arising from this change the *configurational heat capacity*. If we call the contribution arising from the excitation of mechanical degrees of freedom the *vibrational heat capacity*, we can express the observed heat capacity in the form

$$C_V(\text{observed}) = C_V(\text{vib}) + C_V(\text{config}). \qquad (4.3)$$

Similarly, the internal energy, the coefficient of expansion, and the compressibility of the liquid can each be regarded as the sum of a vibrational and a configurational contribution.

The term 'vibrational' may be slightly misleading in this context, since the degrees of freedom that contribute to $C_V(\text{vib})$ may be rotational and translational as well as vibrational. In steam near 100 °C, for example, increases in the kinetic energy of molecular rotation and translation each contribute $\frac{3}{2}R$ to the heat capacity, or a total of $3R = 5 \cdot 96$ cal/mol–°C. This is only slightly less than the observed C_V of steam at 100 °C, $6 \cdot 2$ cal/mol–°C (see Fig. 4.10), so that changes in the potential energy of the molecules with temperature contribute very little to C_V. In any case if we stretch our use of the term 'vibrational' to include rotational and translational degrees of freedom, then the heat capacity of steam, like that of ice, is 'vibrational'.

A simple calculation confirms that the heat capacity of ice is largely vibrational. Suppose that a mole of ice executes $6N$ modes of intermolecular vibration: $3N$ hindered translations and $3N$ librations. If it is further assumed that the frequencies of both types of modes are distributed in Debye spectra having characteristic Debye frequencies of ν_T and ν_L, the temperature dependence of C_V can be easily evaluated from tables (for example, Pitzer 1953). Let us take $\nu_T = 200$ cm^{-1} and

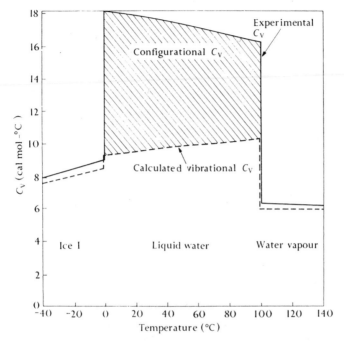

FIG. 4.10. Separation of the experimental heat capacity of H_2O into vibrational and configurational contributions. The vibrational contribution was calculated as described in the text; the configurational contribution is the difference between the experimental and the vibrational values. The calculation of the vibrational contribution for the liquid region is described on p. 179. Data from Dorsey (1940, p. 104) for 100–140 °C, from Fig. 4.9 for 0–100 °C, and from Giauque and Stout (1936) for −40 to 0 °C. Experimental curve from −40 to 0° C is actually C_P, which is probably several tenths of a cal/mol–°C greater than C_V.

$\nu_L = 800$ cm^{-1}, frequencies near the maxima of the ν_T and ν_L absorption bands in ice (Section 3.5 (a)). Fig. 4.10 shows C_V between −40 and 0 °C calculated from these frequencies. Though this model is certainly too simple to represent the lattice vibrations of ice accurately, the calculated heat capacity agrees well enough with experiment to indicate that most of the heat capacity of ice is vibrational in origin.

In contrast to the heat capacities of ice and steam, the heat capacity of liquid water is much too large to arise entirely from thermal excitation of mechanical degrees of freedom. This is evident from another simple calculation. It is well known that each fully excited mode of vibration contributes R to the heat capacity (for example, see Kauzmann 1966). If each molecule in liquid water participates in six modes of lattice vibrations (three hindered translations and three librations; Section 4.7 (c)) then the maximum heat capacity of the liquid arising from vibrations is $6R = 11 \cdot 9$ cal/mol–°C, only about two-thirds of the observed heat capacity. In fact, the heat capacity arising from vibrations is certainly less than $6R$ since the librational modes are not fully excited at room temperature. Moreover, if some water molecules undergo free rotation and translation instead of librations and hindered translations, the maximum heat capacity will be smaller, because rotational and translational motions together can contribute a maximum of $3R$ to the heat capacity.

Clearly the configurational contribution to the heat capacity of liquid water is of the same order of magnitude as the vibrational contribution, and it is this contribution that is responsible for the marked increase in the heat capacity at the melting-point. This large configurational contribution is undoubtedly associated with the distortion, and perhaps the breaking, of hydrogen bonds. With these ideas in mind, let us see how different models for the structure of water account for the observed heat capacity and related properties.

Interpretation in terms of hydrogen-bond breaking

One interpretation of the thermal energy of water is based on the premise that heating breaks hydrogen bonds. The models that use this interpretation are those that postulate a mixture or an interstitial model for water.† Though these studies differ in the specific model taken for the liquid structure, they all assume that the thermal energy is governed by the equilibrium

$$\text{O–H}\cdots\text{O} \rightleftharpoons \text{O–H} + \text{O},$$

for which ΔH^0 is positive. Thus as the temperature is raised, the equilibrium shifts to the right and the configurational potential energy of the system increases.

Two parameters are common to most of these studies: the energy required to break a hydrogen bond and the fraction of broken hydrogen bonds in the liquid at some temperature. Let us comment on these parameters here and consider the values they are given in several studies. More detailed descriptions of the models adopted in these studies, and discussion of the accuracy with which the various models are able to

† These studies include the ones of Grjotheim and Krogh-Moe (1954), Frank and Quist (1961), Némethy and Scheraga (1962, 1964), Marchi and Eyring (1964), and others.

reproduce thermodynamic properties, will be presented in Chapter 5. We shall find that a consistent interpretation of the thermal energy of water can be given in terms of broken hydrogen bonds, provided the mathematical model contains sufficient flexibility in the way of adjustable parameters.

The usual meaning of the expression 'the energy of the hydrogen bond in liquid water' is the energy required to convert a hydrogen-bonded O–H group in the liquid to a non-hydrogen-bonded group still in the liquid:

$$(O-H \cdots O)_{\text{liquid}} \rightarrow (O-H)_{\text{liquid}}. \tag{4.4}$$

Let us denote this energy $E_{\text{H-bond-L}}$. The problem of determining $E_{\text{H-bond-L}}$ is similar to that of calculating the energy of the hydrogen bond in ice from Definition 4 of Section 3.6 (a).[†] The basic difficulty is that a non-hydrogen-bonded O–H group in the liquid still interacts with neighbouring molecules through dispersion and other forces, and the energy of these interactions cannot be evaluated by any direct means. In fact, it seems likely that the energy of this reaction depends on temperature and pressure, since the energy of a hydrogen bond is sensitive to the environment of the bond (Section 3.6 (c)). Various procedures have been used to estimate $E_{\text{H-bond-L}}$, and the resulting values range widely (see Table 4.2). Each procedure constitutes an operational definition for $E_{\text{H-bond-L}}$, so it is not surprising that differing values are found. Whether any of the values in Table 4.2 corresponds to the energy of the reaction depicted by eqn (4.4) is not certain.

The fraction of broken hydrogen bonds at each temperature is a second parameter common to several interpretations of the thermal energy based on mixture and interstitial models. Estimates of this parameter also cover a wide range: a recent compilation of values for 0 °C (Falk and Ford 1966) includes eighteen estimates that range from 0·02 to 0·72. The temperature dependences of a few estimates are shown in Fig. 4.11. The estimates of Némethy and Scheraga and of Haggis et al. are based on thermodynamic data, that of Grjotheim and Krogh-Moe on molar volume data, and that of Walrafen (1966) on the intensity of the ν_T band (Section 4.7 (a)) in the Raman spectrum. Haggis et al. ascribe almost the entire energy of vaporization to hydrogen-bond breaking. They thus predict fewer broken bonds in the liquid than do the other authors, all of whom ascribe a large part of the energy of vaporization to other forces.

[†] See Section 3.6 (a) for a discussion of the meaning of the term 'hydrogen-bond energy'.

Even spectroscopic estimates of the fraction of broken hydrogen bonds range widely. Walrafen (1966) estimated from the intensity of the ν_T band that over 80 per cent of hydrogen bonds are broken at 65° C, whereas Wall and Hornig (1965) estimated from the ν_s band that less

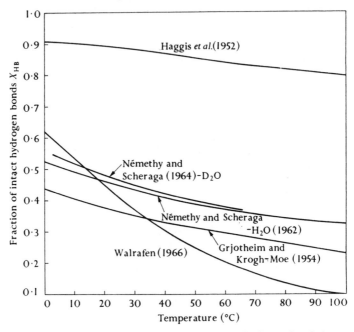

FIG. 4.11. Several estimates of the fraction of intact hydrogen bonds in water, X_{HB}, as a function of temperature.

than 5 per cent of hydrogen bonds are broken at the same temperature. These and other spectroscopic studies are discussed at length in Section 4.7.

The discrepancies among the estimates for both $E_{H\text{-bond-L}}$ and the fraction of broken bonds in the liquid may have to do with the nature of the potential energy surface for the interaction of water molecules. The shape of this surface may be such that the term 'broken hydrogen bond' is not useful for the description of interactions of water molecules in the pure liquid. This possibility is considered in Section 4.8 (a).

Interpretation in terms of hydrogen-bond distortion

Models depicting water as an irregular network of molecules linked by distorted hydrogen bonds have been proposed (Sections 4.2 (b) and 5.3), so it is important to ask whether such models can account for the thermal energy of the liquid. A simple calculation suggests that they can. In the

TABLE 4.2

Estimated values for the energy of a hydrogen bond in liquid water,
$E_{\text{H-bond-L}}$

Authors	$E_{\text{H-bond-L}}$ (kcal/mol-of-hydrogen-bond)	Method of estimation
Némethy and Scheraga (1962)	1·3	Fit of thermodynamic functions derived from a model to experimental values.
(1964) for liquid D_2O	1·5	Fit of thermodynamic functions derived from a model to experimental values.
Grjotheim and Krogh-Moe (1954)	1·3 to 2·6	From molar volume as a function of temperature, and a model of the liquid.
Worley and Klotz (1966)	2·4	From temperature dependence of overtone region of infra-red spectrum.
Walrafen (1967 b)	2·5	From the temperature dependence of the uncoupled O–D stretching band in the Raman spectrum (Section 4.7 (b)).
Walrafen (1966)	2·8	From the temperature dependence of the intensity of the ν_T band in the Raman spectrum (Section 4.7 (a)).
Scatchard et al. (1952)	3·4	From thermodynamic properties of hydrogen peroxide–water mixtures and auxiliary assumptions.
Haggis et al. (1952) Pauling (1940)	4·5	From Definition 3 of Section 3.6 (a).

first step of this calculation we estimate the vibrational heat capacity and vibrational internal energy of water. By subtracting the vibrational internal energy from the experimental energy, we obtain the configurational contribution to the energy. We then show that if the frequency of the O–H stretching vibration of water molecules is taken as an index of hydrogen-bond energy, distortions of hydrogen bonds will account for the configurational energy.

We compute the vibrational heat capacity for liquid water just as we did above for ice. We again assume that the hydrogen-bonded network of water molecules executes $6N$ modes of vibration, and that these modes are distributed in two Debye spectra, this time having characteristic frequencies of 654 cm^{-1} and 168 cm^{-1}. The 654 cm^{-1} frequency is obtained by scaling the frequency used in the ice calculation by the ratio of the experimental infra-red absorption frequencies of the ν_L band in water and in ice I (Sections 3.5 and 4.7). The 168 cm^{-1} frequency comes from a similar scaling of the 200 cm^{-1} frequency used in the ice calculation with the observed infra-red frequencies of the ν_T band. Using these frequencies we find the vibrational contribution to C_V of the liquid shown in Fig. 4.10. Note that $C_V(\text{vib})$ is slightly larger for liquid water than for ice. Hydrogen bonds are more easily distorted in the liquid and thus the vibrating molecules take up more thermal energy than H_2O molecules in ice.

The difference between the observed and vibrational heat capacity is the configurational heat capacity, which, in the model we are considering, arises from the increasing distortion of hydrogen bonds as water is

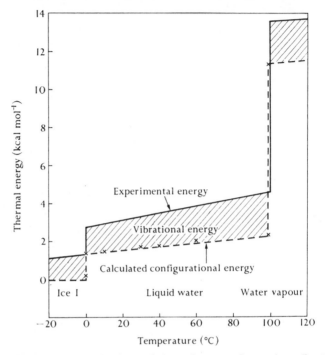

FIG. 4.12. Separation of the observed thermal energy of water into vibrational and configurational contributions. The vibrational contribution (shaded areas) was calculated as described in the text and the configurational contribution was obtained by subtracting the vibrational energy from the observed energy. The crosses indicate the configurational energy calculated from eqn (4.5) and experimental O–H stretching frequencies. For the vapour the 'vibrational' contribution is $3RT$, from molecular translation and rotation. Spectroscopic data come from Falk and Ford (1966) for ice and liquid water and from Benedict et al. (1956) for water vapour. The O–H stretching frequency of liquid water at 0 °C was estimated by extrapolation of Falk and Ford's data.

heated. From Fig. 4.10 it can be seen that C_V(config) is about 50 per cent of the observed C_V at 0° and decreases to about 35 per cent of C_V at 100 °C. These are roughly the same values of the configurational heat capacity as those found by Davis and Litovitz (1965) from a mixture model for water.

The calculated vibrational contributions to the thermal energy of ice and liquid water, based on Debye spectra with the same characteristic frequencies as used in the heat-capacity calculations, are shown in Fig. 4.12. The 'vibrational' contribution to the energy of water vapour is the calculated kinetic energy of molecular rotation and translation, $3RT$. As with the heat capacity, the configurational contribution is obtained by subtracting the vibrational contribution from the experimental quantity. On the basis of this calculation, the configurational energy is roughly 50 per cent of the observed energy over the temperature range 0–100 °C.

The question we must now consider is whether distortions of hydrogen bonds can account for this configurational energy. With an accurate potential function for the distortion of hydrogen bonds we might be able to answer this question directly; in the absence of such a function we can still obtain a tentative answer by using the O–H stretching frequency as an index of hydrogen-bond strength. From spectroscopic studies it is known that when an O–H group forms a hydrogen bond, its stretching frequency is reduced and that stronger hydrogen bonds are associated with greater reductions in frequency. Relationships of the form

$$-\Delta H^0 \text{ (kcal/mol)} = C \times \Delta\nu_{\text{O-H}} \text{ (cm}^{-1}) + K, \qquad (4.5)$$

where C and K are constants, have been proposed for the shift in O–H stretching frequency $\Delta\nu_{\text{O-H}}$ when a hydrogen bond of strength ΔH^0 is formed. Singh et al. (1966) found, for example, that eqn (4.5) with $C = 0.010$ and $K = 2.37$ fitted the data for ninety-seven hydrogen-bonded phenols reasonably well.

For liquid water, Wall and Hornig (1965) suggested that the frequency of the maximum of the uncoupled[†] O–H stretching band is characteristic of the average hydrogen-bond energy, more distorted hydrogen bonds having higher frequencies. If this suggestion is correct, and if the configurational energy arises from distortions of hydrogen bonds, it should be possible to correlate the frequency of the maximum of the uncoupled O–H stretching band with the configurational energy. It turns out that such a correlation is possible using eqn (4.5). The quantity $\Delta\nu_{\text{O-H}}$ in (4.5) is taken as the frequency difference of O–H stretching of HDO vapour (3707 cm^{-1}) and the maximum of the uncoupled O–H stretching band in liquid water or ice. The quantity ΔH^0 is taken as the difference of the configurational energy, per mole of hydrogen bonds, of water vapour at 100 °C and of liquid water or ice at some lower temperature. With $C = 0.007$ and $K = 2.70$, the configurational energy

† This term was defined in Section 3.5 (a). Wall and Hornig's paper will be discussed in Section 4.7 (b).

computed from (4.5) agrees closely with the configurational energy derived above for all three phases (see Fig. 4.12). This correspondence suggests that the configurational energy of water may be accounted for by increased distortion of hydrogen bonds as the liquid is heated. Thus it seems that a model depicting water as a network of distorted hydrogen bonds is not inconsistent with the observed thermal energy of water.

(b) Pressure–volume–temperature relations

The molar volume of H_2O at atmospheric pressure is shown as a function of temperature in Fig. 4.13, along with the molar volumes of several other isotopes. Upon fusion, the molar volume of H_2O ice drops by 8·3 per cent to 18·0182 cm³. As the temperature is raised the molar volume of the liquid continues to fall, reaching 18·0158 cm³ at 4 °C, and then gradually increases to 18·798 cm³ at the boiling-point. Note that the decrease in volume between 0 and 4 °C amounts to only 0·013 per cent of the volume at 4°, and to only 0·31 per cent of the increase from 4 to 100 °C. The molar volume of liquid D_2O passes through a minimum value of 18·1082 cm³ near 11·2 °C.

Several investigators have maintained that the temperature dependence of the molar volume of water exhibits abrupt changes of slope or 'kinks'. For example, Lavergne and Drost-Hansen (1956) performed a statistical analysis of the accurate density measurements of Chappuis. They concluded (Drost-Hansen 1965 a) that 'the data points in the range from approximately 5 to 41 °C (as far as Chappuis's data go) may possibly be better represented by three different, distinct curve segments' than by a single curve. Another kink was reported by Antonoff and Conan at 50·5 °C (1949). Subsequently Kell and Whalley (1965) searched for this kink but failed to find it. They measured the specific volume of water at 0·25 °C intervals from 47·5 to 52·0 °C and found it smooth to 1 ppm. Falk and Kell (1966) examined numerous reports of kinks in the properties of water, including those mentioned here; they concluded that the sizes of the reported kinks were in all cases comparable to the precision of the measurements.

The derivatives of the molar volume with respect to temperature and pressure are given by the coefficients of thermal expansion and compressibility. The isopiestic coefficient of thermal expansion, $\beta = (1/V)(\partial V/\partial T)_P$, is shown in Fig. 4.14. It is negative from 0 to 4 °C where water contracts with increasing temperature, and positive above 4 °C. This figure also shows the region of negative thermal expansion of ice below 63 °K. Fig. 4.15 shows the isothermal coefficient of compressibility, $\gamma_T = -(1/V)(\partial V/\partial P)_T$. It decreases as water is heated from 0 °C, passes through a minimum at 46 °C, and then increases.

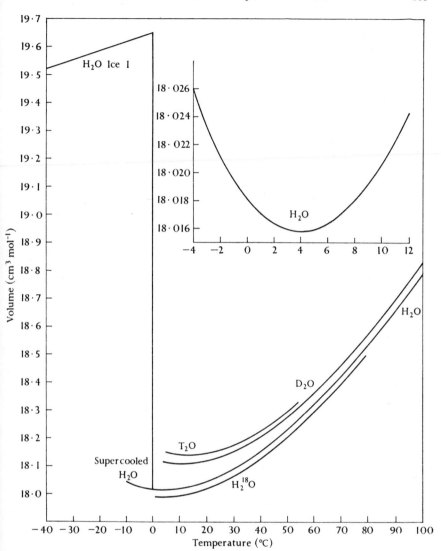

Fig. 4.13. The molar volumes of H_2O ice I and four isotopic liquid waters at 1 atm pressure. The inset is an enlargement of the curve for liquid H_2O between -4 and $+12\,°C$. The data for ice I are from Table 3.10 (b). The curves for the liquid were calculated from eqn (4.6) and the following molecular weights: H_2O, 18·0153; D_2O, 20·028; $H_2^{18}O$, 20·015; T_2O, 22·04.

Kell (1967) fitted mathematical functions to the best available P–V–T data for water at 1 atm pressure. For the temperature dependence of the density he used the expression

$$\rho_0 = \frac{\sum_{n=0}^{5} a_n t^n}{1 + b_1 t}, \tag{4.6}$$

where t is the temperature in °C. The coefficients producing the optimum fit to the data for H_2O, D_2O, $H_2{}^{18}O$, $D_2{}^{18}O$, and T_2O are listed in Table 4.3. The standard error of eqn (4.6) in representing the data is generally smaller than the estimated

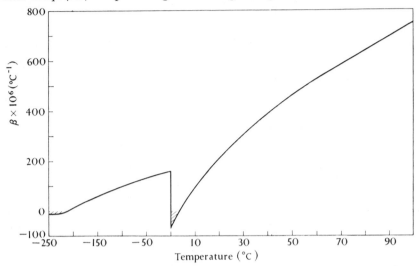

Fig. 4.14. The isopiestic coefficient of thermal expansion, β, for ice I and liquid water at 1 atm pressure. Regions of negative β are shaded. Note that the temperature axis is contracted below 0° C. The data for ice I are from Table 3.10 and Dantl (1962); those for liquid water are from the compilation of Kell (1967).

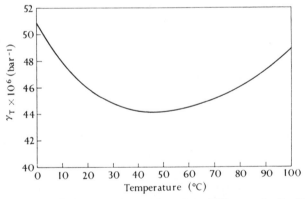

Fig. 4.15. The coefficient of isothermal compressibility, γ_T, for liquid water at 1 atm pressure. Data from Kell (1967).

accuracy of the data themselves. The valid temperature range of eqn (4.6) for the different isotopic species is also given in the table.

To fit the isothermal compressibility at one atmosphere pressure, Kell (1967) and Kell and Whalley (1965) used the power series

$$\gamma_T = \left(\sum_{n=0}^{5} c_n t^n \right) \times 10^{-6} \text{ bar}^{-1}, \tag{4.7}$$

where t is the temperature in °C and the coefficients are

$c_0 = 50 \cdot 9804$, $c_1 = -0 \cdot 374957$, $c_2 = 7 \cdot 21324 \times 10^{-3}$,

$c_3 = -64 \cdot 1785 \times 10^{-6}$, $c_4 = 0 \cdot 343024 \times 10^{-6}$, $c_5 = -0 \cdot 684212 \times 10^{-9}$.

This expression represents the data from 0 to 150 °C to within $0 \cdot 04 \times 10^{-6}$ bar^{-1}.

The negative thermal expansion of water from 0 to 4 °C and the decrease in compressibility from 0 to 46 °C are anomalous: the compressibilities and volumes of other liquids increase monotonically as they are heated. Bridgman (1912, 1931) found that these anomalies disappear as water is compressed. The minimum in the compressibility near 50 °C becomes less pronounced as pressure is applied and disappears altogether near 3000 atm. The behaviour of the volume near 0 °C is more complicated and is summarized in Fig. 4.16 (a). The uppermost plot of volume against temperature is for nearly atmospheric pressure and shows the familiar minimum at 4 °C. As the pressure is increased to 1000 kg cm^{-2}, the minimum is displaced to lower temperatures. By 1500 kg cm^{-2} a maximum appears near -10 °C in addition to the minimum near -4 °C. At 2500 kg cm^{-2}, the maximum and minimum merge into a point of inflexion, and at still higher pressures the volume increases smoothly with temperature. Thus, under high pressure, the molar volume of water behaves like that of most liquids.

The change with pressure of the thermal expansion of water is also complex, as is evident from Fig. 4.16 (b). At 0 °C the coefficient of thermal expansion increases as water is compressed to about 4000 kg cm^{-2}, but then decreases upon further compression. The thermal expansion is nearly independent of pressure at 40 °C; at higher temperatures it decreases with pressure, as do the thermal expansions of most substances. Bridgman summarized the effect of compression on the thermodynamic properties of water by saying that water becomes a 'normal liquid' at high pressures.

Molecular basis of P–V–T properties

From the density of water and the structure of ice I, Bernal and Fowler (1933) reasoned that water must have a more open structure than the disordered, close-packed structures of simple liquids such as argon and neon. They noted that the intermolecular separation of water molecules in ice I is about $2 \cdot 8$ Å, corresponding to a 'molecular radius' of about $1 \cdot 4$ Å. A disordered, close-packed assembly of molecules with radius $1 \cdot 4$ Å would have a density of $1 \cdot 84$ g ml^{-1}. Hence, to account for the observed density of water, $1 \cdot 0$ g ml^{-1}, one must assume either that liquid water is a close-packed liquid in which the effective molecular radius has

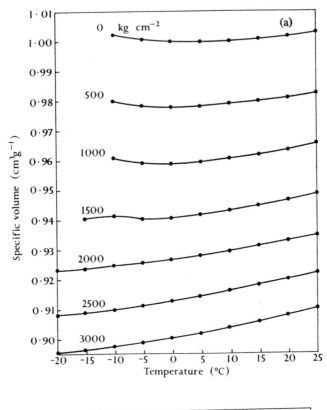

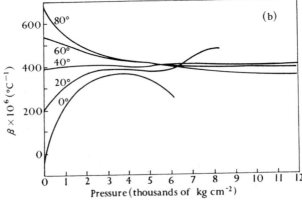

FIG. 4.16. *P–V–T* properties of water at high pressures. (*a*) Specific volume
of water as a function of temperature for several fixed pressures. The pressures
in units of kg cm⁻² are indicated above the curves (1 kg cm⁻² = 0·968 atm).
Based on data from Bridgman (1912). (*b*) The coefficient of thermal expansion
of water, *β*, as a function of pressure for several fixed temperatures. From
Bridgman (1931).

TABLE 4.3†

Coefficients for the representation of the density of water by eqn (4.6) and properties of the equation

Coefficients, g cm⁻³	H_2O	D_2O	$H_2^{18}O$	$D_2^{18}O$	T_2O
a_0	0.9998396	1.104690	1.112333	1.215371	1.21293
$10^3 a_1$	18.224944	20.09315	13.92547	18.61961	11.7499
$10^6 a_2$	−7.922210	−9.24227	−8.81358	−10.70052	−11.612
$10^9 a_3$	−55.44846	−55.9509	−22.8730	−35.1257	
$10^{12} a_4$	149.7562	79.9512			
$10^{15} a_5$	−393.2952				
$10^3 b_1$	18.159725	17.96190	12.44953	15.08867	9.4144
Range of function (°C)	0–150	3.5–100	1–79	3.5–72	5–54
Estimated accuracy of data (ppm)	0.5–20	10	50	100	200
Temp. of maximum density (°C)	3.984	11.185	4.211	11.438	13.403
Maximum density (g cm⁻³)	0.999972	1.10600	1.11249	1.21688	1.21501

† Taken from Kell (1967).

expanded from its value of 1·4 Å in ice to 1·72 Å, or that the arrangement of molecules is much more open in water than in close-packed liquids. Bernal and Fowler were able to rule out the former possibility from the X-ray diffraction pattern of water (Section 4.2 (a)). As mentioned above, they attributed the relatively open structure of water to the presence of extensive four-coordination of molecules in the liquid.

Interpretations of the temperature dependence of the molar volume of water are usually based on the supposition that two competing effects take place as water is heated:

(1) The open structure arising from the four-coordination of molecules weakens or breaks down, thus reducing the volume. This process may be regarded as a continuation of fusion.

(2) The amplitudes of anharmonic intermolecular vibrations increase, thus enlarging the volume.

Effect (1) is dominant below 4 °C where the thermal expansion is negative, and effect (2) is dominant above 4 °C.

We can consider these two effects as the configurational and vibrational contributions to the coefficient of thermal expansion. Effect (1) is the configurational contribution, since it is associated with changes in the average configuration of molecules in the liquid as water is heated. This contribution to β is negative. Effect (2) is the vibrational contribution to β; it is positive in sign and, above 4 °C, larger in magnitude than the configurational contribution.

Let us briefly consider how these effects are treated in studies which assume different models for the structure of water (Section 4.2 (b) and Chapter 5):

Mixture models (for example, Grjotheim and Krogh-Moe 1954, Némethy and Scheraga 1962): hydrogen-bonded clusters are assumed to have a larger molar volume than non-hydrogen-bonded water. Hence the conversion of clusters to non-hydrogen-bonded molecules as water is heated gives rise to a negative ΔV and accounts for effect (1). Vibrational thermal expansion of both the clusters and the non-hydrogen-bonded molecules accounts for effect (2).

Bridgman (1931, p. 144) stated that a mixture model can completely explain the temperature dependence of the molar volume at high pressures (Fig. 4.16 (a)). It must be assumed that the clusters are more compressible than the rest of the liquid. As the pressure is increased, the molar volume of the clusters approaches that of the rest of the liquid, and effect (1) becomes less pronounced. Eventually the volumes of the two components are identical and the liquid exhibits normal thermal expansion.

A different explanation for the high-pressure data is the following: owing to the smaller volume of the non-hydrogen-bonded molecules, pressure shifts the equilibrium between clusters and non-hydrogen-bonded molecules towards the latter. At high pressures, fewer molecules remain in clusters and effect (1) becomes less important than effect (2). According to this view, the part of the compressibility that arises from the shift in equilibrium can be considered the configurational contribution, and the part that arises from compression of the individual components can be considered the vibrational contribution. If one could measure the compressibility of the liquid within a very short time (say within 10^{-11} s), only the vibrational contribution would be detected since the diffusional jumps of molecules that give rise to the configurational contribution cannot take place. Rapid measurements of the compressibility can be made by ultrasonic methods. Slie *et al.* (1966) estimated from ultrasonic measurements on glycerol–water mixtures that the configurational contribution to γ_T of pure water is about 64 per cent of the observed γ_T at 0 °C. Davis and Litovitz (1965) calculated a similar value for the configurational contribution from a mixture model for water.

Interstitial models (for example, Samoilov 1965, Danford and Levy 1962): as hydrogen bonds are broken, molecules move from the framework into cavities. This is accompanied by a negative ΔV, and accounts for effect (1). Effect (2) arises from increased vibrational amplitude of the framework at higher temperature.

Distorted hydrogen-bond model (Pople 1951): as described in Section 4.2 (*b*), the bending of hydrogen bonds in liquid water brings the non-nearest neighbours of a molecule much closer on the average than they are in ice I. Pople (1951) showed that the ΔV of fusion may be attributed to this process. Heating water continues this collapse to a small extent, and thus accounts for effect (1). Effect (2) is attributed, as in other models, to increased vibrational amplitudes.

4.4. Static dielectric constant and NMR chemical shift

The static dielectric constant and the NMR chemical shift of water are properties characteristic of the D-structure of the liquid. Both properties are measured by means of electromagnetic waves having frequencies in the range 10^3–10^8 c/s. During a single oscillation of a 100-Mc electromagnetic field an average molecule experiences at least 1000 diffusional jumps, so that these properties yield no direct information about the arrangements of molecules during very short intervals of time (10^{-11} s).

(*a*) *Static dielectric constant†*

Among the most accurate determinations of the static dielectric constant of water, ϵ_0, is that of Malmberg and Maryott (1956). These

† Hasted (1961) has reviewed the literature on the dielectric properties of water.

investigators measured ϵ_0 at 5° intervals from 0 to 100 °C at atmospheric pressure and believe that their results have a maximum uncertainty of ± 0.05 units. Their data, which are shown in Fig. 4.17, fit the equation

$$\epsilon_0 = 87 \cdot 740 - 0 \cdot 40008t + 9 \cdot 398 \times 10^{-4}t^2 - 1 \cdot 410 \times 10^{-6}t^3, \qquad (4.8)$$

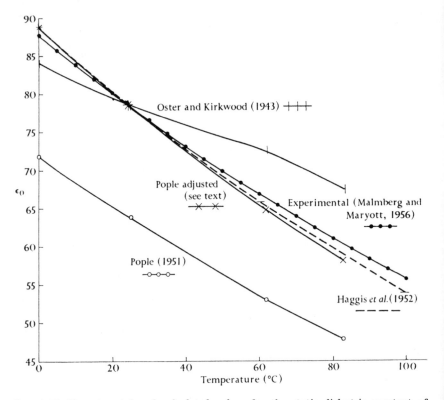

FIG. 4.17. Experimental and calculated values for the static dielectric constant of liquid water as a function of temperature.

where t is the temperature in °C. The data show nearly the same temperature dependence as the earlier measurements of Wyman and Ingalls (1938) but the values are smaller by about 0·25 units; the values are also smaller, by up to 0·17 units, than the more recent determination of ϵ_0 from 0 to 40 °C by Vidulich et al. (1967). The temperature coefficient $(\partial \ln \epsilon_0 / \partial T)_P$ derived from eqn (4.8) is nearly constant at $-4\cdot 55\,(\pm 0\cdot 03)\times 10^{-3}$ °C^{-1} from 0 to 100 °C. Owen et al. (1961) measured the pressure coefficient of ϵ_0. They found that $(\partial \ln \epsilon_0 / \partial P)_T$ increases from $45\cdot 1\times 10^{-6}$ bar^{-1} at 0 °C to $52\cdot 4\times 10^{-6}$ bar^{-1} at 70 °C.

A search by Rusche and Good (1966) for a kink reported to exist near

15 °C in the temperature dependence of ϵ_0 (Drost-Hansen 1965 b) yielded negative results.

The static dielectric constant of water in equilibrium with its vapour was measured by Akerlof and Oshry (1950) over the temperature range from the boiling-point to the critical point. They found that the dielectric constant falls continuously to 9·74 by 370 °C. It may be described over this temperature range by the equation

$$\epsilon_0 = 5321\,T^{-1}+233\cdot76-0\cdot9297\,T+0\cdot1417\times10^{-2}T^2-0\cdot8292\times10^{-6}T^3,$$
(4.9)

where T is the temperature in °K.

Malmberg (1958) determined ϵ_0 of liquid D_2O over the temperature range 4–100 °C and found that the data fit the equation

$$\epsilon_0 = 87\cdot482-0\cdot40509t+9\cdot638\times10^{-4}t^2-1\cdot333\times10^{-6}t^3, \quad (4.10)$$

where t is the temperature in °C. The dielectric constant of D_2O is slightly smaller than that of H_2O at the same temperature, the difference being no more than 0·5 unit over the 4–100 °C range.

Calculations of the dielectric constant from models

Several calculations of the dielectric constant of water have been based on Kirkwood's theory of polar dielectrics. The reader will recall from Section 3.4 (a) that Kirkwood's equation (eqn (3.6 a)) gives the dielectric constant of a substance in terms of two properties that can be calculated from a model: m, the average magnitude of the dipole moment **m** of a molecule immersed in the substance; and g, the correlation parameter (eqn (3.7)) that expresses the degree of angular correlation of the dipole moments of neighbouring molecules with the dipole moment of an arbitrary central molecule.

Oster and Kirkwood (1943) calculated the dielectric constant of water by assuming that molecules in the liquid are approximately tetrahedrally coordinated. They supposed that neighbouring molecules are connected by rigid hydrogen bonds, but that free rotation is possible about the bonds. They took the area under the first peak of the radial distribution curves of Morgan and Warren (Table 4.1) as the number of nearest neighbours, although they noted that these non-integral coordination numbers larger than four (between 4·4 and 4·9) are not entirely consistent with their simple model. This procedure led to a value for m of about 2·35 D. In calculating g, they assumed that the directions of only the nearest neighbours are correlated with the direction of the central molecule:

$$g = 1+N_1\langle\cos\gamma_1\rangle,$$

where N_1 is the number of nearest neighbours as determined from the radial distribution function at a given temperature, and $\langle \cos \gamma_1 \rangle$ is the mean cosine of the angles between the dipole moments of the neighbours and of the central molecule. The resulting values of g range from 2·63 at 0 °C to 2·82 at 83 °C. Together with the value of m, they yield the calculated dielectric constant shown in Fig. 4.17. The calculated value agrees with experiment at 25 °C, but decreases too slowly with increasing temperature. As Oster and Kirkwood noted, this discrepancy is related to their questionable result that the g values increase as the temperature is raised: the greater thermal agitation at higher temperatures would be expected to distort or break down the tetrahedral structure, and thus to decrease the angular correlation of molecules.

Pople (1951) applied Kirkwood's equation to his own distorted hydrogen-bond model (Section 4.2 (b)). He found that g for this model is given by

$$g = 1 + \sum_{i=1}^{\infty} N_i \, 3^{1-i} \cos^{2i}\alpha \left\{ 1 - \left(\frac{kT}{k_\phi}\right) \right\}^{2i},$$

where i refers to the ith coordination shell of hydrogen-bonded neighbours, 2α is the H–O–H angle, and k_ϕ is the 'hydrogen-bond bending-force constant' (see Section 4.2 (b)). Pople used the values of k_ϕ and N_i that he determined from the radial distribution function to evaluate g from this expression. He found that the first, second, and third shells contribute 1·20, 0·33, and 0·07 respectively to g at 0 °C. Thus $g \cong 2$·60 at 0 °C; it decreases to 2·46 by 83 °C. In calculating m, Pople assumed that this quantity differs from μ because of the dipole field of its four nearest neighbours. His result, $m = 2$·15 D at 0 °C decreasing to 2·08 D at 83 °C, is almost certainly too small, because the field arising from further neighbours as well as from the higher electrostatic moments of all neighbours is neglected.

The dielectric constant calculated by Pople is shown in Fig. 4.17. The temperature dependence is correct but the absolute value is about 20 per cent too low. Pople (1951) suggested that the discrepancy arises from the small values for m. Better estimates for m can be made by including the effects of neighbours beyond the nearest four, the only ones considered by Pople in his calculation of m. A simple method of doing this is to calculate m in ice I, first by taking into account the electrostatic field arising from three shells of neighbouring molecules, and then a second time, taking into account only the field arising from the dipole moments of the nearest four molecules. The present authors have done this calculation, using values for the electric field given in a paper by

Coulson and Eisenberg (1966 a). The ratio of these two values of m ($= 1 \cdot 14$) was then multiplied by the moments calculated by Pople to obtain revised estimates for m in liquid water. These new estimates for m are 2·45 D at 0 °C decreasing to 2·37 D at 83 °C. When these values for m are combined with Pople's g parameters, the calculated dielectric constant is close to experiment (see 'Pople adjusted' curve of Fig. 4.17).

Haggis *et al.* (1952) based their calculation of the dielectric constant of water on a mixture model. They assumed that a certain fraction, $1 - X_{HB}$, of hydrogen bonds are broken at a given temperature T, and that the liquid is a mixture of molecules forming 0, 1, 2, 3, and 4 hydrogen bonds. They chose $1 - X_{HB} = 0 \cdot 09$ at 0 °C to give agreement with dielectric data, and determined the temperature variation of X_{HB} (see Fig. 4.11) from thermodynamic considerations. Taking the energy required to break a hydrogen bond as 4·5 kcal mol^{-1}, they calculated the mole fraction of each of the five species as a function of temperature. By assuming a tetrahedral structure for the four-bonded species, which has three coordination shells at 0 °C and one coordination shell at the critical point, they estimated that g for this species decreases from 2·81 at 0 °C to 2·34 at 370 °C. The g parameter for the zero-bonded species was taken as unity; the g parameters for the remaining species were determined by interpolation. The authors assumed that $m = 2 \cdot 45$ D for the four-bonded species at 0 °C and decreases with increasing temperature. For the zero-bonded molecules, they took $m = 1 \cdot 88$ D, and interpolated to find values of m for the other species. When the resulting values for m and g, weighted by their respective mole fractions, are inserted in Kirkwood's equation, the agreement with experiment is quite good (Fig. 4.17).

Conclusions

Kirkwood's theory shows that the large dielectric constant of liquid water arises not only from the polarity of the individual molecules, but also from the correlated mutual orientations of the molecules. In ice, as we have discussed in Section 3.4 (a), the tetrahedral arrangement of molecules results in a partial alignment of the dipole moments of neighbouring molecules with the moment of an arbitrary central molecule. This produces a large value of g; it also produces a large value of m, since the electric field of the neighbouring molecules induces a sizeable additional moment in the central molecule. The same effects are present in liquid water, but to a lesser extent.

Let us picture the D-structure of water as an average over space of many local V-structures. Around some molecules the neighbours assume a fairly orderly, tetrahedral arrangement. These regions are associated with relatively large values of g and m, perhaps almost as large as those for ice I. Around other molecules, the hydrogen bonding is more distorted or broken down, and the values of g and m are smaller. The average values of g and m for the liquid as a whole are therefore somewhat less than those for ice I. As the temperature is raised and hydrogen bonding about more molecules becomes distorted or broken down, the average values of g and m decrease further. This produces a decrease in the dielectric constant that is greater than the decrease arising from the opposition of thermal agitation to alignment of the dipoles in the external electric field.

Both the distorted hydrogen-bond model of Pople (1951) and the mixture model of Haggis *et al.* (1952) are able to account for the high dielectric constant of water. These models are similar in that they assume that few hydrogen bonds are broken in the liquid below 100 °C. Pople, of course, assumed that no hydrogen bonds are broken. Haggis *et al.* obtained best agreement with experiment by assuming that only 9 per cent of hydrogen bonds are broken at 0 °C; their theory predicts that only 20·2 per cent of the hydrogen bonds are broken at 100 °C. Indeed, as noted by Pople (1951), the high value of the dielectric constant of water is strong evidence for the presence of extensive tetrahedral coordination in the liquid at temperatures up to 100 °C.

(b) NMR chemical shift

When a proton is placed in a magnetic field it occupies one of two energy levels, depending on whether a component of its magnetic moment points in the direction of the field or in the opposite direction. If an alternating electromagnetic field of the proper frequency is then applied, it causes transitions of the proton between the two energy levels, and the proton is said to be in resonance with the field. For a magnetic field strength of 10 000 G, proton resonance takes place in an alternating field of about 4×10^7 c/s. The precise value of the magnetic field strength for resonance depends on the local environment of the proton. For example, when an O–H group of a water molecule forms a hydrogen bond the magnetic field strength required for resonance decreases, and it is said that 'the signal shifts downfield'. Thus the change, with temperature and other variables, of the magnetic field strength required for resonance can be used as an index of the change in the average local environment of all protons in the sample.

The chemical shift, δ, is the usual measure of the change in magnetic field strength, H, required for resonance when the environment of a proton changes. The chemical shift found for the condensation of water vapour to liquid water (sometimes called the 'association shift') is given by (Schneider *et al.* 1958, Muller 1965):

$$\delta = \frac{H\ (\text{liquid water, } t\ °C, 1\ \text{atm}) - H\ (\text{water vapour, } 180\ °C, 10\ \text{atm})}{H\ (\text{water vapour, } 180\ °C, 10\ \text{atm})}$$

$$= -4 \cdot 58 + 9 \cdot 5 \times 10^{-3} t \quad (4.11)$$

in parts per million, where t is between 25 and 100 °C. Thus the NMR signal shifts downfield as steam is condensed, and shifts further downfield as water is cooled. Similar shifts are observed for other substances forming hydrogen bonds, the shifts usually being larger for molecules which form stronger hydrogen bonds. Moreover, the magnitude of the chemical shift upon condensation is roughly proportional to the change in X–H stretching frequency during condensation (Schneider *et al.* 1958). The latter quantity is often taken as an index of the strength of hydrogen bonding.

Theoretical interpretation

Let us consider why the formation of a hydrogen bond produces a large chemical shift, and then why the chemical shift of liquid water depends on the temperature.

The strength of the applied magnetic field, H, which produces resonance is not generally equal to the strength of the local magnetic field *acting on the proton*, H_{loc}. These quantities differ because the applied field induces currents in the electrons surrounding the proton, and these in turn produce a secondary magnetic field of strength σH that opposes H. It follows that the total magnetic field acting on the proton is

$$H_{loc} = H(1-\sigma), \quad (4.12)$$

where σ is a constant called the *screening constant*, which depends on the electronic environment of the proton. Now when an O–H group enters into a hydrogen bond, the electronic environment of the proton changes in such a way that σ is reduced. Consequently, by eqn (4.12), the magnetic field acting on the hydrogen-bonded proton must be larger for a given applied field, and resonance occurs for a smaller value of the applied field than it did before the environmental change. Thus the downfield shift upon hydrogen-bond formation is associated with the reduction of σ.

Pople *et al.* (1959) explained the reduction of σ during hydrogen-bond formation by two effects:

(1) The presence of O_B in the O_A–H$\cdots O_B$ hydrogen bond alters the distribution of electronic charge in the O_A–H bond, and thereby changes the value of σ for the O–H system. Viewing the hydrogen bond as an electrostatic interaction between O_B and O_A–H, Pople *et al.* noted that the electric field of O_B tends to draw the proton away from the electrons in the O_A–H bond, and thus reduces the electron density around the proton. This has the effect of reducing σ and thus causing a chemical shift downfield.

(2) Induced electron currents in O_B will produce a magnetic field at the proton. This effect is significant only if the magnetic suscepti- bility of O_B is anisotropic. It may either reduce or enlarge σ, but in either case it is probably less important than effect (1).

The dependence of the chemical shift of liquid water on temperature has been interpreted in terms of both hydrogen-bond breaking and hydrogen-bond distortion. The interpretations in terms of hydrogen- bond breaking (for example, Muller (1965) and Hindman (1966)) are based on the assumption that the observed chemical shift at temperature T, $\delta(T)$, is an average of the chemical shifts of hydrogen-bonded and non-hydrogen-bonded protons in the liquid (denoted δ_{HB} and δ_{N-HB} respectively). Within this approximation, the observed chemical shift may be written

$$\delta(T) = X_{HB}(T).\delta_{HB}+\{1-X_{HB}(T)\}\delta_{N-HB}, \qquad (4.13)$$

where X_{HB} is the mole fraction of intact hydrogen bonds at temperature T. The resonance signal of the hydrogen-bonded proton, as mentioned above, is considerably downfield from that of a proton in the vapour, whereas the chemical shift for a non-hydrogen-bonded proton in the liquid is presumably very small. Thus if it is supposed that X_{HB} decreases as water is heated, it follows from eqn (4.13) that $\delta(T)$ becomes less negative with increasing temperature.

To derive numerical values of X_{HB} from eqn (4.13), it is necessary to estimate magnitudes for δ_{HB} and δ_{N-HB}. This was done by Hindman (1966), who introduced numerous assumptions about the character of hydrogen bonding in the liquid and estimated that the fraction of non- hydrogen-bonded water molecules increases from 0·155 at 0 °C to 0·35 at 100 °C. Muller applied eqn (4.13) in a slightly different way: he appraised estimates for X_{HB} based on various models for water by inserting the estimates into (4.13) and comparing the resulting values of δ_{HB} and

$\delta_{\text{N-HB}}$ with values he considered to be correct. He concluded that the estimate of Davis and Litovitz (1965) (X_{HB} equal to 0·82 at 0 °C, decreasing to 0·69 at 70 °C) was the most satisfactory of those he examined.

Muller and Reiter (1965) showed that the temperature dependence of the chemical shift of hydrogen-bonded substances probably arises in part from the stretching of hydrogen bonds. According to these authors, increasing the temperature excites the hydrogen-bond stretching mode to higher vibrational levels. Owing to the anharmonicity of the vibration, the average separation between the proton and O_B in the O_A–H$\cdots O_B$ hydrogen bond increases with temperature. This increases the screening around the proton and causes a chemical shift towards high field, because of effect (1) above. In calculating the value of $d\delta(T)/dT$ for the O_A–H$\cdots O_B$ hydrogen bond, Muller and Reiter used several potential functions to describe the stretching vibration, and several functions to relate δ to the H$\cdots O_B$ separation. Different combinations of these functions produced values of $d\delta(T)/dT$ between 2×10^{-3} and 8×10^{-3} parts per million. The experimental value of $d\delta(T)/dT$ for liquid water (eqn (4.11)) is $9\cdot5 \times 10^{-3}$ parts per million.

Hindman (1966) also emphasized that the stretching and bending of hydrogen bonds probably contribute to the chemical shift of water. He found that both the calculated chemical shift resulting from the fusion of ice, and the observed shift on heating water from 0 to 100 °C, can be accounted for by hydrogen-bond bending and stretching. Both effects can also be accounted for by a bond-breaking model, as well as by various combinations of bending, stretching, and breaking. Hindman noted that if the amounts of bond breaking and bond stretching in the liquid are known, the chemical shift data impose limits on the amount of bond bending which can take place.

4.5. Optical properties

(a) Refractive index

Tilton and Taylor (1938) determined the refractive index of water for visible light to an estimated accuracy of $\pm 1 \times 10^{-6}$ units over the temperature range 0–60 °C. The shortest wavelength they studied was the Hg line at 4046·6 Å, and the longest was the He line at 7065·2 Å. For all wavelengths studied, the refractive index was observed to increase with decreasing temperature, and at the longer wavelengths it was found to pass through a maximum between 0 and 1 °C. They found, for example, that the refractive index for the Na D-line (5892·6 Å) increases from 1·3272488 at 60 °C to 1·3339493 at 0 °C. At a given temperature, the refractive index is slightly smaller for longer wavelengths of light. It should be noted that the values of the refractive index given by Tilton and Taylor are expressed relative to air; these may be transformed to values relative to vacuum (Tilton 1935).

The refractive index of H_2O is slightly greater than that of D_2O for the same temperature and wavelength of light (Shatenshtein *et al.* 1960). For the Na D-line, the difference is 0·004687 at 20 °C. The maximum of the refractive index of D_2O as a function of temperature is at about 6·7 °C (Reisler and H. Eisenberg 1965). Thus for both H_2O and D_2O the maximum in the refractive index occurs about 4–5 °C below the maximum in the density.

Considerable effort has been directed towards finding a simple expression that relates the refractive index to thermodynamic variables. An expression giving the refractive index, n, as a function of the density, ρ_0, and one constant is the Lorenz–Lorentz formula:

$$P(\lambda) = \frac{n^2-1}{n^2+2} \frac{1}{\rho_0}. \qquad (4.14)$$

The quantity $P(\lambda)$ is called the *specific refraction*; it is related to the molecular polarizability and is a function of the wavelength of the light used in measuring the refractive index. If the environment of each water molecule were either random or had cubic symmetry (so that the field acting on a molecule is the Lorentz field, $\{(n^2+2)/3\}E$, where E is the external field), then

$$P(\lambda) = \frac{4\pi N \bar{\alpha}}{3M},$$

where N is Avogadro's number, M is the molecular weight, and $\bar{\alpha}$ is the molecular polarizability. Normally one would expect the polarizability to be a molecular property so that $P(\lambda)$ would be independent of the temperature and the pressure. For water it is found that $P(\lambda)$ does vary slightly with both of these variables: it decreases as the temperature rises (from 0·206254 at 0 °C to 0·205919 at 60 °C for the Na D-line; Tilton and Taylor 1938), and it also decreases with increasing pressure (by about 0·5 per cent on raising the pressure to 1100 bars; Waxler *et al.* 1964). This variation of $P(\lambda)$ presumably reflects the absence of conditions leading to the Lorentz field in water and possibly also a variation in the polarizability of the water molecule with density and temperature.

Recently H. Eisenberg (1965) found a slightly more complex expression that describes the temperature and pressure dependence of the refractive index of water with great accuracy. This expression is given by

$$f(n) = \frac{n^2-1}{n^2+1} = A\rho_0^B \exp(-CT), \tag{4.15}$$

where A, B, and C are empirical constants independent of temperature and pressure. By differentiating this equation, it is found that B and C are related to derivatives of $f(n)$ and P–V–T properties:

$$B = \frac{1}{\gamma_T}\left(\frac{\partial \ln f(n)}{\partial P}\right)_T, \tag{4.15 a}$$

$$C = -\left(\frac{\partial \ln f(n)}{\partial T}\right)_P - B\beta. \tag{4.15 b}$$

Here γ_T is the coefficient of isothermal compressibility and β is the coefficient of expansion. Equation (4.15) describes Tilton and Taylor's (1938) refractive-index data correctly to within a few digits of the seventh decimal place, using single values of A, B, and C for each wavelength of light. It also describes the variation of n with pressure observed by Waxler et al. (1964); these observations extend only to pressures of 1100 bars, however. The constant B that gives the best fit of eqn (4.15) to experimental refractive-index data is equal to the value of B calculated directly from eqn (4.15 a), using the experimental values of $(\partial n/\partial P)_T$, γ_T, and β. For the Na D-line, $A = 0.2064709$, $B = 0.88538$, and $C = 6.2037 \times 10^{-5}$.

The physical significance of the constant C was discussed by Reisler and H. Eisenberg (1965) and by H. Eisenberg (1965). They found that the refractive indices of methanol and benzene are adequately described by eqn (4.15) when C is set equal to zero. They concluded that C 'expresses the deviation in the behaviour of such liquids as H_2O and D_2O from "normal" behaviour'. A non-zero value of C, they suggested, may reflect a change with temperature of either the concentration of 'ice-like' structures or the average polarizability of water molecules.

Refractive index at infra-red frequencies

Liquid water has several strong absorption bands in the infra-red region of the spectrum (Section 4.7). It is well known (for example, Böttcher 1952, and Kauzmann 1957) that the refractive index of a substance in the vicinity of an absorption band depends strongly on the frequency of radiation. As the frequency is decreased through the region of the absorption band, the refractive index first decreases, then increases sharply, then decreases again (see Fig. 4.18). It is certain that the refractive index of water for infra-red radiation exhibits a number of these *dispersions*, but very little is known about them.

Kislovskii (1959) calculated the refractive index of water as a function of frequency in the infra-red region from the scant absorption, reflection,

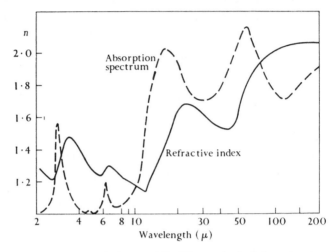

FIG. 4.18. The refractive index, n, of liquid water in the infra-red region of the spectrum. Redrawn from Kislovskii (1959).

and dispersion data available prior to 1959, and from a model for the absorbing system. His model treats an absorption as a forced vibration of a damped harmonic oscillator. His results are shown in Fig. 4.18. The four prominent absorption bands in the figure correspond roughly to the ν_s, ν_2, ν_L, and ν_T bands that are discussed in Section 4.7. The visible region is off to the left of the figure: it can be seen that the refractive index at the shortest wavelength shown is near to the value 1·33 found for visible light. One dispersion region is present for each of the four absorption bands. At the longest wavelength shown, the refractive index is 2·04, roughly the square root of the high-frequency dielectric constant (Section 4.6 (*a*)).

(*b*) *Light scattering*

When a layer of pure water is irradiated with a beam of monochromatic visible light, most of the light is either transmitted through the layer or reflected from the surfaces of the layer, but a fraction of the light is scattered in other directions. The conventional measure of the light scattered in a direction that forms an angle θ with the incident beam is the Rayleigh ratio, $R_u(\theta)$, given by

$$R_u(\theta) = \frac{I_\theta d^2}{I_0}, \tag{4.16}$$

where I_θ is the intensity of light scattered by a unit volume of the sample at the angle θ, I_0 is the intensity of the incident beam passing through the sample, and d is the distance between the sample and the point at which I_θ is measured. The subscript u signifies that the incident light is unpolarized. We should note that a very small fraction of scattered light differs in frequency from the incident beam. This is the phenomenon of Raman scattering, which we shall discuss in Section 4.7; in the present section we are concerned only with Rayleigh scattering, that is, with scattered light having the same frequency as the incident beam.†

The scattering of light by liquids arises from two distinct effects:

(1) The incident beam induces oscillating dipole moments in the molecules, and the oscillating dipoles act as sources of secondary light waves. These scattered waves have the same frequency as the incident beam. If the molecules were regularly arranged, as in a crystal, the scattered waves from different molecules would interfere destructively with one another, and scattered light would be visible only at a few angles of observation. Owing to the fluctuations in density in the liquid that accompany thermal motions, however, different numbers of molecules are simultaneously present in the adjacent volume elements of a liquid, so that destructive interference is incomplete. Smoluchowski and Einstein considered the effect of these inhomogeneities on light scattering and found that they contribute a factor to the Rayleigh ratio given by

$$R_u^{iso}(90) = \frac{2\pi^2 n^2}{\lambda^4} \frac{kT}{\gamma_T} \left[\frac{\partial n}{\partial P} \right]_T^2, \tag{4.17}‡$$

where λ is the wavelength of incident light, n is the refractive index for wavelength λ, γ_T is the isothermal compressibility, and the other symbols have their usual significance. The quantity $R_u^{iso}(90)$ is sometimes called the isotropic Rayleigh ratio. It refers, of course, to light scattered at an angle of 90° to the incident beam.

---

† When a beam of Rayleigh scattered light is examined with a high-resolution spectroscope, it is found to consist of three lines, one line exactly at the frequency of the incident beam, and two stronger lines displaced symmetrically on either side of the incident beam. For water at 20 °C this displacement is only 0·147 cm⁻¹ (Cummins and Gammon 1966). This small displacement arises from the Doppler shift of the scattered light that is reflected from sound waves in the liquid (see, for example, Oster 1948 and Cummins and Gammon 1966).

‡ See Kauzmann (1957) for a derivation of this equation.

(2) The anistropy of polarizability of molecules causes some additional scattering. Cabannes showed that this contribution can be experimentally determined from the *depolarization ratio*, ρ_u. This quantity is the ratio of intensities of the horizontally polarized component and the vertically polarized component in the beam that is scattered in the $90°$ direction. The Cabannes factor, f, which describes the additional scattering, is given by

$$f = \frac{6+6\rho_u}{6-7\rho_u}. \tag{4.18}$$

The total Rayleigh ratio for light scattered at an angle of $90°$ to the incident beam is thus

$$R_u(90) = R_u^{iso}(90) \times f. \tag{4.19}$$

Several investigators have directly measured $R_u(90)$ and ρ_u for water; some of the more recent determinations are shown in the second column of Table 4.4. Accurate measurements of $R_u(90)$ are difficult. Small amounts of dust or fluorescent material in the sample or stray light in the instrument can cause significant overestimation of $R_u(90)$ (see Kratohvil *et al.* 1965 and Cohen and H. Eisenberg 1965 for discussion of these problems); thus the smaller values of $R_u(90)$ in Table 4.4 are probably more accurate. Values of $R_u(90)$ and ρ_u for D_2O at 25 °C are also shown in Table 4.4. These were determined by Cohen and H. Eisenberg, who also measured $R_u(\theta)$ as a function of θ and temperature for both H_2O and D_2O.

The Rayleigh ratio can be calculated from eqn (4.19) using experimental values for both ρ_u and the quantities appearing in eqn (4.17). Several such calculations are shown in the third column of Table 4.4. Note that the calculated values of Cohen and H. Eisenberg (1965) are within 4 per cent of their experimental values.

Interpretation of light-scattering measurements

Most investigators now agree that the Rayleigh ratio contains no direct information on the V-structure of liquid water. The opposite view was put forward by Mysels (1964), who maintained that the difference between the experimental and calculated Rayleigh ratios reflects the extent of structural heterogeneities in the V-structure of a liquid. Let us consider Mysels's proposal and then some criticisms to which it has been subjected.

According to Mysels, the observed Rayleigh ratio has two additive contributions. In his view, 'one of these contributions is made by fluctuations in density caused by pressure variations due to thermal

TABLE 4.4

Light scattering of water: values for the Rayleigh ratio, $R_u(90)$, and for the depolarization ratio, ρ_u†

Authors	$R_u(90)$ experimental (10⁻⁶ cm⁻¹)		$R_u(90)$ calculated‡ (10⁻⁶ cm⁻¹)		ρ_u experimental	
	$\lambda = 436\ m\mu$	$\lambda = 546\ m\mu$	$\lambda = 436\ m\mu$	$\lambda = 546\ m\mu$	$\lambda = 436\ m\mu$	$\lambda = 546\ m\mu$
Kraut and Dandliker (1955)	2·89	1·05			0·083	
Mysels (1964)				0·932		
Kratohvil et al. (1965)						
'Technique C'	2·45	1·08			0·100	0·116
Best estimate	< 2·6	< 1·0	2·59§	0·987§	∼ 0·108	
Cohen and H. Eisenberg (1965)						
H_2O	2·32	0·865	2·42‖	0·885‖	0·087	0·076
D_2O	2·30	0·843	2·32‖	0·848‖	0·090	0·079

† All values are for 25 °C and unpolarized incident light; values are for H_2O except where noted.

‡ Calculated from eqns (4.17), (4.18), and (4.19), using the corresponding experimental value of ρ_u in the last column. Mysels (1964) takes $\rho_u = 0.083$.

§ The authors noted that if ρ_u is taken as 0·06 instead, then $R_u(90) = 2.33$ and 0·885 for $\lambda = 436\ m\mu$ and $\lambda = 546\ m\mu$ respectively.

‖ Derived by the present authors from data in original paper.

agitation, the other is made by local differences in structure which occur independently of pressure variations'. Mysels stated that only the former contribution is accounted for by eqn (4.19). Thus the difference between the observed Rayleigh ratio and the Rayleigh ratio calculated by eqn (4.19) is the contribution arising from local differences in structure. In applying this idea to water, Mysels chose Kraut and Dandliker's (1955) experimental value of 1.05×10^{-6} cm^{-1} for $R_u(90)$ at 546 mμ, and he calculated a value of 0.932×10^{-6} cm^{-1} for $R_u(90)$. He then compared the difference of these two quantities to the Rayleigh ratio that might be expected from the structural heterogeneities associated with various models for the V-structure of water. Mysels found that structural heterogeneities in the interstitial model of Frank and Quist (1961) are small enough to be consistent with this difference, but that those in the mixture model of Némethy and Scheraga (1962) are too pronounced to be consistent with the difference. He concluded that models involving 'compact icebergs of many water molecules or any large proportion of randomly distributed holes of molecular dimensions' are probably inconsistent with light-scattering measurements.

Kratohvil *et al.* (1965) and Cohen and H. Eisenberg (1965) criticized Mysels's (1964) interpretation of light-scattering data. They noted that the bulk properties such as γ_T and $(\partial n/\partial P)_T$ that appear in the Smoluchowski–Einstein expression for the isotropic Rayleigh ratio (eqn (4.17)) are characteristic of the liquid as a whole; these bulk properties reflect all microscopic density fluctuations that occur in the liquid. Thus, if the Smoluchowski–Einstein expression is applicable to water, eqn (4.19) should account completely for the light scattering of water. This means that light-scattering measurements can give no direct information on the V-structure of a liquid in the way that Mysels suggested. One could, of course, using a suitable statistical mechanical theory, compute the isotropic Rayleigh ratio associated with a given model for the V-structure of a liquid. Such a calculation, however, would be equivalent to a calculation of γ_T and the other bulk properties that appear in eqn (4.17). It appears, therefore, that measurements of the angular distribution of scattered light provide no information on the structure of water beyond that given by bulk properties such as γ_T.

Kratohvil *et al.* (1965) and Cohen and H. Eisenberg (1965) also noted that the most accurate experimental determinations of $R_u(90)$ for water are in good agreement with values calculated from eqn (4.19) (see Table 4.4). This indicates that the Smoluchowski–Einstein expression is indeed applicable to water.

4.6. Properties depending on the rates of molecular displacements

The properties of water that differ greatly from those of ice nearly all involve the rates of molecular displacements. Whereas the values of the volume, entropy, compressibility, heat capacity, static dielectric constant, and vibrational frequencies for water differ by at most a factor of 2 from the corresponding values for ice at 0 °C, the viscosity of water is about 10^{-14} times that of ice, and the dielectric relaxation time is about 10^{-6} times that of ice. Viscosity and dielectric relaxation time (like ultrasonic absorption, relaxation time for nuclear magnetization, and rate of self-diffusion) are properties that are determined by the rates of molecular reorientation and translation. Indeed, the most obvious difference between ice and water—the solidity of ice and the fluidity of water—arises entirely from the different rates of molecular movements in the two phases.

Investigations of the dielectric relaxation time and the other rate properties just mentioned have provided fairly accurate values for the rates of molecular reorientation and translation in liquid water. The general method in such studies is to apply a stress to liquid water and to measure the time required for the liquid to come into equilibrium with the stress; alternatively, the stress is removed and the time required for the liquid to return to equilibrium is measured. For dielectric relaxation the stress is an applied electric field, for self-diffusion it is a gradient in the concentration of an isotope, for viscosity it is a shearing stress, and so forth. Studies of the rate properties of water have not, however, produced a detailed picture of the movements of water molecules, and it seems likely that before we obtain such a picture it will be necessary to await further developments in the fundamental theory of non-equilibrium processes.

A recurring concept in the following sections is that of a *correlation time*. Roughly speaking, this is the average period of time for which some property of a molecule—say its orientation in space—persists with little or no change. Correlation times can be more rigorously defined in terms of correlation functions; let us consider the correlation function for dielectric polarization as an example. This is a function of time, t, given by (Glarum 1960):

$$C(t) = \frac{\langle \mathbf{m}(0) \cdot \mathbf{m}^*(t) \rangle}{\langle \mathbf{m}(0) \cdot \mathbf{m}^*(0) \rangle},$$

where $\mathbf{m}$ and $\mathbf{m}^*$ have the same significance as in Section 3.4 (a), and the brackets denote an average in the absence of an external field. Clearly, at any arbitrary zero of time, $C(t) = 1$. It is also clear that as time goes on and the molecule whose moment is **m** changes its orientation in space, $C(t)$ approaches zero. The simplest functional form which $C(t)$ may assume is

$$C(t) = \exp(-t/\tau_{rd}). \tag{4.20}$$

The quantity τ_{rd} in this equation is the rotational correlation time, the subscript d denoting that it is determined from dielectric relaxation measurements. Under other circumstances, $C(t)$ has the more complex form

$$C(t) = \sum_{i=1}^{N} \rho_i \exp(-t/\tau_{rdi}), \quad \sum_{i=1}^{N} \rho_i = 1$$

and the time development of $C(t)$ cannot be precisely described by a single correlation time.

(a) Dielectric relaxation

The study of molecular reorientation in ice by means of dielectric relaxation measurements was described in Section 3.4 (b); this technique is also useful in studying reorientation in liquid water. For liquid water, as for ice, the dielectric constant falls to a small high-frequency value ϵ_∞ as the frequency of the applied field is increased. For both phases this decrease in dielectric constant with increasing frequency, called the *Debye dispersion*, is described reasonably well by a single relaxation time τ_d for every temperature. The chief difference in the behaviour of ice and water is that the relaxation time for water is six powers of ten smaller than that of ice; this shows, of course, that H_2O molecules reorient much more frequently in water than in ice. The mechanism of molecular reorientation in water cannot be deduced from the relaxation data, though the data are sufficient to suggest some characteristics of the mechanism and to rule out some proposed mechanisms altogether.

Studies of the dielectric relaxation of water are summarized in Table 4.5. Collie *et al.* (1948) found that for each temperature they considered, the data may be described by the Debye equation (eqn (3.10)), with a single relaxation time and a value of 5·5 for the high-frequency dielectric constant ϵ_∞. They found that the dielectric relaxation time τ_d decreases from $17\cdot8 \times 10^{-12}$ s at 0 °C to $3\cdot22 \times 10^{-12}$ s at 75 °C. The value of τ_d for D_2O is greater than that of H_2O by a factor which decreases from 1·3 at 10 °C to 1·2 at 60 °C.

In another study, Grant *et al.* (1957) found that the data are better described by a very small spread of relaxation times and a value of 4·5 for ϵ_∞. The reader will recall from Section 3.4 (b) that the deviation

TABLE 4.5

Dielectric relaxation of water: values for the relaxation time, τ_d, the high-frequency dielectric constant, ϵ_∞, the enthalpy of activation, $\Delta H^\ddagger$, the entropy of activation, $\Delta S^\ddagger$, and the dispersion parameter for the spread of relaxation times, α

Authors	Temperature (°C)	τ_d (in units of 10^{-12} s)† H_2O	τ_d D$_2$O	$\Delta H^\ddagger$ (kcal/mol)‡ H_2O	$\Delta S^\ddagger$ (cal/mol/°C)‡ H_2O	ϵ_∞	α
Collie et al. (1948)	0	17·8	..			5·5	0
				4·5	7·4		
	5	..	20·4				
	10	12·7	16·6				
				4·2	6·1		
	20	9·55	12·3				
				4·0	5·4		
	30	7·37	9·34				
				3·5	4·0		
	40	5·94	7·21				
				3·5	4·0		
	50	4·84	5·89				
				3·2	3·0		
	60	4·04	4·90				
				2·8	1·8		
	75	3·22	..				
Grant et al. (1957)	20	9·26				4·5	0·02 ±0·007
Rampolla et al. (1959)	20	10·0				6·0	
Garg and Smyth (1965) Water in dilute benzene solution	20	1·0					

† Calculated from values of the relaxation wavelength, λ_s, reported in original papers, using the relationship $\tau_d = \lambda_s/(2\pi c')$, where $c' = 2\cdot998 \times 10^{10}$ cm s^{-1}.

‡ The values of $\Delta H^\ddagger$ and $\Delta S^\ddagger$ are averages over the temperature interval which straddles the entry.

from zero of the dispersion parameter α is a measure of the spread of relaxation times. Grant et al. found $\alpha = 0\cdot020\pm0\cdot007$. These authors noted that available data are insufficient to show whether or not ϵ_∞ is dependent on temperature. Rampolla et al. (1959), in a third study, obtained $10\cdot0\times10^{-12}$ for τ_d at 20 °C and $6\cdot0$ for ϵ_∞.

A value for τ_d for water in dilute benzene solution was reported by Garg and Smyth (1965); it is $1\cdot0\times10^{-12}$ s at 20 °C, about one-tenth of τ_d for liquid water at the same temperature.

Interpretation of dielectric relaxation data

In analysing the dielectric relaxation data for water, let us consider the magnitude and temperature dependence of τ_d first, then the spread of relaxation times, then the origin of the high-frequency dielectric constant, and finally possible mechanisms for reorientation of water molecules.

In our discussion of the dielectric relaxation time τ_d, it should be kept in mind that this quantity is a measure of the rate of decay of macroscopic polarization when the applied field is removed (Section 3.4 (b)). It is somewhat longer than the rotational correlation time, τ_{rd}, which is the interval between molecular reorientations. According to Powles (1953) and Glarum (1960),

$$\tau_d = \left(\frac{3\epsilon_0}{2\epsilon_0+\epsilon_\infty}\right)\tau_{rd}, \qquad (4.21)$$

where ϵ_0 is the static dielectric constant.

A question we must consider is why the dielectric relaxation time of water is so much shorter than that of ice. The transition-state theory for dielectric relaxation (Glasstone et al. 1941, Kauzmann 1942) is of some help here. According to the transition-state theory, the relaxation time is given by

$$\tau_d = \frac{h}{kT}\exp(\Delta G^{\ddagger}/RT) \qquad (4.22)\dagger$$

$$= \frac{h}{kT}\exp(\Delta H^{\ddagger}/RT)\exp(-\Delta S^{\ddagger}/R), \qquad (4.22\,a)\dagger$$

where $\Delta G^{\ddagger}$, $\Delta H^{\ddagger}$, and $\Delta S^{\ddagger}$ are, respectively, the free energy, the enthalpy, and the entropy of activation for dielectric relaxation. The values of

† The quantities $\Delta G^{\ddagger}$, $\Delta H^{\ddagger}$, and $\Delta S^{\ddagger}$ refer to molecular processes, and should therefore be calculated from τ_{rd} rather than from τ_d. Most investigators have calculated these quantities from τ_d, however, and we do the same here for consistency. It should be noted, though, that if τ_{rd} were used instead of τ_d, $\Delta S^{\ddagger}$ would be more positive by about 0·8 cal/mol/°C.

$\Delta H^{\ddagger}$ and $\Delta S^{\ddagger}$ for water are easily determined from the temperature dependence of τ_d; they are shown in Table 4.5. Let us compare $\Delta H^{\ddagger}$ and $\Delta S^{\ddagger}$ for water at 5 °C to the corresponding quantities for ice at 0 °C (based on the data of Auty and Cole (1952), $\Delta H^{\ddagger} = 12.7$ kcal/mol and $\Delta S^{\ddagger} = 9.6$ cal/mol/°C for ice I at 0 °C). The values of $\Delta S^{\ddagger}$ for the two phases are not very different near 0 °C, but $\Delta H^{\ddagger}$ for ice is 8 kcal/mol larger than $\Delta H^{\ddagger}$ for water. Evidently the relaxation time of water is shorter than that of ice primarily because the enthalpy of activation is smaller in water.

The Debye dispersion of water, as mentioned above, can be described by a small spread of relaxation times. The dispersion parameter α for water (0.02) is close to the value of zero that is observed for a single relaxation time, and less than the values for ice III ($\alpha = 0.04$) and ice VI ($\alpha = 0.05$). The non-zero values of α for several of the ice polymorphs have been attributed to the presence of several different molecular environments in each of these crystals (Wilson et al. 1965). Since molecular environments are certainly more varied in liquid water than in any of the ices, the very small spread of relaxation times in water is a phenomenon that is difficult to explain.

One possible explanation is that molecular reorientation in water is a co-operative process involving a large number of molecules. In this case, variations in the environments of individual molecules would not affect the relaxation time. Such a process was invoked by Denney and Cole (1955) to explain their observation that mixtures of methanol and *n*-propanol exhibit a single principal relaxation time although the pure liquids have quite different relaxation times. For the case of water, however, $\Delta H^{\ddagger}$ and $\Delta S^{\ddagger}$ seem too small for a process that disrupts large regions of the liquid; we shall discuss this below.

A second possible explanation is that, although molecular environments are varied in water when viewed over a time scale of 10^{-13} s (Section 4.7 (*b*)), they are relatively uniform when viewed over an interval of $\sim 5 \times 10^{-12}$ s. A small spread of relaxation times would be consistent with such an averaging of molecular environments. It is difficult to imagine, however, what molecular motion might account for such an averaging.

Let us now consider the origin of the high-frequency dielectric constant. From data in Table 4.5 it is apparent that ϵ_{∞} lies within the range 4.5–6.0. This may or may not be larger than the square of the refractive index in the far infra-red region of the spectrum (Section 4.5 (*a*)); it is certainly larger than the square of the refractive index at optical frequencies—about 1·7. It is also somewhat larger than the value 3·1 for ϵ_∞ of ice I (Section 3.4 (b)).

Two explanations for the relatively large value of ϵ_∞ have been put forward. Haggis *et al.* (1952) and Hasted (1961) suggested that ϵ_∞ for liquid water is larger than ϵ_∞ for ice because of the rotations of those molecules in the liquid that form zero and one hydrogen bond, and also because of rotations of 'unsymmetrical two-bonded molecules'. These are molecules having one O–H bond and one lone-pair of electrons engaged in hydrogen bonds. According to these authors, at high frequencies of the applied field, the three- and four-bonded molecules do not reorient fast enough to come into equilibrium with the field, and it is only zero-, one-, and unsymmetrical two-bonded molecules that contribute to the dielectric constant.

The large ϵ_∞ may, however, arise entirely from the dispersions associated with hindered translational and librational modes of vibration in the liquid. The difference $\epsilon_\infty - n^2$ for ice, where n is the optical refractive index, is attributable to these dispersions (Section 3.4 (b)). Magat (1948) suggested that librations of water molecules account for the difference $\epsilon_\infty - n^2$ and gave a qualitative explanation for this effect: in the absence of an applied field, water molecules exhibit hindered rotations about a position of minimum potential energy. Magat noted that when a field is applied, the librations are biased in the direction of the field and this produces a small polarization in the liquid. Such a mechanism would be expected to give rise to a larger value of $\epsilon_\infty - n^2$ in the liquid than in ice because hydrogen bonds are more easily distorted in the liquid (Section 4.7 (c)), and hence the polarization caused by the applied field would be larger.

Available data do not favour one of these explanations over the other; when measurements of the dielectric constant or absorption coefficients at higher frequencies become feasible, however, it should be possible to choose between them. The zero-bonded and one-bonded molecules would certainly have relaxation times as long as, or longer than, the $1·0 \times 10^{-12}$ s relaxation time observed for water in dilute benzene solution (Table 4.5). In contrast, the hindered translational and librational motions of water molecules have absorption bands near 200 and 700 cm^{-1}, so they must produce a dispersion of the dielectric constant at frequencies around 10^{13} s^{-1} (Section 4.7 (c)). Thus it should be possible to distinguish between the two mechanisms once the dielectric or absorption behaviour is determined quantitatively for the frequency range 10^{12} to 10^{13} s^{-1}.

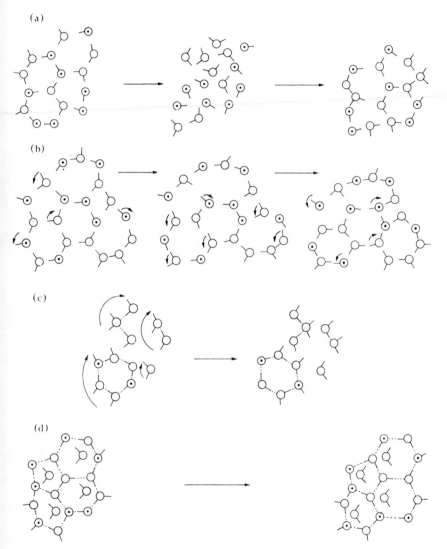

FIG. 4.19. Possible mechanisms for molecular reorientation in liquid water. Oxygen atoms are shown by circles and O–H bonds by lines. A black dot in the centre of an oxygen atom represents an O–H bond that extends above or below the page. (*a*) A representation of the 'flickering cluster' mechanism of Frank and Wen (1957). (*b*) A mechanism involving orientational defects like those thought to exist in ice. Small arrows show the direction in which a molecule is about to rotate. (*c*) Reorientation by rotation of small polymeric groups of water molecules. (*d*) Reorientation of interstitial molecules.

Possible mechanisms for reorientation of water molecules

Fig. 4.19 shows four possible mechanisms for the reorientation of molecules in liquid water. These drawings are highly schematic: they are not presented as serious representations of molecular arrangements in the liquid but rather as aids in developing a qualitative picture of molecular reorientation.

Panel (*a*) is an attempt to depict the 'flickering cluster' mechanism proposed by Frank and Wen (1957). They postulated 'that the formation of hydrogen bonds in water is predominantly a co-operative phenomenon, so that, in most cases, when one bond breaks, then, typically, a whole cluster will "dissolve". This gives a picture of flickering clusters of various sizes and shapes, jumping to attention, so to speak, and then relaxing "at ease".' A hydrogen-bonded cluster, shown on the left, dissolves into a chaotic group of non-hydrogen-bonded molecules (centre), and these coalesce to form a new cluster with the molecules oriented differently from the original cluster. In the presence of an external electric field, molecules would tend to form clusters with their dipole moments oriented in the direction of the field. Frank and Wen believe that the dielectric relaxation time is a measure of the half-life of a cluster.

Consideration of the 'flickering cluster' mechanism in terms of the transition-state theory indicates that the postulated dissolution of clusters would require larger values of $\Delta S^{\ddagger}$ and $\Delta H^{\ddagger}$ than those which are actually observed. The dissolution of a cluster, as described by Frank and Wen, seems to correspond to a 'vaporization' of molecules in a local region of the liquid. Now Kauzmann (1942) pointed out that if the process of activation is pictured as a local vaporization, the ratio of $\Delta S^{\ddagger}$ to the molar entropy of vaporization should be approximately equal to the number of molecules involved in the activation. The entropy which we require for comparison with $\Delta S^{\ddagger}$ is the entropy of vaporization of liquid water to water vapour occupying a volume equal to the 'free volume' of the liquid. This quantity is given by

$$\Delta S'_{\text{vap}} = \Delta S_{\text{vap}} - R \ln(V_{\text{vap}}/V_{\text{f}}),$$

where ΔS_{vap} is the observed entropy of vaporization, V_{vap} is the molar volume of water vapour at its equilibrium vapour pressure, and V_{f} is the free volume of liquid water. If we accept Némethy and Scheraga's (1962) estimate of V_{f} ($= 0.26$ cm^3 mol^{-1}), we find that the ratio $\Delta S^{\ddagger}/\Delta S'_{\text{vap}}$ decreases from 1·1 at 5 °C to 0·5 at 67·5 °C. It should be pointed out that Némethy and Scheraga's value for V_{f} is very small, but larger values only serve to decrease our estimate of the number of molecules involved in the activation process. Hence this calculation suggests that the re-orientation of a water molecule does not involve the movement of a large number of neighbouring molecules by the simultaneous rupture of many hydrogen bonds.

A similar estimate of the number of molecules in a dissolved cluster, based this time on the observed value of $\Delta H^{\ddagger}$, also produces a number that is too small to be consistent with the flickering-cluster mechanism. The quantity $\Delta H^{\ddagger}$ is the enthalpy required to produce one mole of the activated complex, which in this case is one mole of 'dissolved clusters'. It we suppose that there are n water molecules in a dissolved cluster, then at least $2nN$ hydrogen bonds must be broken in producing a mole of the activated complex. To estimate $\Delta H^{\ddagger}$ we must assume some value for the energy of a hydrogen bond in liquid water. Let us take the value of 1·3 kcal mol^{-1} recommended by Némethy and Scheraga (1962); this is the smallest of the values listed in Table 4.2. Thus $\Delta H^{\ddagger}$ is at least 2·6n kcal mol^{-1}. Recalling that the observed $\Delta H^{\ddagger}$ is 4·5 kcal mol^{-1} at 5 °C and decreases as the temperature rises, we see that n, the number of molecules in a flickering cluster, is less than $4·5/2·6 = 1·7$ at 5 °C and decreases at higher temperatures. Thus if the dissolution of the clusters is considered to be a local vaporization and if the dissolved regions are considered to contain more than one or two molecules, the observed values for both $\Delta H^{\ddagger}$ and $\Delta S^{\ddagger}$ are inconsistent with the flickering-cluster mechanism.

Panel (b) of Fig. 4.19 shows a mechanism for reorientation involving orientational defects similar to those believed to exist in ice. An irregular hydrogen-bonded network having all hydrogen bonds intact is shown on the left-hand side of the panel. Several molecules, those forming particularly distorted hydrogen bonds with their neighbours, break some of the bonds and rotate, thereby producing orientational defects similar to the D- and L-defects discussed in Section 3.4 (b). Subsequent rotation of molecules adjacent to defects causes the defects to migrate through the liquid. An external electric field would influence the migration of the defects and thus induce an orientational polarization in the liquid. The observed values of $\Delta S^{\ddagger}$ and $\Delta H^{\ddagger}$ do not seem to be inconsistent with this mechanism: $\Delta S^{\ddagger}$ at 5 °C is slightly less than $\Delta S^{\ddagger}$ for ice I at 0 °C, which is reasonable if the mechanisms in the two phases are similar. The drop in $\Delta H^{\ddagger}$ of ~ 8 kcal mol^{-1} in going from ice at 0 °C to water at 5 °C could conceivably be associated with weaker hydrogen bonding in the liquid. It is not clear that this mechanism would give rise to a narrow spread of relaxation times.

A somewhat similar interpretation of dielectric relaxation data was given by Haggis *et al.* (1952). The reader will recall (from Section 4.4 (*a*)) that these authors treated water as an equilibrium mixture of molecules that form 4, 3, 2, 1, and 0 hydrogen bonds. In their discussion of dielectric relaxation, they did not specify the geometric arrangement of molecules near a rotating molecule except to say that the rotating molecules are those that form only two intact hydrogen bonds to neighbouring molecules. The rate-limiting step in molecular reorientation, according to these authors, is the formation of two-bonded molecules from three- and four-bonded molecules; the two-bonded molecules rotate more quickly than they are formed.

Panels (*c*) and (*d*) show two other conceivable mechanisms for molecular reorientation in water. Panel (*c*) depicts water as a mixture of small polymeric units. This mechanism is almost certainly incorrect; if water were composed of small polymeric units of various sizes which cohere for as long as 10^{-11} s, the rotations of these units would produce a wide distribution of relaxation times. Yet a very narrow distribution is actually observed. Panel (*d*) depicts water as a cage structure with interstitial molecules (Section 4.2 (*b*)) that are free to undergo rotations. It seems likely that the reorientations of molecules forming the cage would be less frequent than those of the interstitial molecules, and consequently that this structure would give two distinct dispersion regions.

(b) Relaxation of nuclear magnetism

As mentioned in Section 4.4 (*b*), each proton in an applied magnetic field occupies one of two energy levels, depending on whether a component of its magnetic moment points in the direction of the field or in the opposite direction. If the magnetic field strength is suddenly increased, more nuclear magnets align themselves with the field, but a period of time is required for the system to reach equilibrium. The time needed to achieve equilibrium along the field axis is called the *spin-lattice relaxation time* and is denoted T_1. This time can be measured by techniques of nuclear magnetic resonance. It is closely related to molecular motions, because a change in the orientation of a nuclear magnet can be induced only by a fluctuation in the magnetic field acting on the nucleus, or, in the case of a nucleus with an electric quadrupole moment, by a fluctuation in the electric field gradient at the nucleus; these fluctuations are caused by rotations and translations of the molecule containing the nucleus.

TABLE 4.6

Studies of nuclear spin-lattice relaxation times of water

Authors (and temperature range of study)	Type of nuclear relaxation studied	Temperature (°C)	Value of τ_{rm}, the rotational correlation time (units of 10^{-12} s)	Other quantities measured and comments
Krynicki (1966) (2·1–95·2 °C)	Proton	0 30 50 75	4·8† 2·0 1·3 0·9	The temperature dependence of T_1 cannot be described by a single value of the activation energy E_A, but the mean value of E_A between 40 and 100 °C is 3·7 kcal/mol.
Smith and Powles (1966) (0–374 °C)	Proton	25 280 374	2·6 0·156 0·0756	The correlation time for molecular angular velocity, τ_{sr}, is roughly $2·87 \times 10^{-15}$ s at 280 °C and $5·06 \times 10^{-15}$ s at 374 °C.
Woessner (1964) (5–100 °C)	Deuteron			The temperature dependence of T_1 above 40 °C can be described by an activation energy E_A of 3·90 kcal/mol.
Powles et al. (1966) (0–374 °C)	Deuteron			Results agree with those of Woessner from 0 to 100 °C.
Glasel (1966) (3–65 °C)	Oxygen-17	25	2·7	In deriving τ_{rm}, the quadrupole coupling constant of ^{17}O in the liquid is assumed to be equal to the value in the free molecule. The activation energy is constant from 4 to 30 °C but shows a distinct break at 30 °C.

† Values estimated from a graph in the original paper.

Spin-lattice relaxation times for water have been measured for the proton, the deuteron, and the oxygen-17 nucleus (Table 4.6), and the method of extracting information about molecular motions depends on which type of nucleus is studied. Let us consider the proton first. The magnetic moment of a proton changes direction when it experiences a fluctuating magnetic field. Such fluctuations may arise from motions of the other proton in the same water molecule and also from protons in neighbouring water molecules. The reciprocal of the observed T_1 may be expressed as

$$\frac{1}{T_1} = \left(\frac{1}{T_1}\right)_{\text{intra}} + \left(\frac{1}{T_1}\right)_{\text{inter}} + \left(\frac{1}{T_1}\right)_{\text{s-r}},$$

where the first two terms on the right-hand side represent contributions from the two effects just mentioned. The third term is called the spin-rotational contribution; it represents the effect of fluctuating magnetic fields that arise from the electric charges of rotating molecules, and is significant only at temperatures above 100 °C. The term $(1/T_1)_{\text{intra}}$ is proportional to a rotational correlation time, if the correlation function that describes molecular reorientation has the form of a simple exponential decay (eqn (4.20); see, for example, Glasel 1967). Let us call this correlation time τ_{rn} to indicate that it is the rotational correlation time determined from nuclear magnetic resonance. Thus to determine τ_{rn}, T_1 must be measured, the contributions $(1/T_1)_{\text{inter}}$ and $(1/T_1)_{\text{s-r}}$ must be evaluated, and these contributions must be subtracted from $(1/T_1)$ to obtain $(1/T_1)_{\text{intra}}$. Methods of evaluating $(1/T_1)_{\text{inter}}$ and $(1/T_1)_{\text{s-r}}$ for water have been proposed by Krynicki (1966), Smith and Powles (1966), and Powles et al. (1966).

Krynicki (1966) measured the proton spin-lattice relaxation time of water from 2·1 to 95·2 °C with an estimated experimental error of ±2 per cent. He found that the temperature dependence of T_1 parallels that of the reciprocal of the dielectric relaxation time: the product $(T_1 \tau_{\text{d}})^{-1}$ equals $3\cdot37 \times 10^{10}$ s^{-2} to within ±3 per cent over the temperature range where data were available. Eliminating the intermolecular contribution to T_1, Krynicki determined τ_{rn} as a function of temperature; the values are listed in Table 4.6. Krynicki noted that the ratio of the dielectric relaxation time, τ_{d}, to τ_{rn} is nearly independent of temperature from 0 to 75 °C and is equal to about 3·7. He interpreted this result in terms of a mechanism for reorientation of water molecules by jumps through small angles.

Smith and Powles (1966) measured T_1 of water under its own vapour pressure from the freezing-point to the critical temperature. They derived the approximate values of τ_{rn} that are given in Table 4.6. Treating the reorientation of water molecules as a Brownian rotational diffusion, they estimated values of the correlation time τ_{sr} for molecular angular velocity (see Table 4.6); this is the time interval for which the angular velocity of a water molecule remains roughly unchanged. From the value of τ_{sr} at the critical point they estimated that the average angle of jump during reorientation is roughly $10°$. They emphasized, however, that if reorientation proceeds by a 'jump and wait' mechanism, the average angle of jump is larger. The two possibilities cannot be distinguished by their measurements.

The deuteron and ^{17}O nuclei have electric quadrupole moments, and thus they change orientations when they experience a fluctuating electric field gradient. Such fluctuations arise primarily from charges in the same molecule as the nucleus under question, so that elimination of inter-molecular effects is not necessary in these studies. For these nuclei, the reciprocal of T_1 has the form

$$\frac{1}{T_1} = AC^2\tau_{rn},$$

where A is a numerical constant and C represents the quadrupole coupling constant of the nucleus. Thus to determine τ_{rn}, C must be known; but this quantity for the water molecule in the liquid state is not available from other sources. Glasel (1966), in his determination of the rotational correlation time in liquid water enriched with $H_2^{17}O$, bypassed this problem by assuming that the quadrupole coupling constant of ^{17}O is the same in the vapour and liquid phases. Woessner (1964) reversed this procedure in studying liquid D_2O; he estimated the rotational correlation time from the dielectric relaxation time and then used this quantity to determine the quadrupole coupling constant of the deuteron in the liquid. He found it to be only $\frac{2}{3}$ to $\frac{3}{4}$ as large as in the free D_2O molecule, but roughly the same magnitude as in D_2O ice. Powles *et al.* (1966) obtained a similar value of the quadrupole coupling constant by comparing T_1 values for liquid H_2O and D_2O. They concluded from this result that hydrogen bonding in water is virtually complete at all temperatures up to $300 °C$.

(c) Self-diffusion

The molecules of a liquid experience frequent displacements from their temporary positions of equilibrium. The *self-diffusion coefficient*, D, is a measure of the rate of such displacements. One method of determining

D is to study the rate of diffusion of an isotopic tracer in the liquid; D for the tracer is then given by Fick's second law:

$$\left(\frac{\partial c}{\partial t}\right)_x = D\left(\frac{\partial^2 c}{\partial x^2}\right)_t, \tag{4.23}$$

where x is the direction of diffusion and $\partial c/\partial t$ is the rate of change of tracer concentration with time. The rate of molecular displacements can also be studied without the aid of isotopic tracers by NMR and neutron scattering techniques.

TABLE 4.7

Values for the self-diffusion coefficient, D, of water

(a) Comparison of values of D, for 25 °C and atmospheric pressure, determined by various techniques

Investigators	Experimental technique	D (10^{-5} cm^2 s^{-1})
Trappeniers *et al.* (1965)	NMR spin-echo measurements	$2 \cdot 51 \pm 0 \cdot 01$
Jones *et al.* (1965)	HTO tracer in continually monitored capillary tube	$2 \cdot 22 \pm 0 \cdot 05$
Wang (1965)	H$_2$^{18}O tracer in capillary tube	$2 \cdot 57 \pm 0 \cdot 02$
Longsworth (1960)	Interferometric detection of boundary between H$_2$O–D$_2$O mixtures. By extrapolation:	
	D for pure H$_2$O	$2 \cdot 272 \pm 0 \cdot 003$
	D for pure D$_2$O	$2 \cdot 109 \pm 0 \cdot 003$
Simpson and Carr (1958)	NMR free precession techniques	$2 \cdot 13$
Wang *et al.* (1953)	HDO tracer in capillary tube	$2 \cdot 34 \pm 0 \cdot 08$
	HTO tracer in capillary tube	$2 \cdot 44 \pm 0 \cdot 06$
	H$_2$^{18}O tracer in capillary tube	$2 \cdot 66 \pm 0 \cdot 12$

(b) Temperature dependence of D determined by the capillary-tube method using H$_2$^{18}O as the tracer

Reported by Wang (1965)		Reported by Wang *et al.* (1953)	
Temperature (° C)	D (in units of 10^{-5} cm^2 s^{-1})	Temperature (° C)	D (in units of 10^{-5} cm^2 s^{-1})
$5 \cdot 00$	$1 \cdot 426 \pm 0 \cdot 018$	$35 \cdot 0$	$3 \cdot 49 \pm 0 \cdot 15$
$10 \cdot 00$	$1 \cdot 675 \pm 0 \cdot 025$	$45 \cdot 0$	$4 \cdot 38 \pm 0 \cdot 11$
$15 \cdot 00$	$1 \cdot 97 \pm 0 \cdot 020$	$55 \cdot 0$	$5 \cdot 45 \pm 0 \cdot 30$
$25 \cdot 00$	$2 \cdot 57 \pm 0 \cdot 022$		

Values of D for water, determined by several methods, are listed in Table 4.7. It can be seen that these are in fair agreement with one another. The discovery that HDO and HTO diffuse no faster than H$_2$^{18}O is especially interesting, because it shows, as noted by Wang *et al.* (1953), that the special mechanism of rapid H$^+$ transfer that accounts for the electrolytic conduction of water (Section 4.6 (*e*)) plays a negligible part in the self-diffusion of water. Longsworth's values for the self-diffusion coefficients of H_2O and D_2O indicate that molecular displacements are slightly more frequent in H_2O than in D_2O at the same temperature. This finding is consistent with the larger viscosity (Table 4.8) and longer dielectric relaxation time (Table 4.5) of D_2O.

Studies of the temperature dependence of the self-diffusion coefficient show that D can be described by the equation

$$D = A \exp\{-E_A/(RT)\}.$$

Wang et al. (1953) found that over the temperature range 1·1–55 °C, E_A is 4·6±0·1 kcal mol^{-1} for HDO and HTO tracers, and 4·4±0·3 kcal mol^{-1} for an $H_2{}^{18}O$ tracer. Wang (1965) reported the results of another study which showed that E_A is 4·8 kcal mol^{-1} for an $H_2{}^{18}O$ tracer over the temperature range 5–25 °C. Some measurements of the pressure dependence of D were made by Cuddeback et al. (1953).

Interpretation of self-diffusion coefficients

Wang et al. (1953) used the transition-state theory of rate processes to interpret their measurements of the self-diffusion coefficients. They noted that the energies of activation for self-diffusion, dielectric relaxation, and viscous flow of water are all about 4·6 kcal mol^{-1} at 25 °C. This observation led them to assume that the mechanism of activation is the same for these three processes. It follows from this assumption and from the transition-state theory that

$$\frac{\lambda^2}{\tau_d} = D \tag{4.24}$$

$$= \frac{CkT}{\eta}, \tag{4.24 a}$$

where λ is the mean distance between two successive equilibrium positions of a diffusing water molecule in the direction of diffusion, τ_d is the dielectric relaxation time, η is the viscosity, and C is a constant that depends on intermolecular separations. Two observations lend support to the validity of this relationship; the quantity $D\eta/T$ is nearly independent of temperature from 0 to at least 55 °C (Wang et al. 1953, Robinson and Stokes 1959), and the values of $\tau_d T/\eta$ for H_2O and D_2O are nearly equal (Collie et al. 1948).

Two important inferences about the displacements of water molecules have been based on eqns (4.24). The first is that λ, the mean length of a diffusive jump in the direction of diffusion, is roughly equal to the separation of nearest neighbours in the liquid. Wang et al. evaluated λ

from eqn (4.24), using their own measurements of D and the values of τ_d determined by Collie *et al.* (1948). They found that λ is nearly constant ($= 1\cdot5$ Å) over the temperature range 0–55 °C. Wang (1965) in a later paper took τ_d to be larger by a factor of 2π and thus arrived at a larger value for λ ($= 3\cdot7$ Å). The second inference from eqns (4.24) is that the unit of the liquid that experiences changes in orientation and position is a single molecule. According to Grant (1957), the magnitude of λ^2/C in eqn (4.24 a) supports this idea. He noted that in the Debye equation for rotational relaxation times, the quantity λ^2/C is replaced by $4\pi a^3$, where a is the 'molecular radius'. He found that the experimental values of the viscosity and dielectric relaxation time, when inserted in eqn (4.24 a), give $a = 1\cdot4$ Å, a reasonable value for the water molecule. He interpreted this result in terms of the ideas of Haggis *et al.* (1952) about reorientation of water molecules in the liquid (Section 4.6 (*a*)).

Information on self-diffusion from scattering of slow neutrons

A technique that promises to be valuable for studying diffusional motions in liquids is the scattering of slow neutrons.† Slow neutrons travel much more slowly ($\sim 10^5$ cm s^{-1}) than X-rays (3×10^{10} cm s^{-1}) and they interact with individual atoms in the liquid over a time interval comparable to the period of molecular jumps. Thus the scattered neutrons contain information on the diffusive motions of molecules. In the case of water, this information is for the hydrogen nuclei, which are the principal neutron scatterers.

One method of extracting this information is to analyse the *quasi-elastic scattering*. The portion of the scattered beam that has exchanged no energy with the lattice vibrations of the substance under investigation is said to have been elastically scattered. For most liquids the spectrum of neutron energies in the 'elastic' portion of the scattered beam is actually somewhat broader than the spectrum in the incident beam, and the scattering is said to be quasielastic. The observed broadening is caused by diffusive motions of molecules.

Among the early investigations of neutron scattering from water was that of Hughes *et al.* (1960). These authors observed no broadening whatsoever in the elastic region, a result that is incompatible with continuous diffusion of molecules. Singwi and Sjölander (1960) interpreted this finding in terms of a jump-and-wait model for diffusion. They were able to fit the experimental results by supposing that a water

† This technique has been described briefly by Palevsky (1966) and at length by Sjölander (1965). Larsson (1965) summarized studies of liquid water by this method.

molecule oscillates about a position of temporary equilibrium for an average of 4×10^{-12} s at 20 °C before experiencing a diffusional jump. This would mean that a water molecule executes roughly 40 inter-molecular oscillations between two jumps. In several other experimental

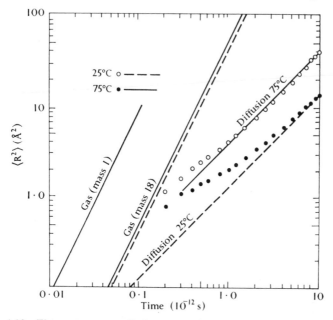

Fig. 4.20. The mean square displacement of a proton in liquid water as a function of time, $\langle R^2 \rangle$, according to Sakamoto *et al.* (1962). The points show the experimental values and the lines show various calculated values. Redrawn from Sakamoto *et al.* (1962).

studies (see Larsson 1965) some broadening of the elastic region was observed. Larsson (1965) found he could fit his own data with the model of Singwi and Sjölander by assuming that the interval between diffusive jumps is $1 \cdot 5 \times 10^{-12}$ s at 20 °C.

Additional support for a jump-and-wait mechanism of diffusion comes from the inelastic-scattering studies of Sakamoto *et al.* (1962). These authors performed a Fourier transform of their data to obtain the time dependence of the mean square displacement of a proton, $\langle R^2 \rangle$. Their results for 25 and 75 °C are shown in Fig. 4.20. Also shown are the calculated variations of $\langle R^2 \rangle$ for continuous diffusion at the two temperatures (based on the diffusion coefficients $D = 2 \cdot 13 \times 10^{-5}$ cm² s⁻¹ at 25 °C and $D = 6 \cdot 27 \times 10^{-5}$ cm² s⁻¹ at 75 °C) and the calculated $\langle R^2 \rangle$ for a gas composed of molecules of mass 18 and of mass 1. Note that at 25 °C the experimental $\langle R^2 \rangle$ is described adequately by continuous diffusion for times greater than $\sim 3 \times 10^{-12}$ s, but not for shorter times. At 75 °C continuous diffusion seems to set in at about 10^{-12} s. Note also that $\langle R^2 \rangle$ is about 4 Å at the onset of continuous diffusion, roughly equal to the square of the intermolecular separation in the liquid. Thus these results support the conclusion of the studies of the quasielastic scattering that, at moderate temperatures, water molecules remain near positions of temporary equilibrium for relatively long periods of time before experiencing diffusional displacements.

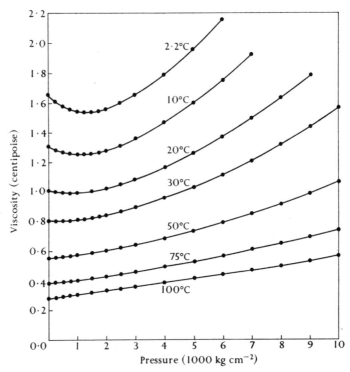

FIG. 4.21. The pressure dependence of the shear viscosity of water according to Bett and Cappi (1965).

(d) Viscosity

The viscosity of a liquid is a measure of its resistance to flow. Since flow takes place by displacements of the equilibrium positions of molecules, studies of the viscosity can yield some information on the nature of these displacements. The shear viscosities of liquid H_2O and D_2O are given in Table 4.8. Heavy water is the more viscous liquid; its viscosity exceeds that of H_2O by a factor that decreases from 1·2 at 30 °C to 1·1 at 250 °C. The energy of activation for viscous flow of H_2O

is also shown; this quantity is slightly larger than the energy of activation for dielectric relaxation at most temperatures.

With the exception of water, liquids become more viscous when pressure is applied to them. The behaviour of water at temperatures below about 30 °C is unique: the initial application of pressure causes the viscosity to decrease. As greater pressure is applied, the viscosity passes through a minimum and then increases. Fig. 4.21 shows that at 2·2 °C the pressure of minimum viscosity is roughly 1500 kg cm^{-2}. Increasing the temperature decreases the pressure of minimum viscosity until, at about 30 °C, the minimum disappears altogether. See Wonham (1967) for a comparison of the results of several investigators on the pressure dependence of the viscosity.

TABLE 4.8

Temperature dependence of the shear viscosity of water, η, and the energy of activation for viscous flow,[†] E_A^{vis}

Temperature (°C)	Viscosity (centipoise)		E_A^{vis} for H_2O (kcal mol^{-1})
	H_2O[‡]	D_2O[§]	
0	1·787		5·5[‖]
5	1·516		4·8[‖]
10	1·306		4·6[‖]
20	1·002		4·2[‖]
30	0·7975	0·969	
40	0·6531		
45	0·5963	0·713	
50	0·5467		3·4[††]
60	0·4666	0·552	
70	0·4049		
75	0·3788	0·445	
80	0·3554		
90	0·3156	0·365	
100	0·2829	0·323	2·8[††]
125	0·2227	0·252	
150	0·1863	0·208	2·1[††]
175	0·1578	0·175	
200	0·1362	0·151	
225	0·1225	0·135	
250	0·1127	0·124	

† $E_A^{vis} = R \, \mathrm{d}(\ln \eta)/\mathrm{d}(1/T)$.

‡ The data for 0–100 °C are those recommended by Stokes and Mills (1965) and presumably refer to 1 atm pressure. Data for 125–250 °C are those of Jaumotte as reported by Heiks *et al.* (1954) and presumably refer to the saturation pressure.

§ Data of Heiks *et al.* (1954) for 99·20 per cent D_2O.

‖ Horne *et al.* (1965) and Horne and Johnson (1966). The values have been estimated by the present authors from graphs in the original papers.

†† Ewell and Eyring (1937).

Pressure also affects the energy of activation for viscous flow, E_A^{vis}. Horne and Johnson (1966) and Horne *et al.* (1965) found that E_A^{vis} increases with decreasing temperature for water at atmospheric pressure down to at least $-0.5\,^\circ\text{C}$. As pressure is applied, E_A^{vis} decreases along all isotherms between 0 and 20 °C. This decrease of E_A^{vis} suggests that compression facilitates molecular displacements, perhaps by weakening or breaking hydrogen bonds.

A second form of viscosity is the *volume* (or *compressional*) *viscosity*. This property cannot be measured with viscosimeters but can be deduced from measurements of ultrasonic absorption and the value of the shear viscosity (see, for example, Litovitz and Davis 1965). The volume viscosity of water is roughly three times as large as the shear viscosity, and accounts for the strong absorption of ultrasonic waves by the liquid. Hall (1948) developed a theory of the volume viscosity in terms of a two-state model for water; his theory has subsequently been modified by several authors. Litovitz and Davis (1965) and Davis and Jarzynski (1967–8) have reviewed this work.

(e) Ionic dissociation and migration

Ionic migration is another process occurring in pure water which involves translational motions on the atomic level. We shall not discuss this topic in detail, as the concentration of ions in pure water is too small at room temperature to affect the structure of the liquid greatly. Readers interested in a more extended discussion are referred to the reviews of Eigen and De Maeyer (1958, 1959).

A small fraction of the molecules in pure water dissociates spontaneously to form H^+ and OH^- ions:

$$H_2O \underset{k_R}{\overset{k_D}{\rightleftharpoons}} H^+ + OH^-.$$

Here k_D is the rate constant for dissociation and k_R is the rate constant for neutralization. The ratio of these quantities, K_{H_2O}, is the dissociation constant. Accurate determinations of K_{H_2O} have been made by measuring the e.m.f. of appropriate galvanic cells (Harned and Owen 1939); the resulting value of K_{H_2O} leads directly to the ionic concentrations, and the temperature dependence of K_{H_2O} leads to the enthalpy and entropy of dissociation (see Table 4.9).

Eigen and De Maeyer (1958) used a relaxation technique to determine the values of k_D and k_R (Table 4.9). The neutralization reaction is extremely fast: Eigen and De Maeyer noted that if a homogeneous mixture of a one-normal-strong acid and a one-normal-strong base could be prepared and then the reaction suddenly initiated, the reaction would run nearly to completion in 10^{-11} s.

Considerable evidence, summarized by Eigen (1964), indicates that the H^+ and OH^- ions in water are strongly hydrated. The heat of hydration of H^+, for example, is about 276 kcal mol^{-1} at 25 °C, exceeding by over 100 kcal mol^{-1} that of any other univalent ion. This suggests that protons in the liquid are strongly bound to water molecules, forming oxonium (H_3O^+) ions, or even larger complexes. Eigen and De Maeyer (1958; Eigen 1964) believe that the $H_9O_4^+$ ion is the most common of the larger complexes. The evidence which they cite for the existence of this ion includes mass spectroscopy, quantum-mechanical calculations, and their interpretation of their own kinetic data (see below). These ions are short-lived: Eigen (1964) estimated that the mean period of association of a proton with a given water molecule, τ_{H^+}, is roughly 10^{-12} s. We can estimate the mean interval between two successive associations of a given water molecule with a proton, τ_{H_2O}, by inserting Eigen's value for τ_{H^+} into the relationship:

$$\frac{\tau_{H_2O}}{\tau_{H^+}} = \frac{[H_2O]}{[H^+]},$$

where the square brackets denote concentrations. This gives $\tau_{H_2O} \approx 5 \times 10^{-4}$ s. Apparently a water molecule experiences many reorientations and translations between two successive associations with a proton. Thus, although proton jumps in water are very rapid, the concentration of jumping protons is small, and consequently the motion of hydrogen atoms in the liquid is governed mainly by the rate of movement of intact water molecules. As noted by Samoilov (1965), this result is consistent with the nearly identical diffusion coefficients found for deuterium and $H_2{}^{18}O$ tracers in water (Section 4.6 (c)).

The mobilities of the H^+ and OH^- ions in water (Table 4.9) have been determined by combining measurements of the conductivity and the transference numbers. It is found that the mobilities of H^+ and OH^- are considerably greater than those of other univalent ions in water (for example, the mobilities of Na^+ and Cl^- at 25 °C are 0.53×10^{-3} and 0.79×10^{-3} cm^2 V^{-1} s^{-1} respectively (Eigen and De Maeyer 1958)). On the other hand, the mobility of the proton in water is smaller than in ice by an order of magnitude (Table 3.13). Eigen and De Maeyer (1958) interpreted these results as follows. The abnormal mobilities of H^+ and OH^- in both ice and water are a consequence of hydrogen bonds between

TABLE 4.9

Constants pertaining to ionic dissociation and migration in pure water at 25 °C†

Ionic dissociation: $H_2O \rightleftharpoons H^+ + OH^-$

Dissociation constant	$K_{H_2O} = \dfrac{k_D}{k_R} = \dfrac{[H^+][OH^-]}{[H_2O]}$	$= 1\cdot821_4 \times 10^{-16}$ mol litre^{-1}
Ionic concentration	$[H^+] = [OH^-]$	$= 1\cdot004 \times 10^{-7}$ mol litre^{-1}
Water concentration	$[H_2O]$	$= 55\cdot34$ mol litre^{-1}
Rate constant for dissociation	k_D	$= 2\cdot5 \times 10^{-5}$ s^{-1}
Rate constant for neutralization	k_R	$= 1\cdot4\ (\pm0\cdot2) \times 10^{11}$ litre mol^{-1} s^{-1}
Enthalpy of dissociation	ΔH	$= 13\cdot5$ kcal mol^{-1}
Entropy of dissociation	ΔS	$= -27$ cal deg^{-1} mol^{-1}

Rates of proton transfer:

$H_2O + H_3O^+ \xrightarrow{\ k_1\ } H_3O^+ + H_2O$	Rate constant k_1	$= 10\cdot6\ (\pm4) \times 10^9$ litre mol^{-1} s^{-1}‡
$H_2O + HO^- \xrightarrow{\ k_2\ } HO^- + H_2O$	Rate constant k_2	$= 3\cdot8\ (\pm1\cdot5) \times 10^9$ litre mol^{-1} s^{-1}‡

Related quantities:

Mobility of H^+	u_+	$= 3\cdot62 \times 10^{-3}$ cm^2 V^{-1} s^{-1}
Mobility of OH^-	u_-	$= 1\cdot98 \times 10^{-3}$ cm^2 V^{-1} s^{-1}
Direct current conductivity (where F is the Faraday constant)	$= F[H^+](u_+ + u_-)$	$= 5\cdot7 \times 10^{-8}\ \Omega^{-1}$ cm^{-1}
Heat of hydration of H^+		$= 276$ kcal mol^{-1}
Heat of hydration of OH^-		$= 111$ kcal mol^{-1}
Mean lifetime of an H_3O^+ ion	τ_{H^+}	$\approx 10^{-12}$ s§
Mean interval between the associations of a given water molecule with a proton	τ_{H_2O}	$\approx 5 \times 10^{-4}$ s‖

† Unless otherwise noted, values are taken from the review of Eigen and De Maeyer (1958).
‡ Meiboom (1961).   § Eigen (1964).   ‖ See text.

molecules; these links facilitate rapid transfer of protons. One of the protons of an H_3O^+ ion, for example, can jump along a hydrogen bond to combine with the adjacent water molecule:

$$H\!-\!H \cdots O\!-\!H \cdots O \quad \longrightarrow \quad O \cdots H\!-\!O \cdots H\!-\!O$$

Similarly, one proton of a water molecule can jump along a hydrogen bond to combine with an OH^- ion:

$$O \cdots H\!-\!O \cdots H\!-\!O \quad \longrightarrow \quad O\!-\!H \cdots O\!-\!H \cdots O$$

Both processes result in the migration of electric charge, and in the presence of an applied field give rise to the flow of current.

According to Eigen and De Maeyer, the mobility of H^+ is smaller in water than in ice because hydrogen bonding is imperfect in the liquid phase. Rapid transfer of protons, of the sort just mentioned, takes place only within the strongly hydrated complex, presumed to be $H_9O_4^+$. Further translation of a proton must await the formation of a strong hydrogen bond at the periphery of the complex. Thus the velocity of proton transfer in water is limited by the rate at which molecules in the vicinity of the hydrated complex come into positions which permit rapid transfer of the proton and thus diffusion of the complex.

The rate constants for the proton transfer reactions have been determined from NMR measurements by Meiboom (1961); they are given in Table 4.9.

(f) Molecular displacements: a summary

We are still far from having a detailed picture of molecular movements in water, but a number of qualitative conclusions can be inferred from the rate properties discussed in the five preceding sections.

(1) Molecules in liquid water near the melting-point experience roughly 10^{11} or 10^{12} reorientational and translational movements per second. Ice molecules near 0 °C experience only about 10^5 or 10^6 reorientational and translational movements per second. This is clearly one of the chief differences between ice and water.

(2) Raising the temperature of water increases the rate of reorientations and displacements, as is apparent from the decreasing viscosity, the decreasing relaxation times, and the greater rate of self-diffusion. The rotational correlation time from NMR studies indicates that when

the critical point is reached, the frequency of reorientations approaches, within a factor of 10, the frequencies of intramolecular vibrations.

(3) The rate of molecular reorientations and translations in liquid D_2O is slower than in ordinary water, as shown by the greater viscosity, the longer relaxation times, and the smaller coefficient of self-diffusion of heavy water.

(4) A number of similarities between those properties that depend on the rate of reorientation and those properties that depend on the rate of displacement, suggest that the processes of reorientation and translation are closely related. The activation energies for dielectric relaxation, self-diffusion, and viscous flow are roughly equal at 25 °C, though the activation energy for self-diffusion appears to be less strongly temperature-dependent than the others. Moreover, the quantity $\tau_d \times T/\eta$ is nearly independent of temperature, which also suggests that molecular translation and reorientation are related. No data seem to be inconsistent with a mechanism that involves jumps of individual water molecules.

(5) Neutron scattering studies indicate that, at least near the melting-point, reorientation and translation proceed by a 'jump and wait' mechanism, rather than by a series of small jumps.

(6) The decrease with increasing temperature of the activation energies for dielectric relaxation and viscous flow may be a reflection of smaller mean hydrogen-bond strengths at higher temperatures. Similarly, the decrease with increasing pressure of the activation energy for viscous flow may indicate that compression tends to weaken or break hydrogen bonds.

(7) Roughly two out of every 10^9 water molecules at 25 °C are ionized, and the resulting protons jump rapidly between molecules. The mean lifetime of a protonated water molecule is $\sim 10^{-12}$ s, and the mean interval between successive associations of a given water molecule with a proton is $\sim 5 \times 10^{-4}$ s.

4.7. Vibrational spectroscopy

Vibrational spectroscopy is a suitable technique for studying the V-structure of liquid water, because the periods of vibration (10^{-13} to 10^{-14} s) for both the intramolecular and intermolecular modes of water are short compared to the average time (10^{-11} to 10^{-12} s) between diffusional motions of molecules. The vibrational spectrum, moreover, is sensitive to the local environments of the molecules. Consequently some idea of the relative positions of molecules during very short time intervals can be derived from vibrational spectra. Interpretation of the spectral data is complex, and since the interpretation given below is based on analysis of the ice spectrum we shall assume that the reader is familiar with Section 3.5 (a).

(a) *Identification of spectral bands*

For every major vibrational band of ice in the range 50–4000 cm^{-1}, there exists a corresponding band in the spectrum of liquid water, though the band maxima are not necessarily at the same frequencies. The band widths in liquid water are not very different from those in ice I near the freezing-point. The bands of the liquid-water spectrum are listed in Table 4.10. Half-widths, extinction coefficients, and temperature dependencies of the band frequencies are given when they are known. Most of the bands can be identified in the infra-red and Raman spectra shown in Fig. 4.22.

Three separate bands are found in the frequency region containing the fundamental modes of water vapour:

(1) By far the most prominent is the broad, irregularly shaped band with its principal maximum near 3490 cm^{-1} in the infra-red spectrum and near 3440 cm^{-1} in the Raman spectrum. This band is associated with O–H stretching vibrations of molecules. It is located at a much lower frequency than the O–H stretching modes of water vapour (3657 and 3756 cm^{-1}) but not at quite so low a frequency as the O–H stretching band of ice (maximum near 3200 cm^{-1}). The first overtone of the H–O–H bending modes of molecules probably contributes to the band.

(2) A band near 1645 cm^{-1} arises from the H–O–H bending modes of molecules. This band also is intermediate in frequency between the corresponding bands in the vapour (1595 cm^{-1}) and ice (~ 1650 cm^{-1}).

(3) The very broad but very weak band with its maximum near 2125 cm^{-1} is the counterpart of the 'association band' in ice. It may be composed of overtones of intermolecular modes, or a combination of the 1645 cm^{-1} band with an intermolecular mode, or both. Williams (1966) proposed the assignment $\nu_2 + \nu_L - \nu_T$ for this band.

Three bands are found at lower frequencies and must arise from intermolecular modes:

(1) The most intense has its maximum in the infra-red spectrum near 700 cm^{-1}, but extends from 300 to above 900 cm^{-1}. In D$_2$O the

TABLE 4.10

Vibrational spectroscopy of liquid water

(Symbols: ν = frequency of band maximum in cm^{-1}; ϵ = extinction coefficient $\times$ 10^{-3} cm^2 mol^{-1} at maximum absorption; $\Delta\nu_{\frac{1}{2}}$ = width of band in cm^{-1} at half maximum intensity; T: x cm^{-1}/°C = a rise in temperature shifts frequency of band maximum by x cm^{-1}/°C.)

Vibrational band	Infra-red			
	H$_2$O	D$_2$O	HDO in D$_2$O	HDO in H$_2$O
Hindered translation ν_{T_2}				
Hindered translation ν_T	Band appears as a prominent shoulder on the ν_L band. $\nu \sim 193^c$ at 30 °C $\quad$ $\nu \sim 187^c$ at 30 °C $\quad\quad T: -0.2$ cm^{-1}/°C$\pm 50\%$			
Libration ν_L	Very broad band, extending from 300 cm^{-1} to 900 cm^{-1}. $\nu \sim 685^c$ at 30 °C $\quad$ $\nu \sim 505^c$ at 30 °C $\quad\quad T: -0.7$ cm^{-1}/° C$\pm 15\%$			
X–O–X' bending ν_2	$\nu = 1645^d$ $\epsilon = 20.8^d$ $\Delta\nu_{\frac{1}{2}} = 75^d$ $\quad\quad T: -0.1$ cm^{-1}/°C^c	$\nu = 1215^d$ $\epsilon = 16.1^d$ $\Delta\nu_{\frac{1}{2}} = 60^d$	$\nu = 1447^h$ $\epsilon = 20\pm 5^h$ $\Delta\nu_{\frac{1}{2}} = 85\pm 5^h$	
Association ν_A	$\nu = 2125^d$ $\epsilon = 3.23^d$ $\Delta\nu_{\frac{1}{2}} = 580^d$ $\quad\quad T: -0.9$ cm^{-1}/°C$\pm 15\%^c$	$\nu = 1555^d$ $\epsilon = 1.74^d$ $\Delta\nu_{\frac{1}{2}} = 370^d$		
O–X stretching ν_s	Very broad band with two principal maxima and a shoulder. At 25 °C: $\nu = 3280^d$ $\epsilon = 54.5^d$ $\nu = 3490^d$ $\epsilon = 62.7^d$ $\nu = 3920^d$ $\epsilon = 0.83^d$ $\Delta\nu_{\frac{1}{2}}$ for entire band $\sim 400^h$	$\nu = 2450^d$ $\epsilon = 55.2^d$ $\nu = 2540^d$ $\epsilon = 59.8^d$ $\nu = 2900^d$ $\epsilon = 0.598^d$ $\Delta\nu_{\frac{1}{2}}$ for entire band $\sim 330^h$	Single, nearly Gaussian band.^{h} At 22 °C: $\nu = 3400$ $\epsilon = 64\pm 5$ $\Delta\nu_{\frac{1}{2}} = 255\pm 5$ At 120 °C: $\nu = 3460$ $\epsilon = 44\pm 5$ $\Delta\nu_{\frac{1}{2}} = 270\pm 5$ $T: 0.67$ cm^{-1}/°C	At 22 °C: $\nu = 2500$ $\epsilon = 42\pm 5$ $\Delta\nu_{\frac{1}{2}} = 160\pm 5$ At 120 °C: $\nu = 2550$ $\epsilon = 26\pm 5$ $\Delta\nu_{\frac{1}{2}} = 180\pm 5$ $T: 0.52$ cm^{-1}/°C

[a] Walrafen (1964, 1966, 1967 a). $\qquad$ [d] Bayly et al. (1963). $\qquad$ [g] Weston (1962).
[b] Larsson and Dahlborg (1962). $\qquad$ [e] Schultz and Hornig (1961). $\qquad$ [h] Falk and Ford (1966).
[c] Draegert et al. (1966). $\qquad$ [f] Wall and Hornig (1965). $\qquad$ [i] Walrafen (1967 a).

man				Inelastic neutron scattering[b]	
)	D_2O	HDO in D_2O	HDO in H_2O	H_2O	D_2O
ak band; intensity decreases with in-asing temperature.[a]				Sharp band with negligible frequency shift between 2–92 °C.	
, 60	$\nu \sim 60$			$\nu \sim 60$	$\nu \sim 60$
eak band; intensity decreases with in-asing temperature in parallel with 60 cm^{-1} .d.[a]				Much less intense band than ν_{T^2} and ν_L bands. Frequency seems to decrease with increasing temperature.	
: 152–175[a]	$\nu = 152$–175^a			$\nu \sim 200$	$\nu \sim 200$
equency of max. decreases from 175 cm^{-1} −5 °C to 155 cm^{-1} at 95 °C.)					
attering may be composed of three bands hin the range of cited frequencies. In-sity decrease with increasing tempera-e parallels that of above bands.[a]				Broad band which further broadens and moves to lower frequencies as temperature is increased.	
~ 450–780[a]	$\nu \sim 375$–550^a			At 2 °C: $\nu \sim 580$ At 92 °C: $\nu \sim 410$	At 5 °C: $\nu \sim 450$ At 95° C: $\nu \sim 270$
= 1640[e]	$\nu = 1208^e$	$\nu \sim 1450^g$	$\nu \sim 1450^g$		
= 126[e]	$\Delta\nu_{\frac{1}{2}} = 67^e$				
pears as very weak, broad band.					
ry broad band with principal maximum at:		Single asymmetric band.[f]			
$\nu = 3439^e$	$\nu = 2532^e$	At 27 °C:	At 27 °C:		
= 407[e]	$\Delta\nu_{\frac{1}{2}} = 306^e$	$\nu = 3439$	$\nu = 2516$		
less intense component is present near:		$\Delta\nu_{\frac{1}{2}} = 278$	$\Delta\nu_{\frac{1}{2}} = 160$		
= 3300[e]	$\nu = 2400^e$		At 65 °C:		
her components may be present near:			$\nu = 2529$		
= 3600[e]	$\nu = 2600^e$		$\Delta\nu_{\frac{1}{2}} = 166$		
= 3500[i]					

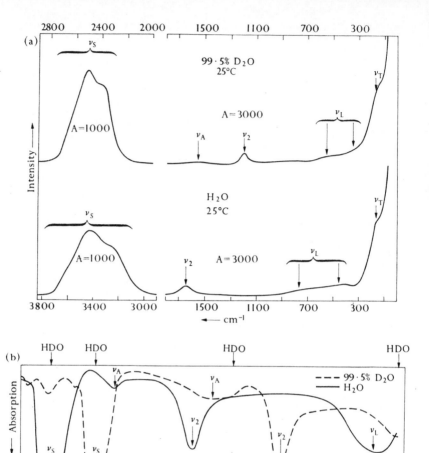

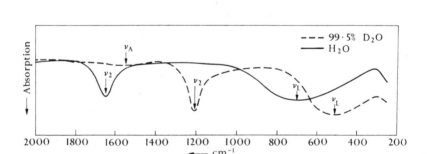

Fig. 4.22. Infra-red and Raman spectra of water. (a) Photoelectric Raman spectra of liquid water and heavy water. Arrows show positions of bands and components of bands. The rise on the right-hand side is due to the exciting arc. A = amplification. (b) Infra-red spectra of liquid water and heavy water. Arrows on top show weak absorptions probably arising from HDO impurities in D_2O. Adapted from Walrafen (1964) with changes of notation.

band maximum is near 500 cm^{-1}. The position of this band and its frequency shift for isotopic substitution suggest that it is the counterpart of the ν_L librational mode of ice. Its frequency is lower than the ν_L mode of ice ($\sim$ 795 cm^{-1} at 0 °C; Zimmermann and Pimentel 1962), and shifts to even lower frequencies as water is heated. This band also appears in the inelastic neutron and Raman spectra (see Table 4.10). In the Raman spectrum two other librational bands may be present near 450 and 550 cm^{-1}.

(2) An infra-red band with its maximum near 193 cm^{-1} appears as a prominent shoulder on the 700 cm^{-1} band. The band frequency shifts only to 187 cm^{-1} in D_2O, so the band must arise from hindered translations of molecules. This mode, which is also detected by Raman and inelastic neutron spectra, undoubtedly corresponds to the ν_T mode of ice.

(3) A narrow band appears at about 60 cm^{-1} in the Raman and in-elastic neutron scattering spectra. Its frequency in D_2O is also near 60 cm^{-1}. This band probably arises from hindered transla-tions and corresponds to the ν_{T_2} mode of ice.

In addition to the above bands, several very small energy transfers (in the range $5\,(\pm 1)$ cm^{-1}) have been observed by several investigators in inelastic neutron spectra (see Larsson 1965). The existence of these energy transfers has not, however, been firmly established.

(b) The O–H and O–D stretching bands

The O–H stretching band is the most thoroughly studied spectral region of liquid water. As in the case of ice, the stretching band of a dilute solution of HDO in either H_2O or D_2O is the key to understanding this spectral band. The HDO bands are simpler because the stretching vibrations of an HDO molecule are only weakly coupled to the vibrations of neighbouring molecules, and also because Fermi resonance with the overtone of ν_2 is absent (Section 3.5 (a)). As a result, the shape of these bands can be interpreted in terms of the local environments of water molecules, or in other words, in terms of the V-structure of the liquid. We shall therefore start by discussing these bands quite thoroughly. We shall then briefly consider the stretching bands in pure H_2O and D_2O.

Fig. 4.23 shows the Raman stretching bands of dilute solutions of HDO in D_2O and H_2O. We shall call these the uncoupled O–H and O–D stretching bands. Panels (a) and (b) are smoothed spectra reported by Wall and Hornig (1965) for 5 mol per cent isotopic solutions. These bands exhibit no structure and only a slight asymmetry. They are

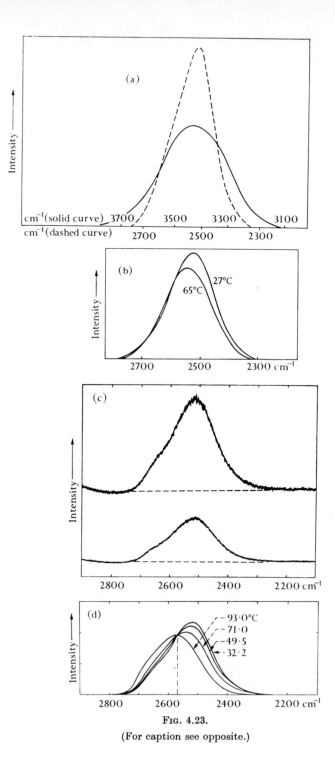

FIG. 4.23.
(For caption see opposite.)

centred at higher frequencies than the corresponding bands in ice I and are about five times broader (Table 4.11). Panel (c) shows the uncoupled O–D band recorded by Walrafen (1967 a, b) for a 6·2 molar solution of D_2O in H_2O, using a laser Raman source and a narrower slit width than that used by Wall and Hornig. The band is similar to the one reported by Wall and Hornig but it is more markedly asymmetric, and the contour on the high-frequency side seems to contain three points of inflexion, indicating the presence of a shoulder. Panel (d) shows the temperature dependence of the uncoupled O–D band as reported by Walrafen (1965 b). The band maximum moves to higher frequencies as the temperature is increased, and the spectra for different temperatures pass through a common point (an *isosbestic point*) at 2570 (± 5) cm^{-1}.

The infra-red spectra of the uncoupled stretching bands have been studied under a greater variety of conditions. Falk and Ford (1966) recorded the infra-red spectra of these bands between 0 and 130 °C. The bands have the same general appearance as the Raman bands in Fig. 4.23 (a) and (b); spectroscopic constants for them are given in Table 4.11. Franck and Roth (1967) studied the infra-red spectrum of the uncoupled band at temperatures and pressures from 30 to 400 °C and from 50 to 5000 bars respectively. For water at a constant density of 1·0 g cm^{-3}, the frequency of the band maximum shifts from 2507 cm^{-1} to 2587 cm^{-1} and the integrated band intensity falls by 40 per cent as the temperature is increased from 30 to 300°. The band becomes more asymmetric at higher temperatures, but the contour is perfectly smooth with no hint of a shoulder. For water maintained at 400 °C, the integrated band intensity decreases by a factor of 6·4 as the density is decreased from 0·9 to 0·0165 g cm^{-3}. At all densities down to 0·1 g cm^{-3}, the band has a smooth contour and no shoulder, and the frequency of maximum absorption shifts gradually from 2605 cm^{-1} to $\sim$ 2650 cm^{-1}. Below 0·1 g cm^{-3}, the rotational fine structure becomes apparent and is very distinct at 0·0165 g

---

Fig. 4.23. Uncoupled O–H and O–D stretching bands in the Raman spectrum of water. (a) Uncoupled stretching bands of 5 mole per cent H_2O in D_2O and D_2O in H_2O, both at 27 °C, as reported by Wall and Hornig (1965).† (b) Effect of temperature on O–D uncoupled stretching band as reported by Wall and Hornig (1965). (c) Argon-ion laser Raman spectra of a 6·2 M solution of D_2O in H_2O at 25 (± 1) °C, as reported by Walrafen (1967 b). The amplification of the upper tracing is twice that of the lower tracing. (d) Effect of temperature on the O–D uncoupled stretching band as reported by Walrafen (1967 b). The dashed vertical line indicates the isosbestic point near 2570 cm^{-1}. These spectra were obtained with conventional mercury excitation and a narrow (15 cm^{-1}) slit width.

† The uncoupled O–H band of panel (a) may have been inverted through its maximum during preparation of the original paper (private communication from Dr. Wall).

TABLE 4.11

Characteristics of uncoupled stretching bands†

Phase	O–H stretching mode		O–D stretching mode	
	Frequency‡ (cm⁻¹)	Half-width§ (cm⁻¹)	Frequency‡ (cm⁻¹)	Half-width§ (cm⁻¹)
Ice I −160 °C (IR)[b]	3277	~ 50	2421	~ 30
Ice II −160 °C (IR)[c]	{ 3373, 3357, 3323	each < 18	{ 2493, 2481, 2460, 2455	each ~ 5
Liquid				
22° (IR)[d]	3400	255 ± 5	2500	160 ± 5
25° (R)[g]	..	..	2507 ± 5	..
27° (R)[e]	3439	278	2516	160
62° (R)[g]	..	..	2550 ± 5	..
65° (R)[e]	..	..	2529	166
120° (IR)[d]	3460	270 ± 5	2550	180 ± 5
200° (IR, 2800 bars)[f]	..	..	2568	195
300° (IR, 5000 bars)[f]	..	..	2587	153
HDO vapour (IR)[a]	3707		2727	

† Raman bands are designated by R and infra-red bands by IR. All entries refer to atmospheric pressure, unless noted otherwise.

‡ Frequency of band maximum. § Width of band at half maximum intensity.
[a] Benedict *et al.* (1956). [b] Bertie and Whalley (1964 *a*).
[c] Bertie and Whalley (1964 *b*). [d] Falk and Ford (1966).
[e] Wall and Hornig (1965). [f] Franck and Roth (1967).
[g] Walrafen (1967 *b*).

cm^{-3}. Other studies of the uncoupled infra-red stretching band were reported by van Eck *et al.* (1958) and Hartman (1966).

Table 4.11 lists the frequencies of the uncoupled stretching bands in the solid, liquid, and vapour states. The frequency of each isotopic band in the liquid (for example, the O–H band for 27° at 3439 cm^{-1}) lies between the ice I (3277 cm^{-1}) and vapour (3707 cm^{-1}) frequencies for the band. Wall and Hornig (1965) interpreted these relative frequencies using the well-known correlation between hydrogen-bond strength and the magnitude of the lowering of the O–H stretching frequency from the vapour value (for example, Pimentel and McClellan 1960). In their view, the relative frequencies 'indicate that the most likely hydrogen bond strength in liquid water is much less than in ice, but still quite strong'. They believe that the small shift in frequency of the band maximum between 27 and 65 °C (see Table 4.11) shows that there is no marked change in the most likely hydrogen-bond strength of liquid water over this temperature range. They suggested that the slight asymmetry of the uncoupled stretching band 'originates in the lower energy of stronger hydrogen bonds'. The frequency distribution of the uncoupled infra-red bands can be interpreted in the same way: the upward shift in frequency as water is heated indicates that the mean hydrogen-bond strength decreases gradually as the critical point is approached.

Wall and Hornig (1965) interpreted the widths of the uncoupled O–H and O–D stretching bands in terms of the local environments of molecules (local V-structures) in liquid water.[†] They first noted that the uncoupled bands are narrower than the stretching bands in pure H_2O and D_2O. For example, the half-width of the O–D stretching band of a dilute solution of HDO in H_2O is about 160 cm^{-1}, whereas the half-width of the coupled O–D stretching band in pure D_2O is roughly 306 cm^{-1} (Schultz and Hornig 1961). But as can be seen from Table 4.11, the uncoupled O–H and O–D bands are still very wide (270 and 160 cm^{-1}, respectively), even when compared with the uncoupled O–H and O–D bands of ice I (50 and 30 cm^{-1}, respectively). Clearly, this residual width cannot arise from vibrational coupling with neighbouring molecules, as this form of coupling has been largely eliminated by using dilute isotopic solutions. Nor can the residual width arise from hydrogen bonding *per se*, since hydrogen bonds are present in ice II, where uncoupled O–D stretching bands are 5 cm^{-1} wide. According to Wall and Hornig, temperature broadening cannot account for the width of the

† The material on which this interpretation is based appears in Section 3.5 (*a*). Readers not familiar with this material may refer to the summary on p. 129.

uncoupled bands; the half-width of the uncoupled Raman band increases by only 6 cm^{-1} over the temperature range of 27–65 °C.

The origin of the breadth of the uncoupled bands, Wall and Hornig concluded, is structural disorder in liquid water. The distribution of oxygen–oxygen separations of nearest neighbours in the liquid gives rise to a distribution of perturbing potentials of the static field type $(U'_j$ in eqn (3.15)) at O–H and O–D groups, and hence to a distribution of O–H and O–D stretching frequencies. The uncoupled stretching bands of liquid water are broader than those of ice I because the range of nearest-neighbour oxygen–oxygen distances is greater in the liquid. Their breadth increases slightly with temperature because the distribution of nearest-neighbour separations becomes more diffuse at higher temperatures.

Two interpretations of the shape of the uncoupled stretching bands in liquid water have been given. The first is that of Wall and Hornig (1965), Falk and Ford (1966), and Franck and Roth (1967), all of whom emphasized that their results indicate an intensity distribution that is continuous and passes through a single maximum (except above the critical temperature at densities below 0·1 g cm^{-3}, where the rotational structure becomes important). They noted that such a distribution seems to be inconsistent with models that depict water as a mixture of a *small* number of distinctly different species of molecules. The basis for this argument is that if a small number of distinct species do indeed exist, then during a period long compared to a molecular vibration, each species is characterized by a distinct molecular environment. Now the uncoupled stretching bands are sensitive indicators of distinct local environments, and should thus manifest these distinct environments. Ice II presents a striking example of this (Section 3.5 (b) and Table 4.11). In this polymorph there are four distinct nearest-neighbour separations, and four separate peaks are visible in the uncoupled O–D stretching band. Hence the apparent absence of structure in the uncoupled stretching band of water seems to rule out the existence of a *small* number of distinct local environments in liquid water. The distorted hydrogen-bond and the random-network models for water, in contrast to the mixture models, require a continuous distribution of nearest neighbouring oxygen–oxygen separations. These models thus seem to be consistent with the shape of the uncoupled stretching band.

On the basis of their interpretation of the uncoupled stretching-band shape, Wall and Hornig estimated the relative frequency of nearest neighbours in liquid water at each intermolecular separation. They did this by means of the well-known correlation between O–H stretching frequencies and oxygen–oxygen separations in hydrogen-bonded crystals (Pimentel and McClellan 1960). They assumed that the same correlation is applicable to liquid water and were thus able to identify an oxygen–oxygen separation with each O–H stretching frequency. Details of this procedure are given in their paper. Their results are shown in Fig. 4.24. The resulting curves resemble the radial distribution curves derived from X-ray diffraction (Section 4.2 (a)): nearest neighbours do not approach within about 2·75 Å of each other, and the most probable separation is about 2·85 Å. Wall and Hornig noted that the agreement between these curves and the X-ray curves gives added support to their hypothesis that the uncoupled band breadth reflects a continuous distribution of intermolecular distances in the liquid. The curves of Fig. 4.24 differ from the X-ray curves in that they refer only to separations of nearest neighbours. Thus the frequency of separations falls off above 2·85 Å and distances as large as 3·10 Å may be present. It should be noted that the slope of the correlation curve which relates O–H stretching frequencies and oxygen–oxygen separation (Wall and Hornig 1965) drops abruptly at about 2·85 Å and has a small value for all larger separations. This means that the information contained in the distribution functions of Fig. 4.24 is much less detailed for separations greater than 2·85 Å than for those less than 2·85 Å.

A second interpretation of the shape of the uncoupled stretching band, based mainly on the uncoupled Raman bands shown in Fig. 4.23 (c) and (d), has been proposed by Walrafen (1967 a, b). He believes that the observed band arises from the superposition of two or three relatively broad, overlapping component bands, each of which is Gaussian in shape. He found that at least two Gaussian components are needed to fit the observed uncoupled O–D Raman band at 25 and 65 °C. One of these components is centred near 2520 cm^{-1}; another is centred near 2650 cm^{-1} and accounts for the apparent shoulder on the high-frequency side of the bands in Fig. 4.23 (c) and (d). As water is heated, the intensity of the high-frequency component increases compared to that of the low-frequency component. Walrafen believes that the low-frequency component is associated primarily with hydrogen-bonded water molecules, and the high-frequency component primarily with non-hydrogen-bonded molecules, and that the increasing intensity of the high-frequency component as water is heated reflects the conversion of hydrogen-bonded molecules to non-hydrogen-bonded molecules. This interpretation is supported by the discovery of an isosbestic point, a phenomenon that

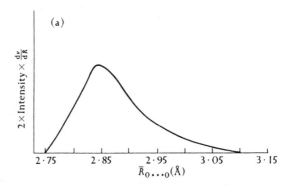

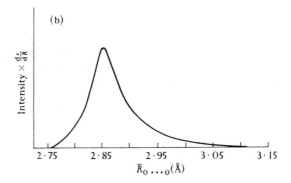

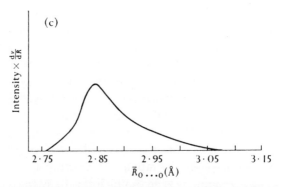

Fig. 4.24. Distribution of nearest-neighbour separations in liquid water, as derived from shape of uncoupled stretching bands. The ordinate of the curve at any given distance is proportional to the fraction of molecules having a nearest neighbour at that distance. (a) From O–H band at 27 °C. (b) From O–D band at 27 °C. (c) From O–D band at 65 °C. From Wall and Hornig (1965).

is often associated with two absorbing species in equilibrium. Moreover, it is consistent with Walrafen's explanation of the shape of the stretching band in pure H_2O (see below) and with his studies of the intermolecular vibrations (Section 4.7 (c)).

This interpretation of the uncoupled stretching band shape rests on the assumption that the component vibrational Raman bands are each Gaussian in shape, since this assumption is used to dissect the observed band into components. Furthermore, the individual component bands that generate the observed band are found to overlap to a considerable extent, so that an appreciable fraction of the different species that are assumed to be responsible for the component bands share a common set of frequencies. Questions can be raised about each of these points.

In the first place, most investigators now agree that the contour of the uncoupled O–H (and O–D) band of water is the envelope of many narrow but overlapping bands, each of which is associated with an O–H (or O–D) oscillator in a particular environment. The same is presumably true of the component band that Walrafen assigns to the hydrogen-bonded species in the liquid. The shape of this band must be determined to a large extent by the distribution of O---O separations in the hydrogen bonds in this component of the liquid. The frequency of maximum intensity corresponds roughly to the most probable O---O separation; frequencies on either side correspond to larger and smaller O---O separations. Now the distribution of these separations is almost certainly not Gaussian in shape: the steep increase of repulsive energy at smaller separations undoubtedly suppresses the relative abundance of hydrogen bonds having lengths smaller than the most probable separation. Thus the component of the observed band that might arise from hydrogen-bonded O–H groups would not be expected to have a Gaussian shape.

Furthermore, it is difficult to see why the component band assigned to the non-hydrogen-bonded species should be as broad as it is. Some variable element in the non-hydrogen-bonded O–H (or O–D) environment must be assumed to exist which is different from a hydrogen bond yet can produce a large shift in the O–H (or O–D) frequency. Indeed, an appreciable fraction of non-hydrogen-bonded O–H (or O–D) groups must exist in an environment which is sufficiently perturbed to produce frequencies that are identical with those of some of the hydrogen-bonded O–H groups. It is difficult to imagine what kind of variability in the environment, other than hydrogen bonding, could be responsible for such large frequency shifts. Of course, if the variability of this environment is ascribed to hydrogen bonding, then the entire analysis becomes virtually equivalent to the alternative one of Wall and Hornig, Falk and Ford, and Franck and Roth. The only remaining difference would be Walrafen's emphasis on grouping the many different environments into two broad classes. The isosbestic point observed by Walrafen suggests that this view may be a reasonable one.

In the opinion of the present authors, the following conclusions may be based on studies of the uncoupled stretching bands: (a) A range of O–H environments, or equivalently of hydrogen-bond strengths, is present in liquid water, as shown by the widths of the bands. (b) Water does not contain a *small* number of *distinctly different* molecular species, as indicated by the relatively smooth band contours that pass through a single maximum. The band shapes, however, do not rule out the possibility that the liquid contains two or more species, each of which exhibits a wide range of molecular environments. Of course, in the limit of many species, or of a wide variability of the environments of each species, this description differs only in semantics from the description of the liquid as a continuous distribution of molecular environments. (c) The presence of some non-hydrogen-bonded O–H groups in the liquid which have environments distinctly different from the majority of O–H groups cannot be excluded on the basis of the band shapes. Non-hydrogen-bonded groups are more difficult to detect by infra-red methods than are hydrogen-bonded O–H groups, because the intensity of absorption of the O–H stretching band increases by a factor of about 10 when the O–H group forms a hydrogen bond (Van Thiel *et al.* 1957, Swenson 1965). Thus it is possible that a sizeable number of non-hydrogen-bonded O–H groups are present in water even below 100 °C, but do not produce a perceptible second maximum at the high-frequency side of the infra-red stretching band because their absorption is too small. The effect of hydrogen-bond formation on the intensity of Raman scattering has apparently not been studied, and it is not inconceivable that free O–H groups might scatter less strongly than O–H···O groups. Indeed, it should be noted that the total integrated intensity of both Wall and Hornig's and Walrafen's Raman spectra (Fig. 4.23) decreases with increasing temperature, as does the integrated intensity of the infra-red spectrum. This behaviour is consistent with the breaking of hydrogen bonds, though it could also be associated with the weakening of hydrogen bonds. Similarly, the apparent shoulder observed by Walrafen (1967 b) on the high-frequency side of the uncoupled Raman band could arise from the presence of non-hydrogen-bonded O–H groups, or, as will be discussed in Section 4.8 (a), it could also be regarded as arising from highly distorted hydrogen bonds.

Several authors have made specific estimates of the fraction of broken hydrogen bonds in the liquid from the distribution of intensity across the uncoupled stretching band. Wall and Hornig (1965) argued on theoretical grounds that 'vapour-like molecules' absorb above 3600 cm^{-1}, and comprise no more than 5 per cent of the liquid. The lower bound of 3600 cm^{-1} for absorption of vapour-like molecules is supported by Stevenson's study (1965) of H_2O in dilute CCl_4 solution; he found that the ν_1 and ν_3 stretching modes are at 3620 and 3710 cm^{-1} respectively. Walrafen (1966, 1967 a) argued, however, that the 3600 cm^{-1} lower bound is at least 100 cm^{-1} too high. Adopting a lower bound of 3500 cm^{-1} on the basis of the Raman O–H stretching band in pure H_2O near the critical point, Walrafen estimated that at least 30 per cent of the water molecules at 27 °C are not hydrogen-bonded.

The stretching bands in H_2O and D_2O

The stretching bands in pure H_2O and pure D_2O are far more difficult to interpret than the uncoupled stretching bands of HDO. The additional difficulties stem from several sources:

(1) The frequencies of the two O–H stretching vibrations, ν_1 and ν_3, and that of the first overtone of the bending vibration, $2\nu_2$, are close to each other.

(2) Each of these vibrations may couple with the vibrations of neighbouring molecules, causing a splitting of each band. Since the band frequencies are closely spaced, the split bands overlap one another.

(3) The overlapping ν_1 and $2\nu_2$ modes may be in Fermi resonance with each other (that is, $2\nu_2$ may borrow intensity from ν_1). Furthermore, owing to perturbations of neighbouring molecules, the two O–H bonds of a given molecule may not be identical; consequently the ν_3 vibration may not be strictly asymmetric, so that it may also participate in Fermi resonance with $2\nu_2$.

The shapes of the stretching bands of pure H_2O and D_2O have not yet been adequately explained in terms of all these effects, but several proposals have been made to explain the main features of the bands. Let us consider three of them.

Cross *et al.* (1937) and Walrafen (1967 a) ascribed the structure in the Raman stretching band (Fig. 4.22 (a)) to the presence of water molecules forming different numbers of hydrogen bonds. This interpretation is based partly on the observation that increasing temperature causes a decrease in intensity of the O–H band in the 3200 cm^{-1} region and an increase in intensity in the 3600 cm^{-1} region. These changes are attributed to larger numbers of broken hydrogen bonds at higher temperatures. Walrafen (1967 a) found that he could fit the observed band at all temperatures from 10 to 90 °C by four Gaussian components, two of which (the lower-frequency ones) decrease in intensity as water is heated and two of which increase. He assigned the components which increase on raising the temperature to the two intramolecular stretching modes of non-hydrogen-bonded molecules, and the components which decrease on heating to two vibrations of hydrogen-bonded molecules. Walrafen interpreted the structure in the infra-red stretching band in the same general way.

Schultz and Hornig (1961) explained the shape of the Raman stretching band in terms of Fermi resonance. They measured the depolarization of Raman scattering as a function of frequency across the band. Using this as a guide, they assigned the slight shoulder near 3600 cm^{-1} to ν_3,[†] the main maximum primarily to ν_1, and the component near 3200 cm^{-1} to $2\nu_2$ in Fermi resonance with ν_1. The variation of band shape with temperature was attributed by them to changes in the Fermi resonance that arise from shifts in frequency of the ν_1, ν_2, and ν_3 vibrations.

A slightly different interpretation of the stretching band shape in water was proposed by Schiffer and Hornig (1967). They believe that collisions of molecules in the liquid give rise to a range of ν_1 and ν_3 vibrational frequencies, the mean ν_1 and ν_3 frequencies being near 3400 and 3600 cm^{-1} respectively. The overtone of ν_2 near 3200 cm^{-1} overlaps the ν_1 vibrations of lowest frequency, and thereby gains intensity from them through Fermi resonance. As water is heated, the mean frequencies of the ν_1 and ν_3 bands increase. This has the effect of diminishing Fermi resonance between the ν_1 and $2\nu_2$ vibrations, and thus of decreasing the band intensity near 3200 cm^{-1}.

(c) *Intermolecular vibrations*

The three vibrational bands arising from intermolecular vibrations were mentioned in Section 4.7 (a). Near 0 °C all three bands are remarkably similar to the corresponding bands of ice. In fact, over the 60–900 cm^{-1} region, the inelastic neutron spectra of ice at −3 °C and of liquid water at +2 °C are virtually identical (Larsson and Dahlborg 1962).

The broad ν_L band (300–900 cm^{-1}), attributed to molecular librations, appears in infra-red, Raman, and inelastic neutron spectra. At 0 °C, the

† Senior and Thompson (1965) disputed this assignment. See their paper for a discussion of the merits of several interpretations of the stretching region.

infra-red band maximum is at ~ 700 cm^{-1} (Draegert *et al.* 1966), somewhat less than the ~ 795 cm^{-1} for ice I (Zimmermann and Pimentel 1962). The band maximum continues to shift to lower frequencies with rising temperature, as does the ν_L band of the inelastic neutron spectrum. In Section 3.5 (*b*) we associated lower frequencies of the ν_L band in some ice polymorphs with more easily bent hydrogen bonds. We also found that the polymorphs having lower ν_L frequencies probably have weaker hydrogen bonds. It seems likely, then, that the lower ν_L frequencies in water as compared to ice indicate that hydrogen bonds in the liquid are more easily bent and are weaker than those of ice. Heating further weakens and aids distortion of the hydrogen bonds.

The less intense ν_T band, attributed to hindered translations, has its maximum near 199 cm^{-1} at 0 °C. This is only slightly less than the maximum of the ν_T band in ice I, ~ 214 cm^{-1} (Zimmermann and Pimentel 1962). With increasing temperature the band maximum in water shifts to lower frequencies by about 0·2 cm^{-1}/°C. A similar shift of the Raman ν_T band has been observed (Walrafen 1966). In Section 3.5 (*b*), the lower ν_T frequencies of some ice polymorphs were attributed to more easily stretched hydrogen bonds in these polymorphs. Thus it seems reasonable to suppose that hydrogen bonds in liquid water are more readily stretched than those in ice, and become increasingly so at higher temperatures.

The intermolecular bands in the Raman spectrum have been investigated by Walrafen (1964, 1966, 1967 *a*). These bands are difficult to study owing to their very low intensities. Walrafen believes that the ν_L band is composed of three Gaussian components, at ~ 440, 540, and 720 cm^{-1}. He found that the integrated intensities of the ν_L, ν_T, and ν_{T_2} bands decrease in parallel with rising temperature. He assigned these bands to specific vibratory motions, and then interpreted their temperature dependence in terms of changes in water structure.

Walrafen assigned the intermolecular bands to the normal modes of vibration of the five-molecule hydrogen-bonded structure shown in Fig. 4.25. This model was chosen on the basis of evidence from X-ray diffraction (Section 4.2 (*a*)) that indicates some water molecules are tetrahedrally coordinated in the liquid. The model is assumed to have C_{2v} symmetry for simplicity. The normal modes include three non-symmetric deformations that correspond to librations about the three molecular moments of inertia, and Walrafen (1964, 1967 *a*) assigned the three ν_L components to these modes. The model predicts four hydrogen-bond stretching modes; Walrafen assigned the ν_T band near 175 cm^{-1} to these. The remaining normal modes are symmetric deformations, corresponding to hydrogen-bond bending. The band at 60 cm^{-1} was assigned to these. Only small isotope effects are expected for the symmetric deformation modes and the hydrogen-bond bending modes, since entire water molecules, not hydrogen atoms, are the vibrating masses in these modes.

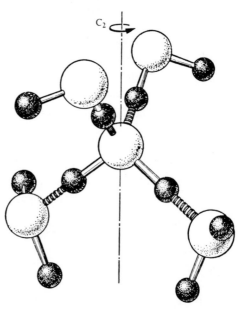

FIG. 4.25. Hydrogen-bonded structure, containing five water molecules, used by Walrafen (1964) to assign intermolecular bands of water to normal vibrations. Small spheres represent hydrogen atoms; large spheres, oxygen atoms; and discs, hydrogen bonds. From Walrafen (1964).

Walrafen (1964, 1966) attributed the decreasing Raman intensities of the intermolecular bands at higher temperatures to the breakdown of tetrahedral groups of water molecules. He represents the breakdown by an equilibrium between 'bound' molecules which are hydrogen-bonded to four neighbours, and 'unbound' molecules which are not: $U \rightleftharpoons B$. Assuming that the integrated intensity of the ν_T band is proportional to the concentration of bound molecules, Walrafen was able to estimate the fraction of hydrogen-bonded molecules at each temperature. His results, shown in Fig. 4.11, are that the mole fraction of hydrogen-bonded molecules decreases from 0·6 at 0 °C to 0·1 at 100 °C. Walrafen (1966) found that ΔH^0 associated with the process $B \rightarrow U$ is 5·6 kcal mol^{-1}. Since complete breakdown of a tetrahedral lattice would necessitate rupture of two hydrogen bonds per molecule, this ΔH^0 corresponds to an average hydrogen-bond energy of $2 \cdot 8$ kcal mol^{-1}.

Other explanations are possible for the decreased Raman intensity at higher temperatures. One was mentioned in passing by Walrafen (1966): he suggested that the decreased Raman intensity of the intermolecular modes might be associated with strongly bent hydrogen bonds. Taking this view, the decreasing intensities at higher temperatures are indicative of larger numbers of distorted hydrogen bonds, and the U molecules correspond to molecules forming only very distorted hydrogen bonds. Alternatively, the decreased intensity might have the same origin as the decrease in intensity with increasing temperature of the main maximum of the ν_T band in the infra-red spectrum of ice I (Bertie and Whalley 1967; Section 3.5 (a)). Bertie and Whalley believe this effect is associated with hot bands.

Clearly, if one accepts Walrafen's first explanation for the decrease in Raman intensity of the intermolecular modes, then one must accept his interpretation of the uncoupled stretching band in terms of an equilibrium between hydrogen-bonded and non-hydrogen-bonded molecules (Section 4.7 (b)). But then, since only 10 per cent of all possible hydrogen bonds are supposed to remain at 100 °C, one must ascribe nearly all the observed changes in the uncoupled stretching band between the liquid and the vapour at 100° C to forces other than hydrogen bonds. These changes in the uncoupled infra-red stretching band consist in an upward shift in frequency of maximum absorption (of ~ 260 cm^{-1}) and a substantial decrease in total integrated intensity. Such changes, however, are just those that usually accompany the breaking of hydrogen bonds (Pimentel and McClellan 1960, p. 70). For this reason one of the other explanations for the decrease in intermolecular Raman intensities seems more likely to the present authors.

(d) Overtone and combination bands

Although no detailed discussion will be given of the spectrum of water at frequencies above 4000 cm^{-1}, we should consider some studies of this region which have led to conclusions about the structure of water.

Buijs and Choppin (1963) observed the temperature dependence of the infra-red spectrum of water in the vicinity of 8000 cm^{-1}.[†] They attributed the absorption of this region to the $\nu_1 + \nu_2 + \nu_3$ combination of water vibrations. They suggested that this absorption is the resultant

[†] Thomas *et al.* (1965) have repeated this work, analysing the data in a slightly different way. They have also studied the corresponding region of the D$_2$O spectrum. Luck (1965) made a similar study covering temperatures from 0 °C to the critical point.

of three component bands whose intensities vary with the temperature. The first component band (8000 cm^{-1}) is prominent in ice, so they assigned it to water molecules with both O–H groups in hydrogen bonds. They assigned the second band (8330 cm^{-1}) to molecules with one O–H group in a hydrogen bond, and the third band (8620 cm^{-1}) to molecules with two free O–H groups. From the temperature variation of the extinction of each component, Buijs and Choppin calculated the relative numbers of the three types of molecules in liquid water. The fraction of molecules having no hydrogen bonds increases from 0·27 at 6 °C to 0·40 at 72 °C; the fraction of molecules having two hydrogen bonds decreases from 0·31 at 6 °C to 0·18 at 72 °C; and the fraction of molecules having one hydrogen bond is nearly constant at about 0·42.

Hornig (1964) disputed the basic assumption of this work: that the temperature dependence of the infra-red band shape around 8000 cm^{-1} is due to changing concentrations of different species of water molecules. Hornig argued that if three distinct species of water molecules are present, and if their presence causes structure in a combination band, then their presence must also cause a similar structure in the uncoupled fundamental stretching bands. Since these bands do not exhibit a similar structure (Section 4.7 (b)), the temperature dependence of the absorption near 8000 cm^{-1} almost certainly has some other cause.†　A more plausible explanation is that heating shifts the frequencies of the fundamental modes, and these shifts alter Fermi resonances between overlapping overtones and combination bands in this region.

4.8. The structure of water: conclusions based on properties

(a) Problems of describing the properties of water in terms of hydrogen bonds

As illustrated by numerous examples in this chapter, the hydrogen bond is a useful concept for correlating data on water. In some instances, however, care must be taken in describing the properties of water in terms of hydrogen bonds; a tendency to view the hydrogen bond as being completely analogous to the covalent chemical bond can be misleading. For example, in several sections (3.6 (a), 3·6 (c), and 4.3 (a)) we have noted that the energy of a hydrogen bond, unlike that of a typical chemical bond at room temperature, depends strongly on the environment of the bond. Let us now consider a related point: the meaning of the term 'break' as applied to hydrogen bonds in liquid water. Though this consideration is largely a matter of semantics, it may explain in part

---

† Buijs and Choppin (1964) replied to this comment, but did not, in the opinion of the present authors, answer Hornig's basic objection to their interpretation.

the wide variation in estimates of the fraction of broken hydrogen bonds in water (Fig. 4.11), and may give some insight into the process of molecular reorientation in the liquid.

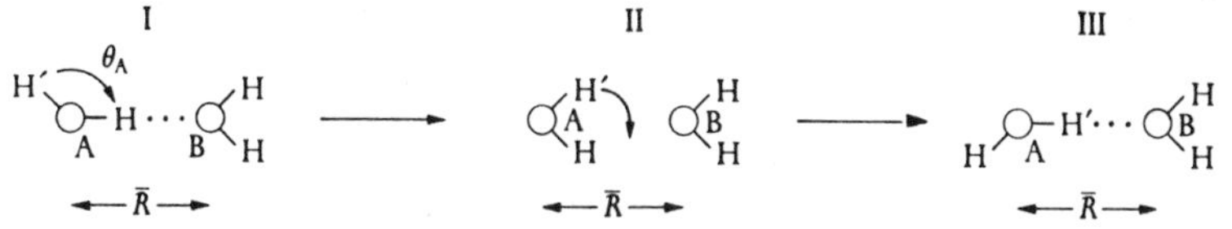

FIG. 4.26. Rotation of an H_2O molecule in liquid water, as discussed in the text.

Suppose that we were able to determine the change in energy that accompanies the rotation of a water molecule in the liquid, as shown in Fig. 4.26. We shall assume that the rest of the liquid adjusts to the rotation of molecule A in this figure, so that the energy of the system is the same in the initial (I) and final (III) configurations. In the intermediate configuration (II), where the hydrogen bond between A and B is highly distorted or broken, the energy is greater. The maximum energy of the two-molecule system is presumably less than that for two isolated molecules, owing to dipole–dipole and other forces between the molecules.

Let us define these energy changes more precisely. The coordinates of molecules A and B, as well as the coordinates of the other molecules $(1, 2,..., N)$ in the liquid, may be specified by a set of nine-dimensional vectors, $\mathbf{R}_A$, $\mathbf{R}_B$, $\mathbf{R}_1$, $\mathbf{R}_2$,..., $\mathbf{R}_N$. Three dimensions are needed for specifying the molecular centre of gravity, three dimensions for the molecular orientation, and three dimensions for the internal coordinates. The potential energy of the liquid may then be written

$$U(\mathbf{R}_A, \mathbf{R}_B, \mathbf{R}_1, \mathbf{R}_2,..., \mathbf{R}_N).$$

The energy we require is the average value of U for a fixed orientation of molecule B (denoted by $\theta_B = 0$) and a series of orientations of molecule A (denoted θ_A), when A and B are constrained to be at a distance $\bar{R}$ apart, where $\bar{R}$ corresponds to a distance near the first maximum in the radial distribution curve of liquid water. This energy can be found from the function

$$\bar{U}(\bar{R}, \theta_A, \theta_B)$$
$$= \frac{\int ... \int U(\mathbf{R}_A, \mathbf{R}_B, \mathbf{R}_1,..., \mathbf{R}_N)e^{-U/kT} \, d\mathbf{R}'_A \, d\mathbf{R}'_B \, d\mathbf{R}_1 ... d\mathbf{R}_N}{\int ... \int e^{-U/kT} \, d\mathbf{R}'_A \, d\mathbf{R}'_B \, d\mathbf{R}_1 ... d\mathbf{R}_N}, \quad (4.25)$$

where the integration is over all coordinates except for those that specify the orientations and relative positions of molecules A and B, and where the primes on $d\mathbf{R}'_A$ and $d\mathbf{R}'_B$ indicate that some of the components of these vectors (those depending on $\bar{R}$, θ_A, and θ_B) have, accordingly, been fixed. Now we wish to consider the dependence of $\bar{U}(\bar{R}, \theta_A, \theta_B)$ on θ_A as molecule A rotates through the configurations I, II, and III of Fig. 4.26, molecule B being held in the fixed orientation given by $\theta_B = 0$.

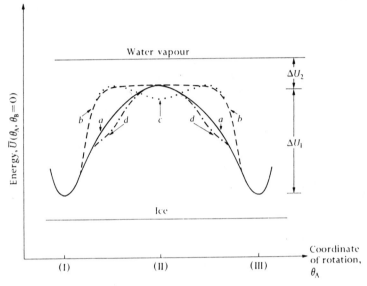

Fig. 4.27. Possible energy curves for the rotation of one water molecule with respect to another, as shown in Fig. 4.26.

Fig. 4.27 shows four conceivable forms for the energy $\bar{U}(\bar{R}, \theta_A, 0)$ as a function of the coordinate of rotation, θ_A. Curve a depicts the energy $\bar{U}$ as rising gradually to a maximum value at configuration II, and then falling gradually. Curve b depicts the energy rising more abruptly, being relatively flat in the region of configuration II, and then falling abruptly. Curve c is similar to b, but has a small minimum around configuration II. Curve d is nearly identical to a, but contains three points of inflexion between the minimum and the maximum, rather than one.

If the energy $\bar{U}$ follows a curve similar to b or c, it is reasonable to speak of 'broken' hydrogen bonds, because the energy of the two-molecule system is distinctly different in configuration II than in configurations I and III. But if the energy follows a curve similar to a, the term 'broken' does not have a well-defined meaning and it is perhaps better to speak in terms of 'distortion' of the hydrogen bond. Indeed, in this case, attempts to infer the fraction of broken hydrogen bonds in liquid water by various experimental and theoretical methods should produce indecisive or even contradictory answers. This is so because, for curve a, a 'broken' bond does not correspond to any well-defined region of the energy curve; consequently different methods of analysis of the properties of water may consider a bond as 'broken' when different points on the curve have been reached. In short, the fraction of broken hydrogen bonds in the liquid may not be a useful parameter for describing water. The situation is less clear if the energy follows curve d, but it still seems better to speak in terms of distortion.

Though it is not yet possible to conclude which, if any, of the curves in Fig. 4.27 is a correct qualitative representation of the energy for this situation, spectroscopic data suggest that curve a or d is closer than the others to the true curve. If curves b or c were correct, one would expect the uncoupled O–H and O–D stretching bands to reflect the presence of two distinctly different O–H environments in the liquid; however, as discussed in Section 4.7 (b), there is no definitive evidence for these distinctive environments. The apparent shoulder observed by Walrafen (1967 b; Fig. 4.23 (c)) is consistent with a curve like d, and thus suggests that d may be more nearly correct than a.

It could conceivably be argued that curve b or c is more nearly correct than a or d, and that two O–H environments are not evident in the un-coupled stretching band because ΔU_2 in Fig. 4.27 is larger than ΔU_1. In this case a non-hydrogen-bonded O–H group in the liquid would be closer in energy to an O–H····O group than to a free O–H group in the vapour. Consequently the presence of non-hydrogen-bonded O–H groups might be reflected merely by an asymmetry in the uncoupled stretching band rather than by two distinct maxima. A small value of ΔU_1 is, however, difficult to reconcile with the large dielectric constant (as well as other properties) of water. The large dielectric constant implies a strong angular correlation of molecules, or in other words, a large value of ΔU_1.

The temperature and pressure dependence of the energy curve for rotation is an interesting topic for speculation. The decrease in activation energy for dielectric relaxation and viscous flow as water is heated suggests that the height of the maximum above the minima (ΔU_1 in Fig. 4.27) decreases with increasing temperature. In agreement with this, the frequency of the ν_L mode (Section 4.7 (c)) decreases as water is heated, indicating that the slope of the potential energy curve in the regions of the minima becomes less steep. Since compression of water at temperatures below 30 °C lowers the viscosity, pressure may have a similar effect.

(b) The V-structure of water: a summary

The vibrationally averaged structure, or V-structure, of a small region in liquid water is the average arrangement of molecules over a period of time longer than that required for intermolecular vibration, yet shorter than that required for diffusive motions of molecules. The V-structure persists in a small region on the average for a time τ_D before being inter-rupted by the translation or reorientation of a molecule; this time depends on the temperature and pressure. The temperature dependence of the viscosity, dielectric relaxation time, and coefficient of self-diffusion all indicate that τ_D decreases when the temperature is raised. At room temperature the relaxation times for molecular displacements are of the order of 10^{-11}–10^{-12} s, so that a molecule completes, on the average, fewer than 100 hindered translations (ν_T mode) and fewer than 1000 librations (ν_L mode) before experiencing a reorientation or translation to a new position of temporary equilibrium. Limited compression of water below 30 °C, like heating, reduces the viscosity and thus apparently shortens τ_D. The value of τ_D for liquid D_2O is slightly larger than τ_D for ordinary water, as shown by the longer relaxation times of D_2O.

Spectroscopic studies have established some basic features of the V-structure of liquid water:

(1) The widths of the uncoupled O–H and O–D stretching bands indicate that in the V-structure there is a considerable amount of variation in the local environments of water molecules, as compared with the relative uniformity of the molecular environments in a crystal of ice I. The frequency span of these bands suggests that some nearest neighbours are as close together as 2·75 Å and others may be as far apart as 3·10 Å or more. The most probable equilibrium separation seems to be about 2·85 Å. The smaller separations are probably associa-ted with strong hydrogen bonds such as those in ice, whereas the larger separations are probably associated with highly distorted, or even broken, hydrogen bonds.

(2) The contours of the uncoupled bands suggest that the V-structure does not contain a *small* number of *distinctly different* molecular environ-ments. These contours, each relatively smooth and having a single maximum, would seem to show that the V-structure contains a wide distribution of environments rather than a small number of distinct environments. The uncoupled stretching bands do not, however,

provide a definite proof that non-hydrogen-bonded O–H bonds are absent from water. Hence, although water contains a large variety of hydrogen-bonded molecules, some distinctly different molecules with non-hydrogen-bonded O–H groups may be present as well.

(3) The uncoupled stretching bands indicate that heating slightly increases the variety of molecular environments in the liquid and decreases the mean hydrogen-bond strength. Water near 0 °C has a greater variety of molecular environments than does ice, as shown by the greater widths of its uncoupled stretching bands. The frequency of the stretching band in water is higher than that in ice, indicating that hydrogen bonds in the liquid are, on the average, weaker. Moreover, the frequencies of the ν_L and ν_T bands of water are lower than those of ice, showing that hydrogen bonds are more easily distorted in the liquid. All these differences are accentuated by increasing the temperature: the uncoupled stretching bands become broader, and hydrogen bonds become weaker and more easily distorted.

Many important questions about the V-structure of water remain unanswered. Very little is known about the distribution of hydrogen-bond angles in the V-structure or about the effect of pressure on the V-structure. The question of the presence of distinctly different non-hydrogen-bonded O–H groups is, of course, also unsettled.

Finally, it is worth noting that we may think of the V-structure as having physical properties which differ from those of the D-structure. If we could make thermodynamic and other measurements during a time of the order of τ_D, the equilibrium positions of molecules would be essentially fixed, and the properties we would measure would be characteristic of the V-structure. Only the vibrational contribution (~ 10 cal/mol/°C) to the heat capacity would be observed, because there would not be time enough for the appearance of the configurational contribution, which arises from changes in the positions and orientations of molecules. Similarly, only the vibrational contributions to the compressibility and coefficient of expansion would be evident. The dielectric constant would have its high-frequency value, ϵ_∞.

(c) The D-structure of water: a summary

The diffusionally averaged structure, or D-structure, of liquid water is the average arrangement of molecules around an arbitrary 'central' molecule over a time interval that is long compared to τ_D. As noted in Section 4.1 (a), the D-structure may also be regarded as the space-average of the V-structures about many different 'central' molecules.

Both the time-average and the space-average views are useful in interpreting experimental data.

Adopting the space-average view of the radial distribution function (Fig. 4.4), we may say that at any given instant many molecules in liquid water near the freezing-point have relatively high concentrations of neighbours at distances of about 2·9 Å, 5 Å, and 7 Å. As discussed in Section 4.2 (a), this sequence of distances, and the area under the first peak of the radial distribution function, suggest that many molecules participate in hydrogen-bonded networks of tetrahedrally coordinated molecules, somewhat like the network found in ice I. The breadths of the peaks in the radial distribution function show, however, that the V-structures around different central molecules vary much more in water than they do in ice. Many molecules in liquid water also have neighbours at a distance of about 3·5 Å, a separation that is not found in ice I. These may be neighbours that are not, at the instant we are considering, part of the hydrogen-bonded network, or they may be members of one of the distorted configurations of hydrogen bonds mentioned on p. 171. As water is heated above room temperature, the densities of neighbours near 5 Å and 7 Å gradually decrease, until at 200 °C the density at all distances greater than 6 Å is essentially equal to the bulk density of the liquid. This shows, of course, that thermal agitation distorts or breaks down the hydrogen-bonded networks.

The large dielectric constant of water is a further indication that, at any given instant, many molecules in water participate in hydrogen-bonded networks. Indeed, all successful theoretical treatments of this property have been based on the assumption that most of the molecules are four-coordinated at room temperature. Among other properties that indicate that a significant proportion of the O–H groups in the liquid are involved in hydrogen bonds are: the large NMR chemical shift of the proton relative to the proton in water vapour, the anomalously high proton mobility in the liquid, and the low quadrupole coupling constant of the deuteron in heavy water.

Thermodynamic properties measured by the usual methods are characteristic of the D-structure of the liquid. The value of a given property (say the heat capacity or the compressibility) may be thought of as having two contributions: a vibrational contribution associated with the changes in the vibrational amplitudes of molecules that are induced by compression or heating, and a configurational contribution associated with the changes in the structure of the liquid. Changes in the liquid structure occur by molecular displacements; these have periods of $\sim 10^{-12}$ s, so that the configurational contribution is apparent if the measurements take longer than this to perform. It seems likely that the configurational contributions arise mainly from changes in the potential energy of hydrogen bonding as water is heated or compressed. Calculations suggest that the configurational contributions to the heat capacity and internal energy are of the order of half of the observed values of these properties. The coefficient of expansion is another property that may be considered to have vibrational and configurational contributions. As water is heated the (anharmonic) intermolecular vibrations increase in amplitude, thereby tending to expand the liquid. This, of course, is the vibrational contribution to the expansion coefficient. At the same time, as the temperature is raised there is greater distortion of hydrogen bonds and this tends to produce a decrease in volume. The negative configurational contribution competes with the positive vibrational contribution to produce the observed minimum in the volume at 4 °C.

5. Models for Liquid Water†

To develop a rigorous, classical theory of the thermodynamic properties of water it is necessary to solve two major problems:

(1) An accurate potential function for the interaction of a group of water molecules is required to specify the Hamiltonian, H, of the system. No such potential function is yet available (see sections 2.1 and 3.6 (b)), but research in this area is active and better potential functions may be developed before long.

(2) The classical partition function

$$Z = \frac{1}{N!h^{3N}} \int \dots \int \exp(-H/kT) \, d\mathbf{R}_1 \dots d\mathbf{R}_N \, d\mathbf{p}_1 \dots d\mathbf{p}_N$$

must be evaluated, where N is the number of molecules and $\mathbf{R}$ and $\mathbf{p}$ are the molecular spatial coordinates and momenta. This is a formidable mathematical task. Nevertheless, notable progress has been achieved in this area for simple liquids such as argon (see, for example, Rice and Gray 1965), and similar methods may eventually be applicable to water.

These problems are so difficult, however, that no serious attempt has yet been made to develop a rigorous theory of liquid water.

Most theories of water are based on a less fundamental but more tractable approach:

(1) A model for water is postulated on the basis of some experimental evidence and some intuition.

(2) The model is translated into mathematical terms. Often a simple partition function containing several variable parameters is devised.

(3) The thermodynamic expressions derived from the partition function are fitted to experimental properties by varying the parameters.

† Reviews and discussions of models for liquid water include, among others, those of Chadwell (1927), Némethy and Scheraga (1962), Frank (1963, 1965), Kavanau (1964), Davis and Litovitz (1965), Wicke (1966), Berendsen (1967), and Davis and Jarzynski (1967–8).

A good fit suggests that the postulated model reflects some elements of the true structure of water; it does not prove that the model is an accurate one. Indeed, as we shall see in Section 5.2 (b) below, several models that appear to be quite different from one another have been fitted by such methods to experimental data. Conversely, a poor fit does not prove that a conceptual model is an inaccurate description of water. A good conceptual model could conceivably suffer distortion when it is introduced into the terms of an approximate partition function.

For these reasons, in discussing models for water, we shall be interested primarily in their consistency with spectroscopic and other data, and secondarily with their ability to reproduce thermodynamic functions. It will be assumed that the reader is familiar with the material on models in Section 4.2 (b).

5.1. Small-aggregate models

A class of models for water, once widely accepted but now of only historical interest, depicted the liquid as an equilibrium mixture of small aggregates of water molecules. Several versions (see Chadwell 1927) treated the liquid as a mixture of H_2O, $(H_2O)_2$, called dihydrol, and $(H_2O)_3$, called trihydrol; another version (Eucken 1946) treated water as a mixture of H_2O, $(H_2O)_2$, $(H_2O)_4$, and $(H_2O)_8$. The dependence of properties on temperature, pressure, and solute concentration was explained by changes in the equilibrium concentrations of the aggregates and for many properties a good fit to experiment was achieved. Dorsey, in his monograph on water (1940, p. 168), summarized the properties of dihydrol and trihydrol in tabular form.

Bernal and Fowler (1933) criticized the small-aggregate models as being 'conceived too much in the manner of molecular chemistry', and as giving an inadequate description of the spatial arrangement of molecules in the liquid. They laid the foundation for most subsequent models by proposing that water is better described as an extended but irregular four-coordinated arrangement of molecules (Section 4.2 (a)). They found that this arrangement could explain most of the same properties that the older models dealt with, and in addition could account for the X-ray diffraction pattern and the properties of water that are unusual when compared with other molecular liquids.

More recent data confirm that small-aggregate models are not correct. Spectroscopic results (Section 4.7 (b)) show that water is not composed of a small number of distinctly different molecular species. The small spread of dielectric relaxation times (Section 4.6 (a)) shows, moreover, that even if small aggregates of different size exist in water, they do not cohere longer than 10^{-11} s. Small-aggregate models cannot account for the strong angular correlation of molecules which, as shown by the high dielectric constant of water, exists in the liquid.

5.2. Mixture and interstitial models

(a) Basic premiss

The basic premiss of most mixture models is that liquid water is composed of a small number of distinctly different molecular species. In the terminology of the previous chapter, mixture models depict the V-structures in the immediate neighbourhoods of different central molecules as being of a small number of distinguishable types. Interstitial models are a class of mixture models in which one of the species forms a hydrogen-bonded framework, and the other species resides in cavities that exist in this framework. The small-aggregate models mentioned in the previous section are another class of mixture models.

In mathematical treatments of mixture models, each species of water molecule is considered to occupy a discrete energy level, commonly called a *state*. Owing to thermal agitation, molecules experience frequent transitions between these states, and consequently over a period of time all molecules are equivalent. A change in the temperature or pressure is supposed to shift the relative populations of the states; the thermodynamic properties of the liquid are explained in terms of these shifts.

Frank (1958, 1963, 1965) advanced theoretical arguments in support of mixture models for water. He noted that Coulson and Danielsson (1954), in a valence-bond theory of the hydrogen bond, found that the following resonance structure contributes to the mutual attraction of a pair of water molecules.

$$H \diagdown O_A^- \quad H_A \text{---} O_B^+ \diagup^H_{\diagdown H}$$

Frank reasoned that the partial negative charge on O_A should attract the protons of other water molecules, and he concluded that the formation of one hydrogen bond promotes the formation of other hydrogen bonds in its vicinity. Conversely, the breaking of a hydrogen bond fosters the breaking of neighbouring hydrogen bonds. The idea that formation and breaking of hydrogen bonds are co-operative processes led Frank and Wen (1957) to postulate the existence of 'flickering clusters' of water molecules in the liquid (Section 4.6 (a)). Furthermore, they suggested that the hydrogen-bonded molecules in the clusters are distinctly different from the non-hydrogen-bonded molecules outside the clusters.

Other considerations indicate that the strength of hydrogen bonding between water molecules is increased by co-operative effects. A comparison of the second and third virial coefficients of steam (Section 2.1 (b)) suggests that some attractive force exists among three water molecules that is not present between two. In addition, calculations on the lattice energy of ice (Section 3.6 (c)) indicate that the mutual polarization of water molecules contributes to their cohesion. In view of this evidence, it seems likely that Frank is correct in concluding that co-operative effects have an important influence on the strength of hydrogen bonding between water molecules. The second conclusion, however, that a small number of distinctly different molecular species are present in water, does not necessarily follow from these considerations. In fact, evidence summarized in Sections 4.7 (b) and 4.8 (b) suggests that this second conclusion is not correct.

(b) Details of several models

The simplest mixture models for water are those in which only two species are postulated. Properties of the liquid are then explained in terms of the equilibrium

$$(H_2O)_{\text{bulky species}} \rightleftharpoons (H_2O)_{\text{dense species}}.$$

In most of these *two-state models*, the bulky species is considered to be an 'ice-like' cluster of hydrogen-bonded molecules, and the dense species is assumed to be more closely packed and to be of higher energy. Thus as the above equilibrium moves to the right, the population of molecules in the state of higher energy increases, and the volume of the liquid decreases. The values of ΔV and ΔE for the equilibrium, as well as the mole fraction of each species, are estimated from one or two observed properties of the liquid. The parameters for several two-state models are summarized in Table 5.1.

Two interstitial models are also listed in Table 5.1. One is the model of Danford and Levy (1962) and Narten *et al.* (1967) mentioned in Section 4.2 (b); the other is Pauling's 'water hydrate' model. Pauling (1959) suggested that the configuration of molecules in liquid water might resemble the clathrate compound, chlorine hydrate. In this model, groups of 20 hydrogen-bonded water molecules form open, pentagonal dodecahedra in which non-hydrogen-bonded water molecules reside. The dodecahedra can be packed together in ways that allow

TABLE 5.1

Principal characteristics of mixture and interstitial models for water[a]

Type of model	Authors	No. of species	Nature of species	Mole fraction of less (least) dense species at 0° C	Difference in energy of the species (kcal mol⁻¹)	Difference in volume of the species (cm³ mol⁻¹)	Data used in determining parameters
Simple two-state models	Hall (1948)	2	(1) 'More ice-like' (2) 'More like that of a simple close-packed liquid'	~ 0·7		8·5	Ultrasonic absorption
	Grjotheim and Krogh-Moe (1954)	2	(1) Distorted, ice-like structure (2) Non-hydrogen-bonded, close-packed structure	0·44	2·6	2·9	Molar volume
	Smith and Lawson (1954)	2	Same as Hall (1948)	0·5	2·6	> 8·0	Velocity of sound
	Litovitz and Carnevale (1955)	2	Same as Hall (1948)	0·3	0·87	8·4	Ultrasonic absorption
	Wada (1961)	2	(1) An 'icy state' of lower density having a quasi-crystalline ice structure (2) A 'packed state'	0·42	2·5	2·8	Molar volume
	Davis and Litovitz (1965)	2	(1) An open, ice-like arrangement of hexagonal rings (2) A close-packed arrangement of hexagonal rings in which each molecule is hydrogen-bonded to two others	~ 0·6	~ 2·7	~ 7	Radial distribution function and molar volume
	Davis and Bradley (1966)	2	Same as Davis and Litovitz (1965) but for D_2O	0·61[b]	2·9	7·2[b]	Radial distribution function and molar volume
Interstitial models	Pauling (1959); Frank and Quist (1961)	2	(1) Hydrogen-bonded, clathrate-like framework (2) Interstitial H_2O molecules that occupy some of the cavities	0·82[b]	~ 2·2		Molar volume and chlorine hydrate structure
	Danford and Levy (1962); Narten et al. (1967)		(1) Anisotropically expanded, ice-I-like lattice (2) Interstitial H_2O molecules that reside in some of the cavities	0·82[b]			Molar volume and radial distribution function

Models associated with partition functions

Model		Description				Properties calculated
Némethy and Scheraga (1962)	5	The 5 species are H_2O molecules forming 0, 1, 2, 3, and 4 hydrogen bonds with neighbouring molecules	0.54[c]	2.6[d]	3.6	Thermodynamic functions
Némethy and Scheraga (1964)	5	Same as Némethy and Scheraga (1962), but for D_2O	0.54[b,c]	3.1[d]	3.5	Thermodynamic functions
Marchi and Eyring (1964)	2	(1) Four-coordinated, hydrogen-bonded framework (2) Freely rotating monomers in some cavities	0.98	6.9	0.5	Thermodynamic functions
Vand and Senior (1965)	3	The 3 species are water molecules whose O–H groups participate in 0, 1, or 2 hydrogen bonds. Molecules of the same species are not confined to a discrete energy level, but rather to a band of levels		2.8[e]		Thermodynamic functions
Jhon et al. (1966)		(1) A cage-like structure of about 46 molecules, having the density of ice I. Mostly destroyed at temperatures above 4 °C (2) A denser, ice-III-like structure, also hydrogen-bonded. Both structures contain 'fluidized vacancies'		0.48	2.0	Thermodynamic functions

[a] All entries refer to 0 °C unless noted otherwise.
[b] At 4 °C.
[c] Total mole fractions of 4-, 3-, and 2-bonded species. These are assumed by Némethy and Scheraga to have the same molar volumes.
[d] Energy difference of 4-bonded and 0-bonded species.
[e] Energy difference of 2-bonded and 0-bonded species.

them to be linked by hydrogen bonds. If they are packed as in chlorine hydrate (Pauling and Marsh 1952), 46 molecules in each unit cell form the hydrogen-bonded framework, and the framework encloses 8 cavities. Assuming that each cavity contains an H_2O monomer, the calculated density of this structure is $0 \cdot 98$ g cm^{-3}, nearly that of liquid water. Pauling noted that a dodecahedral complex of 21 water molecules contains 30 intact hydrogen bonds, or $71 \cdot 5$ per cent of the maximum possible number; no complex of 21 molecules cut out of an ice I lattice contains as many as 60 per cent of the maximum possible number.

The thermodynamic implications of Pauling's model were explored by Frank and Quist (1961). By allowing a variable degree of occupancy of the interstitial sites they found they could account for the P–V–T properties up to 30 °C and 2000 kg cm^{-2}. Since the degree of occupancy changes only slightly with temperature, the configurational heat capacity is only about $0 \cdot 55$ cal/mol °C, and thus the model does not account for the large heat capacity of water. Frank and Quist concluded that, although structures of the type proposed by Pauling may exist in water, the liquid cannot be composed entirely of framework and interstitial molecules. The kinetic properties of water show that V-structures in the liquid are constantly changing, and thus at any instant some fraction of the molecules must be in transition between framework and interstices. Frank and Quist suggested that these transitional structures are responsible for most of the configurational heat capacity.

The remaining models in Table 5.1 are those for which more detailed mathematical descriptions have been developed. For each of these models a partition function was devised. In most cases the difference in energy of the states was taken as a variable parameter, and then determined by fitting the calculated thermodynamic properties to experimental data. Vand and Senior (1965), however, assumed energy spacings consistent with the spectroscopic study of Buijs and Choppin (1963; Section 4.7 (d)). The calculation of Vand and Senior (1965) also differs from the others in that the molecules are not confined to discrete energy levels, but are spread in Gaussian energy bands around the mean energy for each of the species. They postulate three bands, corresponding to H_2O molecules that form 0, 1, and 2 hydrogen bonds; the spread within each band is meant to represent the spread of hydrogen-bond energies and molecular coordination numbers in the liquid. This model thus incorporates characteristics of both the strict mixture models, in which a small number of distinguishable molecular species is assumed, and the models discussed in Section 5.3 in which a continuous spread of molecular environments is assumed. Fig. 5.1 shows the energy states assumed in several models for water.

The calculated thermodynamic properties associated with these models are summarized in Table 5.2. Each of the models is able to reproduce the experimental thermal energy functions fairly well, even

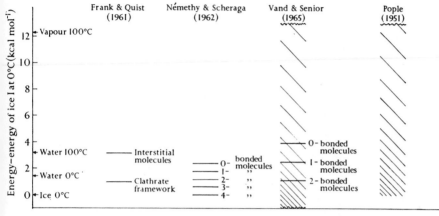

FIG. 5.1. The molecular energy states in liquid water as assumed in several models for the liquid. The experimental internal energies of liquid water at 0 and 100 °C and of water vapour at 100 °C are shown at the left for reference. In Vand and Senior's model, the energy states occupied by molecules are distributed in three Gaussian bands about the mean energies, which are shown by lines; thus the energy states accessible to molecules extend from $-\infty$ to $+\infty$. The energy states accessible to molecules in Pople's model extend from 0 to $+\infty$.

though each is a different description of the V-structure of water. This fact in itself suggests that it is dangerous to draw detailed conclusions about the V-structure of water on the basis of calculations from parametrized models; the mathematical flexibility permitted by ten or more parameters seems to be sufficient to fit numerous models to the experimental thermodynamic functions, and thus a good fit is not sufficient proof that the model is correct. Nevertheless, the ability of the models listed in Table 5.2 to describe the thermal energy and P–V–T properties probably shows that they all reflect some of the basic characteristics of the structure of water. They all, for example, provide for a large configurational heat capacity (by assuming that hydrogen bonds are broken as water is heated), and those which reproduce the experimental minimum in the molar volume provide for both configurational and vibrational contributions to the coefficient of expansion.

Let us consider one of these models—that of Némethy and Scheraga (1962, 1964)—in greater detail. These authors assumed that every water molecule

TABLE 5.2

Calculations of thermodynamic properties of water from mixture models†

Authors	Number of adjustable parameters	Quality of fit of calculated properties to experiment	
Némethy and Scheraga (1962)	2 in addition to 9 vibrational frequencies	E, S, A within 3·8% over 0–100° C range. C_V 18% too high at 0° C 28% too low at 100 °C	P–V–T properties at atmospheric pressure fitted with several (about 6) additional parameters. V shows minimum at 4 °C and is within 0·5% of experimental value between 0 and 70 °C
Marchi and Eyring (1964)	14	Good fit of S and A. C_V too low (= 10 cal/mol °C)	Good fit of vapour pressure over range 0–140 °C. V within 0·3 cm³ mol⁻¹ over range 0–180 °C. Does not show minimum at 4 °C
Vand and Senior (1965)	12 plus 6 spectroscopic constants	E, S, A, and C_V within 1·5% over 0–100 °C range	
Jhon et al. (1966)	9	Excellent fit of S and A over range 0–150 °C. C_V within 12·3% over range 0–100 °C	V within 1% over range 0–150 °C. Vapour pressure within 3·2% over same range

† See Table 5.1 for brief descriptions of the models.

occupies one of five energy levels, depending on whether it forms 0, 1, 2, 3, or 4 hydrogen bonds to neighbouring molecules. The molecules are assumed to be either in compact clusters, or unbonded, but not to form small polymeric units. By building models, Némethy and Scheraga determined expressions for the fractions of 4-, 3-, and 2-bonded molecules in the clusters in terms of n_0, the average number of multiply bonded molecules in a cluster, and y_1, the fraction of all molecules in clusters which are singly bonded. They then described their model by a partition function of the form

$$Z = \sum_{n_0, y_1, X_u} g(n_0, y_1, X_u) \prod_{i=0}^{4} \left\{ f_i \exp\left(-\frac{E_i}{RT}\right) \right\}^{NX}$$

where

X_u is the mole fraction of unbonded (0-bonded) molecules,

N is Avogadro's number,

X_i is the mole fraction of the ith species,

E_i is the energy level of the ith species,

$g(n_0, y_1, X_u)$ is a combinatorial factor $= N!/(N_4! N_3! N_2! N_1! N_u!)$, N_i being the number of molecules of the ith species per mole of water, and f_i is the weighting factor that describes the degrees of freedom of the ith species.

The form of f_i is

$f_i = f_v$ for $i = 1, 2, 3, 4$ and

$f_i = f_t f_r f_v$ for the unbonded molecules,

where

$$f_v = \prod_{j=1}^{s} \left\{ 1 - \exp\left(-\frac{h\nu_{ij}}{kT}\right) \right\}^{-1}$$

and where $s = 6$ for $i = 1, 2, 3, 4$, and $s = 2$ for $i = u$;

$$f_t = (2\pi m k T/h^2)^{\frac{3}{2}} V_f \quad \text{and} \quad f_r = (2\pi/\sigma)(2\pi I k T/h^2)^{\frac{3}{2}}.$$

In these expressions, the subscripts t, r, and v refer to translation, rotation, and vibration, respectively; σ, m and I are the symmetry number, the mass, and a moment of inertia of the water molecule. V_f is a variable parameter called the free volume.

Némethy and Scheraga evaluated the partition function by equating it to its maximum term, as described in their paper. The thermodynamic functions are given by the well-known expressions, $A = -kT \ln Z$, etc. Then by varying the free volume V_f and the spacing between the levels (and also by choosing reasonable values for the frequencies ν_{ij}) they fitted the calculated thermal energy functions to experimental data; the fit they achieved is described in Table 5.2.

In calculating the P–V–T properties of the liquid, Némethy and Scheraga assigned to the clusters the molar volume and coefficient of expansion of ice I. Then the volume and coefficient of expansion of the non-hydrogen-bonded molecules were determined by fitting the total molar volume to the experimental points at 0, 4, and 25 °C; these quantities were found to have values comparable with those of polar liquids. The mole fraction of clusters, determined previously by fitting the thermal energy, was used in this procedure. The calculated molar volume exhibits a minimum at 4 °C; moreover, when the procedure was applied to D_2O (Némethy and Scheraga 1964) the minimum at 11·2 °C was reproduced to within 1 °C, although no new parameters other than the mole fraction of clusters in D_2O were introduced.

(c) Consistency of mixture models with experimental data

The basic premiss on which most mixture models are founded—that liquid water is a mixture of a small number of distinctly different species —is not in accord with experimental data. Studies of the uncoupled stretching bands (Section 4.7 (b)) show that the liquid contains a variety of molecular environments, and thus that water cannot be correctly described in terms of a small number of discrete states. Though the uncoupled stretching bands do not prove the total absence of distinctly different non-hydrogen-bonded groups in water, they do indicate that the liquid is characterized by a wide distribution of species, and models that take no account of this cannot be accurate representations of liquid water.

Even if some distinctly different molecular species do exist in water, the common verbal descriptions of them are inaccurate. 'Ice-like' clusters cannot possibly be like ice. If significant numbers of O–H groups in water had environments similar to those of O–H groups in ice, one would expect to observe a sharp maximum near 3300 cm^{-1} in the un-coupled O–H stretching band. No such peak is observed. Furthermore, the ease with which pure water can be supercooled shows that ice-like nuclei do not exist in the liquid (for example, Koefoed 1957). Evidence against a significant fraction of 'vapour-like' molecules in liquid water at room temperature has been assembled by Stevenson (1965). He formulated several operational definitions for vapour-like molecules in the liquid, and showed that by each of the definitions the fraction of vapour-like molecules is less than 0·01 over the temperature range 0–100 °C. One of his definitions was based on the relative vacuum ultra-violet absorption of liquid and vapour; another was based on the infra-red absorption of a dilute solution of H_2O in CCl_4.

A frequently cited justification for adopting a mixture model is that, with proper choice of parameters, a partition function based on the model can reproduce a number of equilibrium properties of the liquid. It should be noted, however, that the equilibrium properties depend on the *average* energy of the assembly of molecules. A correct average energy can be computed from a judiciously selected set of discrete energy levels, even if the true energy spectrum is continuous. A far better criterion for judging a model of the V-structure of water is that the model is consistent with what is known from spectroscopy about the molecular environments in the liquid. Most mixture models are not acceptable by this criterion; hence it is illogical to draw conclusions from them about molecular parameters such as the average cluster size or the number of broken hydrogen bonds in the liquid.

5.3. Distorted hydrogen-bond models

The distorted hydrogen-bond model of Pople (1951) and the closely related random-network model of Bernal (1964) were described briefly in Section 4.2 (b). In these models, hydrogen bonds are regarded as distorted to varying degrees, rather than as either intact or broken as in mixture models. Water molecules in the liquid, like those in the ices, are considered to be four-coordinated; but the networks of linked molecules in the liquid are depicted as irregular and varied, in contrast to the orderly networks of a few basic types that are found in the ices. Bernal (1964) believes that five-membered rings are a frequent configuration in the liquid, but that rings containing four, six, seven, or even more molecules are also part of the networks.

These distorted hydrogen-bond models have received less attention to date than have mixture and interstitial models. Pople and Bernal showed that these models are consistent with the radial distribution function of water (Section 4.2 (b)), and Pople demonstrated that his model can account for the dielectric constant of water (Section 4.4 (a)) and for the decrease in volume of ice I upon melting. In Section 4.3 (a) a simple calculation is given that suggests that such a model may be able to account for the heat capacity and thermal energy of water.

Pople (1951) showed how one might estimate the average angle of distortion of hydrogen bonds in water. He assumed that the mutual orientation of two water molecules in the liquid is determined only by the energy required to distort the hydrogen bond between them. He described this energy by a 'hydrogen-bond bending-force constant' k_ϕ, which has been defined in eqn (4.2) and Fig. 4.7. Making the further assumption that the distortion of hydrogen bonds may be treated by classical statistics, Pople estimated the average angle ϕ between the O–H bond (or lone-pair) direction and the O····O axis of two hydrogen-bonded neighbours (see Fig. 4.7). Noting that the energy of distortion for small angles of bend is given by $-k_\phi \cos \phi$, he wrote the probability of an angle ϕ being between ϕ and $\phi + \mathrm{d}\phi$ as

$$p(\phi)\sin\phi\,\mathrm{d}\phi = \frac{\exp\{(k_\phi\cos\phi)/kT\}\sin\phi\,\mathrm{d}\phi}{\int\limits_0^\pi \exp\{(k_\phi\cos\phi)/kT\}\sin\phi\,\mathrm{d}\phi}$$

$$= \frac{k_\phi/kT}{2\sinh(k_\phi/kT)}\exp\{(k_\phi\cos\phi)/kT\}\sin\phi\,\mathrm{d}\phi.$$

Thus the mean value of $\cos\phi$, $\overline{\cos\phi}$, is given by

$$\overline{\cos\phi} = \int\limits_0^\pi p(\phi)\cos\phi\sin\phi\,\mathrm{d}\phi = \coth(k_\phi/kT) - kT/k_\phi.$$

As noted in Section 4.2 (b), Pople derived a value of k_ϕ ($= 3\cdot78 \times 10^{-13}$ erg/radian) from his study of the radial distribution function; this leads to values of 26° and 30° for $\cos^{-1}(\overline{\cos\phi})$ at 0 and 100 °C respectively.

The distorted hydrogen-bond models seem to be in accord with most of what is known about the structure of water from experiment. The range of molecular environments postulated in these models is consistent with the large half-widths of the uncoupled stretching bands of water (Section 4.7 (b)). Extensive hydrogen bonding, an intrinsic part of these models, can account for the large dielectric constant and energy of vaporization of water, the abnormal proton mobility of the liquid, and the low quadrupole coupling constant of deuterons in liquid D_2O. One observation that is difficult to reconcile with these models is the small spread of dielectric relaxation times found for water; but it should be noted that this observation is equally hard to reconcile with mixture and interstitial models. Some authors (for example, Némethy and Scheraga 1962) have objected to Pople's model, arguing that a liquid so extensively hydrogen-bonded would be highly viscous. This argument presumes that a broken hydrogen bond in the liquid is fundamentally different from a highly distorted bond, or in other words, that curves b and c of Fig. 4.27 are better descriptions of the energy of molecular rotation in water than are curves a and d. As mentioned in Section 4.8 (a), present evidence suggests that there is no fundamental distinction between broken and highly distorted hydrogen bonds in liquid water. Another objection to Pople's model was based on qualitative arguments to the effect that highly distorted hydrogen bonds are unlikely in liquid water (for example, Frank 1958). Such arguments have less force now that highly distorted hydrogen bonds have been discovered in the high-pressure ices (Section 3.2). Ices II, III, V, and VI all contain distorted hydrogen bonds, yet have internal energies only several tenths of a kcal mol^{-1} larger than ice I; liquid water at 0 °C has an internal energy 1·44 kcal mol^{-1} larger than ice I.

The present authors believe that distorted hydrogen-bond models merit further investigation. Pople's 'hydrogen-bond bending-force constant' is clearly too simple to give a good representation of the forces between water molecules. Calculations based on more realistic potential functions would be extremely interesting.

Addendum

The water molecule

Properties from experiments (Section 1.1e)

Ben Aryeh (1966) determined a value for the derivative of the molecular dipole moment with respect to valence angle $(\partial\mu/\partial\alpha)$ from the integrated intensity of the ν_2 infra-red band.

Spin-rotation constants for the hydrogen nuclei in H_2O, HDO, and D_2O were reported by Bluyssen *et al.* (1967) and Treacy and Beers (1962). Stevenson and Townes (1957) measured the quadrupole coupling constant of the ^{17}O nucleus in $HD^{17}O$, and from this the gradient of the electrostatic field at the oxygen nucleus can be derived.

Calculation of properties (Section 1.2d)

Harrison (1967) and Aung *et al.* (1968) calculated numerous properties of the water molecule from accurate wave functions. Harrison used the wave function of Whitten *et al.* (1966) mentioned in Section 1.2d. The contributions to molecular properties arising from the zero-point vibrations of the nuclei were evaluated by Kern and Matcha (1968). Arrighini *et al.* (1967) calculated the components of the molecular polarizability tensor.

Ice

Structure and properties of the ices (Sections 3.1, 3.2, 3.3, 3.4d, 3.5c)

Brill and Tippe (1967) measured the lattice parameters of ice I over the temperature range 15–200 °K by X-ray methods, and derived values for the coefficients of expansion along the *a*- and *c*-axes. Calculations of the residual entropy of ice associated with hydrogen atom disorder were extended by Lieb (1967).

The ordering of hydrogen atoms in ice III upon cooling below −65 °C was studied by Whalley *et al.* (1968). They proposed a new designation (ice IX) and specific hydrogen positions for the ordered structure. Kell and Whalley (1968) found that older thermodynamic data which had suggested a disorder-order transition at higher temperatures were in error. Ghormley (1968) reported new measurements of the thermal properties of vitreous ice and ice Ic.

Barnaal and Lowe (1967) measured the NMR second moment for protons in ice I, and concluded that its magnitude is consistent with an O—H bond length of 1·00 Å and an H—O—H angle of 109·5° for H_2O molecules in the crystal. The quadrupole coupling constant of ^{17}O in D_2O ice I was determined by Waldstein and Rabideau (1967) and compared to the corresponding quantities for the liquid and vapour phases.

Ramseier (1967) studied the self-diffusion of tritium in Ice I, and concluded that entire water molecules diffuse by a vacancy mechanism.

Hydrogen bonding (Section 3.6)

A detailed discussion of the experimental techniques used to study hydrogen bonding in solids has been given by Hamilton and Ibers (1968).

Morokuma and Pedersen (1968) performed a quantum mechanical calculation of the interaction energy of two water molecules. In the most stable configuration, one O—H group of the donor molecule is collinear with the twofold axis of the acceptor molecule; the binding energy is 12·6 kcal mol^{-1} and the equilibrium O····O separation is 2·68 Å. Weissmann *et al.* (1967) discussed the results of several previous calculations of the hydrogen bond energy in ice.

Liquid water

Vibrational spectroscopy and general discussions of water structure (Sections 4.7, 5.2, 5.3)

Walrafen (1968a) extended his Raman spectral studies of the uncoupled stretching bands to the O—H bond, and emphasized the differences between his results and those of Wall and Hornig (1965). In a detailed review of his work on water, Walrafen (1968b) interpreted the temperature dependence of the Raman spectrum in terms of an equilibrium among various species of water molecule. He explained intensity changes of both the stretching and intermolecular bands in terms of a step-wise breakage of hydrogen bonds during heating, and showed that this breakage can account for the configurational heat capacity of water.

Luck (1967) discussed the correlation of spectroscopic and thermodynamic properties from a different point of view. His paper is followed by a discussion of the structure and properties of water to which Dr. Luck, Prof. H. S. Frank, Prof. M. Magat, and a number of others contributed noteworthy comments.

Stevenson (1968) reported further observations of the UV and infra-red absorption of water. He concluded that his results are not compatible with 'the description of liquid water in terms of a discrete number of sharply defined hydrogen-bonded species'.

Kamb (1968) reviewed studies of the high pressure ices, and considered the extent to which configurations of water molecules similar to these structures might be present in liquid water. His thorough discussion covers thermodynamic, electrical, and spectroscopic properties, among others.

Thermodynamic properties (Section 4.3)

Vedam and Holton (1968) gave tables of P-V-T data for liquid water at temperatures between 0 and 100 °C and pressures of 1 to 1000 kg cm^{-2}, and at 30 to 80 °C for pressures of 1 to 10000 kg cm^{-2}. These data were derived from accurate measurements of the pressure and temperature dependence of the sound velocity by Wilson (1959) and Holton et al. (1968). The data are in good agreement with those of Bridgman quoted in Chapter 4. Vedam and Holton also tabulated adiabatic and isothermal compressibilities, thermal expansion coefficients, C_P, and C_P/C_V for the temperature and pressure ranges given above.

Other properties (Sections 4.3, 4.4b, 4.5b)

In a paper on the theory of light scattering from water, Litan (1968) showed that the Einstein–Smoluchowski–Cabannes expression (eqn (4.19)) underestimates the amount of scattering, but that the discrepancy is within the range of experimental error.

Florin and Alei (1967) measured the ^{17}O NMR chemical shift in liquid $H_2^{17}O$.

Kuhns and Mason (1968) reviewed studies on the supercooling and freezing of small water droplets.

Models for liquid water (Section 5.2)

A two-state interstitial model for water was developed in a series of articles by Gurikov (1965, 1966) and Vdovenko et al. (1966, 1967).

Perram and Levine (1967) criticized the derivation of the combinatorial factor in Némethy and Scheraga's treatment of the statistical mechanics of water.

Bibliography

AKERLOF, G. C., and OSHRY, H. I. (1950). *J. Am. chem. Soc.* **72**, 2844.

ANTONOFF, G., and CONAN, R. J. (1949). *Science* **109**, 255.

ARRIGHINI, G. P., MAESTRO, M., and MOCCIA, R. (1967). *Chem. Phys. Lett.* **1**, 242.

AUNG, S., PITZER, R. M., and CHAN, S. I. (1968). *J. chem. Phys.*, in press.

AUTY, R. P., and COLE, R. H. (1952). *J. chem. Phys.* **20**, 1309.

BADER, R. F. W. (1964*a*). *J. Am. chem. Soc.* **86**, 5070.

—— (1964*b*). *Can. J. Chem.* **42**, 1822.

—— and JONES, G. A. (1963). *Can. J. Chem.* **41**, 586.

BAIN, R. W. (1964). *National Engineering Laboratory Steam Tables 1964.* H.M.S.O., Edinburgh.

BARNAAL, D. E., and LOWE, I. J. (1967). *J. chem. Phys.* **46**, 4800.

BARNES, W. H. (1929). *Proc. R. Soc.* A **125**, 670.

BASS, R., ROSSBERG, D., and ZIEGLER, G. (1957). *Z. Phys.* **149**, 199.

BAYLY, J. G., KARTHA, V. B., and STEVENS, W. H. (1963). *Infrared Phys.* **3**, 211.

BEAUMONT, R. H., CHIHARA, H., and MORRISON, J. A. (1961). *J. chem. Phys.* **34**, 1456.

BELL, S. (1965). *J. molec. Spectrosc.* **16**, 205.

BEN ARYEH, Y. (1966). *Proc. phys. Soc.* **89**, 1059.

BENEDICT, W. S., CLAASSEN, H. H., and SHAW, J. H. (1952). *J. Res. natn. Bur. Stand.* **49**, 91.

—— GAILAR, N., and PLYLER, E. K. (1953). *J. chem. Phys.* **21**, 1301.

—— —— —— (1956). *J. chem. Phys.* **24**, 1139.

BERENDSEN, H. J. C. (1967). *Theoretical and experimental biophysics* (ed. A. COLE) **1**, 1.

BERNAL, J. D. (1937). *Trans. Faraday Soc.* **33**, 27.

—— (1964). *Proc. R. Soc.* A **280**, 299.

—— and FOWLER, R. H. (1933). *J. chem. Phys.* **1**, 515.

BERTIE, J. E., CALVERT, L. D., and WHALLEY, E. (1963). *J. chem. Phys.* **38**, 840.

—— —— —— (1964). *Can. J. Chem.* **42**, 1373.

—— and WHALLEY, E. (1964*a*). *J. chem. Phys.* **40**, 1637.

—— —— (1964*b*). *J. chem. Phys.* **40**, 1646.

—— —— (1967). *J. chem. Phys.* **46**, 1271.

BETT, K. E., and CAPPI, J. B. (1965). *Nature, Lond.* **207**, 620.

BISHOP, D. M., and RANDIĆ, M. (1966). *Molec. Phys.* **10**, 517.

BJERRUM, N. (1951). *K. danske Vidensk. Selsk. Skr.* **27**, 1.

—— (1952). *Science,* **115**, 385.

BLACKMAN, M., and LISGARTEN, N. D. (1957). *Proc. R. Soc.* A **239**, 93.

—— —— (1958). *Adv. Phys.* **7**, 189.

BLUE, R. W. (1954). *J. chem. Phys.* **22**, 280.

BLUYSSEN, H., DYMANUS, A., REUSS, J., and VERHOEVEN, J. (1967). *Phys. Lett.* **25A**, 584.

BÖTTCHER, C. J. F. (1952). *Theory of electric polarisation.* Elsevier, London.

BRADY, G. W., and ROMANOW, W. J. (1960). *J. chem. Phys.* **32**, 306.

BRAGG, W. H. (1922). *Proc. phys. Soc. Lond.* **34**, 98.

BRAND, J. C. D., and SPEAKMAN, J. C. (1960). *Molecular structure.* Arnold, London.

BRIDGMAN, P. W. (1912). *Proc. Am. Acad. Arts Sci.* **47**, 441.

—— (1931). *The physics of high pressure.* Bell, London.

—— (1935). *J. chem. Phys.* **3**, 597.

—— (1937). *J. chem. Phys.* **5**, 964.

BRILL, R. (1962). *Angew. Chem. (Int. edn)* **1**, 563.

—— and TIPPE, A. (1967). *Acta crystallogr.* **23**, 343.

BROWN, A. J., and WHALLEY, E. (1966). *J. chem. Phys.* **45**, 4360.

BUCKINGHAM, A. D. (1956). *Proc. R. Soc.* A **238**, 235.

—— (1959). *Q. Rev. chem. Soc.* **13**, 183.

BUIJS, K., and CHOPPIN, G. R. (1963). *J. chem. Phys.* **39**, 2035.

—— —— (1964). *J. chem. Phys.* **40**, 3120.

BURNELLE, L., and COULSON, C. A. (1957). *Trans. Faraday Soc.* **53**, 403.

CAMPBELL, E. S. (1952). *J. chem. Phys.* **20**, 1411.

—— GELERNTER, G., HEINEN, H., and MOORTI, V. R. G. (1967). *J. chem. Phys.* **46**, 2690.

CHADWELL, H. M. (1927). *Chem. Rev.* **4**, 375.

CHAN, R. K., DAVIDSON, D. W., and WHALLEY, E. (1965). *J. chem. Phys.* **43**, 2376.

CHIDAMBARAM, R. (1961). *Acta crystallogr.* **14**, 467.

COHAN, N. V., COTTI, M., IRIBARNE, J. V., and WEISSMANN, M. (1962). *Trans. Faraday Soc.* **58**, 490.

COHEN, G., and EISENBERG, H. (1965). *J. chem. Phys.* **43**, 3881.

COLLIE, C. H., HASTED, J. B., and RISTON, D. M. (1948). *Proc. phys. Soc.* **60**, 145.

COLLINS, J. G., and WHITE, G. K. (1964). In *Progress in low temperature physics* (ed. C. J. GROTER), Vol. IV.

COTTRELL, T. L. (1958). *The strengths of chemical bonds.* Butterworths, London.

COULSON, C. A. (1951). *Proc. R. Soc.* A **207**, 63.

—— (1957). *Research* **10**, 149.

COULSON, C. A. (1959 a). *Spectrochim. Acta* **14**, 161.

—— (1959 b). In *Hydrogen bonding* (ed. D. HADZI), Pergamon Press, London.

—— (1961). *Valence*, 2nd edn. Clarendon Press, Oxford.

—— and DANIELSSON, U. (1954). *Ark. Fys.* **8**, 239, 245.

—— and EISENBERG, D. (1966 a). *Proc. R. Soc.* A **291**, 445.

—— —— (1966 b). *Proc. R. Soc.* A **291**, 454.

CROSS, P. C., BURNHAM, J., and LEIGHTON, P. A. (1937). *J. Am. chem. Soc.* **59**, 1134.

CUDDEBACK, R. B., KOELLER, R. C., and DRICKAMER, H. G. (1953). *J. chem. Phys.* **21**, 589.

CUMMINS, H. Z., and GAMMON, R. W. (1966). *J. chem. Phys.* **44**, 2785.

DANFORD, M. D., and LEVY, H. A. (1962). *J. Am. chem. Soc.* **84**, 3965.

DANTL, G. (1962). *Z. Phys.* **166**, 115.

DARLING, B. T., and DENNISON, D. M. (1940). *Phys. Rev.* **57**, 128.

DAVIDSON, D. W. (1966). In *Molecular relaxation processes*. Academic Press, New York.

DAVIS, C. M., Jr., and BRADLEY, D. L. (1966). *J. chem. Phys.* **45**, 2461.

—— and JARZYNSKI, J. (1967–8). *Adv. molec. Relaxation Processes*, **1**, 155.

—— and LITOVITZ, T. A. (1965). *J. chem. Phys.* **42**, 2563.

DEBYE, P. (1929). *Polar molecules*. Dover, New York.

DENGEL, O., and RIEHL, N. (1963). *Phys. Kondens. Materie*, **1**, 191.

DENNEY, D. J., and COLE, R. H. (1955). *J. chem. Phys.* **23**, 1767.

DENNISON, D. M. (1940). *Rev. mod. Phys.* **12**, 175.

DiMARZIO, E. A., and STILLINGER, F. H., Jr. (1964). *J. chem. Phys.* **40**, 1577.

DORSEY, N. E. (1940). *Properties of ordinary water-substance*. Reinhold, New York.

DOWELL, L. G., and RINFRET, A. P. (1960). *Nature, Lond.* **188**, 1144.

DRAEGERT, D. A., STONE, N. W. B., CURNUTTE, B., and WILLIAMS, D. (1966). *J. opt. Soc. Am.* **56**, 64.

DROST-HANSEN, W. (1965 a). Scientific Contribution No. 628 from the Marine Laboratory, Institute of Marine Science, University of Miami, Miami, Florida (preprint of paper from the Proceedings of the First International Symposium on Water Desalination).

—— (1965 b). *Ann. N.Y. Acad. Sci.* **125**, 471.

DUNCAN, A. B. F., and POPLE, J. A. (1953). *Trans. Faraday Soc.* **49**, 217.

DUNITZ, J. D. (1963). *Nature, Lond.* **197**, 860.

EDSALL, J. T., and WYMAN, J. (1958). *Biophysical chemistry*, Vol. I. Academic Press, New York.

EIGEN, M. (1964). *Angew. Chem. (Int. edn)* **3**, 1.

—— and DE MAEYER, L. (1958). *Proc. R. Soc.* A **247**, 505.

—— —— (1959). In *The structure of electrolyte solutions* (ed. W. J. HAMER). Wiley, New York.

—— —— and SPATZ, H. Ch. (1964). *Ber. Bunsenges.* **68**, 19.

EISENBERG, D., and COULSON, C. A. (1963). *Nature, Lond.* **199**, 368.

—— POCHAN, J. M., and FLYGARE, W. H. (1965). *J. chem. Phys.* **43**, 4531.

EISENBERG, H. (1965). *J. chem. Phys.* **43**, 3887.

ELLISON, F. O., and SHULL, H. (1955). *J. chem. Phys.* **23**, 2348.

EUCKEN, A. (1946). *Nachr. Akad. Wiss. Göttingen*, p. 38.

EWELL, R. H., and EYRING, H. (1937). *J. chem. Phys.* **5**, 726.

FALK, M., and FORD, T. A. (1966). *Can. J. Chem.* **44**, 1699.

—— and KELL, G. S. (1966). *Science* **154**, 1013.

FISHER, I. Z. (1964). *Statistical theory of liquids.* University of Chicago Press, Chicago.

FLORIN, A. E., and ALEI, M. (1967). *J. chem. Phys.* **47**, 4268.

FLUBACHER, P., LEADBETTER, A. J., and MORRISON, J. A. (1960). *J. chem. Phys.* **33**, 1751.

FRANCK, E. U., and ROTH, K. (1967). *Discuss. Faraday Soc.* **43**, 108.

FRANK, H. S. (1958). *Proc. R. Soc.* A **247**, 481.

—— (1963). *Desalination Research Conference Proceedings, National Acad. of Sciences—National Research Council, Publication* 942, p. 141.

—— (1965). *Fedn Proc. (Fedn Am. Socs. exp. Biol.)* **24**, Supplement 15, S1.

—— and QUIST, A. S. (1961). *J. chem. phys.* **34**, 604.

—— and WEN, W. Y. (1957). *Discuss. Faraday Soc.* **24**, 133.

FRENKEL, J. (1946). *Kinetic theory of liquids.* Clarendon Press, Oxford.

FRIEDMAN, A. S., and HAAR, L. (1954). *J. chem. Phys.* **22**, 2051.

GARG, S. K., and SMYTH, C. P. (1965). *J. chem. Phys.* **43**, 2959.

GHORMLEY, J. A. (1956). *J. chem. Phys.* **25**, 599.

—— (1968). *J. chem. Phys.* **48**, 503.

GIAUQUE, W. F., and ASHLEY, M. (1933). *Phys. Rev.* **43**, 81.

—— and STOUT, J. W. (1936). *J. Am. chem. Soc.* **58**, 1144.

GINNINGS, D. C., and CORRUCCINI, R. J. (1947). *J. Res. natn. Bur. Stand.* **38**, 583.

GLAESER, R. M., and COULSON, C. A. (1965). *Trans. Faraday Soc.* **61**, 389.

GLARUM, S. H. (1960). *J. chem. Phys.* **33**, 1371.

GLASEL, J. A. (1966). *Proc. natn. Acad. Sci. U.S.A.* **55**, 479.

—— (1967). *Proc. natn. Acad. Sci. U.S.A.* **58**, 27.

GLASSTONE, S., LAIDLER, K. J., and EYRING, H. (1941). *The theory of rate processes.* McGraw–Hill, New York.

GLEN, J. W. (1958). *Adv. Phys.* **7**, 254.

GRÄNICHER, H. (1958). *Z. Kristallogr. Kristallgeom.* **110**, 432.

—— (1963). *Phys. Kondens. Materie,* **1**, 1.

—— JACCARD, C., SCHERRER, P., and STEINEMANN, A. (1957). *Discuss. Faraday Soc.* **23**, 50.

GRANT, E. H. (1957). *J. chem. Phys.* **26**, 1575.

GRANT, E. H., BUCHANAN, T. J., and COOK, H. F. (1957). *J. chem. Phys.* **26**, 156.

GRJOTHEIM, K., and KROGH-MOE, J. (1954). *Acta chem. Scand.* **8**, 1193.

GURIKOV, YU. V. (1965). *J. struct. Chem.* (translation of *Zh. strukt. Khim*) **6**, 786.

—— (1966). *J. struct. Chem.* (translation of *Zh. strukt. Khim.*) **7**, 6.

HAAS, C. (1960). *Technical Report* #5, Frick Chemical Laboratory, Princeton University, Princeton, N.J.

—— (1962). *Phys. Lett.* **3**, 126.

—— and HORNIG, D. F. (1960). *J. chem. Phys.* **32**, 1763.

HAGGIS, G. H., HASTED, J. B., and BUCHANAN, T. J. (1952). *J. chem. Phys.* **20**, 1452.

HAKE, R. B., and BANYARD, K. E. (1965). *J. chem. Phys.* **43**, 657.

HALL, L. (1948). *Phys. Rev.* **73**, 775.

HAMILTON, W. C., and IBERS, J. A. (1968). *Hydrogen bonding in solids*. Benjamin, New York.

HARNED, H. S., and OWEN, B. B. (1939). *Chem. Rev.* **25**, 31.

HARRIS, F. E., and O'KONSKI, C. T. (1957). *J. phys. Chem. Ithaca* **61**, 310.

HARRISON, J. F. (1967). *J. chem. Phys.* **47**, 2990.

HARTMAN, K. A. (1966). *J. phys. Chem. Ithaca* **70**, 270.

HASTED, J. B. (1961). *Prog. Dielect.* **3**, 103.

HEATH, D. F., and LINNETT, J. W. (1948). *Trans. Faraday Soc.* **44**, 556.

HEEMSKERK, J. (1962). *Recl Trav. chim. Pays-Bas Belg.* **81**, 904.

HEIKS, J. R., BARNETT, M. K., JONES, L. V., and ORBAN, E. (1954). *J. phys. Chem.* **58**, 488.

HENDRICKSON, J. B. (1961). *J. Am. chem. Soc.* **83**, 4537.

HERZBERG, G. (1950). *Molecular spectra and molecular structure*, 2nd edn. Van Nostrand, New York.

HINDMAN, J. C. (1966). *J. chem. Phys.* **44**, 4582.

HIRSCHFELDER, J. O., CURTISS, C. F., and BIRD, R. B. (1954). *Molecular theory of gases and liquids*. Wiley, New York.

HOLLINS, G. T. (1964). *Proc. phys. Soc.* **84**, 1001.

HOLTON, G., HAGELBERG, M. P., KAO, S., and JOHNSON, W. H. Jr. (1968). *J. Accoust. Soc. Am.* **43**, 102.

HONJO, G., and SHIMAOKA, K. (1957). *Acta crystallogr.* **10**, 710.

HORNE, R. A., COURANT, R. A., JOHNSON, D. S., and MARGOSIAN, F. F. (1965). *J. phys. Chem. Ithaca* **69**, 3988.

—— and JOHNSON, D. S. (1966). *J. phys. Chem. Ithaca* **70**, 2182.

HORNIG, D. F. (1950). *Discuss. Faraday Soc.* **9**, 115.

—— (1964). *J. chem. Phys.* **40**, 3119.

—— WHITE, H. F., and REDING, F. P. (1958). *Spectrochim. Acta*, **12**, 338.

HUGHES, D. J., PALEVSKY, H., KLEY, W., and TUNKELO, E. (1960). *Phys. Rev.* **119**, 872.

HUMBEL, F., JONA, F., and SCHERRER, P. (1953). *Helv. phys. Acta*, **26**, 17.

ITAGAKI, K. (1964). *J. phys. Soc. Japan* **19**, 1081.

JACCARD, C. (1959). *Helv. phys. Acta* **32**, 89.

—— (1965). *Ann. N.Y. Acad. Sci.* **125**, 390.

JHON, M. S., GROSH, J., REE, T., and EYRING, H. (1966). *J. chem. Phys.* **44**, 1465.

JONES, J. R., ROWLANDS, D. L. G., and MONK, C. B. (1965). *Trans. Faraday Soc.* **61**, 1384.

KAMB, B. (1964). *Acta crystallogr.* **17**, 1437.

—— (1965 *a*). *Science* **150**, 205.

—— (1965 *b*). *J. chem. Phys.* **43**, 3917.

—— (1967). Private communication.

—— (1968). In *Structural chemistry and molecular biology* (ed. A. RICH and N. DAVIDSON). Freeman, San Francisco.

—— and DATTA, S. K. (1960). *Nature, Lond.* **187**, 140.

—— and DAVIS, B. L. (1964). *Proc. natn. Acad. Sci. U.S.A.* **52**, 1433.

—— PRAKASH, A., and KNOBLER, C. (1967). *Acta crystallogr.* **22**, 706.

KATZOFF, S. (1934). *J. chem. Phys.* **2**, 841.

KAUZMANN, W. (1942). *Rev. mod. Phys.* **14**, 12.

—— (1948). *Chem. Rev.* **43**, 219.

—— (1957). *Quantum chemistry*. Academic Press, New York.

—— (1966). *Kinetic theory of gases*. Benjamin, New York.

KAVANAU, J. L. (1964). *Water and solute–water interactions*. Holden–Day, San Francisco.

KELL, G. S. (1967). *J. chem. engng Data* **12**, 66.

—— and WHALLEY, E. (1965). *Phil. Trans. R. Soc.* A **258**, 565.

—— —— (1968). *J. chem. Phys.* **48**, 2359.

KENNEDY, G. C., KNIGHT, W. L., and HOLSER, W. T. (1958). *Am. J. Sci.* **256**, 590.

KERN, C. W., and MATCHA, R. L. (1968). *J. chem. Phys.*, in press.

KETELAAR, J. A. (1953). *Chemical constitution*, p. 90. Elsevier, New York.

KEYES, F. G. (1949). *J. chem. Phys.* **17**, 923.

—— (1958). *Trans. Am. Soc. mech. Engrs*, **78**, 555.

—— SMITH, L. B., and GERRY, H. T. (1936). *Proc. Am. Acad. Arts Sci.* **70**, 319.

KIRKWOOD, J. G. (1939). *J. chem. Phys.* **7**, 911.

KIRSHENBAUM, I. (1951). *Physical properties and analysis of heavy water*. McGraw-Hill, New York.

KISLOVSKII, L. D. (1959). *Optics Spectrosc.* **7**, 201.

KOEFOED, J. (1957). *Discuss. Faraday Soc.* **24**, 216.

KOPP, M., BARNAAL, D. E., and LOWE, I. J. (1965). *J. chem. Phys.* **43**, 2965.

KRATOHVIL, J. P., KERKER, M., and OPPENHEIMER, L. E. (1965). *J. chem. Phys.* **43**, 914.

KRAUT, J., and DANDLIKER, W. B. (1955). *J. chem. Phys.* **23**, 1544.

KRYNICKI, K. (1966). *Physica* **32**, 167.

KUCHITSU, K., and BARTELL, L. S. (1962). *J. chem. Phys.* **36**, 2460.

KUCHITSU, K., and MORINO, Y. (1965). *Bull. chem. Soc. Japan* **38**, 814.

KUHN, W., and THÜRKAUF, M. (1958). *Helv. chim. Acta* **41**, 938.

KUHNS, I. E., and MASON, B. J. (1968). *Proc. R. Soc.* A **302**, 437.

KUME, K. (1960). *J. phys. Soc. Japan* **15**, 1493.

KYOGOKU, Y. (1960). *J. chem. Soc. Japan* (Pure Chemistry Section) **81**, 1648 (NCR Technical Translation 953).

LA PLACA, S., and POST, B. (1960). *Acta crystallogr.* **13**, 503.

LARSSON, K. E. (1965). In *Thermal neutron scattering* (ed. P. A. EGELSTAFF). Academic Press, New York.

—— and DAHLBORG, U. (1962). *J. nucl. Energy* **16**, 81.

LAVERGNE, M., and DROST-HANSEN, W. (1956). *Naturwissenschaften* **43**, 511.

LEADBETTER, A. J. (1965). *Proc. R. Soc.* A **287**, 403.

LENNARD-JONES, J., and POPLE, J. A. (1951). *Proc. R. Soc.* A **205**, 155.

LEVINE, M. (1966). Undergraduate thesis, Princeton University. Unpublished.

LIEB, E. H. (1967). *Phys. Rev.* **162**, 162.

LIPPINCOTT, E. R., and SCHROEDER, R. (1955). *J. chem. Phys.* **23**, 1099.

LITAN, A. (1968). *J. chem. Phys.* **48**, 1059.

LITOVITZ, T. A., and CARNEVALE, E. H. (1955). *J. appl. Phys.* **26**, 816.

—— and DAVIS, C. M. (1965). In *Physical acoustics* (ed. W. P. MASON). Academic Press, New York.

LONDON, F. (1937). *Trans. Faraday Soc.* **33**, 8.

LONG, E. A., and KEMP, J. D. (1936). *J. Am. chem. Soc.* **58**, 1829.

LONGSWORTH, L. G. (1960). *J. phys. Chem. Ithaca* **64**, 1914.

LONSDALE, K. (1958). *Proc. R. Soc.* A **247**, 424.

LUCK, W. (1965). *Ber. Bunsenges.* **69**, 626.

—— (1967). *Discuss. Faraday Soc.* **43**, 115.

MAGAT, M. (1948). *J. Chim. phys.* **45**, 93.

MALMBERG, C. G. (1958). *J. Res. natn. Bur. Stand.* **60**, 609.

—— and MARYOTT, A. A. (1956). *J. Res. natn. Bur. Stand.* **56**, 1.

MARCHI, R. P., and EYRING, H. (1964). *J. phys. Chem. Ithaca* **68**, 221.

MARCKMANN, J. P., and WHALLEY, E. (1964). *J. chem. Phys.* **41**, 1450.

MARGENAU, H. (1939). *Rev. mod. Phys.* **11**, 1.

—— and MYERS, V. W. (1944). *Phys. Rev.* **66**, 307.

McCLELLAN, A. L. (1963). *Dipole moments.* Freeman, San Francisco.

McMILLAN, J. A., and LOS, S. C. (1965). *Nature, Lond.* **206**, 806.

McWEENY, R., and OHNO, K. A. (1960). *Proc. R. Soc.* A **255**, 367.

MEGAW, H. D. (1934). *Nature, Lond.* **134**, 900.

MEIBOOM, S. (1961). *J. chem. Phys.* **34**, 375.

MERWIN, H. E. (1930). *Int. crit. Tabl.* **7**, 17.

MILLS, I. M. (1963). *Infra-red spectroscopy and molecular structure* (ed. M. DAVIES). Elsevier, London.

Moccia, R. (1964). *J. chem. Phys.* **40**, 2186.

Moelwyn-Hughes, E. A. (1964). *Physical chemistry*, 2nd edn. Macmillan, New York.

Moore, C. E. (1949). Atomic energy levels, *National Bureau of Standards Circular* 467, Vol. 1.

Morgan, J., and Warren, B. E. (1938). *J. chem. Phys.* **6**, 666.

Morokuma, K., and Pedersen, L. (1968). *J. chem. Phys.* **48**, 3275.

Moskowitz, J. W., and Harrison, M. C. (1965). *J. chem. Phys.* **43**, 3550.

Muller, N. (1965). *J. chem. Phys.* **43**, 2555.

—— and Reiter, R. C. (1965). *J. chem. Phys.* **42**, 3265.

Mysels, K. J. (1964). *J. Am. chem. Soc.* **86**, 3503.

Nagle, J. F. (1966). *J. math. Phys.* **7**, 1484.

Narten, A. H., Danford, M. D., and Levy, H. A. (1966). *Oak Ridge National Laboratory Report ORNL*-3997.

—— —— —— (1967). *Discuss. Faraday Soc.* **43**, 97.

Némethy, G., and Scheraga, H. A. (1962). *J. chem. Phys.* **36**, 3382.

—— —— (1964). *J. chem. Phys.* **41**, 680.

Nowak, E. S., and Grosh, R. J. (1961). *A.E.C. Technical Report ANL*-6508.

—— —— and Liley, P. E. (1961*a*). *J. Heat Transfer* **83C**, 1.

—— —— —— (1961*b*). *J. Heat Transfer* **83C**, 14.

Ockman, N. (1958). *Adv. Phys.* **7**, 199.

Oliver, G. D., and Grisard, J. W. (1956). *J. Am. chem. Soc.* **78**, 561.

Onsager, L. (1936). *J. Am. chem. Soc.* **58**, 1486.

—— and Dupuis, M. (1960). *Rc. Scu. int. Fis. 'Enrico Fermi'* **10**, 294.

—— —— (1962). *Electrolytes* (ed. B. Pesce). Pergamon Press, London.

—— and Runnels, L. K. (1963). *Proc. natn. Acad. Sci. U.S.A.* **50**, 208.

Orttung, W. H., and Meyers, J. A. (1963). *J. phys. Chem. Ithaca* **67**, 1905.

Orville-Thomas, W. J. (1957). *Q. Rev. chem. Soc.* **11**, 162.

Oster, G. (1948). *Chem. Rev.* **43**, 319.

—— and Kirkwood, J. G. (1943). *J. chem. Phys.* **11**, 175.

Owen, B. B., Miller, R. C., Milner, C. E., and Cogan, H. L. (1961). *J. phys. Chem. Ithaca* **65**, 2065.

—— White, J. R., and Smith, J. S. (1956). *J. Am. chem. Soc.* **78**, 3561.

Owston, P. G. (1958). *Adv. Phys.* **7**, 171.

Palevsky, H. (1966). *J. Chim. phys.* **63**, 157.

Papoušek, D., and Plíva, J. (1964). *Colln Czech. chem. Commun. Engl. Edn* **29**, 1973.

Partington, J. R. (1928). *The composition of water.* Bell, London.

Pauling, L. (1935). *J. Am. chem. Soc.* **57**, 2680.

—— (1940). *The nature of the chemical bond*, 2nd edn. Cornell, Ithaca, New York.

—— (1959). In *Hydrogen bonding* (ed. D. Hadzi). Pergamon Press, London.

PAULING, L. (1960). *The nature of the chemical bond*, 3rd edn. Cornell, Ithaca, New York.

—— and MARSH, R. E. (1952). *Proc. natn. Acad. Sci. U.S.A.* **38**, 112.

PERRAM, J. W., and LEVINE, S. (1967). *Discuss. Faraday Soc.* **43**, 131.

PETERSON, S. W., and LEVY, H. A. (1957). *Acta crystallogr.* **10**, 70.

PIMENTEL, G. C., and McCLELLAN, A. L. (1960). *The hydrogen bond.* Freeman, San Francisco.

PISTORIUS, C. W. F. T., PISTORIUS, M. C., BLAKEY, J. P., and ADMIRAAL, L. J. (1963). *J. chem. Phys.* **38**, 600.

PITZER, K. S. (1953). *Quantum chemistry.* Prentice–Hall, Englewood Cliffs, New Jersey.

—— and POLISSAR, J. (1956). *J. phys. Chem. Ithaca* **60**, 1140.

PITZER, R. M. (1966). Private communication.

—— and MERRIFIELD, D. P. (1966). Private communication from Professor Pitzer.

PLÍVA, J. (1958). *Colln Czech. chem. Commun. Engl. Edn* **23**, 1839.

POPLE, J. A. (1950). *Proc. R. Soc.* A **202**, 323.

—— (1951). *Proc. R. Soc.* A **205**, 163.

—— SCHNEIDER, W. G., and BERNSTEIN, H. J. (1959). *High-resolution nuclear magnetic resonance.* McGraw–Hill, New York.

POSENER, D. W. (1960). *Aust. J. Phys.* **13**, 168.

POWELL, R. W. (1958). *Proc. R. Soc.* A **247**, 464.

POWLES, J. G. (1953). *J. chem. Phys.* **21**, 633.

—— RHODES, M., and STRANGE, J. H. (1966). *Molec. Phys.* **11**, 515.

PRICE, W. C., and SUGDEN, T. M. (1948). *Trans. Faraday Soc.* **44**, 108.

RAMPOLLA, R. W., MILLER, R. C., and SMYTH, C. P. (1959). *J. chem. Phys.* **30**, 566.

RAMSEIER, R. O. (1967). *J. appl. Phys.* **38**, 2553.

REID, C. (1959). *J. chem. Phys.* **30**, 182.

REISLER, E., and EISENBERG, H. (1965). *J. chem. Phys.* **43**, 3875.

RICE, S. A., and GRAY, P. (1965). *The statistical mechanics of simple liquids.* Interscience, New York.

ROBINSON, R. A., and STOKES, R. H. (1959). *Electrolyte solutions.* Butterworths, London.

ROENTGEN, W. K. (1892). *Ann. Phys. Chim. (Wied.)* **45**, 91.

ROOTHAAN, C. C. J. (1951). *Rev. mod. Phys.* **23**, 69.

ROSSINI, F. D., KNOWLTON, J. W., and JOHNSTON, H. L. (1940). *J. Res. natn. Bur. Stand.* **24**, 369.

—— WAGMAN, D. D., EVANS, W. H., LEVINE, S., and JAFFE, I. (1952). Chemical thermodynamic properties, *National Bureau of Standards Circular* 500.

ROWLINSON, J. S. (1949). *Trans. Faraday Soc.* **45**, 974.

—— (1951 a). *Trans. Faraday Soc.* **47**, 120.

—— (1951 b). *J. chem. Phys.* **19**, 827.

—— (1954). *Q. Rev. chem. Soc.* **8**, 168.

RUSCHE, E. W., and GOOD, W. B. (1966). *J. chem. Phys.* **45**, 4667.

RUSHBROOKE, G. S. (1962). *Introduction to statistical mechanics.* Clarendon Press, Oxford.

SAKAMOTO, M., BROCKHOUSE, B. N., JOHNSON, R. G., and POPE, N. K. (1962). *J. phys. Soc. Japan*, **17**, Supp. B-II, 370.

SALEM, L. (1960). *Molec. Phys.* **3**, 441.

SAMOILOV, O. YA. (1965). *Structure of aqueous electrolyte solutions and the hydration of ions.* Consultants Bureau, New York.

SÄNGER, R., and STEIGER, O. (1928). *Helv. phys. Acta* **1**, 369.

SCATCHARD, G., KAVANAGH, G. M., and TICKNOR, L. B. (1952). *J. Am. chem. Soc.* **74**, 3715.

SCHIFFER, J., and HORNIG, D. F. (1967). Private communication.

SCHNEIDER, W. G., BERNSTEIN, H. J., and POPLE, J. A. (1958). *J. chem. Phys.* **28**, 601.

SCHULTZ, J. W., and HORNIG, D. F. (1961). *J. phys. Chem. Ithaca* **65**, 2131.

SEARCY, A. W. (1949). *J. chem. Phys.* **17**, 210.

SELWOOD, P. W. (1956). *Magnetochemistry.* Interscience, New York.

SENIOR, W. A., and THOMPSON, W. K. (1965). *Nature, Lond.* **205**, 170.

SHARP, W. E. (1962). The thermodynamic functions for water in the range −10 to 1000 °C and 1 to 250 000 bars, *Report of the Lawrence Radiation Laboratory, University of California UCRL-7118.*

SHATENSHTEIN, A. I., YAKOVLEVA, E. A., ZVYAGINTSEVA, E. N., VARSHAVSKII, YA. M., ISRAILEVICH, E. J., and DYKHNO, N. M. (1960). *Isotopic water analysis*, 2nd edn. United States Atomic Energy Commission translation *AEC*-tr-4136.

SHIBATA, S., and BARTELL, L. S. (1965). *J. chem. Phys.* **42**, 1147.

SIMPSON, J. H., and CARR, H. Y. (1958). *Phys. Rev.* **111**, 1201.

SINGH, S., MURTHY, A. S. N., and RAO, C. N. R. (1966). *Trans. Faraday Soc.* **62**, 1056.

SINGWI, K. S., and SJÖLANDER, A. (1960). *Phys. Rev.* **119**, 863.

SJÖLANDER, A. (1965). In *Thermal neutron scattering* (ed. P. A. EGELSTAFF). Academic Press, New York.

SLATER, J. C. (1939). *Introduction to chemical physics.* McGraw-Hill, New York.

SLIE, W. M., DONFOR, A. R., and LITOVITZ, T. A. (1966). *J. chem. Phys.* **44**, 3712.

SMITH, A. H., and LAWSON, A. W. (1954). *J. chem. Phys.* **22**, 351.

SMITH, D. W. G., and POWLES, J. G. (1966). *Molec. Phys.* **10**, 451.

SMYTH, C. P. (1955). *Dielectric behavior and structure.* McGraw-Hill, New York.

STEPHENS, R. W. B. (1958). *Adv. Phys.* **7**, 266.

STEVENSON, D. P. (1965). *J. phys. Chem. Ithaca* **69**, 2145.

—— (1968). In *Structural chemistry and molecular biology* (ed. A. RICH and N. DAVIDSON). Freeman, San Francisco.

STEVENSON, M. J., and TOWNES, C. H. (1957). *Phys. Rev.* **107**, 635.

STIMSON, H. F. (1955). *Am. J. Phys.* **23**, 614.

STOCKMAYER, W. H. (1941). *J. chem. Phys.* **9**, 398.

STOKES, R. H., and MILLS, R. (1965). *International encyclopedia of physical chemistry and chemical physics*, vol. 3, p. 74. Pergamon Press, Oxford.

SWENSON, C. A. (1965). *Spectrochim. Acta* **21**, 987.

TAFT, R. W., and SISLER, H. H. (1947). *J. chem. Educ.* **24**, 174.

TAMMANN, G. (1900). *Annln Phys.* **2**, 1.

TAYLOR, M. J., and WHALLEY, E. (1964). *J. chem. Phys.* **40**, 1660.

THOMAS, M. R., SCHERAGA, H. A., and SCHRIER, E. E. (1965). *J. phys. Chem. Ithaca* **69**, 3722.

TILTON, L. W. (1935). *J. Res. natn. Bur. Stand.* **14**, 393.

—— and TAYLOR, J. K. (1938). *J. Res. natn. Bur. Stand.* **20**, 419.

TOYAMA, M., OKA, T., and MORINO, Y. (1964). *J. molec. Spectrosc.* **13**, 193.

TRAPPENIERS, N. J., GERRITSMA, C. J., and OOSTING, P. H. (1965). *Phys. Lett.* **18**, 256.

TREACY, E. B., and BEERS, Y. (1962). *J. chem. Phys.* **36**, 1473.

TRUBY, F. K. (1955). *Science* **121**, 404.

TSUBOI, M. (1964). *J. chem. Phys.* **40**, 1326.

TSUBOMURA, H. (1954). *Bull. chem. Soc. Japan* **27**, 445.

VAND, V., and SENIOR, W. A. (1965). *J. chem. Phys.* **43**, 1878.

VAN ECK, C. L. VAN P., MENDEL, H., and FAHRENFORT, J. (1958). *Proc. R. Soc.* A **247**, 472.

VAN THIEL, M., BECKER, E. D., and PIMENTEL, G. C. (1957). *J. chem. Phys.* **27**, 486.

VDOVENKO, V. M., GURIKOV, YU. V., and LEGIN, E. K. (1966). *J. struct. Chem.* (translation of *Zh. strukt. Khim.*) **7**, 756.

———— ——— (1967). *J. struct. Chem.* (translation of *Zh. strukt. Khim.*) **8**, 14, 358, 538.

VEDAM, R., and HOLTON, G. (1968). *J. Accoust. Soc. Am.*, **43**, 108.

VEDDER, W., and HORNIG, D. F. (1961). *Adv. Spectrosc.* **2**, 189.

VEGARD, L., and HILLESUND, S. (1942). *Avh. norske VidenskAkad. Oslo* No. 8, 1.

VERWEY, E. J. W. (1941). *Recl Trav. chim. Pays-Bas Belg.* **60**, 887.

VIDULICH, G. A., EVANS, D. F., and KAY, R. L. (1967). *J. phys. Chem. Ithaca* **71**, 656.

WADA, G. (1961). *Bull. chem. Soc. Japan*, **34**, 955.

WAGMAN, D. D., EVANS, W. H., HALOW, I., PARKER, V. B., BAILEY, S. M., and SCHUMM, R. H. (1965). *National Bureau of Standards Technical Note* 270–1.

WALDSTEIN, P., and RABIDEAU, S. W. (1967). *J. chem. Phys.* **47**, 5338.

WALDSTEIN, P., RABIDEAU, S. W., and JACKSON, J. A. (1964). *J. chem. Phys.* **41**, 3407.

WALL, T. T., and HORNIG, D. F. (1965). *J. chem. Phys.* **43**, 2079.

WALRAFEN, G. E. (1964). *J. chem. Phys.* **40**, 3249.

—— (1966). *J. chem. Phys.* **44**, 1546.

—— (1967 a). *J. chem. Phys.* **47**, 114.

—— (1967 b). Private communication. Subsequently published in *J. chem. Phys.* **48**, 244 (1968).

WALRAFEN, G. E. (1968a). Private communication, to be published.

—— (1968b). In *Equilibria and reaction kinetics in hydrogen bonded solvent systems* (ed. A. K. COVINGTON). Taylor and Francis, London. In press.

WANG, J. H. (1965). *J. phys. Chem. Ithaca* **69**, 4412.

—— ROBINSON, C. V., and EDELMAN, I. S. (1953). *J. Am. chem. Soc.* **75**, 466.

WATANABE, K., and JURSA, A. S. (1964). *J. chem. Phys.* **41**, 1650.

WAXLER, R. M., WEIR, C. E., and SCHAMP, H. W. (1964). *J. Res. natn. Bur. Stand.* **68A**, 489.

WEIR, C., BLOCK, S., and PIERMARINI, G. (1965). *J. Res. natn. Bur. Stand.* **69C**, 275.

WEISSMANN, M. (1966). *J. chem. Phys.* **44**, 422.

—— BLUM, L., and COHAN, N. V. (1967). *Chem. Phys. Lett.* **1**, 95.

—— and COHAN, N. V. (1965). *J. chem. Phys.* **43**, 119.

WESTON, R. E. (1962). *Spectrochim. Acta* **18**, 1257.

WHALLEY, E. (1957). *Trans. Faraday Soc.* **53**, 1578.

—— (1958). *Trans. Faraday Soc.* **54**, 1613.

—— (1967). Private communication.

—— and DAVIDSON, D. W. (1965). *J. chem. Phys.* **43**, 2148.

—— —— and HEATH, J. B. R. (1966). *J. chem. Phys.* **45**, 3976.

—— —— —— (1968). *J. chem. Phys.* **48**, 2362.

WHITTEN, J. L., ALLEN, L. C., and FINK, W. H. (1966). Private communication from Dr. Whitten and Dr. Fink.

WICKE, E. (1966). *Angew. Chem. (Int. edn)* **5**, 106.

WILLIAMS, D. (1966). *Nature, Lond.* **210**, 194.

WILSON, A. H. (1957). *Thermodynamics and statistical mechanics.* Cambridge University Press, Cambridge.

WILSON, E. B., DECIUS, J. C., and CROSS, P. C. (1955). *Molecular vibrations.* McGraw–Hill, New York.

WILSON, G. J., CHAN, R. K., DAVIDSON, D. W., and WHALLEY, E. (1965). *J. chem. Phys.* **43**, 2384.

WILSON, W. (1959). *J. Accoust. Soc. Am.*, **31**, 1067.

WOESSNER, D. E. (1964). *J. chem. Phys.* **40**, 2341.

WONHAM, J. (1967). *Nature, Lond.* **215**, 1053.

WORKMAN, E. J., TRUBY, F. K., and DROST-HANSEN, W. (1954). *Phys. Rev.* **94**, 1073.

WORLEY, J. D., and KLOTZ, I. M. (1966). *J. chem. Phys.* **45**, 2868.

WYMAN, J., and INGALLS, E. N. (1938). *J. Am. chem. Soc.* **60**, 1182.

ZAREMBOVITCH, A., and KAHANE, A. (1964). *C. r. hebd. Séanc. Acad. Sci. Paris* **258**, 2529.

ZEMANSKY, M. W. (1957). *Heat and thermodynamics.* McGraw–Hill, New York.

ZIMMERMANN, R., and PIMENTEL, G. C. (1962). *Advances in molecular spectroscopy* (ed. A. MANGINI), p. 762. Macmillan, New York.

Author Index

Subject Index